Charles Henry Pearson, William Henry Blaauw

The Barons' War

Including the battles of Lewes and Evesham. Second Edition

Charles Henry Pearson, William Henry Blaauw

The Barons' War
Including the battles of Lewes and Evesham. Second Edition

ISBN/EAN: 9783337012458

Printed in Europe, USA, Canada, Australia, Japan

Cover: Foto ©ninafisch / pixelio.de

More available books at **www.hansebooks.com**

THE BARONS' WAR.

Cambridge:
PRINTED BY C. J. CLAY, M.A.,
AT THE UNIVERSITY PRESS.

THE BARONS' WAR

INCLUDING THE

BATTLES OF LEWES AND EVESHAM.

BY

WILLIAM HENRY BLAAUW, ESQ., M.A.

> "'Tis wonderful
> What may be wrought out of their discontent."—
> SHAKESPEARE.

SECOND EDITION

WITH ADDITIONS AND CORRECTIONS.

London:
BELL AND DALDY, YORK STREET,
COVENT GARDEN.
LEWES: BAXTER AND SON.
1871.

AUTHOR'S PREFACE.

THE distant view of the Castle and Battle Field of Lewes having led the Author to examine, with additional interest, the causes and circumstances of the great event which has given them a place in history, he felt that the mere details of a sanguinary contest would be unsatisfactory, unless, in some degree, illustrated by the manners and temper of the times, as well as by the characters and motives of the chief actors. He has not therefore scrupled to digress widely with that object, and the intended narrative of a day has insensibly swelled into a sketch of many years; but on considering the importance of that period of British history, it did not appear that justice would otherwise be done to the subject.

Surprise may well be felt by those who are not conversant with the rude materials from which History has to be constructed, at the confusion and contradictions of the various chronicles relating to these times: many of these have been consulted by the author in manuscript, and of several important papers which have been lately published free use has been also made. Much of their discrepancy, however, becomes corrected by the authentic test of public documents, and much by a due consideration of the circumstances of the writers. While party bias, for they had party even in those days, often induced some to distort facts, others, from the seclusion of their habits, had no means of accurately ascertaining even contemporary events; not a few wrote a century too late for collecting original evidence, and many in their indiscriminate records did not refuse even "profane and old-wives' fables." Later writers in succession, glad of an easy path, have often contentedly followed such authorities, as on a sheep-track, without further enquiry. The weight of each witness thus requiring adjustment in the balance, a list of the principal references has been subjoined, somewhat explanatory of their relative value.

Several specimens of the quaint but characteristic poetry of the age have been purposely introduced in evidence of the opinions then current, and the aspect of their antique phraseology has been occasionally rendered less forbidding by translation.

To the kindness of friends the author is much indebted for some of the illustrations*, and for some

* These have been omitted from the present edition.—*Editor*.

notices on the family of Simon de Montfort in its foreign branches.

The following pages were not intended as a disquisition on the origin and nature of Parliaments, so ably treated by others, and being but "an ancient tale new told," may not present many new facts to the historical student, yet it is hoped that the details, freshly gathered from their original sources, and here newly combined, may impart to some readers a clearer view or a warmer interest in so remarkable a crisis of British history.

W. H. B.

BEECHLAND, NEWICK,
January, 1844.

EDITOR'S PREFACE.

AFTER Mr Blaauw's death, I learned that he had been preparing a second edition of the Barons' War when he was struck down by the illness that eventually carried him off. There was a difficulty in finding any one who could see the sheets through the press. Under these circumstances I volunteered to give what aid I could. When the papers came into my hands, I found that the author had scarcely touched the text except to make a few verbal corrections, most of which had been suggested to him by his friend, the well-known archæologist, Mr Weston S. Walford. On the other hand there was a mass of notes, many of which were quotations from modern authors or picturesque extracts from chronicles that had struck Mr Blaauw's fancy. Altogether, I think, several pages had been transcribed from Jocelin de Brakelond. It was clearly unnecessary to reprint these, and I have therefore had the difficult task of sifting what was to be retained from what ought to be excluded. My practice has been to keep all that was derived from unprinted sources, and all that related to family history : while I have left out mere illustrations and extracts from books that are now generally accessible. I have adhered rigidly to Mr Blaauw's spelling, even where it is now antiquated ; and wherever I have thought it necessary to make a change or add a note have distinguished what is my own by spaced lines [ ] or by the initial P. In a few cases where Mr Walford's notes had not been transcribed by Mr Blaauw (I believe merely from the interruption of illness), I have added them and distinguished them by the letters W. S. W.

I need not say that no care of an editor can in any appreciable degree replace the last touchings and remodellings of an author. Nevertheless judged by what it is, I believe Mr Blaauw's work will long continue to hold a high place among works of its kind. It may serve as some evidence of the care with which he explored the sources of history, that the invaluable publications of the Record Commission during the last fourteen years have not, I think, contained a book except the Annals of Dunstaple, which he had overlooked, while many of the Manuscripts he cites are unfortunately to this moment without an Editor. I confess to thinking that the Barons' War is even now unsurpassed as a history of the particular period it deals with. Some day it will no doubt be superseded, for there are still unused records to be drawn upon. So thorough and modest a student as Mr Blaauw would have been the first to disclaim the praise of having left nothing for his successors to add: the last to wish that his own work should be final.

I have to return my best thanks to Mr F. J. Furnivall, who kindly collated a MS. for me in the British Museum; and more particularly still to the Rev. H. R. Luard, who besides doing me the same good office, has supplied many valuable corrections throughout the book. The Index is due to the author's son, Mr T. St Leger Blaauw.

CHARLES H. PEARSON.

TRINITY COLLEGE, CAMBRIDGE,
May 28, 1871.

REFERENCES.

* denotes those who were of the Royalists' party, and † the Baronial.

Anglia Sacra. . . . . . . By Henry Wharton, folio, London, 1691, contains the account of the affairs of Durham Cathedral from 1214 to 1336, by Robert de Graystanes, Sub-Prior of Durham, who was elected Bishop by his convent 1332, and consecrated in spite of the king's prohibition.—He was afterwards superseded, and died of vexation. A graphic intelligent writer.

Art de vérifier les Dates—3 T. folio, Paris, 1783.

Ann. Burt.† . . . . Annals written in the monastery of Burton contain many interesting documents, and end abruptly with the King's intention to annul the Oxford Statutes. [Edited by Fulman, and more lately by the Rev. H. R. Luard for the Record Commission. Annales Monastici, Vol. I.]

[Ann. of Dunstaple . . . Edited by Hearne, and more lately by the Rev. H. R. Luard for the Record Commission. Annales Monastici, Vol. III.]

Anon. Langued. . . . . . Chronicle by an impartial Languedocian of the Albigensian war, from 1202 to 1219. Recueil des Histoires de la France, Tom. XX. 1840.

Archiv. du Roy. . . . . There are many interesting MSS. relating to English history in the vast collections of the Archives du Royaume, at Paris. An imperfect catalogue of them has been printed in Trésor des Chartes.

Carlav. . . . . Siege of Carlaverock (from MSS. Cott. Caligula A. XVIII.), a poem in French, by Walter, a Franciscan monk of Exeter, describing the siege of that castle (6 m. south of Dumfries) by Edward I., in July, 1300, edited by N. H. Nicolas, 1828.

REFERENCES.

Chr. Dover† . . . . . . Chronica paucorum, continued to 1286 by a monk of S. Martin in Dover. The MS. (Cott. Julius D. V.) is much burnt and shrivelled by fire in the pages relating to 1264-5.

Chr. Jocelin. . . . . . . Chronica Jocelini de Brakelond, a monk of S. Edmund's Bury, relating the affairs of the monastery from 1173 to 1202, during the Abbacy of Samson de Totington, or Totigtune, in the hundred of Weyland, Norfolk,—a picturesque account in amusing detail of the manners, &c. of the interior of the Abbey,—published by the Camden Society from MS. Harl. 1005.

Chr. Lanerc.† . . . . . Chronicle of Lanercost Abbey, in Cumberland, MSS. Harl. 3425. Cotton MSS. Claud. D. VII. 13: "Historia Anglorum ab 1181 ad 1346—per quemdam Canonicum de Lanercost."—The Cotton MS. is much better than the more recent transcript in Harl. MS. Printed by the Maitland Club in 4to. 1839. The battle of Lewes is described on the authority of a nobleman there present (protestante mihi uno nobili qui ibi fuerat), and also that of Evesham (ore tenus attestante mihi uno illorum qui adversus eum dimicavit).

Chr. Laud.*. . . . . . . Chron. Laudunense a Bruto usque ad 1338.—MSS. Cott. Nero, A. IV., 8vo. At p. 110 is a rude drawing of the capture of Henry III., and the death of Simon de Montfort.

Chr. Lewes.* . . . . . . Chronicle by a monk of Lewes to 1312 contains a concise but authentic account of the battle.—MSS. Cott. Tib. A. X.

Chr. Mailr.† . . . . . . Cotton MS. Faustina B. IX. Chronicle by the monks of Mailros, in Galloway, begun 1235, and continued to 1270 by various hands, from 1262 by one partial to the Barons in Rerum Anglic. Script. Vet. T. I.

Chr. Oxen. . . . . Chronicle of John de Oxenede, Benedictine monk of S. Hulme, continued to 1293.—MSS. Cott. Nero D. II. Cotton MS. Faustina B. XIV. is apparently similar. [Edited by Sir H. Ellis for the Record Commission.]

Chr. Peterb. . . . . . . Chronicle of John de Raleto, Abbot of Peterborough, and Robert Boston, monk of Spalding, continued to 1368.

Chr. Ramsey . . . . . . Chronicle by a monk of Ramsey, written before 1267.—MSS. Cott. Otho D. VIII., partly burnt.

REFERENCES. xiii

Chr. Roff.† . . . . Chronica de primis incolis Hyberniæ et de rebus Britannicis, &c., ad coronationem Edwardi I., folio MS. Cott. Nero, D. II., by a monk of Rochester, with some rude drawings at the bottom of the pages, one at p. 176 representing the mutilation of Simon de Montfort's body.

Chr. Shepis. . . . . Chronicle of William de Shepisheved, MSS. Cott. Faust. B. VI.

Chr. Taxter . . . . Chronicle of Taxter, a monk of Bury, from 1245 to 1265, MSS. Cott. Julius, A. I., quoted in notes to Rishanger's Chr. de Bellis L. et Ev. [Printed by Mr. Thorpe in the second volume of Florence of Worcester, as the continuation of that author.]

Chr. Trivet. . . . . Chronica Triveti, Harl. MSS. 4322, written during Edward I.'s reign...printed in the Spicilegium of Luc d'Achery, and edited by Mr Hog for the English Historical Society.

Chr. Worc. Wigorn. . . Chronicle of Worcester, MSS. Cott. Calig. A. 10 to 1308 A. D. [Edited by Rev. H. R. Luard for the Record Commission. Annales Monastici, Vol. IV.]

Epist. Ad. de Marisco . Epistolæ Adamæ de Marisco, a Franciscan monk of much learning. The MS. (Cott. Vitell. C. VIII.) is much shrivelled by fire in the upper part of each page, but is mostly legible, and contains many curious letters to Q. Eleanor, Simon de Montfort, his Countess, &c. [Edited by the Rev. Professor Brewer for the Record Commission. Monumenta Franciscana.]

Fabyan † . . . . Chronicle of Robert Fabyan, Alderman of London, Sheriff 1493; a good authority for details relating to London.

Gugl. Pod. Laur. . . . . Guglielmi de Podio Laurentii Historia Albigensium, a monk of Puy Laurent, near Albi, born about 1210, died after 1272. Recueil des Hist. de la France, tome XX., 1840.

Walt. Heming.† . . . . Chronicle of Walter Hemingford, a monk of Gisburn, where he died 1347. He had good opportunities of obtaining information from eye-witnesses for his history, which extends to 1308. [Printed in Gale, and edited (as Hemingburgh) by Mr Hamilton for the English Historical Society.]

Hist. F. Fitzw. . . . . . Histoire de Foulques Fitz Warin, Paris, 1840, edited from MS. in Br. Mus. by M. Michel, who refers this curious biography erroneously to the Fitz

REFERENCES.

	Warin drowned at Lewes, instead of to his father. Some parts printed as prose appear to be verse.
Househ. Exp.	Manners and Household Expenses in England in the 13th century, comprising the Roll of the Countess of Leicester's Expenses in 1265, from the parchment MS. in Br. Mus. Add. MSS. 8877. Privately printed for the Roxburghe Club by Beriah Botfield, Esq., M.P., 1841, and contains much interesting matter, ably illustrated by the editor, Mr. Turner.
Joinv.	Histoire de S. Louis by his friend and fellow-crusader the Sire Jean de Joinville, born 1224, died 1317.
W. Knight.†	Chronicle of William Knighton, who, flourished in the time of Richard II. His account of the battle of Lewes is copied verbatim from W. Hemingford. [Printed in Twysden's Hist. Ang. Scrip. X.]
Peter Langtoft's Chronicle in Verse.	[Edited by Hearne, and more lately by Mr. Aldis Wright for the Record Commission.]
Lib. de ant. leg.†	Liber de antiquis legibus, a copy, in MSS. Harl. 690, of the London chronicle possessed by the corporation, a register of contemporaneous events. [Edited by Mr. Stapleton for the Camden Society.]
MS. in Antiq. Soc. . . .	Habingdon MSS.
MS. of D. of Bedford at Woburn, written by Richard Fox, a prose Chronicle following R. de Gloucester.	
MSS. Harl. 542.	Mr. John Stowe's Collections.
MSS. Lansdowne, 255.	
MSS. Add. 5444† . . .	In Br. Mus., copied from one that was destroyed by fire, Otho B. III. This "son of a burnt father" is a chronicle written by Londoners from time to time as the events occurred from 1195 to 1307.
MSS. Harl. 548.	The Rules drawn up by R. Greathead, Bishop of Lincoln, for the Countess of Lincoln.
Mat. Par.†	Chronicle of Matthew Paris, monk of S. Alban's, is of the best authority for events during his life; he died 1259. He frequently describes personal interviews with Henry III., but his chronicle, according to the usual custom, was not made public till after the King's death.
Mat. Westm.*	Chronicle of Matthew of Westminster, who flourished 1375, a decided Royalist in his compilation.
Mirac. S. de Mont.† . .	Miracula Simonis de Monteforti, printed with Rishanger's Chr. by the Camden Society, from .SM

Cott. Vespas. A. VI., probably written from time to time by the monks of Evesham, between 1265 and 1278.

Nangis† .... Histoire de S. Louis, by William de Nangis, a monk of S. Denis. Annals to 1300 in French and Latin —good contemporaneous authority. Rec. des Hist. Fr. T. XX., 1840.

Nichols, Leicest. ..... History of Leicestershire by J. Nichols, F.S.A. Edin., contains an excellent account of Simon de Montfort by Rev. Sambrook N. Russell, in Part I. Vol. 1.

Nobility .... Catalogue of, compiled by Robert Cooke, Clareucieux, from MS. 1440 Harl. Art. 23. f. 17. 55. MS. of Rev. H. Wellesley.

Nobility of England from 1066 to 1602. MS. of Rev. H. W.

Petr. Vall. Sarn. ..... Petri Vallium Sarnaii Història Albigensium, a monk of Vaux Sernai Abbey, near Paris, born about 1170-80, living 1218, a furious bigot engaged in the Albigensian war.

Polit. Songs ...... Political Songs of England from K. John to Edward II., edited by Mr T. Wright for the Camden Society; a very curious and interesting collection of contemporary evidences of popular feeling.

Raspe .... Critical essay on oil painting, proving that the art of painting in oil was known before the pretended discovery of John and Hubert Von Eyck, to which are added Theophilus, de Arte Pingendi, and Eraclius de Artibus Romanorum, &c. ; by R. E. Raspe, London, Cadell 1781.

W. Rish.† .... Chronicle of William Rishanger, monk of S. Alban's, continuing that of Matthew Paris from 1259 to 1312, and published with it. A competent contemporary authority. [Edited by Mr. Riley for the Record Commission.]

W. Rish. de bello Lew.† Another chronicle by the same author, "de Bellis Lewes et Evesham," lately printed by the Camden Society from MS. Cott. Claud. D. VI.

Rob. Brune .... The chronicle of English History, written in French verse by Peter Langtoft, Canon of Bridlington, was translated by Robert Manning, called R. de Brune (from Bourne, near Deping, co. Lincoln), begun 1303. [This is now being edited for the Record Commission by Mr. F. J. Furnivall.]

Rob. Glouc.† ...... Chronicle in English verse, by Robert of Gloucester, who resided at Oxford. Camden and Usher con-

REFERENCES.

	sider him to have lived in the time of Henry III.; G. Ellis in the time of Edward I.
Rolls of Arms	Roll 1240—1245 made about 1308-14, published from MS. in Br. Mus. by N. H. Nicolas, 1828.
Rymer	The invaluable series of documents relating to English history, Rymer's Fœdera, Vols. I and II.
Starke	Historiæ Anglicanæ Scriptores. Fol. Lond. 1723, containing Chr. Walteri de Whyttleseye, cænobii Burgensis Hist. (Burgh, originally Medeshamstede until burnt by the Danes, named Peterborough when restored, A. D. 970).
W. Thorn	Chronicle of W. Thorn, a monk of S. Augustine in Canterbury, who flourished 1380.
Trésor des Chartes	To be published in 9 4to. Vols. at Paris by command of Nap. III. by M. Henri Plon; 17,000 documents from A. D. 755 to 1559.
T. Wyke*	Chronicle of Thomas Wyke, an Augustine Canon of Osney, to 1290; an historian of good authority. In Hist. Anglic. Scriptores V. [Edited also with the parallel annals of Osney by the Rev. H. R. Luard for the Record Commission. Annales Monastici, Vol. IV.]

CONTENTS.

CHAP.		PAGE
I.	INTRODUCTION	1
II.	HENRY III. AND HIS COURTIERS	9
III.	SIMON DE MONTFORT	41
IV.	THE OXFORD STATUTES	66
V.	WAR AND TRUCE	100
VI.	THE AWARD OF AMIENS	112
VII.	WAR RENEWED	125
VIII.	NEGOTIATIONS AT LEWES	139
IX.	THE MARCH UPON LEWES	163
X.	THE BATTLE OF LEWES	187
XI.	THE MISE OF LEWES	213
XII.	GOVERNMENT OF THE BARONS	221
XIII.	PARLIAMENT	244
XIV.	TREACHERY AND HOSTILITIES	256
XV.	THE BATTLE OF EVESHAM	270
XVI.	THE DISINHERITED	297
XVII.	ELEANOR DE MONTFORT AND HER SONS	313
XVIII.	THE MURDER AT VITERBO	336
	AUTHOR'S APPENDICES, A TO E	354—363
	EDITOR'S APPENDICES, F. G.	363—380

ERRATA.

p. 45. Note 1, l. 7, instead of "*de* Bald," read "*the* Bald."

p. 129. End of Note 6 from p. 128, add [John de Cranford was also there. New Rymer, I. p. 450].

p. 149. Note 1, col. 3, l. 3, of pedigree, instead of "1177?" read "c. June 1240."

p. 165. Note 3, col. 2, l. 16, instead of "ceulæ" read "ceulx."

p. 169. Note 3, l. 1, for "Grenequer," read "Crevequer."

p. 251. Note 3, col. 2, l. 1, insert "the bishop of" before Norwich.

p. 321. Note 2, *dele* the last sentence.

p. 326. l. 9, instead of "Earl of Lincoln," read "descended from the old Earls of Lincoln."

THE BARONS' WAR.

CHAPTER I.

"Stand upon that elevation of reason, which places centuries under our eye, and brings things to the true point of comparison, which obscures little names and effaces the colours of little parties, and to which nothing can ascend, but the spirit and moral quality of human actions."

BURKE.

THE attention of the present age is not easily attracted to the records of past times : eager to enjoy the luxuries which commerce and science are yearly multiplying for their use, few are disposed to turn back to a distant period of British History, when a very different state of things prevailed; when the seeds of those blessings, now so habitual, were cast upon an unfriendly soil, requiring the watchful guard of a bold mind, and an armed hand for their growth and maturity. The fierce struggles for freedom or power, and the miseries of civil war, once necessary to secure the rights of the community, are now read with a traditional assent, indeed, to the verdict of history, but with little scrutiny into the justice which has thus stamped some transactions with honour, and branded others with disgrace; has considered some conspicuous characters as patriots, others as rebels.

This has been remarkably true as to the great events of the thirteenth century, which established the main prin-

B

ciples of liberty in this land. Magna Charta now passes current everywhere as a household word, the hallowed type of a successful assertion of political rights; while the Barons' war and the battle of Lewes, though also great moral lessons of permanent influence occasionally forced upon monarchs, have dropped away as if unimportant from general remembrance.

There are, indeed, too many battlefields strewed over the face of England, where no really national interest was at stake, where blood flowed only to gratify or thwart the ambition of an individual, or where some point of a disputed pedigree trembled in the balance. From such selfish contests, if they could have been decided by personal combat without involving the welfare of a whole nation, the mind would shrink with less regret; but the Barons' war, of which the Battle of Lewes was a main incident, does not deserve to be forgotten or confused with such. It occurred in stirring times, when every man readily took his side, the proud noble and the half-enfranchised commoner uniting their strength with zealous earnestness; the contest was of a nature which we now consider the most awful and irreconcilable, a war of principles, the conflicting claims of royal prerogative, and of popular control, there met at length in active hostility, after the fruitless trial, for many years, of more pacific means.

There would have been no need to revive this remote subject, which, as Drayton[1] said of his own story of some later wars, "is surely fit matter for trump or tragedy," had it fortunately attracted the electric spark of Shakspeare's genius. Such alchemy would long since have transmuted it into current gold, and would have fixed in the popular mind the sterling worth of the personages and facts, undisturbed by the doubts of philosophers or historians. The silence of the dramatist, however, having prevented them becoming so familiar to us as the events he has handled, we can only feel

[1] Preface to his poem Barons' War.

sure that he would have depicted the chief actors in the reign of Henry III., if at all, with their usual mixture of good and evil qualities, as he has done all his characters, whether historical or self-created[1].

It is not from men of the thirteenth century that we could expect the performance of great actions from pure and unmixed motives; it is not so in the nineteenth. Great and gross vices then prevailed in every class, and public opinion did not require even that decorous homage to virtue, which modern vice is content to render. United with the genuine patriotism of one party, no doubt ambition, self-interest, and revenge played their part, while the conscientious maintenance of long used prerogative on the other side, was embittered by love of despotic power and by personal resentment; and though the warm incentives of religion were called in aid by both parties, each at times displayed an almost ostentatious perjury. A modern hand cannot presume to trace out all the various influences then at work in the breast of individuals: all was not pure, for the agents were human; but nothing can evince more strikingly the soundness of the views adopted by the party victorious at Lewes, than the fact that during their short year of triumph, English freedom rose to so vigorous a manhood, and acquired so confirmed a development, as to enable the spirit of their principles long to survive the downfall of their promoters, and to this day we are enjoying the full maturity of their effects.

There were some powerful engines of agitation to ruffle the surface of society in the thirteenth century. The

[1] Gibbon (see Miscell. Works, Vol. I. p. 106) at one time selected the Barons' War for an historical subject, but soon abandoned it. In a letter (April, 1761) he writes that he had fixed upon the expedition of Charles VIII. into Italy; but in another letter, dated Beriton, Aug. 4, 1761, he states that he had "renounced Charles VIII. I successively chose and rejected the Crusade of Richard I., the Barons' Wars against John and Henry III., the History of the Black Prince, the lives and companions of Henry V., the Emperor Titus, Sir Philip Sydney, the Marquis of Montrose: at length I have fixed on Sir Walter Raleigh for my hero." In July, 1762, he drops Raleigh for the Swiss, and the Medici.

Crusades, those furious efforts of wild credulity, the glory of their own age, though now its reproach and scorn, furnished allurements yet sufficient to assemble hosts too vast for use or restraint; and the Popes of Rome, besides exciting these outbursts of foreign adventure, put forward also at this period their most extravagant pretensions. A war preached in the name of God is indeed an awful matter; but not content with sending crowds of zealots to destruction in Pagan Syria, they wielded the same weapon against all nearer opposition, and repeatedly exhibited the strange anomaly of organizing Crusades against the disciples of the Cross[1]. The simpler faith of the Albigenses was thus crushed by fire and sword; dethronement and a holy war were decreed against our own King John and other monarchs; the political disputes with the Empire were decided in a similar way, although the Popes met occasionally with a stout resistance. Gregory IX. was thus in 1227 publicly denounced by the excommunicated Emperor Frederick as "the Great Dragon and the Antichrist," although, indeed, he retorted on him as "the beast of blasphemy, and the king of plagues." When this Emperor found himself, in 1243, excommunicated for the third time, and his crown declared to be forfeited, he desired his attendants to see if his crown were really lost from his jewel chest, and on its being produced, put it firmly on his head, and stood erect, saying, "I have neither lost it, nor will I do so with impunity for any Pope or Council. As to the Pope presuming to depose me, his superior, so much the better; I was before bound to obey him in some measure, or at least to respect him, but now I am absolved from any sort of love, veneration, or peace towards him[2]." This practical refutation of

---

[1] Lo principe dè nuovi Farisei,
Avendo guerra presso a Laterano,
E non co' Saracin nè con Giudei;
Che ciascun suo nimico era Cristiano.   Inf. xxvii. 85.
This Prince of modern Pharisees delights
Close to the Lateran his war to wage:
Not against Saracens or Jews he fights;
On Christians only he vents all his rage.

[2] M. Paris.

the Pope's power forms a strong contrast to the abject spirit of King John.

The head of the Church insisted not only on the independence but the supremacy of its members, for as the soul is superior to the body (they sophistically[1] argued) so should spiritual authority govern and punish secular power. No civil court being allowed to interfere for the punishment of their most heinous offences, it is said that Henry II. found that one hundred murders had been committed by the clergy unpunished. These and other monstrous abuses might well justify King Richard's satirical bequest of his favourite vices to the different orders of clergy; and the long enduring submission to such arrogance is the strongest proof of prostrate intellect during the dark, or, what modern courtesy terms, the middle ages.

From such prevailing influence, even the French King Louis IX., though eminently distinguished for strength of mind, and resolutely maintaining the rights of his national Church, was unable wholly to free himself. Coming to the throne in early youth, he retained such a lofty purity of conscience and such a mixed spirit of piety and enterprize, that he attracted the universal respect of his contemporaries, who frequently referred their disputes to his arbitration, as we shall have occasion to notice in connexion with the battle of Lewes.

The love of distant adventure, and the spirit of priestly ambition, were felt in England, as well as elsewhere, during the reign of Henry III., while the social condition of the country not only exhibited a civilization inferior to many parts of the continent (for an insular position, until commerce becomes general, necessarily retards its progress), but was still powerfully influenced by the great Norman conquest. The heaviness of a foreign yoke had not yet ceased to gall the conquered, whose debasement had been complete. The Conqueror had seized the estates not only of all who

[1] Thomas Aquinas (who died 1274) quoted in Hallam's Hist. Lit.

had opposed him at Hastings, but even of those who had intended to be there; and, indeed, many of the Normans had done homage to him before the expedition, for lands about to be conquered[1]. To his fellow-soldiers, accordingly, many of them poor and lowly at home, were vast tracts of English land granted.

It is due to King William's discretion, to observe that in Domesday there occurs only once, perhaps by an oversight, a phrase indicating conquest[2], the more usual term referring to so great a change being the courteous one "after the King came to England[3];" and it is also remarkable, that there was no grant of a single acre to any of his own sons.

When Domesday reports but two or three ploughs in a large parish, it is obvious that land of so little value was indeed the cheapest reward in the King's power, and of this he made an unsparing use, giving, for example, to his son-in-law, William, Earl de Warenne, 298 manors. The wholesale nature of the confiscation may be made more palpable, perhaps, by stating that all the three adjoining counties of Kent, Surrey, and Sussex[4], were thus in the hands of 56 proprietors, very few indeed of whom were Saxons.

Kent was the property of 12 owners, all Normans, except the clergy.
Surrey —————————— 41 including 6 Saxons, who held only 8 manors.
Sussex —————————— 15 { of the 3489[5] hides, 2649 belonged to the King and Normans, 833 to the Church, and 10 only to Saxons.

———
68

The King, however, being reckoned in each county, and 10 of the 15 Sussex proprietors holding lands also in Surrey,

---

[1] Chr. de Norm. Thierry, Conq. d'Angl.
[2] "Postquam Wilhelmus Rex conquisivit Angliam."
[3] "Postquam Rex venit in Angliam."
[4] Kent, Sussex, and Surrey being the first counties occupied, and comprising many estates that belonged to Harold, his family and his adherents, suffered in proportion more than the rest of England. P.
[5] The numbers given amount to 3492. My own calculation of the hidage of Sussex makes it under 3200. P.

a deduction of 12 would reduce the number to 56. In all Domesday, which does not include four Northern counties, there are only 600 named proprietors[1].

The few Normans thus enriched, and scattered over the face of the country, became by the very condition of their scanty numbers, and their masses of property, too proud and powerful for easy control, and gradually imbibed from the soil of their new country the inherent maxims of Saxon freedom. They who had conquered the land with the Conqueror, were little ready to give up the privileges which they had so earned, and as, fortunately, no difference of religious creed separated them from the humbled Saxons, though of another race and language, common interests and intercourse gradually led to mutual respect. The Norman landholders were, indeed, but little of patriots, and set slight value on the good of the people, but being jealous of the royal authority, they readily combined with them in the coercion of their King. They had grievances too of their own, heavy burthens repugnant to their feelings, arising from their feudal tenures, which, on every fresh occasion, revived heart-burnings and rebellions among them. Some of these hardships—the unfixed alienation fines, the inability to devise fiefs by will, and the control of the crown over the marriage of wards—had been unknown to them in Normandy[2].

The more refined arts and manners of their foreign dominions naturally attracted the early Norman kings to frequent residence in the country of their birth. During the 36 years of his reign, Henry I. passed but 5 summers in England. Henry II. visited Normandy annually for 26 years, and died there. Richard I. was abroad for 9 years,

---

[1] Mr Blaauw here refers to a passage in Brady's Introduction (pp. 170, 171), "there were not in William the Conqueror's reign (as appears by an alphabetical catalogue made out of Domesday Book) 700 tenants in capite besides Bishops, Abbots, Priors, and great Churchmen," &c. Kelham, however, only enumerates 435, besides Bishops and Churches. Sir H. Ellis, reckoning in Ecclesiastical Corporations and King's Thanes, says "The Tenants in capite amounted scarcely to 1400." Introduction to Domesday, Vol. II. p. 511. P.

[2] Hallam, Middle Ages.

except a few months in England. The long absences of their kings afforded greater opportunity to the barons to establish themselves on an independent footing. After the lapse of four or five generations, they began to consider themselves as Englishmen, and resented as such the tyrannous caprice and corruption of the court. It must be remembered that at this period there was no permanent tax, and no standing army; the physical strength of the crown was but occasional, and the revenue casual. When the Sovereign, therefore, in his need grasped at forbidden profits, his rapacity was resisted at once by the feudal Barons as an unlawful interference, not so much with their rights as subjects, as with their individual privileges and property. These were much more intelligible to them and more dearly cherished, for "what we now call public rights were then private ones," as has been remarked by a sagacious historian[1];" and it was under these impulses that their combined efforts of resistance won the Great Charter.

[1] Guizot, Civilisation en Europe.

CHAPTER II.

HENRY III. AND HIS COURTIERS.

> "Our coffers with too great a court
> And liberal largess are grown somewhat light."
> RICH. II.

MAGNA CHARTA, to which it is remarkable that Shakspeare makes no allusion whatever in his King John, required about thirty confirmations from subsequent kings to enforce its provisions, although its renewal in the ninth year of Henry III. is now referred to as an existing statute, and was of so little avail to check discord, that it was while a foreign Prince was occupying the country and claiming the Crown (in behalf of his wife, John's niece), that Henry III., a boy of nine years old, first inherited the throne.

Nothing but the wisdom and courage of the Regent William, Earl of Pembroke, which won over the chiefs of the opposite party, preserved England from then becoming a tributary province to France, and until his death (in March, 1219) the councils of the young Prince were swayed by his prudence; nor did the defects of the King's character become apparent, until deprived of this statesman.

This Earl, by his marriage with the heiress of Strongbow, the conqueror of Ireland, had acquired immense estates in that country, which extended over 124 miles in length and 74 in breadth. Leaving ten children, his earldom was successively held by each of his five sons, after whom his five daughters became, in 1245, the co-heirs of the property[1]. This failure of male heirs was looked upon as fulfilling the curse of a priest, from whom he had seized some lands. The zealous churchman, when urged by the King to remove the excommunication after his death, stuck steadily to his text, while professing compliance; and though he ceremoniously absolved the soul of the Earl, it was on the express condition of previous restitution by his heirs of the lands in question[2].

An ambitious native of Poictou, Peter de Roches, Bishop of Winchester, succeeded as Regent. Having been an active knight in earlier life, he was employed, in 1234, by the Pope, long after his episcopacy, to command his troops[3]; and this soldier-prelate made the weak King for many years the passive instrument of his own power, inspiring him with those arbitrary principles of government, which so often en-

---

[1] William, the Marshal, Earl of Pembroke, married Isabella, only child of Richard de Clare, Earl of Pembroke, surnamed Strongbow. He died March, 1219, and lies buried in the Temple Church. His arms were "Party per pale, or and vert, a lion rampant, gules."

1. William, 2nd Earl, his eldest son, a gallant soldier, one of the 25 guardians of Magna Charta, died April, 1231, and is buried in the Temple. He married Princess Eleanor, daughter of King John, in 1224, but they had no children, and she remarried, January, 1238, Simon de Montfort, Earl of Leicester.

2. Richard, 3rd Earl, rebelled, and was killed in Ireland, 1234.

3. John, defeated Prince Louis at sea, 1217, and died unmarried.

4. Gilbert, 4th Earl, implicated in the rebellion of Earl Richard (Archæol. Journal, 1863, p. 165), a Crusader, in 1236, suddenly dismissed by Henry III., 1239, died at a tournament, May, 1241, and is buried in the Temple; he married Margaret, a princess of Scotland.

5. Walter, 5th Earl, died December 4, 1245.

6. Anselm, 6th Earl, Dean of Salisbury, died December 22, 1245.

7. Matilda, the eldest daughter, carried the hereditary title of Earl Marshal into her husband's family, with whose descendants it still remains. She died 1248, having married, first, Hugh le Bigod, Earl of Norfolk, and, secondly, John de Warenne, Earl of Surrey.

8. Joan, married Warin de Monchensi. Their daughter carried the earldom of Pembroke to her husband, William de Valence, half brother of Henry III.

9. Isabella married, first, Gilbert de Clare, Earl of Gloucester, who died October, 1230; and, secondly, Prince Richard, Earl of Cornwall, April, 1231. Her incised memorial was lately found at Beaulieu Abbey. Archæol. Journal, 1863, p. 107.

10. Sybilla, married William de Ferrers, Earl of Derby.

11. Eve, married William de Braose (see Calend. Geneal. I. p. 227. P.), who died 1254.

[2] M. Par.
[3] Ibid.

dangered his throne, and even monarchy itself. He is thus described in a contemporary satire[1]:

Wintoniensis armiger	The Winchester Bishop—Knight
Præsidet ad Scaccarium,	At th' Exchequer sits paramount,
Ad computandum impiger	Slow to read Gospel aright
Piger ad Evangelium,	Tho' nimble the money to count;
Regis revolvens rotulum;	The King's Rolls handling all day,
Sic Lucam lucrum superat,	He looks more to lucre than Luke,
Marco marcam præponderat	Marcs their namesake Saint outweigh,
Et libræ librum subjicit.	He ponders on pounds, not his book.

The inherent caprice of the King's "waxen heart"[2] in favour or hatred, evinced a natural incapacity for governing. The only fixed point in his character seems to have been his devotion, if it can be so called; in his movements, either in England or on the continent, he never failed to visit all the churches and shrines of mouldering relics within reach, and not content with three public masses a day, he attended others in private, practising religious ceremonies as diligently and with as little self-discipline of conduct as any man of his times[3].

The anomaly of a governor without either the talent of governing or of selecting others fit to do so, is a heavy affliction upon a nation; the obedience of a willing people requires to be met by the affectionate care and wisdom of a Sovereign, especially when no system of popular control has been devised. Imbecile virtue upon a throne, as affording scope to the evil passions of others, often weighs as grievously upon a people as the daring crimes of ambitious tyranny. Dante, nearly the contemporary of Henry III., puts him into his Purgatory as a man of simple life, singing psalms

---

[1] Polit. Songs, p. 10.
[2] "Cor cereum regis."—M. Par.
[3] Louis IX. advised Henry III. to hear more sermons, and fewer masses, but he replied, that he preferred to hear of his friend more seldom, and to see him the oftener. Chr. Triveti.—See Archæol. Journal, 1860, p. 316, the same anecdote fully reported from Add. MSS. Br. Mus. 4573, p. 57; it occurred in 1259, and in explanation of K. Henry having been delayed by his attendance on masses in his way from meeting the French king in due time for Parliament.

among flowers and odours in a narrow valley, typical of his contracted views.

"Vedete il Re della semplice vita
"Seder là solo, Arrigo d'Inghilterra."—Purg. vii. 130.

But, perhaps, the judgment of later times would pass a sterner sentence on the cause of so much misery and confusion.

Peter de Roches would not allow that there were any peers in England as in France, and considered all the barons therefore liable to his jurisdiction. He encouraged the King in such a distrust of his own nobles, that all the English were dismissed in 1233, and their offices and the command of the royal castles committed to foreigners, 200 of whom came over on his invitation. The King was in vain warned that, to avoid the shipwreck of his kingdom, he must shun stones and rocks, in allusion to the names of Pierre de Roches; his preference for foreigners unhappily continued to prevail long after the disgrace and death of the first suggester.

Among the aliens thus promoted was the well-known legate Pandulf, who, on his return to Rome, after his memorable scenes with King John, had taken priest's orders and was raised to the bishopric of Norwich[1]. This advancement of a man, who had for three days ostentatiously withheld the crown from the King of England, must have been peculiarly distasteful to loyal feeling. After being employed confidentially in the King's service, and procuring from Rome the unusual grant of the firstfruits of his diocese for himself and his successors in the see, he died, greatly enriched, in Dec. 1226.

Among other foreigners who shared the rises and falls of De Roches, were Peter de Rivaulx, the treasurer, and Robert de Passilewe, his underling. The latter is, indeed, sometimes

---

[1] He writes as Bishop Elect from Chichester, in May, 1220, reporting an unsuccessful mission in Wales, to H. de Burgh (Rymer), but was not consecrated until 1222.

designated "as a degenerate Englishman[1]," and at any rate was a crafty courtier, who recommended himself by his contrivances to extort money for his master. As a means of receiving increased wealth, he became a priest, and though his election to the see of Chichester (in 1244) was successfully resisted, large benefices in Durham and Ely, as well as the archdeaconry of Lewes, were conferred upon him[2].

The great rival of de Roches was Hubert de Burgh[3], one of the few nobles of unshaken loyalty to King John, for whom he firmly defended Dover against all the assaults of Prince Louis. Shakspeare has made his name familiar and odious to us, representing him as taunted by the Earl of Norfolk with " Out, dunghill ! dar'st thou brave a nobleman ? " (K. John, IV. 2.) His father had, however, been high in office and favour with Henry II. Hubert was so much esteemed, that, besides obtaining the earldom of Kent, he was made Justiciary of England for life in 1228, and though of a violent disposition and surrounded by many enemies at court, especially de Roches, there seems no reason to doubt his good faith and loyalty. The King, however, reproached him with personal insult as a traitor, and he was made to feel all the bitterness of serving a fickle prince, who alternately caressed and persecuted him in his old age, until, after surrendering part of his estates, he died in 1243, in comparative neglect. It speaks well for him, that in the depth of his adversity, when the furious King was urging others to take his life, he met with two pleasing instances of sympathy: when dragged out of Brentwood Chapel by soldiers, in 1232, a blacksmith refused to put fetters upon " him who had fought so well against the French, and who had preserved England from

[1] "Degener Anglicus."—M. Par.
[2] M. Par. In 1233 the King appointed Ralph de Neville, Bishop of Chichester, to hold the King's seal *for life,* and to be Chancellor of England and Ireland. Rymer, I. 208. R. de Passilewe's election was annulled. Chancellor Neville rose and fell with Hubert de Burgh. Passilewe died in 1252. His arms were "Bendy or, and azure, on a quarter argent, a leopard passant, guardant, gules."— Roll of Arms.
[3] " De Burgh " arg. on fess sable 3 bezants.

aliens;" and when the King was compelled by the indignant clergy to replace him in the Sanctuary[1], and was there starving him by a blockade, his former chaplain, Luke, the Archbishop of Dublin, offered himself as a substitute with the most earnest entreaties and tears[2].

Stephen de Segrave[3], an alien patronised by De Roches, who had obtained the grant of many castles and lands, while his knighthood was yet recent, for he had been a priest, succeeded De Burgh as Justiciary. [July, 1232.] "Judgement (says the indignant chronicler[4]) was then entrusted to the unjust, the laws to outlaws, peace to the turbulent, and justice to wrongdoers." He became not only obnoxious to the barons, but went through the same vicissitudes of royal favour and disgrace as his predecessor, dying, in 1251, concealed in the Abbey of Leicester, where he had taken refuge.

It would appear that the King had proposed to himself perpetual continence[5], and was much disturbed by the remonstrances of his council calling on him to marry for reasons of state. Five unsuccessful treaties for his marriage with different princesses had been proposed, and in one instance so far advanced that the Pope's dispensation was required to annul his previous betrothal to Joanna, afterwards Queen of Castile, when he was at length, at the age of 29, in January, 1236, married to the beautiful Eleanor, one of the four queenly daughters of Raymond, Count of Provence. Used to the superior refinement of arts and manners of her own country, herself highly accomplished and a

---

[1] Those who took refuge in a sanctuary were obliged by law to swear before the coroner that they would go out of the kingdom, and not return without leave. They were to go to some port assigned for their embarkation, carrying a cross to prove that they were under the protection of the Church, and to embark within two tides, unless the winds were contrary, in which case they were obliged to walk into the sea up to their knees daily, as a token of their readiness. The protection ceased in forty days, unless they returned to the sanctuary. In later times they were marked by the coroner with A (abjured) on the ball of the right thumb.—Grose.

[2] M. Par.—Luke died 1255, after a blindness of many years.

[3] "Vir flexibilis, de clerico factus miles."—M. Par.

[4] Wendover, Vol. IV. p. 265.

[5] Chr. Lanerc.

poet[1]; it was by sending specimens of her talent in this respect, that she introduced herself to the notice of the English Court.

The young Princess was brought over by her uncle, William, Count of Champagne, an artful man, who soon acquired great influence over the King, and from this time all patronage was in the hands of the Queen's relations and adherents. The Pope had given him the bishopric of Valence, in order to secure his military talents in the war against the Emperor, and King Henry was so bent on making him Bishop of Winchester, that he would probably have succeeded, had not the news of his death, by poison, at Viterbo, in 1239, prevented the scheme. The King's grief at his loss was so outrageous, that he tore his clothes, cast them into the fire, and with loud groans shut himself up in total seclusion[2].

The Queen's influence prevailed in welcoming others of her own family with grants of wealth and offices of dignity, to the disgust of the neglected English.

> "Thoro the Quene was so muche Frenss folc ibrougt
> That of Englisse men, me tolde as right nought;
> And the King hom let hor wille, that each was as King,
> And nome povere menne god, and ne paiede nothing[3]."
>
> ROBT. GLOUC.

Peter of Savoy, another uncle, was raised to the chief place at the council, and received grants of the vast domain of Richmond[4], in Yorkshire, soon after his arrival in 1241.

---

[1] Arms in S. aisle of Westminster Abbey, "Or, 4 pallets gules." In Sandford's General Hist. p. 57, are two seals of Queen Eleanor of Provence. Some MS. poems of hers are still extant at Turin.—See Strickland's Queens.

[2] M. Par.

[3] Through the Queen was so many French folk brought, that Englishmen were reckoned as right nought, and the King let them have their will, so that each was as a King, and they took poor men's goods, and paid nothing.

[4] Peter de Savoy received Richmond 1241, allowing John, son of Peter, Earl of Brittany, who had resigned it 1237, a pension of 2000 marcs. On the marriage of John, Earl of Brittany, in 1259, with Beatrice, daughter of Henry III., Richmond was claimed by him, and finally surrendered to him, July 1268, by Peter de Savoy, who accepted the Honor of Hastings in its place. By patent 126_, the

The castles of Pevensey and Hastings were quickly added, besides the wardship of the young Earl of Warenne and Surrey[1], by which Lewes Castle also came under his extended influence in Sussex, a circumstance which may have decided the King, at a later period, in the selection of that county for his field of battle. The honour of knighthood was conferred on him with great pomp in Westminster Abbey. On one occasion, he returned from the continent (1247) bringing with him a bevy of fair damsels, as destined mates to the young nobles held in ward by his courtiers; an unnecessary importation, sure to provoke the jealousy of all the affronted sex. The wealthy earls of Lincoln, of Devon, of Kent, of Gloucester and of Warenne[2] were thus provided with foreign countesses in their early youth, before they had the power of exercising any choice. Peter became a Crusader in 1255, and was employed repeatedly in embassies to France. The Savoy in London still keeps up the remembrance of another grant to him, which, with his other property, he bequeathed at his death, in 1268, to the Queen and his brothers[3].

King had granted to his executors 7 years' revenue after his death, and, 1262, allowed Peter de Savoy to dispose of his lands by will.—Whitaker's Hist. Richm. Rymer. Gell's Registrum Honoris de Richmond, 1722.
[1] Sept. 23, 1341.
[2] Edmund de Lacy, Earl of Lincoln (who died 1258), married, 1247, Alice, daughter of Marchese Saluces. His arms in S. aisle Westm. Abb. are, "Quarterly gules and or, a bendlet sable, and a file of 5 lambeaux argent."
Baldwin de Ripariis, Earl of Devon, married, 1257, a Savoyard, kinswoman of the Queen.
Richard de Burgh, Earl of Kent, married another kinswoman in 1247.
Gilbert de Clare, son and heir of the Earl of Gloucester, married, 1253, Alice, daughter of Guy Count of Angoulême.
John de Warenne, Earl of Warenne and Surrey, married Alicia, the King's half sister, who died 1256, while yet young.
Peter de Geneve, a Provençal favourite of the King, of low origin, was married to one of the wealthy daughters of Walter de Lasci.—M. Par.
[3] On the seal Petri de Sabaudia appended to the deed confirming the peace with France in 1259, there is a lion rampant, not included within an escutcheon. Archiv. du Royaume cart. 629. 10. In Roll of Arms, t. Henry III., Peter de Savoy's arms are "gules, a cross argent," being assumed by Amadeus V. at the request of the Knights Hospitallers of St John, patron of Lombardy, after the raising the siege of Rhodes in 1315. [In his first edition Mr Blaauw had said: "His marble effigy in complete ring-armour, covering even his hands is still extant on an altar-tomb at Aquabella in Savoy." He afterwards added in a (corrected) note, from information sup-

His brother, Boniface, exercised a similar influence over the King, and, in 1241, to the great scandal of the Church, this stranger was, by dint of royal compulsion, chosen Archbishop of Canterbury, although so reluctant was the chapter to elect him, that many of its members abandoned their stalls in disgust, and became Carthusian monks. His person was tall and elegant, but his youth, ignorance, and overbearing manners[1] made him incompetent for such a dignity, and the offence was the more striking from his contrast with the sainted Edmund[2], whom he succeeded, and who had retired to a foreign monastery, where he died hopeless of reforming the Church.

Boniface was enthroned, with great pomp, in 1249, in presence of the Royal family, and afterwards freely mingled in the intrigues and wars of the Continent, together with his brother Philip, Archbishop of Lyons, neglecting his see, and draining off its revenues for 13 years[3]. The well-known anecdote of his visitation at the convent of St Bartholomew may illustrate his views of episcopal duty, though somewhat startling to modern clergy, accustomed to the serene tranquillity of such an occasion. Though he was met with every mark of respect, and led in procession, with ringing of bells, to the choir, yet his authority being there questioned, the archbishop so far forgot himself as to assault the aged sub-prior with his fist, beating his breast and grey head, and crying out with horrid oaths, "This, this is the way to attack English traitors," while the example was naturally followed by the attendants, who attacked the canons in the

---

plied by Mr Walford: "The eagle of the empire is on his shield. The arms of Savoy as a fief of the empire were, or, an eagle displayed, sable." But he finally wrote, "The effigy at Aquabella is more probably that of Peter de Maurienne, his brother, or that of his nephew Thomas, Count of Maurienne, who founded the Church at Aquabella." P.]

[1] M. Par. — " Plus genere quam scientiâ coruscus." "Morum et scientiæ mendicum." Add. MSS. 5444, "inutilis minister," Chr. Lanerc. "homo honestus, curialis et compositus sed admodum literis indoctus."

[2] He was canonized 1246, and Nov. 16 appointed as his Feast.

[3] When he died in 1270, "tota lætatur Anglia specialiusque Cantuarium."—Add. MSS. 5444.

same manner. It is even said that in this disgraceful affair, the prelate's robes becoming discomposed betrayed armour beneath. The beaten party presented themselves in their bruised and bleeding state to the Bishop of London, who at once forwarded them to the King, but at the palace-door they waited in vain for an audience, and were obliged without any redress to betake themselves, with prayers for vengeance, to their patron saint, who having, according to the legend, been flayed alive, must be considered a good judge in matters of torture. The good citizens of London losing all patience at such a scene, rang the tocsin, and fairly hunted the archbishop back to Lambeth[1]. Such conduct justifies our applying to this prelate the bold address of a satirical song, composed about this time:

" Tu qui tenes hunc tenorem	Thou, with that greedy haughty face,
Frustra dicis te pastorem,	No shepherd thou, but hireling base!
Nec te regis ut rectorem	In all the world's intrigues plunged deep,
Rerum mersus in adorem!	In vain your forfeit rank you keep.
Hæc est alia	Spawn of the horseleach, whom well fed
Sanguisugæ filia	The grasping Court may fitly wed.
Quam venalis curia	
Duxit in uxorem."[2]	

It was for bishops of this character, that the King's brother, Richard, candidly expressed his wish at a later

[1] M. Par. That the violence and doubtful principles of a monk did not disqualify him for the mitre, may be seen by the early life of Robert de Stichill, who was elected Bishop of Durham, 1260. When yet a monk, at first "nimis levis fuit, et quâdam die Dominica cum propter levitatem suam et rebellionem esset injunctum sibi, ut super sellam in medio chori solus sederet, ut sic rubore confusus maturesceret, *sellam per pedem arripuit, et extra chorum inter populum projecit.* Dicitur etiam quod, ipso apostare cogitante, cum per crucem ex aquilonari parte chori noctanter transire conaretur, monitus est, per vocem emissam cœlitus, ut rediret, et si stare vellet de episcopatu promissum accepit—sic *igitur* dimissis levitatibus et puerilibus cœpit maturescere." Anglia Sacra, R. de Graystones, p. 739.

[2] Polit. Songs, from MS. Cotton, Jul. D. vii. Boniface died abroad— on his tomb was the following inscription, "Hic jacet Bonifacius de Sabaudia Cantuarensis episcopus, operibus et virtutibus plenus; obiit autem apud S. Helenam, A.D. 1270, 18 die Julii. Magister Henricus Calonensis fecit hanc tumbam." Hist. Chron. Piedm. p. 353 in Godwyn de Presulibus.

period. His letter to Prince Edward from Aix la Chapelle, 1257, after boasting of his friend, the Archbishop of Mainz, having in person defeated and nearly captured the Archbishop of Treves, remarks, "See what spirited and warlike prelates we have in Germany! I think it would not be wholly without its use to you, if similar ones were created in England, whose services you might then safely employ against the troublesome attacks of your rebels[1]." For such hints to be current even in a confidential letter, sufficiently stamps the character of the court.

In 1243, the Queen's mother, Beatrice, Countess of Provence, visited England, a lady of remarkable beauty, manners, and prudence. Already mother of two queens, she lived to see her two other daughters bear the same title, an uncommon fortune, recorded by Dante,

> "Quattro figlie ebbe e ciascuna reina
> Ramondo Berlinghieri."—PAR. vi.

Before her death, indeed, in 1268, by the marriages of grand-daughters, Beatrice saw six[2] queens descended from her. Well might she be proud of her progeny, like a second Niobe, to whom a chronicler[3] compares her.

She was received by the King with all the honour due to accomplishments and rank. Nobles met her at Dover, and conducted her in procession through London, where the streets were adorned with gay trappings, and, by a very necessary compliment, rendered passable for the occasion by clearing away the mud and other impediments of the highway[4]. The festivities at the marriage of her daughter,

---

[1] Latin letter in Ann. Burton, dated May 18, 1257.
[2] Her daughters were Margaret, Queen of France, whose daughter became Queen of Navarre; Beatrice, Queen of Sicily; Senchia, Queen of the Romans; and Eleanor, Queen of England, mother of the Queen of Scotland.
[3] M. Par.
[4] Blonde of Oxford, l. 5622.—This poem of the 13th cent. describes a similar preparation of the town of Dammartin to receive the Earl of Oxford:

"La novele tost s'estendi
Parmi la vile, et espandi
Que li peres leur dame vient,
Dist luns à l'autre, 'Or nous con vient
Faire la vile netoüer.'
Qui donque veist desploüer

Senchia[1], with Prince Richard were of unparalleled prodigality, and when she left England, she was attended by the King and court on foot to the sea-side.

Her distinguished reception, blamable only on the score of extravagance, naturally induced her to repeat the visit five years afterwards, as a widow, and she was then accompanied by her brother, Thomas, Count of Maurienne, "both thirsting for fresh draughts from the well-known fountain of royal bounty[2]." Thomas had been previously welcomed with such unsuitable pomp, as to excite the ridicule of the English, but he, too, must have been merry, when he went back after only a few days' visit with the King's gift of 500 marcs (£333. 6s. 8d.), and a grant of the same sum as an annual charge for twenty years upon the Exchequer. Another deed was prepared which would have given him a groat on every sack of wool exported, but to this the keeper of the King's seal, Simon Norman, positively refused to affix its authority, and for this act of sturdy patriotism was disgraced (1239) and turned out of office[3].

Count Thomas, who had married the Pope's niece, was besieged in 1255, in Turin, until his brothers, the two valiant archbishops of Lyons and Canterbury, went to his rescue, and the English court again contributed money. Although so weak as to be carried in a litter, it was to King Henry he once more repaired, in 1258, when in need of fresh supplies for his ransom, and readily procured from him a thousand marcs (£666. 13s. 4d.). He died abroad, in 1259, by poison.

Another turbulent and ambitious Savoyard was raised by court favour, in 1240, to be Bishop of Hereford. This was Peter de Aigue Blanche (Aquablanca), who had been chap-

Toilles de lin et couvrir rues
Si donc que mis ni voit les nues;
Et es costés par les fenestres,
Perdre tant couvertoirs aestres,
Tant drap d'or et tant d'escarlate,
Qui ne sont pas fourré de nate,
Mais de vair, de gris et d'ermine."
[1] Her name in the Latin treaty of marriage (Rymer) is Senchia; in Cal.

Pat. 28° H. III., Shencia. By different authors she is variously named as Sanctia, Scientia, Cynthia, and Cincia.
[2] M. Par. "Ad notum fontem sitientes."
[3] M. Par. The seal was delivered to Richard, Abbot of Evesham.

lain and steward to William, the Queen's uncle, and it was by his advice that all the preferments in the Church were given to foreigners. He accompanied the Crusade of 1250, and was the principal agent in Italy when the Sicilian crown was given to the English King's son. Being at Rome in 1256, with Robert Waleran[1], a knight, engaged in raising money for the payment of the King's debt to the Pope, he there devised the remarkable expedient of sending over bills of exchange, drawn upon the English clergy, to which the legate was instructed to require their signatures, each acknowledging the debt inscribed. This method of transacting business had arisen but shortly before this period in Italy, then the great mart of commerce, and Aigue-blanche derived much credit for his ingenuity in thus perverting it to the purposes of extortion. Fulk de Basset, the Bishop of London (who is boldly praised by a contemporary[2], as "the anchor of the whole kingdom and the shield of its safety"), strenuously resisted this base expedient, and on being threatened with the loss of his mitre, made his memorable reply that "he would then put on his helmet." Aigue-blanche continued under the patronage of the King, notwithstanding his bad character[3], and ignorance of the language and interests of England, although even that patronage failed when attempting to procure him the sees of Lincoln or Lichfield. On a subsequent occasion also, we shall find that he was made to suffer the effects of his personal unpopularity.

Among all the oppressions that vexed the subjects in this reign, none galled their pride or irritated their feelings more than this ostentatious preference of foreigners at court. To enrich them, the choicest gifts of the royal prerogative were willingly lavished; the most lucrative wardships of the young nobles, implying the enjoyment of their estates, the direction of their education, and the disposal of their mar-

[1] Waleran the Hunter—sepulchral slub at Steeple Langford, Wilts.— Arch. Journal, 1858, p. 75.
[2] M. Par.
[3] M. Par. "infamia."

riages, fell into the ready hands of these insolent favourites. "We have nothing to do with your English laws or customs[1]," was their bold reply to all complaints, after acts of violence or plunder, and their impunity induced even some of the English to imitate them: "there are so many tyrants already in England (they argued) that we too may as well set up for such."

The jealousy of foreigners thus became, by force of circumstances, the bond of union between the Normans and Saxons, once so hostile to each other; but the one party was now anxious to retain what they had, and the other dreaded the fresh swarms of oppressors. High and low were therefore eager to exclude these aliens, and it is not surprising that Queen Eleanor herself, by whom they had been introduced, should partake largely of their unpopularity. It was, indeed, to her own foreign steward, William de Tarento, "who fastened on plunder as a leech does on blood[2]," that she transferred the important wardship of William de Cantilupe and the Earl of Salisbury[3], which had been granted to her. This man, a Cistercian monk, had earned her gratitude by raising money for her on the pledge of monastic lands.

For many years her friends had enjoyed a monopoly of court bounties, and it was resented by them as an interference, when another flight of needy foreigners, from a different quarter, arrived in 1247, to bask in the same sunshine.

Isabella, the King's mother, had, four years after King John's death, married[4] her first affianced husband, Hugh le

[1] M. Par.
[2] M. Par.—" Qui quasi sanguini sanguisuga emolumentis inhiabat." He died in 1258.
[3] The wardship of the lands and heirs of William, grandson of William Longespie, Earl of Salisbury, was granted in 1257 to Queen Eleanor. But according to Dugdale, whom Sir Harris Nicolas follows, the earldom did not pass beyond the first William. P.
[4] Queen Isabella's letter to her son Henry III. announcing her marriage with the Lord Hugh de Lusignan, who had "remained alone and without heirs in Poictou," explains that his friends would not allow of his marriage with her daughter Joanna (born 1203), affianced to him, on account of her tender age, and therefore, lest he should take a wife

Brun, Count de la Marche. This gallant troubadour, whose songs are still extant, not only avenged himself for the loss of her broken alliance by a rebellion in Poictou, but with a poetic chivalry remained unmarried until accepted by the lady in her 34th year. She retained, indeed, the undiminished charms of her English dower, and the title of Queen, which she never relinquished. By this connexion, King Henry was subsequently entangled in an inglorious war with France, which rendered the Count unpopular with the English, and on the Queen Dowager's death, in 1246, all their children[1] were sent to thrive under the protection of their royal half-brother. Although they arrived poor, their condition was soon altered; the most confidential offices, and the highest stations in the Church were considered due to them, and, in 1256, the King even commanded that his chancery seal should never be affixed to any deed to their detriment.

William de Valence[2], the third, was, in 1247, made go-

in France, "which if he had done, all your land in Poictou and Gascony would be lost. We seeing the great peril that might accrue if that marriage should take place, when our counsellors could give us no advice, ourselves married the said Hugh, Earl of March, and God knows that we did this rather for your benefit than our own." M. A. E. Wood's Letters of Royal and Illustrious Ladies, Vol. I. p. 38, from the Latin, Royal Letter, No. 392 in Tower. King Henry does not seem to have had previous notice of his mother's marriage, yet he wrote to congratulate the court on hearing of it, May 20, 1220, "gavisi sumus et plurimum lætati."—Rymer. Particulars relating to the family of Le Brun are given in Archæol. Journal, 1853, pp. 359, 360.

[1] 1. Hugh, married Joland, daughter of Peter de Dreux, Duke of Brittany.
2. Guy, Count of Angoulême, whose daughter, Alice, married Gilbert de Clare, Earl of Gloucester.
3. William de Valence, Earl of Pembroke, died 1296, buried in Westminster Abbey, married Joan de Monchensi.
4. Geoffry de Lusignan.
5. Aymer, Bishop elect of Winchester.
Margaret, married Raymond, Count of Thoulouse.
Alicia, married, 1247, John, Earl of Warren.
Isabella, wife of Maurice de Croham.

[2] Arms, burelle d'argent et d'azure de 10 pieces, orle de martlets gules—his tomb in Westminster Abbey, engraved in Stothard's Monumental Effigies. An enamelled casket (see Shaw's Ancient Furniture) bearing the arms of England, Angoulême, Valence, Dreux, Duke of Brittany, Brabant Lacy, and "azure, a lion rampant purpure," is extant, was exhibited in 1862 at Archæol. Institute's Enamel Exhibition, by G. Chapman, Esq. (Arch. Journ. p. 285), and may

vernor of Goodrich Castle, and married to Joan, a great heiress of the Monchensi family, grand-daughter to the great Earl of Pembroke, a title afterwards borne by himself, in virtue of the estates at Pembroke, which he held (by grant, 1250) on the tenure of doing suit for them to his wife. On the death of her father, Warin de Monchensi, in 1255, who is said to have bequeathed more than 200,000 marcs (£133,333. 6s. 8d.), the wardship of his son, William, was granted to this foreigner.

It was on a solemn occasion, that the King conferred knighthood on his half-brother. The pious monarch had passed on foot through the muddy and uneven streets to Westminster Abbey, himself clad in the humblest dress, though following a procession of full-robed clergy. In his uplifted hands he held a crystal vase, containing what had been sent from the Holy Land by the Templars, as the blood of our Saviour[1]; he had prepared himself by previous fasts and watches for this ceremony, the fatigue of which nearly overpowered him, but which he thought so important at the time, that he charged his historian, Matthew Paris, whom he invited to dinner, especially to record all the circumstances of the day. The pride of his knightly belt, thus publicly invested, led William de Valence to try his prowess too soon afterwards against some English nobles at a tournament, at Newbury, where, being yet young and not grown to his full strength, he got "egregiously cudgelled[2]" by the tough veterans.

His command of Hertford Castle gave him the opportunity, in a hunting-party, of first poaching in the Bishop of

---

have been his or his son Aymer's— the work perhaps of the artist who has left his enamelled coats of arms on W. de V.'s tomb: the casket is 7 in. long, 3¾ high, 5¼ broad.

[1] By the Pope's Bull, a promise of six years and 116 days of pardon from the pains of purgatory was made to all who came to reverence this relic.

On another occasion, when King Henry obtained a Papal Bull, permitting him to eat meat on a Saturday, a very sensible condition was annexed to the frivolous privilege, that he should also feed 1000 poor persons on that day.

[2] "Egregie baculatus."—M. Par.

Ely's park at Hatfield, and then unceremoniously making free with his cellar. The bishop being absent, he broke down the doors, cursed the beer as sour, and pulled the spigots out of all the casks, leaving the choicest wines to run waste, after serving it out to all the grooms and huntsmen, until the whole party were drunk[1]. The good bishop, when told of this outrage, remarked, with a most courteous reproof, "Why plunder and spoil what I would readily have given away on a civil request[2]?"

His qualities as a soldier made him of importance, however unpopular; and he steadily adhered to, and fought for, the King,—surviving, indeed, to share in the Welch wars of Edward I., and though killed at Bayonne in 1296, in battle, his body was brought over for burial in Westminster Abbey, where his conspicuous tomb still remains, and where his epitaph[3] (now destroyed) praised him with the accustomed truth of such memorials, as placid, courteous and humble.

The next brother, Guy, though the object of profuse gifts in 1251 and 1253, was not personally obnoxious to the English, who remembered in his favour that he had, during the war in Poictou, given the King timely warning of some intended treachery on the part of his own father. He became a Crusader, and returned so poverty-stricken that he could not make his way up to London without borrowing some horses on his road from the Abbot of Feversham, a loan, indeed, which he forgot to restore[4].

Aymer, the youngest brother, was a priest, and, in spite

---

[1] "Usque ad nauseam."—M. Par.
[2] A similar specimen of the abrupt manner in which the clergy were liable to be plundered, is given in the Chronicles of Barnewell Monastery, in 1266. "A tall knight, Philip Champion, roused the Prior out of his bed at dawn, saying, 'I want all your wheat, all your beer, and all your larder. Give me the keys.'"— Cart. Barn. MSS. Harl., 3601. in notes to Rish. Chr.
[3] " Qui valuit validus, vincens virtute valorem,
Et placuit placidus sensus morumque vigore,
Dapsilis et habilis immotus prælia sectans,
Utilis ac humilis devotus præmia spectans."
Stoth. Mon. Eff.
Not far from his own tomb is that of his son and successor, Aymer, whose widow founded Pembroke College, in Cambridge.
[4] M. Par.

of the King's recommendation, was rejected by the chapter of Durham, in 1249, as insufficient in age and learning for the bishopric. In the following year, however, the King repaired in person to the chapter-house at Winchester, the more effectually to influence the election there, and by dint of his persuasion, Aymer became bishop elect of that see, and long enjoyed its emoluments, though he was never consecrated. When, subsequently, on a dispute with his clergy, he shut them up in the church for more than three days without food, they looked upon it as a just retribution for their guilt in having elected, under constraint, "such a youth, ignorant even of grammar, unable to speak English, and incompetent to perform any clerical offices[1]."

The subordinate offices about court, as well as the higher dignities, swarmed likewise with aliens. The Queen's trea-

[1] M. Par. Many years afterwards, the interest of a foreign queen was sufficient to bring an incompetent bishop into the church. In 1318, Louis de Beaumont was recommended to the clergy of Durham for election to that see by Queen Isabella (of French blood), to whom he was related by the marriage of her first cousin Princess Catherine, sister of Philip VI. to Robert de Beaumont. The Earls of Lancaster, Hereford and Pembroke with Henry de Beaumont, his brother, a successful soldier, waited during the election in the church, threatening if a monk should be chosen in preference, to split his shaven crown. Henry de Stamford was nevertheless chosen, but the Queen made Edward II. reject him ("ipsa nudatis genibus corruit coram eo"), and the Pope, in consideration of a large bribe (which was paid with difficulty in 14 years), appointed Louis de Beaumont. On his road to consecration, he was plundered and seized by Gilbert Middleton, who carried him off 60 miles to Mitford Castle (of which he was the governor, not the proprietor), and who exacted a heavy ransom. Middleton was afterwards surprised at Mitford by treachery and executed at London. The bishop's consecration at Westminster, March 26, 1318, was a difficult task to a man ignorant of Latin, and is graphically described by a contemporary chronicler (Robert de Graystanes): "Castus erat sed laicus—Latinum non intelligens, sed cum difficultate pronuncians; unde cum in consecratione suâ profiteri debuit, quamvis per multos dies ante instructorem habuisset, legere nescivit, et cum auriculantibus aliis cum difficultate ad illum verbum, 'Metropoliticæ,' pervenisset et diu anhelans pronunciare non posset," he broke out into his native French, "*Seit pur dite*," let it pass as if said. Coming next to the phrase, "in ænigmate," he again confessed his distress with "*Par Seynt Lowys il ne fu pas curteis qui ceste parole ici escrite.*" Beaumont afterwards obtained of the Pope Bulls to vest the appointment of Prior in himself, and also to devote one-fourth of the revenues of the Church to the Scotch wars, but the chapter would not act upon them: "sed quod istæ Bullæ impetratæ erant tacita veritate et suggesta falsitate, noluit ejus concilium eis uti." See Chr. Graystanes, c. 33, in Anglia Sacra. Surtees' Durham, xxxviii. folio 1816.

surer, Peter Chaceporc, became a privy councillor, and was so high in favour, that, after his death, in 1254, the King went expressly to visit his tomb at Boulogne. As he is extolled for bequeathing money to a monastery, he probably died enriched[1]. When one Poictevin Hurtald, who was the King's councillor, died, another succeeded him, Peter de Rivallis; to Elias de Raban, an estate of 500 marcs (£333. 6s. 8d.) was readily granted, in 1252, even when the King was himself extremely pressed for money. The Queen's physicians were Henry of Montpelier and the Italian Leopardi; another, who is highly praised in his friend De Marisco's letters, Peter, rector of Wimbledon, may indeed have been an Englishman[2].

Even in those remote times, a royal kitchen was naturally attractive of foreign artists; accordingly, we find the King appointing Robert de Monte Pessulano, to mix choice, delicate beverages for him at his feast, in 1250; bestowing 200l., in 1258, on William de S. Hermite, a Poictevin, for holding his napkin and carving his meat; and following the example of the Conqueror, who rewarded a successful dainty of his cook, Tezelin, with a manor[3]. In such days of gross feeding,

[1] M. Par.
[2] Ep. Ad. Maris. MS. Cotton, Vitell., c. viii. John de Kaleto or Cauz, a native of Normandy, is said by Gunton (Hist. Peterb.) to have been allied to Q. Eleanor, and was made abbot of Peterborough, Jan. 15, 1250. Pope Innocent IV. granted leave in 1250 to the monks, in consideration of the coldness of climate, to perform service in the church hooded. He was made a justiciary, and also the King's treasurer. He died March, 1262. See Dugd. Mon. i. 356.
[3] Addington in Surrey. "Tezelinus coquus tenet de Rege Edintone; valet et valuit c solidos."—Domesday. It passed, by the marriage of Isabella de Caisneto (Cheney), to her husband, Peter, son of Henry Fitz Aylwin, first Mayor of London; he held the moiety, 1199, by service of the kitchen. In 1233, W. Aguilon and on the Excheq. Roll is allowed "non debet servicium militare de terris—sed serjanteriam, scilicet, inveniendi unum cocum in coronatione Regis ad faciendum cibum, qualem Senescallus preceperit in coquina Regis." In 1294, Margaret, Countess of Devon, died seized of it, by gift of Robert Aguilon, and held it, "de Domino rege in capite per servicium unius ferculi die coronationis Domini Regis, et vocatur illud ferculum—*Maupygernon.*" In 1330, on death of Thomas, Lord Bardolf, he had held it by the service of serving up to the King at his coronation, three dishes of a certain mess called Maupygernoun, one to be set before the King, another for the archbishop, a third for a nobleman selected by the lord of the manor in lieu of all service. In 1379, William Bardolf held it,

the refined skill of a French cook must have had a double value; and trustworthiness, as a protection against poison, being of the highest importance, the office was often filled by persons of consideration. When the papal legate was on a visit at Osney Abbey, in 1238, his own brother was his cook, and, like other great artists, so jealous of interruption when exercising his high functions, that he angrily threw some of the scalding broth he was cooking at a poor Irish student, who stood at the kitchen door, provoking thereby a dangerous riot and even his own death[1]. The Queen's favourite cook, Richard de Norreys, was rewarded by the grant of Ocholt manor, in Berkshire; he died, in 1255[2], possessed of more than 5000 marcs (£3,333. 6s. 8d.), and the mansion, built by his descendants, at Ockwell, in Henry the Sixth's time, still exists, to testify with its quaint gables and the founder's wholesome mottoes, ("Ffenthfully serbe," "Humble et loiall,") that the foundations of a family may be as firmly laid in services of peace as in deeds of war and violence[3].

The rivalry between these Poictevins, Provencals and Savoyards, naturally produced violent quarrels, and the court was divided into separate parties, as "King's men and Queen's men[4]." Their successive plunder recalled to the minds of the sufferers the scriptural image: "That which the palmer-worm hath left, hath the locust eaten; and that which the locust hath left, the canker-worm hath eaten; and that which the canker-worm hath left, hath the caterpillar eaten."

Besides the grievance of these court favourites, Rome,

"in capite per servitium serjanterie coquine, qualiter et quo modo ignorant (juratores)." See Mr Stapleton's Preface to Liber de Antiquis Legibus.

[1] M. Par.

[2] M. Par.—He was the ancestor of Lord Norris, of Rycote, now represented by the Bertie family. John Norreys, who built Ockwell, and died 1467, married the coheiress of William Mountfort, of Lapworth, by Rose Braundeston. In the painted glass of the hall, the arms are, "Argent, a chevron between three eagles' heads erased, sable."—Lyson's Berks.

[3] 'Le Cordon Bleu' of Lady Morgan.

[4] M. Par.—"Regales contra Reginales, Pictavenses contra Provinciales."

during all this reign, turned to profit King John's illegal homage. He has been often blamed for his baseness in surrendering the crown to the Pope[1], but the illegality of such a transfer is still more apparent. No sovereign, even at that time, could acquire a personal right to subject his own nation to a foreign power, and it is remarkable that the French nobles, in 1216, as if alarmed at the precedent, unanimously protested in council against such a doctrine. John's homage was void from want of consent of the party interested, although there were, indeed, some bishops and nobles[2] (among whom we regret to find the earls of Pembroke, Warren and Arundel) who sanctioned this degradation with their formal assent. At a later period, in 1301, the barons of England boldly protested to Pope Boniface VIII., that they would not relinquish the independence of their country, even if the King were willing to do so.

It may be satisfactory to know that the record of national disgrace, "that detestable charter of England's tribute[3]," did not long survive its abject author[4], the document having been destroyed in an accidental fire in the Pope's palace, at Lyons, in 1245.

The Pope, however, naturally would not forego the advantages which the acknowledgment of his supremacy seemed to give him, and long lists of Italian priests were sent with peremptory claims upon the first vacant benefices in England, setting aside all previous rights of patronage. A calculation of the value of the benefices held by aliens, in 1252, which amounted to more than 70,000 marcs (£46,666. 13s. 4d.)[5] a

[1] The surrender of the crown is said to have taken place at the house of the Knight Templars on the ridge of the western heights at Dover. The remains of a tower, called Bredenstone, were discovered there in 1806, the ruins being five feet above ground.
[2] Rymer.
[3] M. Par.—He calls it also "Illa non formosa sed famosa subjectio."

[4] When King John's tomb was examined in 1797, he was found to have been buried in the fitting shroud of a monk's cowl, while his hands, with a curious inconsistency, were in white jewelled gloves.
[5] The collection of Peter's pence (Romfeoh) was irregular, and the proceeds often intercepted by the collectors, so that Rome received little. Originally a royal Anglo-Saxon grant,

year, was forwarded to Rome by Grethead, the excellent Bishop of Lincoln. The Pope, who did not relish such arithmetic, asked, "Who is this ridiculous old madman?" and took no notice of the letter, although informed, by a Spanish Cardinal near him, of Grethead's superior scholarship and piety[1]. The parishes thus in the hands of non-residents, enjoyed neither the offices nor comforts of religion.

It is curious to observe, that, even in these early times, there prevailed on the Continent an idea of the great wealth of England, the Pope professing to look upon it as "an inexhaustible well of money[2]." When the nobles resisted his demands, he extorted contributions with a greedier hand from the King and clergy, from whom he often required a tallage of a twentieth, a tenth, or even more. An unholy barter of patronage and plunder was thus established: the King, in awe of the Barons, relied on the protection of the Pope, and therefore encouraged his exactions; while the Pontiff, on the other hand, sold his spiritual thunders to guard the throne, for the privilege of draining the country of its riches.

No pains were taken to conceal the King's preference for his alien clergy: how bitterly this degradation was felt, may be seen in a contemporary poem[3], written probably by a native ecclesiastic.

" Ja fu cleregie	Once was the clergy
franche e à dessus,	Looked up to and free,
Aimée e cherie	Cherished and loved
nule nen pot plus;	None more could be.
Ore est enservie	Now all enslaved,
E trop envilée	Trampled, debased,
e abatu jus.	They lie full low.

it was regulated by William I., payment by a lord of manor being an acquittance for all in his demesne. The popes frequently complained that the money, though collected, did not reach them, and indeed they did not expect much, and would have been content with 300 marks—it was reserved in K. John's surrender to the Pope (salvis per omnia denariis Petri) in addition to 1000 m. a year, to be paid by the King as the Pope's feudatory. See Archd. Hale's Domesday of St Paul's, cxviii and cxxvii.

[1] M. Par.
[2] M. Par.—"Puteus inexhaustus quem nullus poterat exsiccare."
[3] Pol. Songs from a MS. Cotton, written, probably, in 1256.

Par iceus est hunie	I dare not name
Dunt dut aver aie,	Who give them shame
Je nós dire plus.	Though help they owe ;
Li rois ne lápostoile ne pensent	Neither Pontiff or King
altrement,	Think of other thing
Mès coment au clers tolent lur	Than how best to grasp and hold
or e lur argent."	The clergy's silver and gold.

The legate was placed in the King's seat at a royal feast, to the great scandal of the English nobles; even the legate's nephew was knighted and pensioned. In the reckless distribution of Church patronage, a valuable benefice was given, in 1252, to a Poictevin chaplain of Geoffry de Lusignan, a mere half-witted jester, kept to amuse the court. Matthew Paris tells us that he saw this man in the orchard of St Alban's Abbey, pelting the King and his master, Geoffry, with hard apples, and squeezing sour grapes into their eyes:

> " The skipping King, he ambled up and down
> With shallow jesters and rash bavin wits,
> Soon kindled and soon burn'd : carded his state,
> Mingled his royalty with capering fools."
> HENRY IV., p. 1, 3. 3.

The King's chaplain and agent, John Mansel, is another instance of the prodigality by which a favourite becomes enriched. The son of a country priest, he had, when young, exerted himself manfully[1] at a siege in Gascony, and nearly lost his life by his eager valour, though he escaped with a broken leg; he appears to have been a good man of business, and was constantly employed afterwards by the court, in diplomacy or other matters. He had been chancellor to the Bishop of London, and received the great seal from one king, 1246, till the feast of St Mary, 1249[2]. Although his highest [ecclesiastical] dignity was that of provost of Beverley, yet he accumulated wealth to a degree and by means which astonished his own times, as well as ours, enjoying, it is said, no less than 700 benefices at once, calculated at 4000[3]

---

[1] M. Par.—" Inter strenuos non ultimus."
[2] 31 Hen. III., Rot. Pat. m. 2. He introduced the " non obstante" clause into grants and patents. John de Lesington succeeded him.
[3] Chr. Mailr. values them higher, at 18,000 marcs (£12,000). Lord

marcs a year (£2,666. 13s. 4d.). This Wolsey of the thirteenth century, as he has been termed, gave a sumptuous feast, in 1256, to all the court, on occasion of the King and Queen of Scotland's visit, the most choice, orderly, and plenteous ever given by a priest. His house at Totbill being insufficient to contain the numerous guests, the banquet, the first course of which was supplied by 700 dishes, was served in several large tents. His sister, Clarice, and her husband, Geoffry, a soldier of mean birth, partook of his good fortune, and received from the King grants of lands, the title to which was disputed by the Abbey of St Albans. Matthew Paris remonstrated personally on this injustice, but the King justified it by the similar pretensions of the Pope, adding, indeed, "Bye-and-bye, however, I will consider this matter:" the memory of such promises, the chronicler remarks, passed away with their utterance.

Subject to the ignominious slights of the court, the great nobles and clergy scarcely needed additional motives for personal resentment and resistance, but the King's conduct in matters affecting the very principles of government, and his avowed contempt for the restraint of law, afforded still stronger grounds for their distrust.

His fear or his fickleness, indeed, caused him again and again to proclaim Magna Charta when in difficulties, but he played this game so often, that the Barons could not but see, that his compliance was only intended to disarm their opposition to his demands for money. He had annulled the charter when he came of age, although he had repeated his oaths to it on many subsequent occasions, and in like manner his vow of a crusade was often used as a convenient form of requiring supplies. So lightly esteemed, indeed, was the King's faith, that even when he publicly fixed[1] the very

Campbell presumes he "presented himself to all that fell vacant and were in the gift of the Crown while he was Chancellor" (Chancellors, I. p. 136). Even this, however, would not account fully for such a number in three years.

[1] This was in 1252, when he named the feast of St John the Baptist, 1256, for his departure on

day for commencing his enterprise, "the bystanders were not the more persuaded of his truth," and, in fact, he never went[1]. On every new perjury the solemnity of the royal pledge seemed to increase: when the oath to the charter was administered in Westminster Hall (May 3, 1258) before all the barons and prelates of the realm, every stringent form which honour or religion could devise to bind the conscience was employed. The awful curse was pronounced aloud, "which excommunicated, anathematized, and cut off from the threshold of holy Church all who should by any art or device, in any manner, secretly or openly, violate, diminish, or change, by word or writing, by deed or advice, either the liberties of the Church, or the liberties and free customs contained in the Great Charter, or the Charter of Forests." The original charter of King John was spread out in sight, and to this solemn confirmation of it, both the King and prelates and barons impressed their seals, "in testimony of the truth to posterity[2]." While others held a lighted taper during the ceremony, it was remarked that the King put his out of his hand, excusing himself as not being a priest, and it is possible that even this frivolous omission may have satisfied his conscience afterwards as to the invalidity of the oath, but he held his hand on his heart all the while, when the torches, amid the ringing of bells, were extinguished; and when the universal cry arose, "So may all transgressors be extinguished and smoke in hell!" he added with a superfluous hypocrisy, "So may God help me as I keep this oath, as a man, as a Christian, as a knight, and as an anointed King[3]!" So few laymen could at this period write their names that the utmost importance was naturally attached to the stamp of

---

the Crusade.— Cal. Rot. Pat., 37° H. III. "Nec tamen hoc circumstantes reddidit certiores."—M. Par.

[1] On the 20th May, 1270, the King writing from Westminster again alludes to his departure for the Crusade with his son Prince Edward as being fixed for the morrow of the approaching feast of St. John, without further delay (sine ulteriori dilatione), going beyond seas to the help of the Holy Land, the Lord so willing.—Rymer.

[2] Rymer.

[3] M. Par.

their seals as the readiest substitute of authentication, and hence the satirical verses[1], written in mixed French and English, on a similar occasion, in Edward II.'s time, humorously suggest that the Charter became invalid because the wax of the seals was held too near the flames and so melted:

"L'en puet fere et defere, Ceo fait il trop souvent; It nis nouther wel ne faire, Therefore Engeland is shent.	To do and undo he'll dare, On change too oft the King's bent; It is neither well nor fair Therefore England is shent.
La Chartre fet de cyre, Jeo l'enteink et bien le crey, It was holde to neih the fire And is molten al away."	'Tis stamped on wax: none need enquire If the Charter's power decay, It was held too nigh the fire And is molten all away.

A modern historian[2] has praised Henry as having "received strong religious impressions," but certainly he was not ambitious of the Psalmist's eulogy of "him that sweareth to his own hurt and changeth not;" and it is revolting to state that immediately after these serious pledges, he reverted to his old course, capriciously quarrelling with some, and oppressing others, promoting aliens, and dealing out his prodigal bounty to his foreign kinsmen as before. A curious instance of his duplicity occurred in 1253, when he ordered the public exhibition of some enormous darts, as a palpable proof of the dangerous weapons he was exposed to in Gascony, demanding fresh supplies to carry on the war, but concealing the fact of his having already concluded a treaty of peace[3]

---

[1] Polit. Songs from Auchinl. MS.
[2] Lingard.
[3] Queen Eleanor, as Regent, and Richard, Earl of Cornwall, write to King Henry III. while absent in Gascony at this time (Feb. 14, 1254), that the Earl Marshal and John de Balliol after a contrary wind for twelve days, had arrived in England, Feb. 4; that before and after their arrival the prelates and barons had been consulted about a subsidy, and had promised if the King should be attacked in Gascony to come over with all their power, but offered no money—the clergy too voted no subsidy, but expected the tenth levied for the Crusade which should begin in that year, to be relaxed; "but from the other laymen who do not sail over to you, we do not think we can obtain any help for your use, unless you write to your lieutenants in England firmly to maintain your great charters of liberty, since by this means they would be more

and alliance with his enemies. Some mistrust naturally arose among the nobles of the council, when they learnt that the Queen and her eldest son had been summoned to this scene of supposed danger, and the unexpected arrival of Simon de Montfort, who knew the truth[1], completed the exposure of this dishonest trick.

The empty title of King of Sicily, being craftily proffered by the Pope[2], was soon afterwards accepted for the King's second son, Edmund, a mere boy of ten years old. This "likeness of a kingly crown," so far from conferring any national advantage, was only the occasion of draining off more of the wealth of England to Italy. In the words of Dante, speaking of another titular King of Sicily:

"Quindi non terra, ma peccato e onta
Guadagnerà, per se tanto più grave
Quanto più lieve simil danno conta."
PURG. XX. 76.

Even when the royal treasury was exhausted, the King was made a responsible debtor for vast additional sums claimed by the Pope for the expenses of asserting this title by force of arms.

Edmund, acting of course as the instrument of his father, lost no time in displaying his unsubstantial power[3], and

strongly animated cheerfully to grant you aid."—Wood's Letters of Royal Ladies, vol. ii. p. 36. Royal and Historical Letters, voL ii. p. 101.
[1] M. Par.
[2] The crown was accepted March 14, 1254, for the English Prince; but Conrad, the King *de facto*, did not die till May 21, 1254, and was then young. The Pope's grant required the payment of 135,541 marcs £90,360. 13s. 4d.) in return. By a brief from Viterbo, xiv. Kal. Feb. (Jan. 19), 1258, Pope Alexander allowed the postponement for three months of the payment of money due for the final settlement of his claims on account of Sicily. By a brief from Anagni, xv. Kal. Jan. (Dec. 18), 1259, the Pope threatened to revoke his grant of the crown of Sicily, unless the money was paid. By a brief from Viterbo iii. Kal. June (May 30), 1258, the Pope pressed urgently for the money (rogandum attentius et portandum sublato obstaculo, &c.).
[3] Pope Innocent IV. having authorized Prince Edmund (May 25, 1254), to make a seal for Sicily; we find the Prince signing, accordingly, "aureâ bullâ nostrâ," at Windsor, March 20, 1261—Rymer. The impression of this seal in the British Museum, represents him seated on his throne with ball and sceptre, inscribed, "Edmundus natus Regis Henrici illustris;" on the other side are the arms of England only, not Sicily, inscribed " Edmundus Dei gratiâ Siciliæ Rex."

granted (Oct. 3, 1254) the principality of Capua to Thomas, Count of Maurienne, the Queen's brother. Aigue-blanche received the investiture of Sicily by a ring, as his proxy, June 22, 1257, not long before the good sense of the English barons renounced the title.

Twice again (in 1255 and 1256) was the great Charter publicly confirmed, and afterwards disregarded; when the barons, whose good faith had been so often abused, at length resolved to secure themselves and the state from the ruinous incompetence of their King. This they put into effect at the great council, summoned at Oxford, in 1258. Their Sovereign

"Broke oath on oath, committed wrong on wrong,
And in conclusion led them to seek out
This head of safety."
HEN. IV. 1

The great civil struggle began in consequence from this period, and before entering into the different events of the contest, it will be well to consider the character of some of the leading actors not before referred to. Among the King's friends, those of superior historical importance were his brother and his son.

The Prince Richard, Earl of Cornwall, prominent by birth and immense wealth[1], was much superior in capacity to the King his brother, and had on several occasions expressed disgust at his arbitrary conduct. Although, when he confederated with other barons (in 1227, 1233, 1237) to enforce the Charter, he had been as often won back to the court party by personal or other motives, yet he fully shared in

---

[1] Prince Richard had a grant of the Stanneries and mines with Cornwall, to be held by the service of five knights' fees, 1239; the castle of Lidford and the forest of "Dertmore" were granted to him.—Dugd. He did not bear the arms of King John, but those of the earldom of Poictou (argent, a lion rampant gules, crowned or) united with those of Cornwall, bezants used as a bordure sable bezantée. Sandford's Gen. Hist. p. 95—a plate of seals of Prince Richard. One represents him as a knight galloping with his arms (lion and bezants) on his shield. The same arms larger are on the reverse, on both sides the words, Sigillum Ricardi Comitis Cornubiæ. Another seal exhibits him as a King seated on his throne, with ball and sceptre.

the universal jealousy of the thriving foreigners who surrounded the King. He often sat in council at the Exchequer to advise the King in money-matters[1]. But he felt so strongly that his influence was not powerful enough to sway the King to better counsels, that, on his departure for the Crusade, in 1240, he confessed his anxiety to be "absent from the sight of those evils which he foresaw would, in consequence, gather upon his family and the kingdom[2]." Some years afterwards his prudence induced him to repel the offer of the Sicilian throne for himself, but it unhappily yielded to the temptation of another title equally profitless, and he was crowned King of the Romans at Aix-la-Chapelle, in May, 1257, by the suffrages of Mainz, Cologne and Bavaria, though never acknowledged by the greater part of Germany. His wealth seems to have been the principal inducement with the electors who raised him to this rank[3].

Prince Edward displayed, in early manhood, decided symptoms of sound principle and energy, in remarkable contrast to the King his father, of whom he soon became the ablest defender and friend.

The Horatian[4] maxim of sons resembling their fathers

[1] He is recorded as present, 1230, with H. de Burgh, the Justiciary, R. Earl of Chester, G. Earl of Glocester, W. Earl of Warenne, W. Earl of Albemarle, H. Earl of Hertford, J. Earl of Huntingdon, and other barons determining, "quod talliæ factæ ante guerram, quæ recognitæ fuerint de Scaccario et non fuerunt hucusque allocatæ, allocentur;" and on Feb. 12, 1270, making better arrangement for the King's debts in Exchequer, with Walter, Archbp. of York, Godfrey, Bp. of Worcester, Prince Edward, W. de Valence, our brother, Roger de Mortimer, Philip Basset, Henry de Aleman, Robert Aguillon, Robert Waleran and others.—Madox, Hist. Exch. 1711, folio.

[2] M. Par.

[3] K. Richard presented his regalia, a crown and robes, to the church at Aix-la-Chapelle according to their archives; his silver crown of Germany is still preserved there, but with a modern addition.—See Archæol. Journ. 1863, p. 197.

[4] "Fortes creantur fortibus et bonis,
——— nec imbellem feroces Progenerant aquiliæ columbam."—4. 4. 29.

Dante gives a fine religious interpretation to the degeneracy of offspring:

"Giacopo e Federigo anno i reami, Del retaggio miglior nessun possiede,
Rade volte risurge per li rami L'umana probitate: e questo vuole
Quei che la dà, porchè da lui si chiami."
—Purgat. VII. 121.

is curiously opposed to the history of British sovereigns. Neither Edward I. nor Edward III. were born of "the great and good;" nor were the dove-like Edward II., Richard II., or Henry VI. true to the eagle-breed of their fathers.

Prince Edward's birth, June 17, 1239, after three years' marriage[1], had been welcomed with the utmost joy by his father and the nation. When only 15 he was betrothed[2] at Burgos to the beautiful Eleanor of Castile, receiving knighthood at the time from his brother-in-law, King Alphonso X.[3], at whose court his gallant demeanor attracted much admiration; his ample dowry consisted of Gascony, Ireland, part of Wales, Bristol, and other lands, the value of which, if deficient, was engaged to be completed to 15,000 marks (£10,000) a year. Such early marriages, or rather espousals, were then common; but a year elapsed before the bride came (about Michaelmas 1255) to her husband, preceded by her brother Senchius, Archbishop-elect of Toledo, though only in his 20th year. The surprise of the English was much excited by so youthful a prelate, and by the unusual luxury of his domestic habits; they were disposed to scoff when the youth raised his hand with the pastoral ring to bless them, and still more when they observed his lodging at the Temple[4] with

---

[1] "Natus est regi filius ex insperato."—Chr. Lanerc.

[2] He recorded his assent to his own marriage by a deed, dated Morrow of Saint Mary Magdalen, 1254.—Rymer. Lous IX., when of the age of 19, had married a queen of 13 years. Alexander III., of Scotland, was only 9 years old when he married the daughter of Henry III. The Bishop of Worcester, Peter de Montfort, and Robert Waleran, were appointed to receive King Alphonso's letters of security for Prince Edward's journey (dated Toledo, Kal. Apr.), and they were to deposit a copy of them at Bayonne, before they went into Spain, for fear of accidents.—Rymer, 1254.

[3] "Vedrassi la lussuria, e'l viver molle

Di quel di Spagna."
Par. 19. 124.

[4] "Fecit tapeciis, palliis et cortinis, etiam pavimentum nimis pomposc adornare."—M. Par. The King by a letter from Nottingham, July 25, 1255, in expectation of the arrival of the Archbishop of Toledo and Garsyas Martini. as ambassadors from the King of Castille, to whom he was anxious especially to do honour (quos rex quam plurimum optat honorari) desires his chamberlain, in London, John de Gysore, to send four casks of good wine to be put in the cellars of the New Temple. By another order of the same date he ordered Richard de Muntfichet, the warden of his forest in Essex, to take ten deer (damos) and cause them to be conveyed to the New Temple. By

tapestry and curtains and carpets. At a time when our kings' palaces were strewn with rushes[1], and the windows had no glass, the introduction of such luxuries by these children of the South was derided as effeminacy: they had probably adopted the use of carpets from the Spanish Mohammedans, among whom, as among all others of oriental[2] origin, the universal habit of sitting on the ground had made them from the earliest times almost necessaries. King Henry displayed much gallantry in preparing the rooms destined for the Princess in a manner similar to those of the archbishop, and on her arrival she found silken hangings[3] on her walls, and carpets on her floors, much to the wonder and envy of the English. Two jongleurs who came in the archbishop's train, received twenty shillings each from the King in return for their entertainment; while another attendant, Garcias Martinez, had an annuity of 100 marcs (£66. 13s. 4d.) granted to him.

Prince Edward was soon forced into conspicuous action by the circumstances of the court. Some Gascon merchants, who considered themselves entitled to his special protection against some illegal exaction, obtained redress by his bold reproaches, although this soon rendered him an object of disfavour at court, and of this he became so conscious that he kept a guard of 200 horsemen about his person. These military comrades unfortunately behaved with so much insolent licence towards the people, helping themselves to the horses and vehicles of other persons with violence and cruelty, that

---

another order, July 26, he desires the mayor and sheriffs of London to receive the said ambassadors with courtesy and honour, and to proclaim that no insult should be offered to any of their suite.—Rymer.

[1] In 1222 there is a grant to Richer de Fonte of 3s. 8d. for rushes to the King's two chambers, and 3s. 4d. for rushes for his great chamber. In 1223, 3s. 11d. for rushes for two chambers, and 15s. 9d. for rushes for the King's houses.— Brayley's Westm. 31.

[2] The Chinese are to this day the only Asiatics who habitually use chairs. Even at Troy, King Priam selected a dozen carpets for Achilles, probably small ones, for sitting.—Il. xxiv. 230.

[3] "Holosericis palliis et tapeciis, ad similitudinem Templi appensis, etiam pavimentum aulæis redimitum, invenit."—M. Par.

some disrepute was reflected back upon the Prince. Though his income was so large, yet his expenses exceeded it, and he was obliged, in 1258, to pledge some of his estates to William de Valence, for a supply to his extravagance[1].

It is but due, however, to the reputation of a Prince who became one of the boasts of British history, to remark that his household as King was both well-regulated and economical; in proof of which may be quoted the account of his expenses during three successive weeks in Lent, 1290, at Langley, co. Bucks. In the first week they were £7. 10s. 4½d., in the second, £5. 19s. 1¼d., and in the third, £51. 2s. 2½d.; or, to take a period of four months, they were but £81. 5s. 10d., a rate of domestic expense which, even allowing for the great difference in the value of money, must appear very small.

From the same account it appears that among the provisions for his Lenten fare, were some strange fish for a King's table; besides the "Aberdeens" (herrings cured there), salmon pasties, oysters, eels, lampreys, pikerels, gurnards, "troites" (trout), and "morud" (cod), there are also mentioned congers, whelks, and a gallon of "menus" (minnows). To complete the picture of these olden times, may be added the weekly charges for "litter for the hall and the chamber twenty pence, and for rushes sixteen pence[2]." Such was the luxury of the thirteenth century.

---

[1] The Prince also endeavoured to raise money by alienating to his uncle Guy de Lusignan the island of Oleron at the mouth of the Charente, which had been granted to him as dower on his marriage. The King wrote to the mayor and prudhommes of Oleron (Westm. 26 Oct., 42°, 1257) stating that such grant had been procured wrongfully (*alio modo quam bono*) without his assent, and desiring them not to obey Guy. He again wrote to the same effect, (Winton, July 11, 42°, 1258,) and Prince Edward was obliged in consequence to acknowledge his forgetfulness of the clause of non alienation in his own grant, and to revoke the life-grant to Guy, from Sutwerk, IV. Nov. 43°, 1258. The King wrote again to assure the authorities of Oleron that he would never alienate them from the Crown, in consequence of their fidelity.—Rymer.

[2] Archæol. 5. 15, from Rotulus Familiæ MS. in the Tower.

CHAPTER III.

SIMON DE MONTFORT.

"Always acting as if in the presence of canonized forefathers, the spirit of freedom carries an imposing and majestic aspect: it has a pedigree and illustrating ancestors; it has its bearings and its ensigns armorial; it has its gallery of portraits, its monumental inscriptions, its records, and titles."

BURKE.

THE ablest and most active chiefs among the barons opposed to the court at the time of the Oxford Parliament were Richard de Clare[1], the Earl of Gloucester and Hertford, and Simon de Montfort, Earl of Leicester, each allied by marriage[2] to the royal family, but exasperated into opposition by personal affronts, as well as by public motives, and each too powerful and ambitious not to be jealous of the other.

De Clare had, as a minor, espoused the daughter of Hubert de Burgh, whose ward he was, but the King anxious himself to dispose of so wealthy an heir, had compelled a divorce, and constrained him to marry another lady. He had distinguished himself in the Crusade and the Welsh

---

[1] Arms in north aisle Westm. Abbey, "Or, 3 chevrons gules."

[2] De Clare's widowed mother had married Earl Richard; de Montfort was the husband of Princess Eleanor. Isabella Marshal, the Countess of Gloucester, died at Berkhamstead, 1239; and, though she had wished to be buried at Tewksbury, near her first husband, Earl Richard, her second, who married her 1230, did not permit this, but buried her at Beaulieu, and founded a chaplain to pray for her soul. She had done the same for her first husband's soul, when a widow—she bequeathed to Tewksbury monastery, besides some silver cups, and some church vestments, a phial sent her by the Pope with relics of various saints, some hairs of S. Elizabeth the virgin, some linen of S. Agnes, de tribus pueris, de sanctis 40 martyribus, &c. —Dugd. Monast. ii. 55.

wars, and was beloved and trusted by all the English nobles on account of his eloquence, prudence, and acquaintance with the laws. The persuasions, however, of the King, and the proffered dower of 5000 marcs (£3333. 6s. 8d.), induced him, in 1253, to yield his eldest son, Gilbert, then about 15, in marriage to Alicia, the daughter of Guy, the King's half-brother, an alliance very distasteful to his friends. De Clare had ever been an active party in upholding the liberties of the subject, and having personally witnessed the King's solemn oaths to maintain them, he considered himself in a manner pledged to insist upon their fulfilment.

The most remarkable person, however, of his party, and the one who has most identified his name with the history of the times, was his compeer, Simon de Montfort, a man of so much energy and talent in war and council, that although allied to the King and born abroad, his acknowledged capacity and honour overcame these disadvantages; and at a time when foreigners were universally odious and the court distrusted, the barons and people of England with one accord ranged themselves under this foreign courtier, as their leader for the recovery of their national liberties. There must obviously have been no common ascendancy of character to produce such a result.

His grandfather, Simon the Bald, the third Count de Montfort, was descended from a King of France, and by his marriage with the heiress of Robert Fitzparnel[1] Earl of Leicester, transmitted to his son the claim of large English estates, and of the dignity of High Steward. This alliance in 1165 with the daughter of Blanchemains, as the earl was called, formed the only tie of connexion between England

---

[1] Petronilla, his widow, furnished the church of Leicester with a curious piece of fancy work, a rope made of her own hair, to suspend the lamp in the choir. — Chr. Knight. She was the heiress of Hugh de Grantemenill, Baron of Hinckley, and by that tenure Hereditary Grand Steward of England. In the Exchequer Roll of Normandy (Ducarel, Ant. Ang. Norm.) the Earl of Leicester is named as owing 10 soldiers and 40 servants for the honour of Grantemenill, and 81 soldiers for the honour of Britolio. —See Pedigree of de Montfort, at page 45.

and the great Simon de Montfort, which enabled him successfully to establish his claim to a place among the nobles of England, in 1232, after a long interval of foreign absence of all the family. On the death of Fitzparnel, accordingly, Simon, the fourth Count de Montfort, became Earl of Leicester, and the estates were, in 1206, divided between Simon and Saiher de Quincy[1], Earl of Winchester. Simon's rebellion soon afterwards caused a forfeiture of his estates, and his own banishment; but he must have had bold and powerful adherents, for King John was some time afterwards startled by a report, a false one indeed, of the barons having elected Simon as their King[2]. Being a good soldier, and remarkable for his stature and strength, he had an opportunity, while an exile from England, of making his "name very precious to all the bigots of that age" (as Hume remarks) by his barbarous crusades against the Albigenses[3]. The cruelties practised are well known, but the fanaticism of the period was widely spread, and the merit of extinguishing heretics so, blinded his contemporary historian, that even after relating

[1] Arms in s. aisle Westm. Ab. "gules, 7 mascles conj. 3, 3, and 1 or."

[2] Chr. Dunst. For an account of Simon de Montfort's incised slab at Carcassonne, see Archæol. Journ. 1855, p. 280.

[3] It is curious to mark the feeling of modern Roman Catholics on this point. Comte de Montalembert, pair de France, in his "Histoire de Ste Elisabeth de Hongrie (1231)," thus expresses himself: Il est reconnu aujourd'hui que ces cruautés contre les Albigeois, &c., étoient du moins réciproques, et l'on n'a pas encore, que nous sachions, trouvé le moyen de faire la guerre, et surtout une guerre de religion, avec aménité et douceur. Celui qui fut dans cette lutte de champion de Catholicisme, Simon de Montfort, a sans doute terni une partie de sa gloire par une trop grande ambition, et par une rigueur que la bonne foi ne sauroit excuser; mais il lui en reste assez pour que *les Catholiques ne rougissent plus de la proclamer hautement.* L'histoire offre assurement bien peu de caractères aussi grands que le sien par la volonté, la persévérance, le courage, le mépris de la mort; et quand on songe à la ferveur et à l'humilité de sa piété, à la pureté inviolable de ses mœurs, à cet *inflexible dévouement à l'autorité ecclésiastique,* qui l'avoit fait se retirer tout seul du camp des croisés devant Zara, parceque le Pape lui avoit défendu de guerroyer contre les chrétiens, ou conçoit tout l'excès de son indignation contre ceux qui troublaient la paix des consciences, et renversaient toutes les barrières de la morale. Son caractère et son époque se peignent à la fois dans ce mot qu'il prononça au moment d'entreprendre une lutte inégale: "Toute l'église prie pour moi, je ne saurois succomber;" et encore lorsque poursuivi par l'ennemi, et ayant passé avec sa cavalerie une rivière, que les gens à pied

Simon's order, at the capture of the castle of Brom, to cut off the noses of a hundred of the garrison, and to pluck out their eyes, with the exception of one eye reserved to a single guide, he immediately praises him as "the mildest of men[1]."

There is, indeed, some reason to hope that the service was unpopular among his troops, and revolted their common feelings of humanity; for Simon, in a letter to Pope Innocent III. (August, 1209), not only urges his own merits for having so rapidly marched upon the heretics, but also puts forward this special reason why he ought to be confirmed in his government over the country, that "he had been obliged to hire soldiers to remain with him at a greater price than in other wars, as he could scarcely retain them, unless rewarded by double pay[2]."

This zealot has been compared[3] to Cromwell, as a hero well fitted for a holy war, and was superior to the meaner superstitions of his time. When his wife came to him greatly alarmed at having dreamed of blood flowing from her arms, he replied, "Do you think we follow dreams and auguries like the Spaniards? If you had even dreamed that I was to die in this war, I should go forward so much the bolder and freer, in order to reprove the folly of such people[4]." The Countess de Montfort, was, indeed not unlikely to have such dreams of blood; for, a Montmorency herself, she shared all her husband's perils of war, at one time (1210) leading to him a reinforcement of 15,000 soldiers, at others enduring, with her children, the miseries of a besieged town[5].

---

ne pouvaient franchir, il là repassé avec cinq hommes seulement, en s'écriant: "Les pauvres du Christ sont exposés à la mort, et moi je resterais en sureté? advienne de moi la volonté du Seigneur, j'irai certainement avec eux."—In accordance with these opinions, the bust of Simon de Montfort is placed in the *great* Salle des Batailles at Versailles, among those Frenchmen who have fought for their country.

[1] "Omnium mitissimus erat."— Pet.Vell. Sarn. Besides clemency, he laid claim to the virtue of truth, and bore "Veritas" as the motto of his seal.—See Montfaucon, pl. 88.
[2] Gugl. Pod. Laur.
[3] Hallam, Middle Ages.
[4] Pet. Vall. Sarn., anno 1213.
[5] At Vaur, 1211, while nursing her sick son; and at Narbonne, 1217, blockaded with her sons and their wives.—Pet. Vall. Sarn.

From such noble and fierce parentage issued the Simon de Montfort[1] of English history, the youngest of four sons, a youth of about eighteen years, at the time of his father's death in 1218.

Large grants had rewarded the terrible services of the sword and torch of religious bigotry; and to these Almeric, the eldest son, succeeded, who is described as "an imitator of

[1] The pedigree of the de Montfort family includes so many historical characters that it is here subjoined for reference.—See Dugd. Baron., Nichols' Leicest., Househ. Exp., Gugl. Pod. Laur.

The children of Simon de Bald, eighth Count de Montfort, were these:—

1. Almeric, Count d'Evreux, which he ceded to the King of France, 1200; died about 1224.
2. Simon, ninth Count de Montfort, Earl of Leicester, 1206; banished rebel, 1208; leader of the war against the Albigenses, 1209; killed at Toulouse, 1218; married Alice, who died 1221, daughter of Bouchard, Sire de Montmorency and Ecouen, Constable of France, who died 1230.
3. Guy, a crusader in Palestine and against Albigenses, received a grant of Castries.
4. Robert, killed at Toulouse, 1218.
5. Bertrade, who died 1231; married to Hugh, Earl of Chester; their son Ranulph died 1231, having had a grant 1215 of the forfeited estates of the rebel Earl of Leicester.

The children of the above Simon, ninth Count were—

1. Almeric, tenth Count de Montfort, knighted 1213; Constable France in succession to his grandfather de Montmorency, 1231; crusader 1238; prisoner there till 1241; died at Otranto, 1241; he married, 1222, Beatrice, daughter of Count de Vienne; their son John, sixth Count de Montfort renounced all English claims, 1248.
2. Guy, a crusader, slain at Castelnauderi, 1220; Count de Bigorre, by his marriage with Petronilla, Countess of Bigorre, 1216; she died, 1251, surviving five husbands; Eskivat was their son; their daughter Alicia died at Montargis.
3. Robert, died unmarried, 1226.
4. Simon, born about 1200, became Earl of Leicester on the cession of his brother Almeric 1232; commanded the Barons' army at Lewes, 1264; killed at Evesham, 1265; married, Jan. 7, 1238, Princess Eleanor, daughter of King John, who was born, 1212; widow of William le Mareshal, Earl of Pembroke, who died April, 1231; she died, at Montargis, 1274.
5. A daughter, in treaty of marriage to a son of the King of Arragon, 1210.
6. A daughter, married 1217, to Ademar Poictou.

The children of Simon, Earl of Leicester, and Princess Eleanor, were—

1. Henry, named after his sponsor, Henry III.; killed at Evesham, 1265.
2. Simon, prisoner at Northampton, 1264; defeated at Kenilworth, 1265; murdered his cousin, Prince Henry, at Viterbo, 1271.
3. Guy, wounded at Evesham, 1265; entered service of Count d'Anjou in Italy; murdered P. Henry at Viterbo, 1271.
4. Almeric, a priest, treasurer of York, 1265; taken prisoner by Edward I. 1273; released, 1283; became a knight in Italy.
5. Richard, left England for Bigorre, 1265, perhaps the ancestor of the Wellysbourne Montforts.
6. Eleanor, left England for Montargis with her mother, 1265; taken prisoner, 1273; married, 1279, to Llewellyn, Prince of Wales.

the goodness and energy of his father in all things[1]." The forfeited English estates had been granted in 1215, to the rebel Earl of Leicester's nephew, Ranulph, Earl of Chester[2]. Perhaps the grant was only temporary and conditional[3], for at his death in 1232, Almeric, who had frequently put forward his claims to the property, became still more urgent for its restoration, and two of his brothers having died, he now sent his only remaining brother Simon with a petition to King Henry, dated from Paris, February, 1232[4]. He described himself in this as Count de Montfort and Earl of Leicester (although no such title had been recognized by the English King for twenty-four years), referring to the lands and rights of his "father of good memory," and offering to be satisfied, if the King would accept of Simon to do homage for them, in case his own claims should be disallowed. Simon, as holding no lands under the King of France[5], could pay a more undivided homage, and on this plea was at length admitted[6] to his hereditary possessions and honours, after the solemn renunciation of Almeric in his favour, with the reversion only in case of failure of heirs male. This took place in the

[1] Pet. Vall. Sarn.
[2] In 1218 des Roches, Bishop of Winchester [had custody], of the estates.
[3] This conjecture is almost certainly true, as the Testa de Nevill (p. 36) mentions the Honour of Leicester as a ward in the King's hands in behalf of Simon de Montfort (c. 1218), and the younger Simon did homage for the Honour of Leicester in Aug. 1231, more than a year before the Earl of Chester's death.—Excerpta e Rot. Fin. I. p. 217. P.
[4] Almeric and Simon, probably the 6th and 7th lords of Montfort, counts of Ecouen (Simon being the father of Simon the Bald, and their brother William being a canon of Chartres), being among the benefactors to the cathedral of Chartres, their effigies appear in the painted glass of the choir, occupying the roses of the 5th and 6th windows in knightly armour, seated on horses at a walking pace, each bearing the arms of de Montfort on his shield (gules, a lion rampant, with forked tail argent), and each carrying a banner for Evreux (party per pale indented gules and argent).—Willemin Mon. Fr. Montfaucon. Winkle's Cath. A contemporary (Anon. Langued.) describes Simon 9th lord as planting on the highest tower of a captured castle "son estendart là ont era pint lo leon." Rolls of arms, 1308-14—" Conte de Leister, goules ung leon rampand d'argent, la cowe fourchée, et banner party endentée d'argent et de goules."
[5] "Simon de Monte Forti expulsus fuit de regno Franciæ propter seditiones suas." Cott. MS. Nero A. IV. is the only authority for such a statement.
[6] Simon's homage was acknowledged by the King, Shrewsbury, May 27, 1232.

presence of the King, at Westminster, soon after Easter, 1232.

This act was probably the result of a private division of the family estates between the two brothers, and when renewed by Almeric's son John, in 1248, it is expressly stated in the deed that "on the other hand, Simon, Earl of Leicester, renounced all the rights in France, which either his father or brother ever had, so that neither the one in England, nor the other in France, could claim anything except by failure of heirs[1]."

Thus replaced, after a long interval, in the possessions and dignities which his family had before enjoyed in England, Simon de Montfort was not slow in rising to favour at the court of Henry III. Béing "a gentleman of choice blood, education, and features[2]," he was perhaps all the more welcome there, because his foreign birth and habits might seem to connect him more readily with the feelings of the other aliens who surrounded the King. In his capacity of High Steward—though the powerful family of Le Bigod also claimed this honour—he attended to hold the basin of water at the feast of the Queen's coronation. Fully sensible of the maxim of a quaint author of his times, that "a woman who has lands of her own is much the most desirable[3]," a maxim not out of date, though six hundred years old, Simon had been twice led by his aspiring views to seek a marriage with widowed ladies of princely blood. The French King, from whose allegiance he had withdrawn himself, interfered on that account, to prohibit the alliances he sought with Matilda, Countess of Boulogne, and afterwards with the great territorial heiress Joan[4], Countess of Flanders.

---

[1] "Nisi per rectam eschaetam."— MSS. Lands., 299. The seal of John represents him galloping on a horse, and bearing the double-tailed lion on his shield and trappings. The reverse has the banner of Evreux.

[2] Short View of a long Reign, by Sir R. Cotton. The Chronicle of Lanercost (p. 39) describes Simon as tall and handsome.

[3] "Quar femme que ad terre en fée serra dássez plus desirrée."— Hist. F. Fitzwarin, p. 10.

[4] Joan, daughter of Baldwin 9, Count of Flanders, widow of a Portuguese Prince. King Louis had made

Baffled in these quarters, Simon next won the affections of another widow, under circumstances of difficulty which might well have deterred a less ardent lover. The King's sister, Princess Eleanor, had in 1224, married William, the second Earl of Pembroke, one of the foremost warriors of his time, and who had been one of the chosen guardians of Magna Charta. He had distinguished himself in repelling and punishing the aggressions of the Welsh in 1223, and when left by the King in command of Brittany (1230) he took some Norman castles with great spirit; and, although on one occasion, 1227, he had sided with Prince Richard to compel the King by force of arms to do him justice, yet he was so much beloved, that on his death, in April, 1231[1], the monarch wept over his corpse and looked upon his loss as an additional punishment for the blood of Thomas Becket. He had but lately, in perfect health, attended the marriage of his sister[2] to his friend Prince Richard, and his death occurring so suddenly, his successor was refused admission to the inheritance of his lands, until it was ascertained whether the widowed Princess was with child, as was rumoured. There was, however, no issue; and the lady in the first anguish of her grief, had publicly taken a vow[3] of perpetual widowhood[4], in the presence of two eminent prelates, both after-

it an express condition in his treaty with her in 1226, "quod nunquam subtrahent se a coronâ et homagio." She married, in 1237, Thomas of Savoy, the Queen's brother, swearing previously that her marriage with Simon de Montfort had not been completed.—Père G. Daniel t. III. 24. Nicholl's Leicest.

[1] He was buried in the Temple Church, where his effigy still remains. Hallam (Middle Ages, Vol. III. p. 242) confuses the persons of the earls of Pembroke, attributing to the father and regent "one of the greatest names in our ancient history," the anecdote of the King's defiance and the earl's rebellion, which can apply only to Richard his second son, who was earl 1231-34, succeeding Princess Eleanor's husband.

[2] Isabella, Countess of Gloucester, who died in childbirth, 1240.

[3] "Solenne votum castitatis emisit, cujus postea prævaricatrix effecta."—T. Wyke.

[4] The following was the form of prayer used on such occasions: "Consecratio vestium viduæ. Inlumina, quæsumus, oculos majestatis tuæ ad benedicendam hanc viduitatis vestem, ut quæ inordinatis vestibus viri sui visibus placuit, in sacratis indumentis benedictionis tuæ servire mereatur. Consolare, Domine, hanc famulam tuam viduitatis languoribus constrictam, sicut consolari dignatus es Saraptinam viduam

wards canonized, the Archbishop Edmund, and Richard, Bishop of Chichester.

To this solemn resolution she had held true for more than six years; but, if we may trust the King's subsequent reproaches, de Montfort was now not only an accepted suitor, but had so forwarded his suit, that a marriage had become necessary for her honour. The ceremony was performed by the King's chaplain, without publicity, on January 7, 1238, and the King himself gave her hand to de Montfort at the altar of St Stephen's Chapel[1], within those walls which have since so often witnessed the eloquence and wisdom of the representatives whom de Montfort's subsequent efforts succeeded in establishing.

Besides his real admiration of her as a beautiful woman, and his pride in so lofty an alliance, de Montfort may have been partly influenced by the dazzling hope[2] of their issue hereafter inheriting the crown, for at the time no children had been born to the King after two years' marriage, and Earl Richard had but one son living. Their union, however, even if it had its origin in policy, continued in affection until death, unchanged by discouragement and trials, and the Royal Princess, with a true woman's heart, invariably

per Heliam Prophetam. Concede ei pudicitiæ fructum, ut antiquarum non memineat voluptatum, nesciat etiam incentiva desiderii, ut soli tibi svbdat propria colla, quo possit pro laboribus tantis sexageminum gradum percipere, munus dilectabile sanctitatis."—Mabillon, De Liturgia Gallicana, Paris, 1685.

[1] The marriage took place "in parvula capella Regis, quæ est in angulo cameræ." There are several notices of this chapel: in 1229, 60s. 10d. paid to Walter, chaplain of St Stephen's Chapel; to Adam of the King's Chapel 30s. 6d.; and annually to the same, 21s. The treasurer ordered at another time to make a new, good, and large door at the upper end of St Stephen's Chapel. 100 wax candles are ordered for St Stephen's day. The chapel was begun to be rebuilt, 1292; was burnt 1298; its building continued by Edward II., and renewed by Edward III., 1330. The Parliament called by the barons met Jan. 20, 1265, "coram omni populo in Magna Aula Westmonasteriensi." In the last two Parliaments of Edward III. the Commons were directed to withdraw to their ancient place in the Chapter House, "à lour ancienne place en la maison du Chapitre de l'Abbeye de Westminstre" (Rot. Parl. II. p. 322 —366)—the peers to the White Chamber. During some Parliaments in Edward III.'s time the Commons met "en la Chambre de Peinte."—Brayley's Westm. 241—424.

[2] M. Paris.

adhered to her husband's interests and fortunes, even when her own kindred stood opposed to him.

On her marriage becoming known, an immediate outcry of sacrilege arose against the lady's broken vows, which, though she had not taken the veil or habit of a nun, were held to be binding on her, and Prince Richard, though so near of kin, was prominent in anger and menaces, because neither he nor the other barons had been consulted on the subject. It was with great difficulty that gifts and the mediation of friends succeeded in appeasing him.

Alarmed however lest his enemies should procure the marriage to be annulled, de Montford resolved to plead his own cause with the Pope, to whom he secretly repaired, after sending the Princess to the castle of Kenilworth[1]. The King did not, as yet, withdraw his favour from him, for he furnished him on his departure with letters to the Pope and cardinals, dated Tewkesbury, March 27, 1238. The letter ran thus: "The King to all the cardinals, health. We have thought it right to send our beloved brother and liege Simon de Montfort to the Apostolical Court for certain business, touching the honour and advantage of ourselves and our kingdom, particularly beseeching your fatherly love to be pleased to give him equally honour and confidence in those matters which the said Simon shall lay before you, and which concern the good of ourselves and of our kingdom[2]." These letters were strengthened by the Emperor's interest, which de Montfort secured in his way to Rome, and by a well-timed distribution of money at the Papal Court. These bribes appear to have been so large, that de Montfort, whether authorized or not by his instructions, included the King as a security for their payment. That no success was to be expected however without such appliances may be

---

[1] This royal castle had been committed to his care. It was granted to the Princess Eleanor, 1248, for her life, but in 1254 it was again granted for the joint lives of the Earl and Countess of Leicester.—Dugd. Warw.

[2] Househ. Exp. from Pat. Hen. III., m. 8.

learned from the opinion of a humourous poet[1] of the times, who even intimates that the word "papa" signifies "pay, pay."

> Cum ad Papam veneris, habe pro constanti,
> Non est locus pauperi, soli favet danti:
> " Paez, paez," dit le mot, si vis impetrare.
> Papa quærit, chartula quærit, bulla quærit,
> Porta quærit, cardinalis quærit, cursor quærit,
> Omnes quærunt, et si quod des uni deerit,
> Totum jus falsum, tota causa perit.
> Das istis, das aliis, addis dona datis,
> Et cum satis dederas, quærunt ultra satis;
> O vos bursæ turgidæ, Romam veniatis,
> Romæ viget physica bursis constipatis.
>
> Rich givers may hope to speed with the Pope,
> Of this be sure, 'tis no place for the poor:
> "Pay, pay's" the word, if you wish him "yes" to say;
> The Pope and his Brief and his Bull cry "pay."
> Cardinal, porter, and lacquey cry "pay,"
> All echo "pay, pay," and if one's left unfeed,
> All your right becomes wrong, your suit goes to seed;
> Give these and give those, empty store after store;
> Give freely to all, they beg a little more:
> Come quick, ye fat unwieldy purses, come,
> Your costive bulk get physicked thin at Rome.

After obtaining by these means such a letter from the Pope to his legate in England as ensured a decision in favour of his marriage, de Montfort hastened back, landing October 14, 1238, and not suffering himself to be detained even by the joyous welcome of the King, repaired at once to his home at Kenilworth, where he arrived in time to hail the birth of a son at Advent. Remembering the King's subsequent imputation on his sister's honour, which may have been but a mean subterfuge to excuse himself towards those who disliked the marriage, it is of interest to note the interval of nearly eleven months between the dates of the marriage and this birth. As far as posterity can judge, Eleanor seems to have well deserved the simple eulogy of the old chronicler[2], as a "god woman thoru out all."

[1] Pol. Song of 13th century from MSS. Harl. 978. [2] Rob. Glouc.

The royal favour continued to betray no symptom of diminution: de Montfort was fully invested as the Earl of Leicester, Feb. 2, 1239. He had been one of the appointed sponsors in the following summer at the baptism of Prince Edward, and came with his countess, as a matter of course, to attend the solemn churching of the Queen, in Westminster Abbey (Aug. 5, 1239), when they were unexpectedly received by the King with the most violent reproaches as to their conduct before marriage, and its sacrilege, to which he pretended his assent had been entrapped, and he angrily prohibited them from entering the church, as if they had been excommunicated. What seems especially to have irritated him, was having been made a security for the payment of the bribe to Rome; but as they could not pacify, even by their tears, this capricious outbreak, they left the palace, and going down the Thames that very evening in a small boat, at once sailed abroad. From this moment de Montfort ceased to be a mere courtier, and though often afterwards caressed at court, when his services were needed, he maintained henceforth, in active employment, the more independent character of a soldier and a statesman.

When he returned indeed in the April following (1240), he was welcomed with all honour by the King, whose resentment seems to have been as unsteady as his favour, but the only object now of de Montfort, who had become a crusader, was to raise money from his estates for that expedition.

His adoption of the cross was perhaps in penance for his marriage, but whether it also required a peculiar hatred of the Jews does not appear. His antipathy to them, however, is curiously recorded in his charter to Leicester, in which, as if conferring a great boon upon the burgesses, "he concedes that for the good of his own soul and that of his ancestors and successors, no Jew or Jewess should ever reside there, either in his own time or that of his heirs to the end of the world[1]." The same prejudice may have indeed led

---

[1] The Jews were banished also from Bury by the Abbot, 1190, "*magnæ*

him to sanction some cruelties on the Jews in London, which will be noticed at a later period.

In Syria the military talents of Simon de Montfort must have made themselves conspicuous, though we have no details; he appears to have been present at the fierce contest near Damascus, where his brother Almeric and other nobles were taken prisoners[1], and his fellow-crusaders thought so highly of him, that the barons, knights, and citizens of Jerusalem, (in a deed[2] still extant) sent a petition to the Emperor Frederick II. for his appointment as governor there during the minority of the King Conrad. This honourable testimony to his merits, however, did not detain him long in Palestine, for when the English Prince, Richard, had generously redeemed the captive crusaders, de Montfort returned

probitatis indicium," according to Jocelin—" et cum emissi essent, et armata manu conducti ad diversa oppida, Abbas jussit solempniter excommunicari per omnes ecclesias, et ad omnia altaria omnes illos qui de cætero receptarent Judæos vel in hospicio reciperent in villa S¦ Edmundi. Quod tamen postea dispensatum est per Justiciarios Regis, scilicet, ut si Judæi venerint ad magna placita Abbatis ad exigendum debita sua a debitoribus suis, sub hac occasione poterunt duobus diebus et duobus noctibus hospitari in villa, tercio autem die libere discedent."—Chr. Jocelin, p. 33. No Jews were allowed to be present at the coronation of Richard I. for fear of their enchantments—the Lion-heart afraid! [Wendover, Vol. III. p. 7. Compare the statement in the Chronicle of Dunstable, p. 57, that at the second coronation of Henry III., in 1220, " Judæi * in turri Londoniarum servabantur * ad cautelam." P.] The Regent Marshal, in 1218, during the King's minority, issued an order to the sheriff of Worcester that throughout his (ballivam) bailiwick Jews should bear on their outer garment, whenever they walked or rode in the town or out of it, two white linen tablets on their breast (factas de lineo panno vel de parcameno), in order that Jews by this sign might openly be distinguished from Christians.—Oxon, 30 March, 1218 — *Teste Comite.*— Rymer. In 1253 the King ordered (providit et statuit) that there should be no more schools for Jews than those allowed in the time of K. John. In synagogues they were to celebrate their rites in a low voice, so that Christians might not hear (submissa voce—ita quod Christiani non audiant), no Christian nurse was to suckle a Jew's child, no Christian to serve a Jew, nor eat with them, nor dwell in their houses. No Jew was allowed *to eat meat in Lent,* nor to enter a church, except to pass through (nisi transeundo).—Rymer.

[1] Almeric was taken prisoner near Jaffa; many fled to Ascalon and on to Ptolemais.— See Gesta Dei per Francos, 2. 216, also Assizes et bons usages, &c., folio, Bourges, 1690, pp. 221—238.

[2] Househ. Exp. from MS. Cotton, Vesp. F. 1. This letter of the " Barons Chevalers et Citeens de Jerusalem," dated from Acre, June 7, 1241, is signed among others by " Philip de Montfort, Seigneur de Thoron," whom Joinville also mentions as Lord of Tyre, in King Louis' crusade.

to Europe with him; his brother Almeric, after his ransom from captivity, died at Otranto[1] in 1241 on his return.

During the war against the French in the following year, de Montfort exhibited no scruple in fighting against his former countrymen, and exerted himself greatly at the battle of Saintes[2]; in England too he was one of the twelve commissioned by the King to retrieve the confusion of his finances. So fully did the sunshine of royal favour now again light upon him, that his influence prevailed even over the competition of the King's brother in obtaining a grant of the rich wardship of Gilbert de Umfraville[3] in 1245. This courtly warmth, however, did not relax his zeal as an earnest reformer of abuses, and his name stands second among the signatures to the remarkable remonstrance to the Pope sent by the barons in 1246. The English Church had been so long goaded and beaten, that like Balaam's ass (such is the unsavoury simile of the chronicler), it now at length opened its mouth in reproaches, and a threat was uttered that unless speedy redress were made, "it would become their duty to raise a bulwark in defence of the house of the Lord, and of the liberty of the realm[4]."

The grievances at home, the prodigality of the court, and the employment of aliens, as well as the decay of commerce by the exactions on merchandize were sternly urged by Leicester and others in 1248, and with such effect as to produce in the King a sudden fit of economy as reckless as his previous bounty; his means had been indeed at one time so exhausted, that being unable to pay 200 marcs (£133. 6s. 8d.) for the wages of those employed in his chapel, he had ordered John Mansel to pawn the image of the Virgin Mary "on condition that it should be deposited in a decent place[5]." In

---

[1] Almeric was buried in St Peter's Church.—MS., Lansd. 299.
[2] M. Par.
[3] Umfraville, arms — gules, a cinquefoil within an orle of crosses patonce or.—Surtees' Durham, 2. 394.
[4] M. Paris. "Oportebit nos ponere murum pro domo Domini et libertate regni."
[5] Smith's Westminster, from Rot. Claus. 27, H. III.

his passion all his vases and silver plate and jewels were now ordered to be at once sold by the weight, without any regard to their real value; his household expenses, his alms, his customary Christmas gifts, even the number of wax candles in the churches were reduced, and he threw himself, an expensive and unwelcome guest, on the hospitality of many abbeys, requiring rich complimentary presents in requital for such honour.

King Henry tried also private persuasion to obtain loans of money, but his credit was gone, and the Bishop of Ely, when applied to, plainly told him so. "Turn out this boor, (cried the King in his anger), and when out, never admit him again[1]." Hugh Northwold however was no niggard, as his beautiful and costly works at Ely remain to testify, and "this boor" continued a pious and liberal prelate for twenty-five years. His present refusal, perhaps, was the motive for the rude rifling of his cellar about this time, before related. The King did not spare even his own brethren from these coarse reproaches, when disappointed of money. On Bishop Aymer coming to take leave of him, he treated him with the utmost discourtesy, and greeted him with—"Go to the devil for not backing me up better in wringing money out of the bishops[2]."

In the meanwhile, Simon de Montfort had been on the point of returning to Palestine[3] with his wife, but was dissuaded from doing so by the King; who needed his services to suppress the rebels of Gascony. Although he soon restored order in that province and sent the chief rebel, Gaston, Count de Bearn, prisoner to England, unfortunately King Henry, who never knew how to choose well either a friend or an enemy, took Gaston into favour, and restored him to his estates, thereby enabling him to repeat his rebellion a few years afterwards. De Montfort was employed also successfully to form a treaty[4] of peace in 1249 with Theobald, King of Navarre, nephew to Berengaria, Queen of Richard I.

---

[1] M. Paris.
[2] M. Paris, anno 1253.
[3] M. Paris, anno 1248.
[4] Clarendon, Jan. 10, 33 Rot. Pat.

During his occasional visits to England, he had been honourably welcomed, though still preserving the same independence of spirit, and on one occasion had remonstrated with effect on some breach of the chartered liberties of London[1], a circumstance which may afterwards have secured him so many friends in that city. His earnestness to redress wrongs may be traced in his friend Adam de Marisco's letters, who represents him as personally exerting himself day after day at Oxford in reconciling a dispute between some officers of the Earl of Cornwall, and of Bishop Grethead[2], and his zeal for the public service induced him to raise money by cutting down his own timber, in order to renew the war in Gascony more effectually.

Some of the castles (Egremont and Chatillon) which he took there from the rebels had been hitherto deemed quite impregnable, and the discontented Gascons, anxious to get rid of so strong a master, intrigued secretly to prejudice the King against him. Though the Archbishop of Bordeaux and others, who headed this mission of complaint, had been convicted traitors, they were readily listened to at court, and de Montfort, finding himself thus accused behind his back of extortion and tyranny, hastened to England, there to meet his accusers face to face. A most extraordinary scene ensued, which the King's previous loss of character could alone have made possible within the precincts of a court. De Montfort appeared in the Council to silence his enemies by the refutation of their charges, and then appealed to the King's personal knowledge of their falsehood and of his own faithful services, reminding him with what promises of support he had encouraged him to undertake the command in Gascony for six years. "Let your words be made good, my Lord King," he exclaimed, "keep your covenant with me, and replace those expenses which I have borne for you to the

---

[1] M. Paris.
[2] Ep. de Mar. p. 105, in a letter addressed to the bishop. [The Simon Fitz Simon of whom Adam de Marisco speaks in the letter referred to is not identified by Professor Brewer with the Earl of Leicester, and seems from the context to have been a person of inferior rank. P.]

notorious beggary of my own earldom." On the King replying that "he did not hold himself bound to fulfil promises made to a false traitor," the affronted earl lost all command of his impetuous temper, and in direct terms openly gave the lie to the King, intimating, too, that the shelter of his royalty alone protected him from instantly feeling the consequences of such a charge. "Who can believe you to be a Christian, or that you ever go to confession? of what use indeed would such a mere form be without repentance and atonement?" The King, though goaded by these insults, did not dare to order his arrest, but gave vent in his reply to his long-harboured hate; "never has my repentance of anything certainly been more sincere, than of having ever suffered you to enter England and to enjoy those estates and honours which now so puff you up[1]."

The interposition of their friends, who were present at this Council, Prince Richard with the Earls of Gloucester and Hereford, put an end to this unseemly wrangle; and the Prince, who had also been forcibly defrauded out of the government of Gascony[2], may well have looked on with complacency at the humiliation of his brother now arising from a similar want of integrity.

The friendly hand of Adam de Marisco[3] has left us an authentic account of these Gascon plots, their favourable reception at court, and the King's contumelious reproaches on Simon de Montfort, but praises "the calmness and moderation with which he endured them." There is, however, reason to distrust this eulogy as too partial, and perhaps even derived from de Montfort's own account, for the popular opinion of his hasty temper and unreserved speech appears in many other contemporary accounts. A curious poem[4] of

[1] M. Paris.
[2] It had been granted to him, 1243.
[3] Marisco mentions the accusation to have been made by both laymen and clergy ("tam clerici quam laici—malitiosis mendaciorum suppositionibus, Comitem Leycestriæ effrenati impetentes—comes passus est contumelias a Domino Rege coram multis"), the Earl observing moderation, gentleness (mansuetudinem), and magnanimity towards the King and his flatterers (adulatores). Ep. A. de Mar. p. 123, &c.
[4] Pol. Songs, from MS. in Bibl. du Roi, 7218.

this time reports a supposed debate on French affairs between the King, Roger le Bigot, and Simon de Montfort, and thus characterizes the quick and haughty bearing of the latter: the King had been talking of setting the Seine on fire, and making the French run away from Paris:—

> Sir Simon à Montfort attendi ce navel,
> Doncques sailli a piez; il ne fout mie bel,
> A dit à rai Inglais, "Pars le cors Saint AneL
> Lessiez or cesti chos: François n'est mi anel."
> * * * *
> "Que dites vous, Symon?" pona Rogier Bigot,
> "Bien tenez vous la rai por binart et por sot?"
>
> De Montford starts up, looking grim to scoff,
> When the boasting King he hears.
> "By the Lamb of God leave this meddling off,
> "For France is no lamb for your shears."
> * * * *
> "Why how now Simon?" le Bigot cries out,
> "Do you set the King down for a fool or a lout?"

In no instance did King Henry's disregard of private rights meet with a more remarkable reproof than from the young Countess of Arundel[1], widow of Hugh, the last earl of the Albini family.

On being refused redress concerning some property, she personally rebuked the monarch in free, but noble language: "Why do you turn away your face, Sire, from justice? Placed as you are between us and God, how can you dare to vex the Church, oppress the barons, and deny us our rights?"

On the King taunting her with being chartered by the barons to plead for them with such eloquence: "No, Sire," she replied; "your barons have given me no such charter, but with respect to that great Charter, granted by your father, and so often solemnly sworn to by yourself, you stand guilty of repeated perjury, on which account not only I as a

---

[1] Isabella de Warenne, whose husband died 1243. She was still very young at the time of this interview (1252): "cum jam vix metas adolescentiæ pertransisset."—M. Paris. She died 1283. The anecdote is erroneously given by Cartwright (Rape of Arundel) to Isabella de Albini, wife of John Fitzalan [who died before her husband, and consequently before 1239].

woman, but all your true-born subjects appeal to the tribunal of the Highest for retribution on you." Her grandfather, Hameline, had been half-brother to Henry II., and her brother, the Earl de Warenne, was married to the King's half-sister; these alliances suggested another answer to the embarrassed King: "You ask this favour perhaps on the strength of being my kinswoman?" "No, Sire," was her abrupt reply on leaving him; "how should I expect any favour from you when I cannot get bare justice[1]?" The contempt of the royal person must have been widely spread indeed to have emboldened a young noblewoman thus to address her Sovereign.

With something of the policy of David towards Uriah, King Henry now desired de Montfort, as he was so fond of war, to go back to Gascony, where he would find plenty of work. "I will cheerfully go," he answered; "nor will I return till I have made the rebels your footstool, however ungrateful you may be." There is an interesting letter of Adam de Marisco, which describes the anxious consultation of Simon and his countess to provide for the education and discipline of their children during his absence at this period: after entrusting them to the care of Grethead[2], the Bishop of Lincoln, he is represented as "embarking with his eldest son Henry for this expedition, cheerfully rejoicing in the protection of the Most High, and proceeding without delay towards Gascony, while the countess earnestly implores the bishop's prayers in behalf of her husband and family at so anxious a period, which had kept them all in suspense, not only day by day, but from hour to hour[3]."

---

[1] M. Paris.
[2] The bishop was in the confidence of another countess, and has left us the rules he drew up for her guidance in the management of her household. "Commences les 27 Reules que le bone Evesk de Liĉoln Robert Grosseteste fist a le Countesse de Liĉoln de garder et gouverner sa terre et son hostel. Ky cestes Reules tient bien et biel, occū bien purra vivre." Harl. MSS. 548, f. 21. Was this the foreign countess, Alice, daughter of Marcheso Saluces, 1247? See p. 16 anto.
[Mr Furnivall has kindly examined these rules for me, and finds that they differ from the seventeen called Grosseteste's, which Professor Brewer has printed in the Monumenta Franciscana, and Mr Furnivall again in the Babees Boke. P.]
[3] Epist. A. de Mar.

The malcontents of Gascony had, in the meanwhile, acquired such strength, that de Montfort found himself sorely pressed by them, in a manner to call forth all his energies as a soldier. It was with the utmost difficulty that he was able to preserve the mastery over them in a battle, during which he was himself unhorsed, and his life in great danger; at another time he was blockaded by them in an unprovisioned town[1], from which, however, he extricated himself by personal activity.

These perilous services were rendered to a thankless master. Soon after his back was turned, the Queen had prevailed upon King Henry formally to strip de Montfort of his military command, and to substitute Prince Edward[2]. The Archbishop of Bordeaux and his partisans, induced by the gifts and feasts of the court, at once performed homage to the young Prince as Seneschal of Gascony, and the King even enjoined the Gascons not to obey Simon de Montfort if he should oppose the arrangement thus made[3].

Released by this treachery from all public duties, de Montfort quitted the scene of his government, and repaired to Paris, where offers awaited him of dignity and power, superior to what he had been deprived of. The affairs of France were in great confusion at the time; King Louis being an absent crusader, and Blanche, the Queen-mother, recently dead, the nobles of France feeling the need of a directing head, invited de Montfort to exercise the powers of Regent over the country. The temptation was great indeed to a man "not without ambition," especially at a moment when he had been recently insulted, discarded, and betrayed by the English King; and yet these flattering proofs of the esteem in which he was held among his former countrymen, could not win him over from his duty towards England, as the country where all his public and private duties now centered.

[1] Montauban.—M. Par.
[2] Windleshoure (Windsor) June 13.
[3] August 27. Cal. Rotul. Patent. 36°., H. III.

The Gascon rebels were in the meanwhile still more irritated by King Henry's destruction of their cherished vineyards, than they had been by the stern warfare of de Montfort, and the English were still more disgusted when they saw the castles they conquered granted by the reckless monarch to Peter de Savoy and other foreigners. Gascony was nearly lost, when relief came from an unexpected quarter; for de Montfort at this crisis again tendered his assistance, which being now welcomed by the King, the very dread of his presence soon so awed the Gascons, that they gradually came back to their allegiance. To this act of generous patriotism[1] it is said that de Montfort was advised by his great master in religious and political matters, Bishop Grethead, who died soon afterwards (1254), in such popularity, that twenty manifest miracles were attributed to the sanctity of his tomb in one year[2], and the University of Oxford petitioned Clement IV. for his canonization. To complete the reconciliation with so useful a soldier, the King now agreed to pay de Montfort a compensation[3] for the three-and-a-half years unexpired term of his command in Gascony, which had been originally granted him for six years.

After Gascony had been thus reduced to order, King Henry indulged himself with an expensive visit to Paris, on

[1] A royalist chronicler even here supposes guilty designs "pro præmeditatâ calliditate."—T. Wyke.
[2] M. Paris. To Grethead are ascribed the completion of the nave, the transept, and the upper story of the central tower of Lincoln cathedral.—"Canonization." The dean and chapter of S. Paul's also petitioned Clement'V. for this honour to Grethead, whom they thus describe: "quem primitus filium et post patrem ipsius ecclesiæ patrona edidit virgo mater, qui, in hujus mundi ergastulo, a vitæ suæ primævo certamine acri et sedulo carnis domuit incentiva, et quanto super cunctos ejus temporis eminebat philosophos, et in Dei scientia et doctrinâ anteibat theologos—verbo edificationis insistens, quod verbis docebat, operibus exhibebat —— quæ signa miracula et virtutes apud nos per usum sunt vetera, et per augmentum quotidie sunt recentia atque nova —— qualis autem erat in carne, et est modo in spiritu, quia sanctus per virtutes et miracula limpide est ostensus —— flexis genibus exoramus—Sanctorum ascribere catalogo confessorem." Non. Julii, 1307.—Wilkins' Conc. II. 287.
[3] In 1254, 7000 marcs (£4666. 13s. 4d.) were paid. Liberate 38°, H. III., m. 8.4. In 1259, several barons pledged themselves for 3000 marcs (£2000) to certain merchants who had advanced the money for the King's debt to Simon de Montfort.— Rot. Pat. 43°, H. III.

his return to England. The Abbey of Fontevraud was in his road, where two of his kingly ancestors lay buried, and where his mother had taken the veil and died; over her remains he caused a tomb to be placed (the mutilated effigy of which was lately discovered[1] among the rubbish of a prison cellar); and he bequeathed his own heart[2] afterwards with an affectionate remembrance to the same spot. After being met at Chartres by his brother-in-law, King Louis, he was conducted to the Old Temple at Paris, as being the only building capacious enough for his suite, which included one thousand beautiful horses, besides sumpter-beasts and carriages. The procession of his entry was graced by the English students at the University of Paris, who appear to have been numerous enough to welcome their King with great splendour. These students, indeed, were apt to bring back to England "false ideas, French nonsense, and corrupt morals;" and are satirically complimented as being very agreeable companions, with only three vices clinging to them, incident to their young blood and jovial tempers[3]. The sumptuousness of the feast given by Henry on the following day astonished the Parisians. All the poor were freely invited to an abundant meal, and afterwards a banquet of unparalleled magnificence was open to the French and English courts, without any restraint of guard or doorkeeper, when to each guest some

[1] Stothard detected it in 1816, but when applied for with a view to remove it to England, it was refused.—Stoth. Mon. Eff. [The old arms of Angoulême were lozengy or and gules. W. S. W.]
[2] It was actually delivered to the abbess at Fontevraud, Dec. 13, 1291, nineteen years after his death, by the Abbot Wenlock, of Westminster.
[3] "Sophismata et ineptias Gallicanas, et inquinatos mores."—Wood, Ant. Oxon., 55.
"Washeyl et Drynkheyl nec non persona secunda,
Hæc tria sunt vitia quæ comitantur eos.

His tribus exceptis nihil est quod in his reprehendas
Hæc tria si tollas cætera cuncta placent."—Nigellus Wireker.
Robert Wace, in his description of the behaviour of the English on the eve of the battle of Hastings, uses the same Saxon words for their jovial pledges in their carousals:
"Mult les veissiez demener
Treper et saillir et chanter,
'Dublie' crient et 'Weisseil'
Et 'Laticome' et 'Drincheheil'
Drinc 'Hindrewar" et 'Drintome'
Drinc helf et drinc tome
Eissi se contindrent Engleis."

gift—a golden clasp, a silver cup, or silken belt was presented by the King. Though it was Lent, yet the fertile variety of the dishes and of delicious drinks are fondly put on record; nor does it appear that the appetite of the French guests at all failed them, as had been apprehended by some, who thought the sight of Richard Cœur de Lion's shield, which hung on the Temple walls, might have that effect[1].

It was perhaps on this occasion that King Louis observed to Joinville: "I believe you would be loth to do what our guest the King of England is now doing, washing, the feet of lepers and then kissing them on this Holy Thursday[2]." Louis' son died during this visit, and, as another instance of menial offices still more unusual in a King, his body was carried to the grave part of the way on the shoulders of King Henry, and the noblemen of the two courts[3]. With a mixed devotion and love of art, both strong impulses with Henry, his first visit at Paris was to the Sainte Chapelle, then in all its fresh beauty, having been rebuilt by Louis IX. in order to receive the genuine Crown of Thorns[4], which had been pawned by the French Emperor of Constantinople. In the satirical[5] poem of the age, before referred to, King Henry is made to covet in a droll manner this architectural gem of Pierre de Montereau[6].

"Par la cinc plais a Dieu,	"By the five wounds of God I swear,
Parris fout vil mult grant,	That at Paris, that very great city,
Il i a i chapel dont je fi coetant;	There's a chapel so choice and rare,
Je le ferra portier a i charrier rollant	I'll have it rolled off in a car
A Saint Amont à Londres toute droit	To my Abbey in London afar,
en estant."	There set it up just as it stands."

During his eight days' residence at Paris, he was much

[1] Père Daniel, H. de Fr.—M. Paris.
[2] Mem. Joinville.
[3] Nangis.
[4] The Holy Cross, Crown of Thorns and other relics had been "pawned" to the Venetians; and redeemed from them for a large sum of money, with the consent of the Emperor Baldwin, by Louis IX., by deed dated S. Germain en Laye, June 1241. Gall. Christ. t. VII. 98.
[5] Pol. S. from MS. 7218, Bibl. du Roi, Paris.
[6] The rebuilding in its present form of this chapel attached to the ancient palace of the courts of Paris was begun 1245, and the consecration April 27, 1248.

struck also with the superior elegance of their plaistered houses, and their height of many stories[1], matters then rare or unknown in England.

The enormous expenses of this royal visit rendered still more urgent the King's want of money on his return to England, and his difficulties were aggravated both by a Welsh invasion, and by the exigencies of the Sicilian crown of Prince Edmund. At the Council summoned in order to procure a supply, William de Valence came to an open rupture with de Clare and de Montfort, who resisted the grant—terming the latter "an old traitor," and giving him the lie with the same rudeness that de Montfort had exercised towards the King on a former occasion. "No, no, William," was de Montfort's answer; "I am neither a traitor myself, nor the son of one; our fathers were not at all the same sort of persons," alluding to the imputed treachery of Hugh le Brun towards King Henry. Had not the King thrown himself between his fierce relations, the affront might have been avenged by blood, and it was remarked that foreigners would scarcely believe it possible that anybody, even of royal blood, should presume so to insult a nobleman like Simon de Montfort, "so much esteemed above all persons native and foreign[2]."

Urged by Simon's passionate claim for speedy redress, and pressed to adopt restraints upon such insolence in future, the King once more, on the tomb of Edward the Confessor, the saint to whom he was specially devoted, pledged his royal word to amend the general grievance.

This led to the meetings of the great Council, first held at Westminster[3], and afterwards at Oxford, June 13, 1258, in order to consider by what means the royal oath should be

---

[1] M. Paris.
[2] "Inter omnes transmarinos et cismarinos præcommendatum."—M. Paris.
[3] Pauli, in his "Simon von Montfort" (s.s. 82, 83), observes that the Earl of Leicester had been nominated for a mission to Italy in June, 1257 (Rymer, I. 360), but probably did not go on it, as he was present at the Parliament of Westminster, May 2, 1258.

made effectual. The vigour and novelty of the statutes enacted at Oxford were the cause of the civil commotions, which acquired the name of the Barons' War, of which the battle of Lewes was one of the most important events; and by some historians the meeting at Oxford has been called the Mad Parliament, the monopoly of which title, however, it has been remarked[1], would be a grievous disparagement to some of its successors.

[1] By Sir F. Palgrave, "Truths and Fictions."

CHAPTER IV.

THE OXFORD STATUTES.

"If then we shall shake off our slavish yoke,
Imp out our drooping country's broken wing
Redeem from broking pawn the blemished crown,
* * * * * *
Away with me"—
RICH. II. ii. 1.

WHILE profusion had brought the King to penury, the dearth of provisions had, at this period, spread misery among the people, and prepared them more readily for some public expression of the general discontent. The bad weather of 1257 had prevented the ripening of all fruits and corn; wheat had remained uncut even to November, and so great was the urgency to carry the harvest, that even Sundays and other church festivals were so employed, if the weather permitted. Wheat, which had in 1255 been at the price of 2s. a quarter, now rose to 20s. or 24s.; horseflesh and even the bark of trees became articles of food[1]. During this famine, the King, by an invidious exercise of his prerogative, seized and forestalled for his own purveyance the corn which Prince Richard had imported from abroad in fifty vessels; London, however, resisted this as a breach of their charters with such effect, that by a legal decision the King was required to come into the market like others, with the

[1] M. Paris. Taxter Chr. (1258), "20,000 Londini attenuati fame."— Chr. Evesh. Lel. Coll. v. 1.

advantage only of buying his corn there at 2d. a quarter below the market price[1].

There was a wide-spread desire and expectancy of some remedy for the long course of mismanagement, and it was at this crisis that many of the great barons confederated with the fixed resolution to devise and enforce a reform of the abuses of the Royal government. All the barons at this time must have had more Norman blood in them than English, but their assimilation in feeling with the country, into whose vital interest the strong hold of the Conqueror had grafted them, was now so far advanced that they resented the intrusion of any fresh stock of aliens into their privileges. Having met therefore at Oxford at the time appointed with their retainers, to the number of 60,000, armed as if prepared for the Welch war, their manifest strength sufficed to overpower the alien faction which had guided the King, and the statutes then enacted, which continued for seven years the source of civil discord, were accepted and sworn to by King Henry with a constrained assent.

Without detailing these well-known enactments, it may be stated here, that they confirmed Magna Charta, provided for the orderly inheritance of property, forbade the disparaging marriages of wards and the wasteful grants to aliens, and required that the officers of state and the fortresses of the kingdom should be put into the hands of Englishmen only. The necessity for this latter stipulation was proved by fifteen[2] of the principal castles, as well as the Cinque Ports, being at this very time under foreign governors. Following the example of Magna Charta, twenty-four persons[3] were appointed to watch over the rigid execution of these laws, twelve being

[1] Fabyan's Chr.
[2] Dover, Northampton, Corfe, Scarborough, Nottingham, Hereford, Exeter, Sarum, Hadleigh, Winchester, Porchester, Bruges, [Bridgewater,] Oxford, Sherburne, and London.—See Nichols's Leicest.
[3] " 24 Conseillers de aide le Roi."

—Rog. Hoved. The King, in his proclamation (May 2, Westminster) had engaged, by oath, to reform the Government according to the advice of twelve elected by himself, and twelve to be elected by the barons at the meeting at Oxford, which was to last a month (in unum mensem).

chosen by each party. On the barons' side, among the most conspicuous, may be named (though the lists of various[1] authors differ) the Earls of Leicester and Gloucester, Humphrey de Bohun, Earl of Hereford, Roger le Bigot the Earl Marshal, Walter Cantilupe the Bishop of Worcester, the powerful Marcher Roger de Mortimer, and Peter de Montfort, a cousin of Simon's; while, on the other side, the twelve nominated by the King comprise but one independent nobleman, John de Plesseys, Earl of Warwick[2], his own three half-brothers, his nephew, Prince Henry, his brother-in-law, Earl de Warenne, his two secretaries, John Mansel, treasurer of York, and Henry Wengham[3], Fulk Bassett, Bishop of London, who was as much a friend of the barons as of the King, and a few inferior persons.

As this "mad parliament" of Oxford sat in deliberation for the unusually long period of a month, and was attended by about 100 barons[4], nearly the whole number then entitled to be summoned, the attendance being commonly but twenty or thirty, the King's continued resistance to such a pressure was evidently hopeless, when he could prevail on so few of the great barons to act as his friends at such a crisis.

The different temper of the parties to these Oxford Statutes was displayed, when the oath of their observance was

Prince Edward and the King's brothers signed this preparatory document.—Rymer.

[1] Roger Hoveden.—Ann. Burton.

[2] He had become earl by marrying Margery, [sister and heiress of the last earl, Thomas de Newburg,] and died without issue, 1263.

[3] On the resignation of William de Kilkenny, Chancellor from 1254 to St. Edward's Day, 1255, the Great Seal was delivered to Henry de Wengham, and as Chancellor made oath to seal with it only according to the directions of the twenty-four barons, appointed by the provisions of the Oxford Parliament, 1258 (Ann. Burton). When he was displaced (Oct. 18, 1260) by Nicholas de Ely, Archdeacon of Ely, the seal was broken up, and the pieces given by the King " to Robert Waleran to be presented to some religious house of the King's gift."—(Rot. Pat. 44° Hen. III.) Lord Campbell's Chancellors, i. 148. Wengham became Bishop of London, 1259, and died 1261, having had a grant from the King to retain two deaneries, ten rich prebends, and other benefices, besides his bishopric (Rot. Pat. 43 H. III).

[4] There were about 250 baronies at this time, but many were in the King's hand, and several barons held a great many each; Prince Richard, Earl of Cornwall, held eighteen.—See Nichols's Leic.

tendered, for "the King who was the first to set them aside, was the first also to swear to them[1]," while Prince Edward followed with avowed reluctance[2]; Prince Henry, who had been recently knighted by his father at Aix-la-Chapelle, excused himself on account of his youth, as needing the sanction of his father, whose absence abroad probably emboldened the barons on this occasion, and having no land of his own to constitute him a baron, his plea obtained a delay of 40 days[3]. The King's half-brothers, and his brother-in-law de Warenne, not only refused compliance, but swore, "by the death and wounds of God," never to surrender the castles which the King had committed to their charge.

Simon de Montfort, on the contrary, declared that he took the oath as a religious tie upon his conscience, "never under any pretence to break the pledge he was solemnly contracting, whatever others might do[4]." It is indeed singularly strange to observe that this rigorous expulsion and exclusion from office of all foreigners should have been guided and executed by a foreigner. But, being himself an alien, de Montfort surrendered accordingly his own castles of Kenilworth and Odiham, and then felt himself entitled to address the recusants, especially his old enemy William de Valence, who had been the most vehement in his protests and defiance: "To a certainty you shall either give up your castles or lose your head."

This threat, coming from a man well known to be able and willing to execute it, was lost upon them, and the recusants stole away unobserved from Oxford, at the hour when others were at dinner, to Wolvesham[5] Castle, where they hoped their brother, the Bishop of Winchester, would be able to protect them. So hot a pursuit, however, was set on foot, that the unpopular fugitives were soon reduced to submission,

[1] Chr. Lanerc.
[2] Four counsellors were appointed to him, probably as sureties for his observance, John de Baliol, John de Gray, Stephen Longespee, and Roger de Montalt.—Ann. Burton.
[3] Letter in Ann. Burton.
[4] Nangis.
[5] "Ulvesham."—Ann. Burt. The palace in Winchester is still called Wolvesey.

and it is even said, that the bishop recommend them to surrender quietly, as being justly punished for their former misdeeds[1]. Though the King, who accompanied the besiegers, used every endeavour to obtain better terms for them, the barons were now inexorable in requiring the immediate exile of all aliens on pain of death, reserving only to Aymer as a bishop, and to William de Valence as Lord of Pembroke, the option of remaining under sureties for good behaviour. These, though thus excepted, would not separate their fate from the others[2], and all accordingly resolved to quit England, venting their spleen even against the Queen, as having, from jealousy of their court favour, contrived their ruin and involved them in her own unpopularity. It is certainly remarkable that her own uncles, Peter of Savoy and Archbishop Boniface, remained unmolested and were publicly employed.

This strong measure of banishment was additionally recommended to the barons, by the treatment they had remarked in two recent instances of English Princesses married to foreign Sovereigns, when their train of English attendants had been scrupulously dismissed both by the Emperor and the King of Scotland—a prudent step on all such occasions, the neglect of which is sure to excite jealousies.

The Earl de Warenne, thus left alone in his opposition to the Oxford Statutes, now at length yielding to circumstances, pledged himself by oath to their maintenance.

Dover and other castles[3] were now put into native hands, and Hugh le Bigot being made Justiciary of England, was "sworn to do justice in spite of the King, the Queen, their sons, or any living person, uninfluenced by hate or love,

---

[1] W. Rish. de bello Lew., inconsistently with his usual opinions, represents the bishop on this occasion as a man of conspicuous sanctity.
[2] R. Hoved. Ann. Burt. W. Rish.
[3] These other castles were, Bamborough, Newcastle-on-Tyne, Scarborough, Haldesham, Nottingham, Northampton, the Tower of London, Rochester, Canterbury, Winchester, Porchester, Corfe, Sarum, Devizes, Exeter, Bridgewater, Gloucester, Hereford, Oxford, Horestan.—Ann. de Burton, p. 453. P.

prayer or price, and never accepting from any one anything, except such matters to eat and drink as are accustomed to be carried to the table of a rich man;" a hazardous permission, implying that no corruption could arise from gifts of dainties. Truly was it now observed in a private letter[1]: "Great and arduous matters have the barons to arrange, which cannot soon or easily be accomplished; they advance fiercely in their business; I wish the issue may be fortunate."

By a safe-conduct to the place of embarkation, dated from Winchester, July 5, 1258[2], to last until the Sunday after S. Thomas of Canterbury (Saturday July 7), the Bishop Aymer, his brothers Guy and Geoffry de Lusignan, and William de Valence, were put under the care and escort of the Earls of Hereford, Warenne, and Albemarle; but a new charge of crime arose against these exiles on their road. At a great banquet in the bishop's palace (it is not clear whether at Winchester or at Southwark[3]) some of the principal guests, including the Earl of Gloucester and the Abbot of Westminster, were taken ill with symptoms of poison. The earl's brother, William, indeed died, but the earl himself, by the care of his physician, John St. Giles, a Dominican monk, escaped after a tedious illness with the loss of his hair, his nails and teeth nearly dropping off, and his skin peeling away. "The Lord was unwilling (observes a chronicler[4] with much feeling) to widow England by his loss, at such a moment of extreme danger and need."

Another victim of this illness, Richard de Crokesley, Abbot of Westminster, who died under it July 18, 1258, was a person of importance by station and talents; learned in canon and civil law, he had been often employed by the King at home and abroad, and was one of the twelve nominated by him at the Oxford Parliament. His death gave

[1] Ann. Burt. litera cujusdam. A very interesting authority, evidently written by one well informed with the persons and transactions around. "Ferociter procedunt Barones in agendis suis : utinam bonum finem sortiantur."
[2] Rymer.
[3] The remains of the episcopal palace have been recently effaced by modern buildings.
[4] H. Knighton.

occasion to his elected successor, Prior Philip de Lewisham, to decline the honour, for the most singular reason, namely, that he was too fat ever to travel to Rome for confirmation, and preferred living at ease in his old way; he died indeed a few months afterwards, before he could learn the Pope's assent.

The sudden illness and death of so many persons of note naturally gave rise to suspicions of foul play, but the evidence of poison as against the departing aliens, though in the temper of the times readily believed, appears very slight; though some concealed stores of poison were said to be found, yet the same illness attacked others after the exiles were gone, and the odium was then transferred to their own cooks. The Earl of Gloucester's steward, Walter de Scotney[1], being accused of taking bribes from William de Valence, for the betrayal of his master in this attempt on his life, fled from the charge, and, when taken some months later, was hanged at Winchester, in spite of his professions of innocence.

Together with the nobler exiles, some meaner aliens were now cast out—the King's favourite carver, William de S. Hermite and Guy de Rochfort, who had converted his trust of Colchester Castle into means of oppression. Another, by his brutal tyranny and arrogance, had made himself so peculiarly obnoxious that he was imprisoned; this was William de Bussy, the steward of W. de Valence, whose usual defiance of all complaints had been, "the King sanctions whatever my master wishes;" when on his trial he endeavoured to plead his tonsure, he was prevented by force and dragged back to a closer cell[2].

The Poictevin brothers had been expressly limited to the sum of 6000 marcs (£4000) to carry away with them, the rest

[1] "1259 Walterus de Scotney *equorum distractione concisus et postmodo patibulo suspensus* periit Wintoniæ pro morte Domini Gulielmi de Clare, fratris Comitis, quem veneno perdidit, ut dicebatur, Comes autem ipse et quidam alii *ad jentaculum Domini Edwardi*, tunc proditione ab Angliâ exulatorum, venenum pauserunt."— Chr. Evesham, Leland Coll. Vol. I. p. 243. His descendants continued in possession of Scotney Castle, in Sussex, until the time of Edward III.
[2] M. Paris.

of their treasures and the rents of their estates being withheld[1], and made responsible in the suits commenced against them in the courts of law. The King, who wrote from Winchester, July 3, commanded the immediate seizure of 3000 marcs (£2000) belonging to W. de Valence, lying in the Abbey of Waltham[2]. Much more than the permitted sum was, however, smuggled out of the country, and the King enjoined de Clare (Woodstock, August 18) to enquire strictly into this evasion[3]. Joan, the wife of W. de Valence, having obtained by petition a sum of 500 marcs (£333. 6s. 8d.) from her own estates, and being refused more, in fear that it would go to her husband, contrived nevertheless to join him at Christmas[4], with a quantity of money concealed in woolpacks. Young Henry de Montfort, with a fresh recollection of their insult to the earl, his father, had followed the Poictevins to Boulogne, and prevailed on the French King to show them no favour, beyond that of a safe passage to Poictou.

That young de Montfort was not alone in his eager hatred against these exiles, is shown by the contumelious terms employed by others at the time, when speaking of them:

> "Totam turbat modica terram turba canum,
> Exeat aut pereat genus tam prophanum." [5]
>
> A paltry set of curs is troubling all the land,
> Drive out or let them die, the base ungodly band.

The new order of things established by the barons soon received the ready assent of the city of London, and of the community, though there may have been some who disliked any innovation upon the accustomed submission of the people to their kings[6]. Owing to de Clare's dangerous illness, however, the former publication of the Oxford Statutes was

[1] W. Rish.
[2] Cal. Rot. Pat.
[3] Rymer.
[4] She travelled in "longa quadriga." Expense Roll. 23-24 Edw. I.

Printed by Hawthorne in Illust. of Domestic Manners, t. Edw. I.
[5] Polit. S. in W. de Rish. Chr.
[6] It is in this spirit that Thomas Wyte, a royalist poet in the begin-

deferred till October 18, 1258, when they were solemnly proclaimed, together with Magna Charta, in every county, with the unusual and striking circumstance of being in Latin, French and English[1].

The latter language, then just emerging into form, being now for the first time, as far as we know, used in any public document, proves the anxiety of the barons to explain their conduct to the people at large, by the use of the best medium of information. While the clergy were familiar with Latin, and the Normans, living either at court or in their own feudal castles, naturally retained their own French, the country people as tenaciously had preserved their Saxon; and though, with the growth of towns, the fusion of the races advanced, yet the use of the three languages in England continued for some time after the present period. It was strikingly marked, during the persecutions of the Templars, under Edward II.; the priests and clerks made their recantation in Latin, the laymen in French principally[2], but "some decrepit Templars, unable to stand from old age,

---

ning of Edward I.'s reign, refers to the Oxford Statutes:
"Degener Anglorum gens, cuæ servire solebat,
Ordine mutato regem cum prole regebat,
Conjurat populus fruiturus lege novella."
—Pol. Songs from MS. Cotton, Vespas. B. XIII.
[1] Ann. Burton.
[2] In the romance of "Blonde of Oxford" (13th c.) are several allusions to the mixed prevalence of the two languages. Even highborn persons are represented as speaking bad French; the young Frenchman, Jehan de Dammartin, made love to the Earl of Oxford's daughter by teaching her better French, and the Earl of Gloucester speaks bad French.
"Un peu parroit à son langage
Que ne fu pas née à Pontoise."
l. 358.

"Et en milleur François le mist
Qu'ele n'estoit quant à li vint."
l. 404.
"Si vaut à lui parler François,
Mais sa langue torne en Englois."
l. 2623.
The Abbot of Bury at an earlier date is chronicled as being able to speak Latin and French in a plain way, and to read English well, though with a Norfolk brogue.—Chr. Jocelin. His remark on the election of a prior (1200) proves that sermons in English were needed, and were not uncommon. "Abbas"—"dicens quod in multis ecclesiis fit sermo in conventu Gallice, vel potius Anglicè ut morum fieret edificatio, non literaturæ ostensio," p. 95. Herebert, the abbot's chaplain, when elected prior, is thus described: "Sobrius et volubilis linguæ in Gallico idiomate utpote Normannus nacione," p. 95.

resorted to English, because they had not the use of any other language[1]."

As in the King's circular letter[2] to each county on this occasion, we have the earliest state paper in English extant, it may be interesting to have a genuine specimen of this King's English, the concluson of which runs thus:

"Widnesse usselven æt Lunden' thane egtetenthe day on the monthe of Octobr' in the two fowertigthe yeare of ure cruninge: and this wes idon ætforen ure isworene redesmen (here follow the names of the councillors), Ætforen othre moge, and al on the ilche worden is isend in to aurihce othre shcire over al thare Kuneriche on Engleneloande ek in tel Irelonde."

The King appears in this proclamation unreservedly to pledge himself and enjoin obedience to the Oxford Statutes.

"Henry, through God's support, King of England, Lord of Ireland, Duke of Normandy and Aquitaine, Count of Anjou, sends greeting to all his liegemen, clerical and lay, in Huntingdonshire; That you may all well know that we will grant, that whatever our Councillors, all or the majority of them, who are chosen by us, and by the people of this land (Landsfolk) in our kingdom, have done or shall do for the honour of God, for our allegiance, and for the good of this land, by the agency of these aforesaid Councillors, be stedfast and lasting in all things without end. And we enjoin all our lieges, by the allegiance which they owe to us, that they stedfastly hold, and swear to hold in this respect to the Provisions that are made or may be made by those aforesaid Councillors, or by the majority of them, as has been also before said; and that each other person help to do that which others ought to do and to bear towards them, and that none, either of my land or elsewhere, through this business be hindered or reversed in any way; and if any man or woman should go against this, we will and command that all our other lieges hold them as most deadly enemies; And because we will, that this be stedfast

[1] July 18, 1281.—Wilkins's Conc. M. Br. 1, 391.
[2] Rymer, from Pat. in Tur. Lond. 43 H. III.

and lasting, we send you this writ open, signed with our seal to keep among your stores. Witness ourself at London the 18th day of the month of October, in the 42nd year of our reign: And this was done before our sworn Councillors—

"Boniface, Archbishop of Canterbury,
"Walter of Cantelop[1], Bishop of Worcester,
"Simon of Montfort, Earl of Leicester,
"Richard of Clare, Earl of Gloucester and Hertford,
"Roger Bigod, Earl of Norfolk, Marshal of England,
"Peter of Savoy,
"William of Fortibus, Earl of Albemarle[2],
"John of Plesseiz, Earl of Warwick,
"John Geoffreyson,
"Peter of Montfort,
"Richard of Grey,
"Roger of Mortimer,
"James of Aldithel[3], and before many others.

"And all and each word is sent into every other shire over all the kingdom of England and into Ireland[4]."

Nearly the same names are also found to a spirited memorial, which the barons at this time sent to the Pope in explanation of their conduct, and which their messengers were desired to deliver and then return without entering into any controversy. Among the chief complaints thus embodied, are "the ruinous disorders, the distress, and the decay of learning to which the introduction of so many Italians into English benefices[5], and the infatuation of the

[1] Cantelow. Oxon MS.
[2] His arms, in the north aisle of Westminster Abbey, are "gules, a cross potence vaire." He sided with the barons throughout, dying 1263, without male heirs.
[3] The curious in surnames should remark that these noblemen, when speaking English, did not prefix "de" to their surnames, but the translation "of."
[4] Another copy of this proclamation was found among the archives of the city of Oxford by Mr Joy, and is published in Dr Ingram's Memorials of Oxford, Vol. III. p. 6. It is directed "To alle his holde ilerde and ileawede on Oxenefordeschir."
[5] As a palliation of this evil, the Pope, in 1253, had permitted patrons to present at once to benefices, even before vacancies, reserving, however, the life interest of the foreigners.— Lingard. A century after this, however (1374), Wicliffe was sent to Rome with the very same complaint.

King, by denying justice against his favourites, had brought the country; the manifesto announced that twelve on each side had been appointed to reform all abuses, while the barons at once renounced the crown of Sicily, which had been accepted for Prince Edmund without their consent. The point, however, most strongly urged upon the Pope, as that most within his competence, was the dismissal of Aymer, from the bishopric of Winchester, denouncing him as leading the King and Prince Edward to perjury, unmindful of his own salvation, and watching only for the disturbance and waste of the kingdom. They supposed his deposition would be the easier, inasmuch as he had never yet been consecrated bishop, but even if the King and barons wished to re-admit him, they stated plainly that the community would not tolerate it, and worse would ensue; the officials of Aymer[1] and the other aliens had been more like robbers, so plundering the poor and ensnaring the simple, that neither could inferiors live under them, nor equals deal with them, nor superiors check them. The barons, however, were resolved to oppose to the subterfuges of their enemies an union so much the more earnest, as well knowing that no faithful brotherhood could exist, unless where there was an entire agreement of will and a cementing together of the very minds[2].

The Pope's answer did not come till two years after (1260), and even then declined to discuss any schemes of church reform with laymen; to the complaint of the decay of literature his reply was remarkable, adroitly denying the fact by complimenting England on its poetry and learning: "On the contrary," he remarked, "so far from finding any scarcity of learned men in England, by the grace of God we cannot discover now-a-days any kingdom or province in the

---

[1] The prior and convent of S. Swithin at Winchester, in a petition to the King, prayed the restitution to them of the manor of Portland, which their late Bishop Aymer had deprived them of unlawfully, under pretence of purchase.—597, Chanc. Rec. 5th Rep.

[2] "Etiam conglutinatio animorum."—Rymer.

whole world, which has a greater, or even so great, an abundance of them. For in this kingdom of England there is found in these present times a most agreeable fountain of Helicon, from the very sweet liquor of which, not only natives, but even foreigners, receive and quaff pleasant draughts, by which their dry hearts and thirsty breasts are copiously refreshed. There reside the liberal arts of philosophy, by which the rude spirits of men are disciplined: from thence proceeds, and has proceeded, an illustrious multitude of learned men, and a succession of saints, in whose company the army of Heaven rejoices, and from the authors of this land also deep springs of writings have burst forth, and are now bursting forth, so as to irrigate the neighbouring provinces with their floods[1]."

What these draughts were of which the Pope had so keen a relish, it is difficult to trace. There were certainly some Englishmen of great learning even in this age[2], when paper was [practically] unknown and parchment scarce, but they were mostly educated at Paris, such as Archbishop Langton, St Edmund, and Bishop Grethead. The latter, indeed, was partly an Oxford scholar, and was not only a good Grecian, but composed, also, a Romançal poem "on the sin of the first man," of 1700 verses, still extant. There were some other poets[3] of little note: William of Wadding-

[1] Rymer.
[2] Even long afterwards the laity were thought unworthy of learning: the enlightened Bishop of Durham, R. de Bury, the great book collector, the author of Philobiblion (finished 1343), the correspondent of Petrarch, the preceptor of Edward III., observes," *Laici omnium librorum communione sunt indigni.*" — Hutch. Durh. The Hamaritic Arabians laid the most jealous restrictions on learning their mode of writing, "characteres eorum—vulgo discere non permittebant; nec cuipiam, nisi post impetratam ab ipsis veniam, iisdem utendi facultatem."—Pocock, Spect. Hist. Arab. p. 161. Foster's Arabia.

[3] Archæol.Vol. xiii. p. 36. [We may perhaps add to these] the twelve lays in French verse by Marie, born in Brittany, but writing in England, and dedicating to a king who understood English. The romances appear taken from Welch or Armoric ones: she introduces English words occasionally, as "fire," translates "Laustic" (Arm.) into Nightgale, and proper names into English.—Harl. MS. 978, translated Cotton Calig. A. 11. She is referred by Fauchet (Œuvres, 579) to middle of 13th century.—Pasquin, Récherches de la France, 8. 1. She also wrote Fables with some English words: Harl. MS. 978 (104 fables)—the prologue refers to Longsword, Earl of Salisbury, who

tou, who translated the poem of "Manuel" into French; the native of Amesbury, who continued Wace's[1] "Brutus;" Denis Pyramus, the author of some free tales at Henry III.'s court; and the "Roman de la Rose," too, was begun in 1250 by William de Loris. Can the Pope have alluded to the wondrous intellect of Roger Bacon[2], to whom all the knowledge preceding and succeeding times seems to have been familiar? Many of his greater works, however, had not then been written.

The barons, having by their union and courage established the government upon principles consistent with public liberty and their own security, saw England now, at length, restored to a peaceful content, which continued for three years. If they, however, are to be charged as rebels when fighting in the subsequent war, they were so now, for they had changed all the powers of the state, and if not justified by the paramount necessity of the case in the battle-field of Lewes, neither were they so now, in effecting a bloodless, but not less complete revolution.

It would be neither easy nor safe to define strictly the point of oppression at which the right of resistance begins— "a right," as has been eloquently observed[3], "terrible and unsocial, for it appeals to force and to war, which is the destruction of society itself, but a right nevertheless which must never be effaced from the inmost heart of man, for its effacement is the acceptance of slavery." No hasty hand, on

---

died 1226; [and she says at the end,] "Marie ai non, si suis de France." La Fontaine took from her the subjects of "The Drowning Woman," "Fox and Cat," "Fox and Pigeon."
[1] Robert Wace, in 1155, turned the Latin Brutus of Geoffry of Monmouth into French verse, ending with 7th century (Cott. Vitell. A. x.). The continuation carried on the annals to 1241. He lived at Amesbury, and alludes to the death of Princess Eleanor of Brittany at Bristol, 1241. He is supposed to have been of a Saxon family, as his Anglo-Norman history is not exact. He relates the choice of the Conqueror's sons, Robert to be a hawk, William Rufus to be an eagle, Henry to be a starling. (Cott. Cleop. A. XII.)
[2] R. Bacon says he only knew four men of his time skilled in mathematics: his own pupil John of London, Peter de Maharn Curia of Picardy, Campan of Novaria, and Nicolas, the tutor of Almeric de Montfort.—Op. Min. Wood, Antiq. Oxon.
[3] Guizot, Civilis. en Europe.

slight cause, should grasp at even the rightful arms of defence; such weapons may well be suspended in the armoury of the Constitution as a token and a warning, without being handled for every-day use. Though custom has limited the term of rebellion to the opposition of subjects to their King, yet all disobedience to the supremacy of the law[1] might, on sound principles, be thus denounced, and such disobedience may equally arise from a King, a House of Commons, a self-exempting Church, or a misled people. In all cases where law ceases, disorder begins; and though it may, according to the agent, at times be called tyranny, and at others privilege or rebellion, it is substantially the same, and deserving of the same reproach. In the present case it was not only the feudal chieftain in his castle, but the men of peace, the bishop in his palace, and the monk in his cell, the busy citizen, and the peasant in his cottage, who felt aggrieved, and who all joined heart and hand in the resistance to Henry III. In the words of Lord Bacon[2], "such men's eyes are upon the business, and not upon the persons, or if upon the persons, it is for the business' sake as fittest, and not for flags and pedigree."

Almost all the memorials of the time teem with approbation of the change resulting from the Oxford Statutes, and with well-considered arguments in their support. The reasons justifying the barons were reviewed with ability in a

---

[1] The venerable H. de Bracton, a judge of this age, maintains the same doctrine throughout in [his treatise on the laws of England]: "Lex omnium rex." " Hoc sanxit lex humana, quod leges suum ligent latorem." "Merito debet (rex) retribuere legi, quia lex tribuit ei, facit enim lex quòd ipse sit rex."—l. 3, c. 9. "Sedem judicandi, quæ est quasi thronus Dei, non præsumat quis ascendere insipiens et indoctus."—l. 1. c. 2. "Supervacuum esset leges condere et justitiam facere, nisi esset qui leges tueretur; * * nihil enim aliud potest rex in terris, cum sit Dei minister et vicarius, nisi id solum quod de jure potest, nec obstat quod dicitur, quod principi placet legis habet vigorem; potestas sua juris est et non injuriæ; quia illa potestas solius Dei est, potestas autem injuriæ Diaboli et non Dei, et cujus horum operum fecerit rex, ejus minister erit, cujus opera fecerit."—l. 3. c. 9. f. 107. "Est enim corona regis facere justitiam et judicium et tenere pacem, sine quibus corona consistere non potest nec tenere."—l. 2. c. 24. Henr. de Bracton, De Leg. et Cons. Angliæ.—Lond. 1569.

[2] Essays.

IV.] THE OXFORD STATUTES. 81

poem[1] written a few months after the battle of Lewes, the condensed spirit of which is worthy of remark.

It urged "that the barons intended no prejudice to the royal honour, but that they felt as much bound by duty to come forward and reform the state, as if the kingdom had been attacked by an enemy; for if the King's real enemies, the wretched false flatterers around him, strove to pervert the prerogatives of the crown to their own pomps, trampling on the native nobles, while contemptible aliens were advanced to high places, did not this amount to an attack by enemies, and if the King, seduced by them or by his own evil will[2], should do wrong, was it not the duty of the barons to reform it? Nor could the analogy of God being a single and supreme governor at all warrant a weak fallible King to claim uncontrolled power. The King might, indeed, urge that he should have the power of selecting whom he pleased to assist his own weakness; such freedom would not, however, be interfered with by restrictions on his doing wrong, to which children and even angels submit. Let him be free then to do all that is good, but let him not dare to do ill; such is God's charter[3]. He, himself, was but the servant of Heaven, and could claim no allegiance from others, unless he owned his to his God; let[4] him feel that the people belong to God, not to himself; he who may be set over a people for a time is soon laid low under his marble tomb, while God's power remains

---

[1] Polit. Songs, from Harl. MS., 978, in Latin rhyme. The inscription on an old tile from Great Malvern (in Gent. Mag., May 1844, pl. 1, fig. vii.) is said to have been anciently used as a talisman against fire, and is found also on a bell at Kenilworth: "Mentem sanctam, spontaneum honorem Deo, patriæ liberationem." It would have been no bad exposition of the professed principles of the barons' party at this period.
[2] "Seu rex ex malitiâ faceret nociva."—V. 590.
[3] "Ergo regi libeat omne quod est bonum,

Sed malum non audeat: Hoc est dei donum."—V. 687.
Compare the lines quoted in the Vision of Piers Plowman. Ll. 281-284, ed. Wright:
"Dum rex a regere dicatur nomen habere
Nomen habet sine re, nisi studet jura tenere."
[4] "Sciat populum non suum sed Dei,
Et qui parvo tempore populo præfertur,
Citò clausus marmore terræ subinfertur."—V. 707.

G

for ever. If a prince, instead of loving his people, should despise and strip them, it would be difficult not to despise and resist in return; for freemen cannot be expected to submit to such treatment. As a King, therefore, depending on his own judgment may readily err, it is very fit that the Commons of the realm should be consulted, to whom the laws and customs are best known, and who can best express public opinion. Men should be chosen as counsellors to the King, who have both the will, knowledge, and courage[1] to be useful, who would feel themselves hurt when the kingdom suffered, and would rejoice when the nation was glad. If the King cannot choose such men, others must, for as the safety or ruin of all must depend on the guidance of the vessel of state, the choice of a competent pilot concerns all. To permit fools in their ignorance to govern cannot be called true liberty[2], which should ever be bounded by the limits of the law, beyond which all is error; for the law is paramount even to the King's dignity[3]; it is the light without which he who guides others must go astray."

After the lapse of six centuries little could be well added to the force and clearness of this argument, which singularly tallies with the soundest constitutional doctrine of the present day, and it may serve as an answer to the reproach of a modern historian[4] upon the revolution effected by the Oxford Statutes, "that its tendency was to a very narrow aristocracy, the end of which would be anarchy or tyranny." By the general concurrence of evidence it is manifest that the people of England judged the reasons sufficient at the time to justify the innovation on the usual forms of their government; and he only, who is ready, in the present day, to avow his passive

---

[1] "Qui velint et sciant
Et prodesse valeant. *   *   *   *
Qui se lædi sentiunt, si regnum
lædatur,
 *   *   *   *   *
Gaudenti congaudeant."—V. 786.
[2] "Nec libertas propriè debet nominari
Quæ permittet stultos dominari;
Sed libertas finibus juris limitetur
Spretisque limitibus error reputetur."—V. 833.
[3] "Legem quoque dicimus regis
dignitatem
Regere."—V. 848.
[4] Hume.

obedience under similar provocation, may presume to reverse their judgment.

King Henry, who, like Proteus, as he was called by a contemporary[1], had so often evaded all the ties of faith and honour, now felt his power effectually restrained by sterner bonds. Though the only means of defence left him were a false heart and a bitter tongue, yet with both these did he continue the struggle. To relieve his conscience from the pressure, however slight, of his oath, he applied at once to the Pope for absolution from it, while he betrayed the vexation of his reduced position by ill-advised speeches.

Going down the Thames one day he was overtaken by so violent a thunderstorm, of which he had a great dread, that he was put on shore at the Bishop of Durham's[2] palace, which was opposite. De Montfort, who was residing there, came out to meet him with all due respect, observing, "What do you fear now, Sire, the tempest has passed?" The King, however, who continued to evince alarm, openly confessed, "I do, indeed, dread thunder and lightning much, but, by the head[3] of God, I tremble before you more than for all the thunder in Heaven." It was in vain that the earl calmly pointed out to him "how unjust and incredible it would seem that he should fear one who had ever been a true friend to him, his family, and the kingdom, when he ought rather to fear his enemies and deceivers[4]." Such hatred of those who now held sway, thus overpowering even his hypocrisy, was not likely to conciliate them.

The barons were, at this time, embarrassed by the expected return of the titular King of the Romans from Germany, whose influence they feared might upset their new arrangements. The Bishop of Worcester, Peter of Savoy, John Mansel, and the Abbot of Bury, were sent over to

[1] M. Par.
[2] In after times it was given by Henry VIII. to Anne Boleyn, and was the residence of Elizabeth, while Princess. The site is now occupied by the Adelphi.
[3] King John had adopted for his habitual oath, "by God's feet."
[4] M. Par.

require his oath to the Oxford Statutes before he landed, and the King, who had hastened to Canterbury to meet him, also exhorted him, by letter[1], not to introduce the exiled aliens by force, which he was evidently expected to do. Though the prince, at first, not only declined the oath, but refused any explanation of his visit, insisting on his right as an earl and prince to be consulted in the reform of abuses, he soon learnt that the barons now in power were not to be trifled with. Troops and ships lined the coast to resist his approach on any terms, and finding all animated with a hearty goodwill to maintain the new state of things, he yielded, and was, at length, permitted to land, with his wife, his second son Edmund, and a very limited suite. Even then he was not allowed to enter the castle of Dover, but, on the following day, was called forward as Earl of Cornwall in the Chapter House at Canterbury by the Earl of Gloucester, who took no notice of his foreign title, and he then publicly and solemnly swore to be a faithful and active helper in reforming the government on pain of forfeiting all his lands.

The Londoners, when they saw him return thus peaceably without his Poictevin brothers contrary to their fears, honoured his entry with unusual welcome (Feb. 2), and he seems to have attended principally to his own affairs and the management of his enormous wealth during his residence. It was soon after this that he obtained the grant of a Guildhall for his German subjects in London, where they might import grain, ropes, linen, steel, &c.[2]

After thus maintaining domestic peace, and disentangling England from the ties of the Sicilian crown[3], the barons exhibited another proof of wiser counsels by a treaty with France, in which the formal resignation was made of Nor-

---

[1] Dated Jan. 18, 1259.—Rymer.
[2] Stow's London. Grant dated Westminster, June 15, 1259.
[3] The King had authorized proxies, one of whom was Simon de Montfort, to renounce the crown of Sicily, "si viderint expedire."—Windsor, June 18. Rymer. There are many Papal briefs pressing for money on account of Sicily, May 30, Dec. 18, 1258.—Rymer.

mandy and other French provinces, long lost indeed, but to which the title had never been disclaimed until now; some territories (Perigord Limousin), long estranged from the English crown, were in return restored, by the conscientious French monarch, and also such a sum of money, as the maintenance of 500 knights for two years ought reasonably to cost, was to be paid to the King of England, to be expended only for the service of God, the Church, or the kingdom, to the satisfaction of the twenty-four councillors[1]. Notwithstanding any precaution, this article to supply the means of keeping on foot a standing army appears a singular, and as the event proved, dangerous device. Commissioners[2] were appointed to settle the amount due under this clause, and as 134,000 livres Tournois (at 2s., £13,400) were subsequently agreed upon, payable by six instalments, we may learn from this, that each horseman was calculated to cost 335 livres Tournois (£33. 10s.)[3] a year, or 28 livres Tournois (£2. 16s.) a month, about 1s. 10½d. a day.

The French treaty was throughout negotiated and concluded by the principal barons in person: the earls of Hereford and Albemarle witnessed King Henry's act of renunciation; Simon de Montfort, Peter de Savoy, and Hugh le Bigot acted as his proctors[4] at its ratification in

[1] Rymer. The text of the treaty is in French, the preamble and conclusion in Latin. The 5th article runs thus: "Derechef li Roi de France donra al Roi d'Angleterre ce que cinc cenz chevalers devroient coster reisnablement a tenir deux anz a lésgard de prodes homes qui seront nomé d'une part et autre * * et li Rois d'Angleterre ne doit ces deniers despendre forsque el service Dieu ou d'Eglise ou al profit del roiaume de Angleterre et ce par la veue des prodes homes de la terre, esleuz par le Roi d'Angleterre et par les hauz homes de la terre."

[2] Rymer, Westminster, May 20.

[3] Spelman values the livre Tournois at this period at 2s., Lingard at 5s. The Abbot of Bury St. Edmund's seems to have paid his four knights in 1198 about 3s. a day each, during their forty days of service. "Abbas autem in instanti eis (quatuor militibus) 36 marcas dedit ad expensas 40 dierum."—Chr. Jocelin. p. 63.

[4] Rymer. In Archives du Royaume, Carton, 629, 4 (Tresor des Chartes, p. 7), there are several seals appended to the original treaty of peace, 1258. 1. Simon de Montfort's arms on a heater escutcheon within a circular seal. 2. Peter de Savoy, a lion rampart (broken). 3. Guy de Lusignan (perfect) Secretum Sigillum, "barry, a lion rampant." 4. Geoffry de Lusignan, a large seal representing him on horseback with his horn, a dog on the saddle behind him. 5. Bigot (is

the presence of the French King, and they with others acted as commissioners to arrange the amount of payments. There was very properly a reservation of private claims on thus surrendering the nominal sovereignty of the French provinces, and there were probably many such to be adjusted, several of the great families settled in England having held lands in Normandy on feudal tenures. In a record[1] of the time of Henry II., among those from whom service to the duchy of Normandy was due, are the following names, familiar in English history:

	Knights.	In his own service.
Humphrey de Boun (Bohun)	2	2
William de Veteri Ponte (Vipont)	2	11¼
Walkelin de Ferrars	5	42¾
Hugh de Mortimer	5	13½
William de Tregoz	1½	...
Ralph de Ver	1	...
Robert de Montfort, for the honour of Caucainvill	5	33
,, ,, for Orbec	2½	...
Geoffrey de Montfort	3½	13½
Hugh de Montfort, for lands held under the church of Bayeux	8	...

Robert Marmiun and Dom. Bardolf neither came nor sent, nor said anything in answer to their summons.

The service of a fractional [knight or heavy-armed soldier] so carefully noted in the register was of course fulfilled by the whole man extending his legal forty days in a similar proportion.

As there was drawn up at the same date with the treaty wanting). To the Confirmation of the Peace by the barons and prelates of England, 1259 (Arch. du Roy. Garton, 629. 10, Fr. des Ch. p. 9,) there are 16 seals appended. 1. Roger de Mortimer, his arms on a heater escutcheon within a circular seal. 2. Hugh le Bigot, Justiciary, lion rampant on a small escutcheon. 3. Peter of Savoy, a circular seal, with a lion rampant, no escutcheon. 4. Richard de Grey, a knight galloping. 5. James de Andridelee (indistinct). 6. Earl of Albemarle, on one side a knight on horseback, on the other his arms. 7. Peter de Montfort, within a circular seal an escutcheon bendy. 8. John Mansel, on one side an antique head with inscription from a Roman Imperial coin, on the other, half of an armed man on a tower, beneath which a kneeling figure. 9. Philippe Basset (large), circular containing arms on escutcheon three bars indented.

[1] Exchequer book of Duchy of Normandy in Ducarel's Antiq. Anglo-Norm. pp. 29—38.

(May 20, 1259) an act[1] to indemnify the Princess Eleanor, Countess of Leicester, for any loss she might sustain by it, an erroneous charge[2] has arisen against her and her husband, as having broken off the treaty under the hope of Normandy becoming the inheritance of their children. So far from this being true, the countess did in fact solemnly resign her claims to any "lands in Normandy, Anjou, Touraine, Maine, Poictou, or in any other part of France," in the presence of both kings and of her husband at Paris, on the Thursday after St Andrew, Dec. 1259[3].

The twenty-four councillors went on thus ruling the country successfully, though absorbing for a time the royal authority; the merits of monarchy however are not unusually seen best in contrast with the experiment of other systems. One of the inevitable evils of multiplied sources of power soon arose, jealousy among co-equals[4]; and though the overpowering weight of the public interests for a time overbalanced the violence of the shock, yet the elements of derangement were in activity, and ultimately produced results fatal to the mechanism of the barons' government.

The dissension which arose between the two great chiefs, de Clare and de Montfort, in their hour of undisputed authority, has been indistinctly assigned to various motives. The supposition of the Countess of Leicester's retention of her private claims has been already disposed of, and another account represents de Clare as reviving against his colleague the refuted accusations of oppression in Gascony; while on the other hand de Montfort is said to have provoked a sharp personal altercation by his straightforward rebukes on the hesitation of his colleagues in enforcing the reforms

---

[1] Rymer. A commission to settle her claims was also appointed on the same day.—Rymer.
[2] M. Par.
[3] Rymer. The seals of Simon de Montfort and his countess are both wanting (apparently torn off) from their Confirmation of the Peace, dated Dec. 4, 1259, in Archiv. du Roy. Cart. 629, 13.
[4] "Nulla fides regni sociis, omnisque potestas
Impatiens consortis erit.
—Lucan i.

determined upon. "What, my lords, after having resolved and sworn, do you still deliberate in doubt, and you especially, my lord of Gloucester, who, as the most eminent of us all, are so much the more strictly bound to these wholesome Statutes? I have no pleasure in dealing with such false and fickle men." Although de Bohun and others of the Council sided with him, he appears to have withdrawn to France in dissatisfaction.

That there was a general apprehension of the barons halting in their career at this period may be gathered from the vehement tone of remonstrance in some contemporary writings, calling upon de Clare, le Bigot, and others, not to flinch from their oaths[1].

The King, though doubtless rejoiced to see any division among the barons, continued yet for some time to dissemble, perhaps waiting for the papal brief of absolution. With the ostensible motive of forwarding the additional articles of the treaty with France, which were arranged during the autumn of 1259[2], he repaired in person to meet the French King,

[1] "O, Comes Glovernæ, comple quod cœpisti,
Nisi claudas congruè, multos decepisti:"
* * *
"O tu Comes le Bygot, pactum serva sanum
Cum sis miles strenuus, nunc exerce manum."
* * *
"O vos magni proceres, qui vos obligatis,
Observate firmiter illud quod juratis."—Pol. Songs. W. Rish.

[2] VI. Cal. Dec. (Nov. 26) 1259, the King of England coming to Paris for peace, was received solemnly in the great church (in ecclesia majori).—Gall. Christ. tome VII. The King evinced some signs of reluctance at Paris in this negotiation of treaty. The Parliament of Paris waited for his presence, as Duke of Aquitaine, before proceeding to business, but he arrived too late, and excused himself to Louis IX. by alleging that he had stopped to hear masses at so many churches in his way from his sister-in-law's, St Germain des Prés. This again happened the next day. To obviate this, the French King secretly ordered all the churches on the road to be shut up, so that King Henry, deprived of this pretext, arrived at the Parliament among the earliest; but when complimented for his punctuality, interposed another objection, "My dearest brother and kinsman, I cannot hold intercourse with people and at a place under an interdict;" and explained his reason for so saying by the fact of having found all the churches on his road shut up, as if under an interdict. The French King was therefore obliged to confess his stratagem, and with somewhat of a taunt, which we should not have expected from so saintly a monarch, asked: "My beloved kinsman, why do you delight in hearing so many masses?" Henry: "And why do you delight in so many sermons?" Louis:

and probably procured promises at least of assistance from him in his intended change of policy, besides drawing upon the fund appointed by the treaty from time to time[1] for his own purposes. He wrote[2] indeed to enjoin Prince Richard "to guard his Cornish coasts from any landing of aliens, his Poictevin brothers having collected arms and horses for invasion;" but the armaments were probably with his connivance, and the prohibition only dictated by the barons. While sickness was detaining him abroad, he was much alarmed by a suspicion that de Montfort was conspiring to prevent his return and to supersede him by Prince Edward. This was probably unfounded[3], but there appears to have been some coolness at the time between the King and his son, whom he would not even admit to his presence on his return, being conscious, as he confessed himself, of his own weakness: "If I see him, I might not be able to resist kissing him," and it required the mediation of Prince Richard to effect a reconciliation. Of de Montfort the King was evidently distrustful, though that nobleman's absence abroad had weakened the barons and excited suspicions[4] of his fide-

---

"It seems to me very sweet and wholesome to hear so often of my Creator." Henry: "And it seems to me sweeter and wholesomer to see Him again and again rather than merely to hear of Him." The result of this incident was that each King was left to attend sermons or masses at his own option, and that the treaty was carried on by the other peers without them. One cannot help suspecting that there was a real unwillingness in the English King to appear as a vassal duke in the French court, disguised under this show of religious zeal.—Archæol. Journ. 1860, p. 316. The articles were signed on the Monday before S. Lucia, December 8, 1259.

[1] Rot. Pat. 44 Hen. III. On the Monday after St Peter and St Paul, 1260, he received 14,513 l. T. from King Louis, who was also to repay 5000 marcs to the King of the Romans for him. Henry III. did homage to King Louis for Aquitaine at Paris, December 9, 1259 ("die Jovis post festum St¹ Andreæ), in presence of Archbishop Boniface of Canterbury, Godfrey de Kinton, Archbishop of York, Benedict de Gravesend, Bishop of Lincoln, Simon de Wanton, Bishop of Norwich, one of the King's Justices, Henry de Wingham, Bishop Elect of London, Richard de Clare, Earl of Gloucester, William de Fortibus, Earl of Albemarle (who died the same year), Dominus Petrus de Montfort, John, Lord de Balliol, John Mansel, Lord Keeper, "cum multis aliis adstantibus."—MS. record attesting it, belonging to P. O'Callaghan, Esq.
[2] Boulogne, April, 1260.—Rymer.
[3] T: Wykes considers it false. MS. Add. 5444 affirms it.
[4] " Nam se quidam retrahunt, qui possunt juvare,
Quidam subterfugium quærunt ultra mare."—W. Rish. Pol. Songs.

lity among his own party. A few days after his return, the King complained of French passports having enabled de Montfort to bring over some horses and arms, "by which (he observes in his letter to the French King) you may more clearly see the disposition of his mind towards us[1]."

Whether this was written confidentially, or in the hope of fomenting the jealousy of the other barons, may be doubted, but as the King was still watching the opportunity to take off the mask, we find the Earl of Leicester a little later officiating, by his special appointment, as steward at the court feast of St Edward, Oct. 13, 1260. King Henry had secretly invited his brother Aymer to return from exile, but he was deprived of what help his violent and unpopular advice might have given him, by the bishop's death at Paris at this time: he had in the meanwhile considerably increased the fortifications of the Tower of London, within which he had entrenched himself with the Queen, preferring such defences to the nobler and firmer guard of his people's love[2]. As this and other symptoms gave occasion to rumours of some intended treachery, he endeavoured to counteract their effects by a proclamation, dated from the Tower, March 14, 1261[3], disavowing any intention of imposing unusual taxes, and ordering "the arrest of any persons who should excite discord between himself and the barons by such reports."

At length there came to him the expected relief to his scrupulous conscience, derivable from a papal absolution, procured by bribes[4]; and it may be as well to reproduce to public scorn a state paper[5] avowedly sanctioning perjury, with some selfish reservations:

---

[1] April 28, 1260.—Rymer. Simon de Montfort had made a temporary visit to England in February, when he offered a precious baldequin at the shrine of St Alban.—Mat. West.

[2] "Però la miglior fortezza che sia, è non esser odiato dal popola; perchè ancora che tu abbi le fortezze, e il popolo ti abbiá in odio, le non ti salvano." A striking remark of Machiavelli (Il Principe), anticipating Burke's "cheap defence of nations."

[3] Rymer.

[4] "Donariis missis."—Oxenede's Chr.

[5] The Latin original is in Rymer. Its author, Alexander IV. (Reinaldo de Conti di Segna, Bishop of Ostia, elected Dec. 12, 1254), died in the next month, May 25, 1261.

"Alexander, bishop and servant of the servants of God, to our dearest son in Christ, the illustrious King of England, health and apostolical blessing.

"It has come to our knowledge, that you, heretofore induced apparently by a certain pressure[1] of the nobles and people of your realm, have bound yourself by your personal oath to observe certain statutes, ordinances and regulations, which they, under the pretext of reforming the state of your kingdom, are said to have made in your name, and to have confirmed by oaths to the diminution of your power and to the detriment of your royal freedom.

"We, therefore, being willing to provide for your dignity in this matter, with our apostolical authority in the plenitude of our power, from this time forwards, entirely absolve you from your oath. If, however, there should be contained in those statutes and ordinances anything concerning the favour and advantage of prelates, churches, and ecclesiastical persons, we do not intend to make such void, or in any way relax the said oath in that respect.

"Let no sort of person, therefore, infringe this charter of our absolution, or oppose it by rash endeavour; if, however, any one should presume to attempt it, let him know that he will incur the wrath of Almighty God and of the blessed apostles Peter and Paul. Given at the Lateran, April 13, 1261."

A similar brief was addressed to the Queen, the prelates, nobles and others who had taken the oath, which the Pope now annulled with the convenient explanation, "that the sanctity of an oath, by which faith and truth should be confirmed, ought not to be made the strengthening bond of wickedness and perfidy[2]." It has been justly remarked[3] that this doctrine of absolution would in civil wars always ne-

---

[1] "Quasi quâdam impressione magnatum et hominum."
[2] Rymer. 3 Kal. Maii, April 30, 1261. On the 20th May, 1259, the King wrote from Westminster letters of thanks to the Cardinals Pietro Capoccio Albo, John Gaytano, Otto-

bono Ottomano, H°. de Seinchier, and R. Hanybal, for promoting his business (negotia), as had been reported to him by William Bonquer.
—Rymer.
[3] Sir J. Mackintosh.

cessitate the extermination of one party by the other, for nothing less would ensure the observance of any terms of peace.

The absolution having been read publicly at Paul's Cross on the second Sunday in Lent, the King by a protean effort again cast loose the restraints of his oath, and proceeded to annul the laws he had sanctioned, but which we have reason to think he had long meditated to get rid of. His courtiers are represented as thus addressing him immediately after the Oxford Parliament:

"Sir, we see thin ille,
Thi lordschip is doun laid, and led at other wille,
*   *   *   *   *
It is a dishonoure to the and to thi blode.
Call agen thin oath, drede thou no menace,
Nowthor of lefe ne loth thi lordschip to purchace;
Thou may full lightly haf abolution
For it was a gilery, thou knew not ther tresoun.
Thou hast frendis enowe in Inglond and in France,
If thou turne to the rowe, the salle drede the chance[1]."

In his proclamation he now accused the barons of not having kept the conditions agreed upon as to his own treatment, or the amendment of the laws: a charge which the exciting circumstances of the period rendered probably true to a certain extent, but a plea by which the King could have no right to benefit, having, in fact, applied for absolution so "lightly had," long before any possible infraction of the terms by the other party.

The Queen had also won[2] over some of the least resolute of the barons, so that Henry now felt emboldened to displace some of the new governors from his castles[3], and Mansel,

---

[1] Rob. Brune, Chr. "Sir, we see thy grievance, thy power is cast down and guided at the will of others. It is a dishonour to thee and to thy blood; recall thy oath, dread thou no menace, either by consent or force, to recover thy power. Thou mayest have absolution very easily, for it was a cheat, thou knewest not their treason: thou hast friends enough in England and France: if thou turnest to resistance they shall dread the chance."
[2] M. Par.
[3] Hugh le Bigot was displaced from Dover.—T. Wyke.

though one of the twenty-four councillors, surrendered[1] to him Scarborough and Pickering in pursuance of the Pope's brief.

All the fruits of the new policy, which had restored England to peace for the last three years, were in evident peril, when the barons, who could not be inattentive to the King's course of reaction, gathered again their formidable strength, and offered for the sake of peace to assent to any reasonable alterations of the Oxford Statutes: a conference between the parties thus prepared for contest having taken place at Kingston[2], they agreed at length (July 9, 1261), upon a *mise* or reference on the disputed points to the decision of the French King Louis, the integrity of whose character, connected as he was by brotherhood with King Henry, received thereby the most honourable tribute.

The King, however, did not allow himself to be checked by this arrangement, and was preparing himself not to acquiesce in any adverse sentence: he had collected troops, shut himself up in the Tower, sent orders to the Cinque Ports for the seizure of any arms, or horses or ships, should Simon de Montfort attempt to land with them[3]; and as another indication of the political struggle on which he was bent, he had in May committed all his crown jewels to the custody of his sister-in-law, the Queen of France, not perhaps so much for their security as to raise money[4] upon their deposit, a practice not unusual in that age. In the list, besides his great crown, three golden crowns, and five "garlands," which were also cinctures for the head, were an alphabet, three gold combs, fifty-two clasps, sixty-six girdles, 208 jewelled rings, and the two golden peacocks, which poured sweet waters from their beaks.

The King had sent urgent summons for the return of his son, who, having left England without his leave, had been

[1] Rymer.
[2] The safe conduct granted to the barons to meet at Kingston, to arrange terms, was dated May 20,
1261.—Pat. Rot.
[3] Rymer.
[4] 5000 marcs borrowed on pledging them.

received with great distinction by the Duke of Burgundy, at whose tournaments he gained great credit[1]; at Paris also the Prince had engaged in similar trials of martial exercise (Feb. 1262), accompanied by his friends and cousins the two sons of Simon de Montfort. When at length, in the beginning of June, the Prince attended his father's call, it was only to reproach him bitterly for his false policy, and to declare[2] that "as for himself, though he had unwillingly sworn, yet he would not be false to his oath, and was ready to risk death for the good of the state, and commonalty of England." He accordingly held himself aloof from the court in order the more strongly to denote his opinions. One of the exiles, William de Valence, whom he had brought over with him, had been compelled to swear to the Oxford Statutes, and to answer any charges made against him; he had been offered indeed the liberty of remaining when the other foreigners were sent away, in consideration of holding the lands of the earldom of Pembroke.

Soon after the *mise* had been arranged, the King justified his own course in a proclamation[3], wherein he announced that "he should no longer consent to the frivolous restraints imposed on him, but should find a remedy for his diminished power, boasting of the long peace enjoyed by England during his reign, explaining that he had recalled some of the aliens in order to profit by their advice, and had lately committed his castles to his own friends, as being persons of greater weight[4], and cautioning his subjects not to listen to any deceitful or false suggestions concerning him."

The arguments on behalf of the King's views in his present position are found not unfairly stated in the poem from which the summary of the barons' reasoning has been already extracted. The King's case was made to rest mainly upon precedent and prerogative, "according to which he would

---

[1] Chr. Dover, "bene in omnibus se habuerat."
[2] Ann. Burt. Chr. Rish.
[3] Rymer.—MSS. Add. 5444.
[4] "Majoris potenciæ."

cease to be a King, if restrained in his power; the free choice of judges, governors, and councillors had always been at the pleasure of the King without any interference from the barons, who might indeed rule over their own property, as the King might over his; while any diminution of his hereditary privileges would reduce him to be their slave[1]." These were the opinions probably not only of himself, but of most of the King's adherents at the time, and were not wholly unwarranted by the previous history of English monarchy.

While awaiting the result of the reference to the French King, there was no relaxation on the part of King Henry in improving his own position. He wrote[2] to desire Louis "to give no credit to the Earl of Leicester, who had gone to France without his knowledge, and for reasons unknown to him"—a satisfactory proof of that statesman's fidelity to the great cause in which he was so deeply engaged, however unexplained his absence may be.

After having so absolutely annulled the Oxford Statutes, the King thought it expedient to grant a formal pardon to the chiefs concerned in framing and executing them, apprehensive probably of their strength, and also glad of the opportunity of thus describing their reforms as crimes which needed his pardon. This document, dated from the Tower, Dec. 7, 1261[3], especially named the twenty-four councillors, who had been exercising the highest authority in the state during the last three years.

A fresh absolution having become necessary to the tran-

[1] " * * Esse desineret rex, privatus jure
Regis, nisi faceret quid vellet.
Non intromittentibus se de factis regis
Angliæ baronibus, vim habente legis
Principis imperio. * * *
Quare regem fieri servum machinantur
Qui suam minuere volunt potestatem.
* * * ne tam ubere valent regnare
Sicut reges hactenus qui se præcesserunt,
Qui suis nullatenus subjecti fuerunt."
—Pol. Songs, from MS. Harl., 978, v. 491, &c.
[2] "Windsor, Sept. 2, 1261."—Rymer.
[3] Rymer, in French.

quillity of his mind in consequence of the death of the Pope who had granted the first, the King wrote, Jan. 1, 1262, from Westminster, to petition the Pope to cancel his oath, as his predecessor had done[1], and found the new Pontiff, Urban IV.[2], as pliant as his predecessor, so that his emissaries, John de Hemyngford and John Lovell, soon brought back another "solemn revocation of all the statutes, ordinances and restrictions which the barons of England had devised in diminution of the King's authority, even though he should have consented and sworn to them, denouncing at the same time the penalties of excommunication on all recusants[3]." Some of the King's party, the Archbishop, Simon de Waltone, Bishop of Norwich, John Mansell and others, were enjoined to publish this in all churches with ringing of bells and lighted tapers[4].

Louis IX. had in the meanwhile been anxiously assisting Henry's agents at Paris, John de Cleyshill and John de Montferrant, in their endeavours to detach Simon de Montfort from the party of the barons, but he was obliged to report with deep regret his inability to find any method by which the Earl of Leicester might return to the peace and favour of his Sovereign, having been assured by the earl indeed just before Lent, that "though he had confidence in the good intentions of King Henry, yet he had none in his advisers, and therefore did not think it comported with his honour to agree to any terms, for certain reasons which he should only give by word of mouth[5]." Even after this answer, which fixes the integrity of de Montfort on the highest testimony, the French King detained the agents at Paris, in the vain hope of ultimate success.

[1] Rymer.
[2] Urban IV., Jacobo Pantaleon, Patriarch of Jerusalem, elected Aug. 29, 1261; crowned Sept. 4; died Oct. 2, 1264.
[3] The absolution is dated "Viterbo, 5 Kal. Mar.(Feb. 5);" and its proclamation in Westminster, May 2, 1262.—

Rymer. "John Lovell," clerk and proctor to the King of England at the Roman court, writes relative to the Bull of Absolution which he had procured from Viterbo, 14th May.—956 Chanc. Rec. 5th Rep.
[4] Rymer.—Chr. W. Thorn.
[5] Rymer, in Latin.

Another attempt at accommodation had been made in England by Commissioners[1] jointly appointed by both parties, and when these could not agree the disputed questions had been referred to the arbitration of Prince Richard. This decision, however, which pronounced[2] in favour of the King's unlimited right of appointing any one he pleased to command his castles, obtained but little general acceptance, however much it encouraged the King to persevere in his unpopular course. Again Henry went to Paris, where he was always treated with the utmost courtesy, and was there so stricken with illness that for some time he could not attend to business; he described himself in a letter to his brother from St Germain[3], Sept. 30, 1262, "so depressed and broken down by his fever, that he could even then scarcely get out of bed, and walk a little; regretting also that he could not yet pay him the money he had borrowed[4] of him through Peter de Savoy, but thanking him for his labours and vexations on his account."

Finding the negotiations with de Montfort now broken off, he cautioned his English adherents to guard against

---

[1] Philip Basset, Walter de Merton the Chancellor, and Robert Waleran, by the King; John de la Haye, Richard Folyot and Richard de Middleton, by the barons. Walter de Merton received the Great Seal "without the consent of the barons," as stated in his Patent (Rot. Pat. 45° Hen. III., m. 8), on the King's requiring its unwilling surrender from Nicholas de Ely, on the Tuesday after the Translation of St Thomas the Martyr (July 7), 1260-1 (Pat. Rot. 45° Hen. III. m. 8). A salary of 400 marcs a year was appointed him. He continued Chancellor till displaced by the barons, when Nicholas de Ely succeeded him, 1263, on the Thursday before S. Margaret the Virgin (Jan. 28), in presence of Simon de Montfort, &c., at Westminster. During the king's absence abroad, both under Merton and Ely, the Seal was always to be attested by H. le Despenser, Justiciary. Walter de Merton was Bishop of Rochester, 1274-77, and founder of Merton College. He was again Chancellor on the death of Henry III. in K. Edward's absence, until Robert Burnel was appointed, Sept. 21, 1274.

[2] In the Latin letters both of the Commissioners and Prince Richard (Rymer) the word "misa" occurs in the sense of reference to arbitration, which was afterwards affixed to the agreement of Lewes; it was, in fact, in common use, as also the term "compromissum:" "de quibus Rex et Barones sui posuerunt se in misam," " per formam misæ supradictæ," "compromissum inter nos et Comitem non processit."

[3] Rymer.

[4] He had borrowed 10,000 marcs of his brother in 1247.—Cal. Rot. Pat., 31° H. III.

his seditious intrigues[1]; but as after his recovery, though still feeble, he unnecessarily prolonged his journey homeward by a visit to Rheims, contrary to the advice of Mansel, he found on his return in December that Simon de Montfort had secretly preceded him early in October[2], and under circumstances well calculated to give him increased importance. Richard de Clare, Earl of Gloucester, the jealous compeer of de Montfort, was lately dead (July, 1262)[3], and had left open to him the undisputed leadership of his party: the common danger had indeed already reconciled[4] these chiefs, and the survivor, "the key of England, who had locked out the aliens for three years," as was said[5] of de Montfort, now seeing all his policy put in jeopardy, when the barons pressed him to assume the guidance of their somewhat weakened party, at once assented, "with a declaration of his equal readiness either to die among bad Christians, fighting for Holy Church, or among pagans as a sworn crusader[6]."

He returned, therefore, at this period to take that decided part in the constitutional struggle, which has made his name famous. His talents well fitted him for the duties he undertook: "he was a man," says a friendly chronicler[7], "of wonderful forethought and circumspection, pre-eminent in preparing and vigorously carrying on war, himself a complete soldier, abounding in excellent stratagems, not degenerate from his high ancestry, and gifted with divine wisdom." There can be no doubt that his influence over the minds of others was powerful: a royalist[8] of this period well

---

[1] In an order to P. Basset, from St Germain, Oct. 8, 1262.—Rymer.
[2] Oct. 3, 1263; according to T. Wyke his return was secret, "clanculo rediit."
[3] Richard de Clare died at Eschemerfield, in Kent, and was buried at Tewkesbury, his funeral being attended by the bishops of Worcester and Llandaff, 12 abbots, and numerous barons and knights. Numerous indulgences were granted by the bishops and the Archbishop of Canterbury to those who should pray for his soul.—Dugd. Mon. II. 55. His son Gilbert was also buried at Tewkesbury, 1295, having died at Monmouth.
[4] "Prius per verba indecentia discordes."—MSS. Add. 5444.
[5] W. de Rish. Chr.
[6] Oxenede Chr.
[7] Chr. Mailros.
[8] T. Wyke.

describes him, "as moulding the barons with his own deep-cut impression, especially the younger ones, who, being ductile as soft wax, followed him not from any love of justice, but from greediness of gain."

Associated with him—though, on account of his youth, unable to command the same deference which had been readily yielded to his father—was Gilbert de Clare; he was indeed married to the king's niece, but the death-bed injunctions of his father, and the wishes of his mother[1], the widowed Countess of Gloucester, secured his important adherence to the barons, and he played a conspicuous, though not a consistent part, in the coming troubles.

[1] Matilda de Lacy, daughter of the Earl of Lincoln. "Gilbertum novitium instigante matre suâ blanditiis allectum, qui prius Regi devotus extiterat, resilire coegit." — T. Wyke.

CHAPTER V.

WAR AND TRUCE.

"The hearts
Of all his people shall revolt from him,
And kiss the lips of unacquainted change."

K. JOHN, III. 4.

THE first actual hostilities, after both parties stood thus in presence, hopeless of amicable compromise, seem to have arisen on the distant frontier of Wales, at the end of 1262. Prince Llewellyn, probably in concert with the barons, if we may judge from their subsequent alliance, attacked the lands of his kinsman Roger de Mortimer, who had openly renounced the authority of the twenty-four councillors, and those of the Savoyard Bishop of Hereford. The disorder soon spread, and in order to remedy it, the King sent the most pressing summons to his son, who kept aloof from court at Bristol, "urging him to make no delay under any pretext of indolence or puerile wantonness[1];" a strange reproach to so enterprising a Prince of twenty-four years old, but indicating probably an expected unwillingness of mind rather than of body. Whether by the danger of his Welsh estates or by the persuasion[2] of the Queen, Prince Edward was at any

---

[1] "Sub pretextu alicujus otiositatis vel lasciviæ puerilis."—Rymer. The Prince had written to his father, March 31, 1263, promising to come at Easter.

[2] "Blanditiis per matrem suam tenuit ex parte patris, et extraneos fovebat et consanguineos."—MSS. Add. 5444.

rate roused into activity, and soon retaliated on the territory of Humphrey de Bohun, giving over what he conquered to de Mortimer. De Bohun, the eldest son of the Earl of Hereford, was possessed of Brecknock and other lands, in right of his wife Eleanor de Braose, daughter of Baron de Cantilupe, whose inheritance she had shared in 1259[1] with her sister Matilda, wife of his enemy de Mortimer. True to the honour of having his family name enrolled among the appointed guardians of Magna Charta, de Bohun had during these troubles pursued an independent line, being one of the first to side with the barons at Oxford, and continuing now to act with them, so as to expose his property to an attack, by which the castles of Hay and Huntingdon were wrested from him[2].

The ravages of war rapidly spread over the border counties, in which plunder and destruction by fire and sword took place. Among the partisans of the barons, who took a leading part in these hostilities, which spared neither houses, parks, or even churches, were Roger de Leybourne and John Gifford[3]. A general persecution was carried on against all

[1] Rot. Pat. 43° H. III.
[2] By the barons he was subsequently appointed governor of Goodrich and Winchester. He died, 1265, possessed of the castle and manor of Hay, and the castle of Huntingdon, and Hinton.—Cal. Inquis., post mortem, 1267. Arms at Carlav: azure, a bend argent, cottised, between six lioncels rampant or.
[3] Chr. Dover. The Giffords descended from Walter Gifford, son of Osbern de Bolebec, and his wife Aveline, sister of Gunnora, Duchess of Normandy, great grandmother to the Conqueror, who created Walter, Earl of Buckingham, and Earl of Longueville in Normandy. Walter was one of the Commissioners to compile Domesday. Elias had joined the barons against King John, and was deprived by him of his estates at Broughton Gifford (Wilts), &c., which were restored by Henry III. John Gifford, his son and heir, 17 years old at his death in 1248, was the first Baron Gifford by writ summoned till his death in 1299. He was employed against the Welsh, 1257-62, and was excommunicated in 1264 by the Archbishop of Canterbury for his depredations. After fighting against the King at Lewes, and against Montfort at Evesham, he received the next year the Royal licence to hunt in all the King's forest south of Trent; in 1281 he had a grant of Free Warren at Broughton, and his other manors in Wilts. Together with Edmund Mortimer he commanded the English on left bank of the Wyo against Llewellyn in 1282, and crossing by a ford, defeated him. Llewellyn's head was sent by him to Rhuddlan, and then to the Tower of London crowned w.th ivy. His wife Matilda (whose first husband was K. John's great nephew, and so related

who could not speak English[1], the people joining in it so eagerly, that many foreigners, both laymen and clerical, fled the country in alarm, and the stewards of the alien clergy were forbidden to pay them any rents, or render them any account, on pain of their lands being laid waste.

The treasures of Peter, the alien Bishop of Hereford, were seized and himself captured in his own palace, or, as some say, in his own cathedral, his former pride now becoming the subject of popular ridicule:—

" Ly eveske de Herefort	The Bishop of Hereford knew full well
Sout bien que ly. Quens fu fort,	That the Earl, if he pleased, could
Kant il prist l'affere:	make his blows tell,
Devant ce estoit mult fer,	When he took the matter in hand:
Les Engleis quida touz manger,	Greedy and proud was the alien before,
Mes ore ne set que fere[2]."	He could eat all the English and crave for more,
	But now he is at his wits' end.

He was imprisoned at Erdesley by de Montfort, but being released at Michaelmas he was present at Amiens with the King in the next year, and perhaps did not return at all. In June, 1265, the King (then under the influence of de Montfort) wrote to him abroad, observing that, "in passing through Hereford, on his way to settle the Marches of Wales, he was grieved to find in the cathedral neither bishop, nor his deputy, neither dean, vicar, nor canons, to perform the due services by day and night[3]." In spite of this threatening summons, he seems to have retired to his native place, Aqua-

to Llewellyn) interceded in vain with Archbishop Peckham to obtain Christian burial for him. She was daughter of Walter de Clifford, and married William Longespée, who died 1257. In 1271, 14 years later, she complained to the king of John Lord Gifford taking her by force from her manor at Canford (Dorset), and marrying her at Brimsfield against her will. He alleged her consent, but paid a fine of 300 marcs for not having obtained the king's licence.

He promoted the Statute De Tallagio non Concedendo to restrict the power of Edward I. while in Flanders. He died May 28, 1299, at Bayton, and was buried at Malmesbury (see Wilkinson's Hist. Broughton Gifford, p. 26, &c.).
[1] Add. MSS. 5444. He who could not speak "in Anglicanâ linguâ in multo vilipendio et despectu haberetur a populo."
[2] Polit. S. from MS. 13th century.
[3] Wilkins's Conc. M. Br. Vol. I.

bella, in Savoy, where he died in peace, Nov. 27, 1268, and where his bronze effigy, a handsome man in pontificals, still exists[1].

Another alien, Mathew de Besil[2], a resolute soldier, was also taken prisoner by the barons. He had forcibly re-instated himself on the King's behalf as Sheriff and Governor of Gloucester, where he made a stout resistance, retreating ultimately to a tower, into which Roger de Clifford and John Gifford, with much difficulty, forced their way by breaking down the door with iron mallets and pickaxes[3]:—

" Ne ł Sire Mathi de Besile	To Sir Mathew de Besile,
Ne lesserent une bile	Neither in town, plain, nor hill
En champ o en vile,	Did they leave a single stick :
Tot le soen fut Besile	The besom swept Besile clean out,
E cointement fu detrusse	Daintily stripped and put to the rout
Par un treget sanz gile[4]."	By a plain-speaking honest pick.

His courage, however, when he would not surrender to threats of death, even after the doors were broken down, extorted the praises of his enemies[5]. He survived the war, and held four manors in 1266[6], probably given him by the King.

In another part of the kingdom, Simon de Waltone, Bishop of Norwich, who had made himself odious as the ready tool of the Pope in publishing the absolution, was obliged to take sanctuary in Bury St Edmunds, meeting with little sympathy on the occasion from a contemporary:—

" Et ly pastors de Norwis	The shepherd of the Norwich fold,
Qui devoure ses berbis	Who fleeces and preys on his sheep,

[1] The effigy was cast by Henry de Cologne. " Hic jacet venerabilis Pater Dominus Petrus Herefordensis quondam Episcopus, fundator, structor et dotator hujus ecclesiæ," &c. —Arch. Vol. xviii. p. 189. His nephew was Dean of Hereford.

[2] At Abingdon, A.D. 1460, the building of a bridge was assisted by one of this name:—
Sir Peris Besillis, knyght curteys and keend,

For his fadir soule and his frendes he did as he scholde.
He gaf them stonys i nowhe into the werkys ende,
Also mony as they nedid, feche hem if they wolde.
—MS. of 15th century; Parker's Domestic Architecture, Vol. III. p. 42.

[3] W. Rish.
[4] Polit. S. from MS. 13th century.
[5] Chr. Roff.
[6] Cal. Inquis. post mortem.

Assez sont de ce conte:	Of Leicester's power need not to be told;
Mout en perdi de ces biens,	His goods from loss he could not keep,
Mal ert que ly lessa riens,	No thanks to him who left him aught,
Ke trop en saveit de honte[1]."	For shame by shame is fitly brought.

In the last year of his life (1266) he again felt the strength of popular revenge, when Norwich was taken and plundered by the disinherited[2].

The armed levies of the barons, who marched forward under the royal standard[3], were daily increasing during their advance by the adherence of the people, when they dispatched Roger de Clifford to require the King's observance of the Oxford Statutes. The King was at this time urged by the warden of his forces in the North, Robert de Neville[4], to summon to his help the great Scotch lords, Bruce, Baliol, Comyn, and others who held fiefs in England, and to garrison Pontefract by the northern potentate Percy, but even de Neville, while insisting on the necessity of resisting the rebels by main force, confessed at the same time to the King that "he had found many lukewarm in their answers to his appeals[5]." So little able, however, was the King to encounter the baronial army on the instant, that this recom-

---

[1] Polit. S. from MS. 13th century.
[2] W. Rish.
[3] Fabyan.—W. Rish.
[4] Robert de Neville, second Lord of Raby of that name, 1258, was the grandson of Robert Fitz Maldred, lineal male heir of Uchtred, Earl of Northumberland, and fifth in descent from the Conqueror's Admiral, Gilbert de Nová Villâ. The castles of Norham and Wark were in his custody.—Hutchinson's Durham, Vol. 1. 211. He died 1282, having married Ida, widow of Roger Bertram; his two next generations disgraced themselves by their passions.—V. Banks' Dorm. Bar. Geoffry de Neville was also a royalist, and was taken prisoner at Lewes. From the Admiral's brother Robert was descended John de Neville, who fought on the barons' side at Evesham and Chesterfield, and Hugh, also of the same party, who was made prisoner at Kenilworth.—V. Rowland's Neville Family.

[5] "Pluresque tepidos in responsis suis ad conservationem pacis invenio."—Rymer. After Easter, 1263, the justices Gilbert de Preston and Richard de Hemington held their assize at Lincoln. The abbey of Peterborough was at great expense in entertaining them. Their "iter remansit indeterminatum," on account of the civil war about Pentecost, "unde *justitiarii timore perterriti latenter* recesserunt." "Facta summonitione servitii per ballivos feodales, prout moris est, tenentes militiam *nihil facere voluerunt*."—Chr. W. de Whittlesey.

mendation of future vigour did not suffice to ward off his present extremity of danger, and he was reduced, in June 1263, on the mediation[1] of his brother Prince Richard, as a preliminary to peace, to prohibit Prince Edward from continuing his hostilities.

The usual demands[2] as to the Oxford Statutes and native governors of castles were comprised in the treaty, and so critical was the King's position that on June 29, he sent the four bishops of London, Worcester, Lincoln, and Coventry, who had endeavoured to reconcile the parties, with the draft to his Chancellor, with special injunctions to revise it, "with all speed, in order that the King and Prince might escape from a great and imminent danger[3]."

An immediate truce took place, and the surrender of Dover Castle having been exacted as a pledge for its continuance, it was now given up by Prince Edmund on July 26, to three of the mediating bishops on the King's requisition to that effect (dated Westminster, July 18), which stated that "the peace between himself and the barons had been reformed and confirmed[4]."

Young Prince Henry had joined this movement of the barons against the King his uncle, and had made an eager pursuit of John Mansel, when that wealthy churchman fled in terror[5] (June 29) to Boulogne, where a French knight,

[1] Rymer. King of the Romans to King Henry, June 28, Itelbord (Nettlebed?). [King Richard had property at Nettlebed, but from the spelling *Istelhard* in note 3 I think the place he dates from is most likely his manor of Isleworth. P.].
[2] W. Rish.
[3] "Ad imminens et formidandum periculum evitandum."—Rymer. By a letter from the king of the Romans to Henry III., dated Istelhard, June 30, we learn that he had arrived at Chippenham on the 29th, and, on hearing that Simon de Montfort was at Reading, had invited him to meet him on the day he wrote (Saturday) at Loddon Bridge to treat for peace: the earl had answered that he could not come or vary his former proposal. Wherefore, finding that Simon de Montfort had that day moved to Guildford, and would be at Reigate on the morrow, he (K. of Romans) had changed his intention, and instead of proceeding to Wallingford, would on the morrow meet the King Henry at London.—No. 413, Tower Records, 5th Report. [Chippenham is no doubt the manor of Cippenham, now Chippenham Liberty in the parish of Burnham, Bucks. King Richard had a palace there. Lipscombe's Buckinghamshire, Vol. III. p. 210. P.]
[4] Rymer.
[5] "Timens pelli suæ."—Chr. Dover.

Gerard de Rodes, honourably received him. The King, aware of Mansel's unpopularity, wrote to Cardinal Ottoboni[1], cautioning him not to credit any slander he might hear against him, having known him from his youth and having always found him faithful[2]. The young Prince, in his incautious zeal against the fugitive, had even crossed over to Boulogne, and had there been seized and imprisoned by Ingelram de Fiennes, to the great indignation of the barons[3], who suspected the Queen[4] to have instigated the act. The present turn of events, however, soon effected his liberation on the request[5] of the King of the Romans, and he was appointed[6] with the Earl de Warenne to arrange the terms of reform by which Prince Edward was to abide. This was probably in reference to the disorder of his private affairs, owing to his debts and improvident mortgages of his property, some of which were cancelled as illegal.

The barons had observed the repeated visits of the King to France since the Oxford Statutes, and knowing the large sums which had been paid him there in pursuance of the treaty, they evinced such a jealousy of his foreign intrigues, that King Henry now postponed his intended visit, writing to Louis the humiliating confession (August 16, 1263)[7], that he did so "because his barons for certain reasons desired some security for his speedy return." Before his departure, accordingly (September 18), he published his oath to "return before Michaelmas, and to do nothing abroad contrary to the advantage or honour of his heirs, or of his kingdom[8]."

[1] Cardinal Ottoboni de Fieschi, Conte di Lavagno, after his mission to England became Pope Adrian V. in July, 1276, and died August in the same year. Dante puts him into Purgatory (P. 19, v. 98) for his avarice:
107. Ma come fatto fui Roman pastore
Così scopersi la vita bugiarla.
* * * * * * *
112. Fino a quel punto misera e partita
Da Dio anima fui, del tutto avara:

Or, come vedi, qui ne son punita.
[2] Chr. Dover.—Chr. Roff.
[3] "Supra quod ultra modum movebantur Barones Angliæ."—Chr. Dover.
[4] "Procuratione ut putabatur Reginæ."—Chr. Roff.
[5] "Berkhampsted, July 10, 1263."—Rymer.
[6] Rymer, in French, dated from Lambite [Lambeth], Saturday after the Assumption.
[7] Rymer.   [8] Ibid.

In spite, however, of this precaution, in itself a strong proof both of the predominance at the time of the barons' party, and of their undisguised distrust of their King, whom they were so loth to lose from their sight for even ten days, it is not unlikely that the two Kings, during their short interview at Boulogne, arranged their measures for extricating Henry from his difficulties; and the fact of this suspicious conference might be remembered afterwards by the opposite party, as casting doubts on the impartiality of Louis when acting as arbitrator.

Some of the chronicles[1] of the times affirm plainly this corrupt concert of the French King, dating his promises of support so far back as when Henry began to fortify himself in the Tower; substantial aid was actually sent under the Count St. Pol, with eighty knights, and as many slingers, while Gerard de Rodes, the same French knight who had welcomed Mansel, led another troop, who received forty days' pay before their arrival in England, the leaders being paid forty marcs (£26. 13s. 4d.) weekly from the Exchequer[2]. Another account[3] considers King Louis actually corrupted by English money; while again a different[4] version represents his compliance with Henry's wishes as proceeding from the softer influence of the two sister Queens.

The hollow armistice formally agreed to seems to have had little effect. It did not prevent the King, under the guidance of Prince Edward and Philip Basset[5], making a vigorous attempt to surprise Dover (December 4), which Richard.de Grey, the Constable of the Castle, successfully resisted, refusing to admit the King unless he entered the fortress with a limited suit of nine persons[6]. Foiled in this, he then hoped, by a rapid march back, to have taken unawares de Montfort and his forces, who were quartered in Southwark. The gates of the city of London having been

[1] W. Rish. Chr. Roff.
[2] "De Fisco."—Chr. Roff.
[3] Oxenede's Chr.
[4] Taxter's Chr.
[5] T. Wyke.
[6] Chr. Dover.

shut, and the keys thrown into the Thames, by the connivance of four citizens of authority, he had nearly succeeded in surprising de Montfort in a position of great peril, had not the zealous Londoners, whose hearts were all in favour of the barons, burst open the barriers of the bridge for him, and crowded to secure his safe entry among them. Though the four traitors were saved by de Montfort from the summary vengeance of the people, a heavy fine[1] exacted from them was devoted to strengthen the chains and defences of the city, and violent death still awaited them, as we shall see, under the most singular circumstances, at Lewes.

Prince Edward, in the earlier part of the year, had been so closely besieged in Gloucester[2], that he was only enabled to escape by imposing on the good faith of the Bishop of Worcester, who, as mediator, prevailed on the barons to withdraw their forces, on the Prince giving hostages—a precaution subsequently remitted from courtesy towards him. When thus freed from the danger, he unfortunately considered himself freed also from his obligations, and immediately levied a fine of 1000[3] marcs on the citizens, after which, under pretence of placing his wife in security there, he occupied Windsor, even at that time an admired spot[4], making every effort to fortify the castle, and to garrison it with the fugitive aliens, and also with Spaniards brought over for the purpose.

A general uneasiness naturally prevailed late in the year 1263[5], and the nominal truce appeared giving way to more

[1] W. Rish., De Bello Lewes. Add. MSS. 5444.
[2] Some chronicles (W. Rish.) name Bristol as the scene of his danger.
[3] W. Rish., De Bello Lewes. Taxter Chr. Pol. S. from Harl. MS. 978, thus refers to the transaction:—
"Cum in arcto fuerit quicquid vis promittit,
Sed mox ut evaserit, promissum dimittit.
Testis sit Glovernia ubi quod juravit

Liber ab angustiâ statim revocavit."—V. 431.
[4] "Sub colore vigilandi uxorem intravit in castrum de Wyndleshor, et ibi se tenuit rex."—Lib. de Antiq. Leg. "Quo non erat splendidius tempore ullo."—Add. MSS. 5444.
[5] It appears to have been about this time that the King addressed a letter to the Sheriff of Oxford (dated Re[a]ding, 23rd Nov. 48°), warning him against certain persons, calling them "Harlotos," who in divers parts of

open hostility, when both parties were again prevailed upon, by the mediation of Louis IX. and the Pope, to consent to a reference or *mise* of the disputed authority of the Oxford Statutes to the decision of the French King. The latter, when urged by Pope Urban to reconcile the English factions, took no unneighbourly advantage of their discord for selfish purposes, as he might have done; and after two conferences had been held in vain at Boulogne[1] on the subject, the *mise* was at length agreed to in the middle of December.

By leaving the Tower early one morning before Christmas[2], the King was able to join his son, at Windsor, and from hence, surrounded by a foreign garrison, he addressed a proclamation to his subjects, dated December 20, 1263, not only protesting anew his "readiness to observe the Oxford Statutes and to defend the people in their liberties, but declaring also that as to aliens, he did not intend to introduce them, nay, that he had not done so, and in fact stood in no need of their aid[3]."

The Queen[4], with more honesty, had never concealed her dislike of the Statutes, and was notoriously averse to the pacification, if such it could be called, which had been agreed upon in the preceding June. To bring about a reaction—

---

the kingdom favoured (congregationes et conventicula) meetings and assemblies, and impudently made illicit contracts according to their method, contrary to the honesty of the church and against good manners, which we will not and ought not to endure (juxta ritum suum contra honestatem ecclesiæ et bonos mores faciunt impudenter quod sustinere nolumus nec debemus). The sheriff is ordered to forbid them.—Lansd. MS. 967.

[1] Hist. de Fr. Père G. Daniel.
[2] Fabyan.
[3] Rymer. "Alienigenas non vocavimus, non vocabimus, nec eorum auxilio indigemus." An order had, indeed, been issued (Westminster, July 20, 1263) for all foreigners who were in garrison at Windsor to leave it, and a safe conduct was granted them, July 26.—Rot. Pat. 47 H. III.

[4] The Queen Eleanor had been appointed Keeper of the Great Seal, Aug. 6, 1253, during the King's absence in Gascony, to act with the advice of Richard, Duke of Cornwall. While holding this office, she was delivered of a Princess, named Catherine, on St Catherine's day, Nov. 25, 1253. She met the Parliament in 1254, and in vain asked for a supply; on May 15, 1254, she resigned the Seal and sailed from Portsmouth to join the king at Bordeaux.—T. &c. Pat. 37° Hen. III. m. 8. She sat as judge in the Aula Regia on the Morrow of Nativity of the Virgin (Sept. 9).—Rot. Thes. Hen. III. Ld. Campbell's Chancellors, Vol. I. p. 140.

"Was evere the Quene thogt, so muche as heo mighte thenche,
  Mid couseil, other mid sonde, other mid wimman wrenche."—Robt. Glouc.[1]

An incident marking the coarse manners of the age, and her own unpopularity, had occurred to her in July.[2] Anxious to enjoy the greater security of Windsor under the protection of her son, she had embarked from the Tower to effect her passage by the Thames. The Londoners, however, assailed her when the barge approached the bridge with every mark of foul indignity and hatred, the rudest curses, the most opprobrious accusations[3] were shouted at her, while mud, broken eggs, and stones were thrown down with so much violence as to compel a retreat to the Tower. She succeeded in retiring, with her son Edmund[4], to the Continent soon after this outrage, and is said to have materially influenced the King of France in his arbitration, or, as an uncourteous chronicler[5] has it, "he was deceived and seduced by the serpent-like fraud and speech of a woman, and by her the King's heart was changed from good to bad, from bad to worse, from worse to worst," adducing as parallels the female influence exerted on Adam, David, and Solomon, to their ruin.

The personal affront thus put upon his mother by the citizens of London, implanted so intense a spirit of revenge in Prince Edward, that his resentment fatally influenced the battle of Lewes.

The Queen was an eager and imprudent politician, and had often, by her ill-bestowed patronage and her counsels of resistance, increased the King's embarrassments; but with

---

[1] "Was ever the Queen's thought, as much as she could think, with advice or messages, or with womanly plots." Even the royalist, T. Wyke, represents her as inclined "animo resilire."

[2] As John Mansel escaped by night from the Tower immediately after this outrage on the Queen, and was carried under Prince Edmund's escort to Dover, which that Prince surrendered to the barons, July 26, it must have happened previous to that date.—Lingard names July 14. Nichols's Leic. July 13.

[3] "Non erubescentes Dominam suam meretricem et adulteram multoties repetitis verbis nuncupare."—T. Wyke.

[4] Chr. Dover.

[5] Chr. Tewks., MS. Cotton, Cleop. 4, VII.

respect to the odious charge of conjugal infidelity rudely cast upon her during this gross unmanly insult, there is nothing known of her conduct as a wife to justify it; and, on the contrary, she ever fulfilled with zealous courage more than all the duties of her station towards her husband during his difficulties. She remained true to his memory, even after his death, retiring to the seclusion of a convent at Amesbury,[1] which had been founded by a previous Queen Dowager, and from hence she wrote to her son, trying to convince him that the sanctity of her late husband had effected a miraculous cure on blindness. Edward I., though with too much good sense to attend to this, always showed her a deference inconsistent with any suspicion of her misconduct, and he even permitted his daughter, Mary, to take the veil at her persuasion, contrary to his own wishes[2]. The Queen, keeping her dowry, took the veil herself, at Amesbury, in 1286,[3] and died there, when Edward, who, on a former occasion of sickness, had hastened to her, came expressly from Scotland to attend her funeral.

[1] It was a cell to Fontevraud, where so many royal Normans were buried.
[2] Princess Mary was born March 11, 1278, and took the veil in 1284. A letter from her, written probably between 1315 and 1317 to her brother Edward II. is in M. A. Wood's Letters, Vol. I. p. 61. She frequently visited court, attended confinements of royal ladies, and visited other nunneries; she died 1333, having survived by some years all her family.
[3] The Queen's profession took place July 1286, after a visit to her relations on the Continent. She afterwards styled herself "the humble nun of Fontevraud."

CHAPTER VI.

THE AWARD OF AMIENS.

"Most righteous judge! a sentence, come prepare."—M. OF VEN.

THE time now approached for the arbitration of the French King, a decision anxiously looked for by all parties, with the hope of putting an end to civil disturbance, and fixing the principles of government on a permanent basis.

The formal instrument, by which such unusual authority was vested in the hands of a foreign King, had been sealed in London, Dec. 13, 1263, by the chiefs of the baronial party, including the Bishops of London and Worcester, the Earl of Leicester, his son Henry, Peter de Montfort, Humphrey de Bohun, jun., Hugh le Despenser, and many others,[1] who took part in the subsequent battles. The deed contained their oath to abide by the award of King Louis concerning the validity of the Oxford Statutes, whether for or against them, and a similar pledge was given by the King in a letter dated

---

[1] "Ralph Bassct de Sapercote, Baldwin Wake, Robert le Ros, Henry de Hastings, Richard Gray, William Bardoulf, Robert Vipont, John Vescy, Nicholas Segrave, Geoffry Lucy."—Rymer, from Thes. Cur. Scacc.—*Geoffry de Lucy* held the Cap of State at the Coronation of Richard I. He married Juliana, widow of Peter de Stokes. During the civil wars he fought for King John, and at Lincoln for Henry III. He was Governor of Jersey, &c., of Porchester, 1238; went on the crusade 1236, and died 1252; his *son Geoffry* sided with the barons at Oxford, and now with Simon de Montfort. He escaped from the battle of Evesham to Gloucester, which however he surrendered to Pr. Edward, on promise of pardon. He died 1284, and was succeeded by his son Geoffry.

from Windsor about the same time, as well as by Prince Edward, Prince Henry, the Earl de Warenne, the Earl of Hereford, William de Valence, and many other distinguished[1] Royalists.

The King repaired to Amiens[2] with several of his adherents, and there met others, who had withdrawn from England in terror, such as the Archbishop Boniface, the Bishop of Hereford, so lately released by the barons, and John Mansel. The latter, indeed, never returned to England; and his fate is as remarkable an instance of fallen fortune as the Wolsey of later times. He, who had often refused bishoprics, both on account of the greater value of the benefices he held, and also because it would have interfered with his[3] free manner of living, now after all his splendour died abroad in poverty and the greatest wretchedness[4].

Simon de Montfort appears to have set out from Kenilworth with the intention of being present at Amiens, but his horse accidentally falling with him on the road near Catesby[5], he was disabled by the fracture of his thigh-bone, and obliged to return home[6]—a misfortune which led to

[1] "Hugh le Bigot, Roger le Bigot, Philip Basset, Robert Brus, Roger le Mortimer, Hugh de Percy, William de Breaus," and many others.—Rymer. The *mise* is frequently referred to in the original: "nos compromisimus in Dominum Ludovicum—super provisionibus Oxoniensibus—de alto et basso."

[2] The King was at Dover, January 1; at Amiens from January 12 to 25; at Boulogne, Feb. 7; at Whitsand, Feb. 14; at Dover, Feb 15.—Rymer. In the time of Richard II. the licensed packet-boats conveyed passengers from Dover to Whitsand at the price of 6d. in summer, and 1s. in winter for a single person; for a horse, 1s. 6d. in summer, and 2s. in winter. By an Act of Edward III. in 1336, nobody was allowed to go to the continent from any other port than Dover; this was repealed 4° Edward IV.

[3] "Quia lubricus erat."—Chr. Mailr.
[4] Chr. T. Wyke. As he had given back some portion of his wealth to the Church by founding a monastery, he is praised as a prudent, circumspect man. — M. Par. All his property, including his mansion of Sedgewick, co. of Sussex, which he had licence to embattle, 1259 (Rot. Pat.), was granted after his death to Simon de Montfort, junior. After the battle of Evesham, William de Braose claimed Sedgewick Castle, as escheated to him as lord; but after a lawsuit with him, it was restored in 1266 to John le Savage, in whose family it had long been; some fragments remain near Horsham.—See Sussex Arch. Coll. vIII. p. 35; Placit., p. 174; Rot. Pat. 47 H. III.

[5] Near Daventry, in Northamptonshire, about 20 miles from Kenilworth.
[6] Chr. Dunst.

unexpected results in the subsequent battle of Lewes. The barons thus temporarily deprived of their chief, wrote, Dec. 31, stating "that being occupied with other matters, they could not attend personally to carry on the *mise*, and therefore appointed Humphrey de Bohun, jun., Henry de Montfort, Peter de Montfort, and others[1], as their proxies for the purpose, inviting the King of France to explain his own ambiguous or obscure words." King Henry's oath to the *mise* was, in like manner, delivered by the proxy of John de la Lynde[2], Knight. The discordant parties thus assembled at Amiens, having pleaded their opposite opinions in presence of King Louis IX., during several days[3], that Sovereign at length delivered his important judgment, with great solemnity, on the 23rd January, 1264.

The deed[4], which is still extant in the archives of Paris, recites with becoming precision the mutual agreement of the contending parties to accept his arbitration, and after thus authenticating his judicial trust, King Louis pronounces that, "having summoned the King and certain barons, and having heard the arguments on both sides, considering the Oxford Statutes and the results that had flowed from them, that much had been done against the right and honour of the King, to the disturbance of the kingdom, the depression and plunder of churches, with grievous damage done to aliens and natives, both clerical and laymen, and that probably worse might happen hereafter, we, in the name of the Father, the Son, and the Holy Ghost, annul and make void the Oxford Statutes and all regulations depending on them, more especially inasmuch as the Pope has already annulled them." He then

---

[1] Adam de Neumarket, William le Mareschal, William le Blund, and Masters Thomas Cantilupe, Geoffry Cuberle, and Henry de Braunceston, clerks.—Rymer.

[2] John de la Lynde was Justice of the Common Pleas, June 1266, and in 1267 was appointed by the King to act as seneschal in command of the city of London, with John Waleran, then Constable of the Tower.—Fr. Chr. He was of Bolebrook, Sussex, which he died possessed of.—Inq. p. mort., 1273.

[3] Hist. de Fr. Père G. Daniel.

[4] The original is in Latin, dated Amiens, on the morrow of St Vincent, 1263.—Rymer. There is also a copy in Lib. de Antiq. Leg.

goes on to forbid all enmities on account of the non-observance of these Statutes, to order all castles to be given up to the King, who was to appoint his own ministers and household as freely as before, the statue of banishment against the aliens to be annulled, and the King to have full power and government in all and over all things as before. "We do not wish, however, or intend, by the present ordinance, to derogate in any thing from the royal privileges, charters liberties, statutes, and laudable customs of the kingdom, which existed before the Oxford Statutes;" desiring, in conclusion, that the King should be indulgent to the barons, and remit all rancour, as the barons, also, on their part should do, neither harassing the other.

Although the obvious meaning of this award seems plain and decisive, yet, as each party put their own construction upon it, and accepted that portion only favourable to their own views, without regard to the rest, it partook in some degree of the ambiguity of an ancient oracle in its effects. While one of the consulting parties could only recognize the total overthrow of the Oxford Statutes, the other noticed only the express reservation in full force of all the great charters of liberty, which those Statues had, in their opinion, only confirmed and enforced. The sanction given by the French decision to the employment of aliens in places of public trust seems the point most open to objection, as contrary to the laws and customs of England; but it seems strange that the high character for equity and chivalrous honour which the kingly arbitrator had established should have blinded the barons to the dangers necessarily attending an appeal to such a tribunal. Even without impugning his honesty, though contemporaries[1] spoke freely on that subject,

[1] "O rex Francorum, multorum causa dolorum,
Judex non rectus, ideo fis jure rejectus."
—Polit. S. from MS. Cott., Otho D. viii. "Rex Francie," " ut dicebatur ob favorem Dominæ Reginæ et Domini Edwardi dictas provisiones quassavit omnino." " Barones ipsius corruptionem intelligentes."—Chr. Wigorn.

they could not have reasonably expected King Louis to decide otherwise than in favour of his brother Sovereign, if they had vigilantly watched the whole tenor of his domestic government, and how successfully he had maintained and extended the prerogatives of royalty in France. It is still more surprising that, a few months later, the same arbitrator should be again appealed to, after the evident failure of the present expedient.

All now seemed satisfactory to King Henry; he had gained his cause, and expected to enjoy the fruits of the verdict.

"But when the Kyng of France had known certeynly
That the Purveiance disherite Kyng Henry,
He quassed it ilk dele thorgh jugement.
The Kyng was paied wele, and home to England went."—R. Brune[1].

Before his embarkation at Whitsand (Feb. 15), he evidenced his sense of all danger being over, by commissioning his Queen and Peter de Savoy to bring back his jewels, which had been deposited at Paris[2].

Vain and brief, however, was the hope of tranquillity, for in less than a month all England was again in confusion and strife. The barons, who, whether wisely or not, had sworn to obey the award of the arbitrator, were almost immediately in arms, alleging his partiality, and yet inconsistently adopting his clause, which exempted the old charters from annulment, as a pretext to justify their resistance. As the King could not well have given fresh occasion for distrust, we must consider that the aggressors on this occasion were the barons and their great chief Simon de Montfort. That which probably had the greatest influence upon them, and which, in fact, might form their readiest justification, was the strong persuasion that the King would not have submitted to an adverse decision more patiently than themselves, or more

---

[1] "But when the King of France had ascertained that the provision disinherited King Henry, he annulled every part of it by his decision. The King was well pleased, and went home to England."
[2] Rymer. Fabyan.

faithfully than he had to his previous engagements. So true is Clarendon's[1] remark, that "the strength of rebellion consists in the private gloss which every man makes to himself upon the declared argument of it, not upon the reasons published and avowed, how spacious and popular soever."

The King, nevertheless, derived some considerable advantages from so solemn a decision in his favour; the castle of Dover was surrendered to him during the short interval of peace, all the members of his own family became more active in his cause, and several of those who had hitherto opposed him, but who now may have fairly considered him as the injured party, also joined him. Prince Henry, the eldest son of the King of the Romans, whom the warlike talents of his uncle the Earl of Leicester, as well as strong ties[2] of affinity, had attached to his banner during the recent commotions, and who had been lately released from prison by his influence, now came forward with a chivalrous candour to announce his resolution no longer to fight against the King, and surrounded his arms with a promise never to bear them against his former leader. His conversion, indeed, has been attributed[3] to the gift of the lordship of Tickhill, by which Prince Edward had won him over; but however that may have been, de Montfort gave him a contemptuous licence to act as he pleased: "I care not for your weapons, my Lord Henry, but for your inconstancy; go your way then, return with your arms, for I am in no ways afraid of them."

Others, also, from interested motives, as is alleged, withdrew with him, and powerfully aided the King's party from this time[4]. Among these were John de Vaux, Hamo l'Estrange, Roger de Cliffort, and Roger de Leyburne. The defection of the two latter was the more noted as they had made themselves conspicuous as partisans of the barons the

[1] Essay xiv.
[2] The young Prince was nephew to the Countess of Leicester in two ways, his mother being sister to her first husband, and his father her own brother.
[3] W. de Rish.
[4] "Muneribus excæcati."—W. de Rish. Their desertion is dated earlier by some.

year before when they were thus praised by a contemporary[1] :—

" Et de Cliffort ly bon Roger	Roger de Cliffort the good,
Se contint cum noble Ber	Like a noble Baron stood,
Si fu de grant justice:	And to all dealt justice fit;
Ne suffri pas petit ne grant	Nor great, nor little, he swore,
Ne arère ne par devant	Behind his back or before,
Fere nul mesprise :	Should any misdeed commit.
Et sire Roger de Leyburne,	And Sir Roger de Leyburne,
Que sà et la sovent se torne,	Who here and there would turn
Mout ala conquerant ;	To conquer, kill, and burn :
Assez mist paine de gainer	Prince Edward had harassed him sore,
Pur ses pertes restorer,	So now he tried hard to restore
Que Sire Edward le fist avant."	His loss and win something more.

Cliffort[2] was the nephew of Walter, who is memorable for having made a King's messenger, when he brought him a disagreeable writ, eat up the document, parchment, wax, and all. His comrade, Leyburne[3], of a violent and unsteady disposition, had been in the service of Prince Edward when abroad, and was his companion at the tournaments there. He must, on his return, have separated himself from the Prince, and thus have given occasion to the hostile attacks which he sought to revenge by his ravages under the standard of the barons.

---

[1] Polit. Songs from MS. of 13th century.

[2] His arms were "chequy or and azure, a fess gules." He became a crusader 1272, and died 1286.

[3] Arms of Leyburne, "azure six lioncels argent."—Rolls of Arms. In Rot. Pat. 36 H. III. m. 1, he is stated to have killed Arnulph de Mountney, "ad rotundam tabulam." "Fuerat cum Domino Edwardo contra voluntatem Baronum, ipsiusque Edwardi denarios ubique tanquam seneschallus expederat, et ipsum in Franciâ ad torneamenta adduxerat." —Chr. Dover. Also Add. MS. 5444. [An interesting account of Sir Roger de Leyburne will be found in an article on the Heart Shrine in Leyburne Church, by the late Mr Larkin, in the Archæologia Cantiana, Vol. II. pp. 133–192. Sir Roger had been steward to Prince Edward, and enjoyed his full confidence till it was estranged by the Queen, who instigated her son to demand a rendering of accounts, which shewed a deficit of £1000. This was probably soon after November, 1260. During the next three years Sir Roger was an ardent partisan of the barons. In 1263 he joined de Montfort in a general raid upon foreigners throughout England, and is accused of meditating an attack upon Dover castle. Mr Larkin, however, believes that Rishanger's insinuation of interested motives is unwarranted, and that Sir Roger considered his work done when aliens were expelled the country, and was anxious to accept an honourable compromise. P.]

He now once more changed sides, and rejoined the royalists, his character thus curiously contrasting with that of his eldest son, so pithily sketched in the poem of Carlaverock:—

"Guillemes de Leybourne ausi Vaillans homs sans mes et sans si[1]."	William de Leybourne valorous wight, With no ifs or buts, but plain downright.

Immediate war being thus the result of the King of France's attempt to produce peace, a French historian[2] remarks that "so celebrated and authentic a judgment had no other effect than to make the least passionate of the rebels return to their duty, those who were dissatisfied with their party being glad of the opportunity to desert it."

In the midst of this abandonment, the courage and determination of Simon de Montfort never faltered. "Though all should leave me," he observed, "yet, with my four sons, I will stand true to the just cause, which I have sworn to uphold for the honour of the Church, and the benefit of the kingdom: in many lands and provinces of divers nations, both Pagan and Christian, have I been, but in none have I found such faithlessness and deception as in England[3]." If the national character for good faith, so opposite to this stern rebuke, has since become proverbial over the world, the happy change may, perhaps, be partly due to the ennobling effects of the principles and forms of liberty, which de Montfort was at this moment struggling to establish.

No breathing time was given, as events hurried on; the barons seem at once[4] to have resolved upon resuming their arms, rather than abandon the restrictions upon the former abuses in the state, and they soon threatened the King with their gathered forces. Henry, after a hasty preparation for

---

[1] In the same spirit Colada, the sword of the great Cid, still preserved in Spain, was inscribed with "yes, yes," on one side, and "no, no," on the other, as if its sharp edge would cut its way through all doubts.

[2] Père G. Daniel.—Hist. de Fr.
[3] W. de Rish. de bello Lew.
[4] "Barones vero non contenti de arbitrio prædicti Regis statim militaverunt."—Lib. de Ant. Leg.

war at Windsor, summoned a council of his adherents, to meet him at Oxford, having repaired to his palace at Woodstock[1]. He betrayed no very high opinion of the good manners of his followers, when, on March 12, 1264, he published an order to clear Oxford of all the students, "in order that they might be out of the great danger of meeting the chieftains, whom, on account of the sudden disturbances, he had summoned, and many of whom were fierce and untamed[2]." This may have been said in especial reference to his new friends, the Scotch, who joined him here in great numbers; but the true motive, probably, was a suspicion of treachery, had he left in the town so many devoted partisans of the barons[3]. It is said that there were 15,000 matriculated on the books of the University at this time, and among the number thus removed, the great Roger Bacon may have been included—for neither learning nor science suffice to exempt men from the miseries of civil war. Should any doubt be suggested, whether it was the ill behaviour of the soldiers or of the students, which occasioned this dispersal of the latter, the honour of Oxford may be gratified by the testimony of Archbishop Boniface, who, at his visitation in 1252, had declared, after his heart had been warmed by abundance of good eating and drinking, that "the University rivalled Paris in its wit, dignity of demeanour, gravity of dress, and severity of manners[4]."

Of the quality of learning at Oxford at this period, we cannot, indeed, have a very high opinion. Two of the most accomplished men of the age, Robert Grethead and Adam de Marisco, had given lectures there, and had urged the study of the Bible, but Roger Bacon ridicules the sermons preached there, as full of "much childish trifling and folly, unsuitable to the dignity of the pulpit," and tells us that Greek was almost unknown. Of the Latin we may judge

[1] Fabyan.
[2] "Magnates multi indomiti, quorum sævitiam de facili reprimere non possemus."—Rymer.
[3] W. de Rish. de bello Lew.
[4] M..Par.

by the formal condemnation, by successive archbishops at their visitations, of the same gross grammatical errors[1].

King Henry had not always been unpopular at Oxford. He had many years previously founded a noble hospital, and had been welcomed there soon after his marriage with festivals and illuminations[2]. His present visit was marked by an incident characteristic of him as "a most devout worshipper of rusty nails and rotten bones[3]." His zealous devotion to the relics of saints, emboldened him, with more strength of mind than usual, to break through the trammels of an ancient[4] superstition, which had for five centuries forbidden the approach of a King to the shrine of Saint Frideswide. That noble lady had, in the eighth century, seen the insults of a Mercian prince, Algar, punished by a sudden blindness, as he was entering Oxford in close pursuit of her,— an affliction as suddenly removed afterwards by her prayers[5]. Universal opinion expected the coy virgin to resent the intrusion of royalty even to her tomb, and Henry accordingly made all befitting preparations for such an arduous enterprise. After a liberal distribution of alms, high mass, and a day's fast, he ventured on foot into the forbidden sanctuary, and there paid his devotions :—

"The King hadde then to gode wille, thoru freren rede,
And hii masson at orisons vast vor him bede,
So that vastinde a day a vote he dude this dede."—Rob. Brune.[6]

Though he was not stricken by blindness on the spot, yet those who clung to the pious prejudice of ages probably looked upon his early defeat at Lewes as a sufficient fulfilment of the omen.

Both parties were now prepared for the struggle, and

---

[1] Archbishops Kilwarby, in 1276, and Peckham, in 1284, each had to argue against the Latinity of " ego currit, currens est ego," &c.—V. Wood's Antiq. Oxon. 59-125.
[2] T. Wyke.
[3] Henry's Hist. v. 7.
[4] " Spretâ illâ veteri supersti-
tione."—T. Wyke.
[5] Leland's Collec.
[6] The King then had a desire towards God by advice of the monks, and ordered high mass quickly before him at orisons, so that fasting a day on foot he did this deed.

each had so much to dread and so much to hope, holding principles long discordant, and so recently proved to be irreconcileable, that the chances of an amicable treaty were indeed slender. It was however attempted, and very nearly succeeded.

The King appointed (March 13[1]) the Bishop of Lichfield[2], and Nicholas de Plumpton, Archdeacon of Norwich, to meet the agents of the barons at Brackley (a few miles from Oxford), under the mediation of the French ambassador, John de Valentia. Their credentials[3] commissioned them to treat concerning the security and tranquillity of the kingdom, so as to strengthen the general peace, promising[4] to assent to what they should arrange.

An earnest summons was, however, issued on the same day by the King, now fully conscious of the extreme peril of circumstances, calling on all his lieges to hasten, by Mid-Lent at latest (March 30), "with their horses and arms to his help, as being necessary to keep his state undamaged by the very serious commotion, which might easily put in imminent danger (though God forbid) both the kingdom and crown of England[5]." The Earl de Warenne, too, at this juncture, repaired, by the King's permission, to Ryegate and Rochester, in order the better to defend his estates there[6].

It is difficult to suppose that either party could sincerely expect a peaceful solution of their dispute at this crisis, but it would seem that the Bishops of London, Winchester, Worcester, and Chichester, were sent by the barons with the offer of submitting to all the other articles of the French award, provided the King would remit the one single article as to the employment of aliens[7]. This exclusion of alien influence

---

[1] Rymer, in Latin. The safe conduct of the barons appointed to treat was to be in force till Saturday before Mid-Lent, March 29, and was dated Oxford, March 17.—Rymer.

[2] Roger de Meyland, bishop from 1258 to 1295.

[3] Dated March 20.—Rymer.

[4] "Ratum habituri et gratum."

[5] Rymer.

[6] W. de Rish. de bello Lew.

[7] MSS. Add. 5444. They humbly prayed "quod saltem unicum et solum remittat articulum, videlicet quod alienigenis ab Anglia remotis, per indigenas gubernetur, et omnibus

seems to have been indeed, throughout these troubles, the vital point of the baronial policy. An agreement[1] was even drawn up in presence of the King to regulate the return of Archbishop Boniface, on five conditions :—1. That he should recall the excommunications which he had fulminated from Boulogne[2], in 1263, against several barons, and two of the younger de Montforts, for their plunder of church property. 2. That the damages done to churches or clergy should be assessed by a council of his suffragans. 3. That no other aliens than his own immediate household should accompany him. 4. That other aliens might return to their benefices on condition of spending all their income at home. And, 5. That the prelate should neither bring with him, nor procure by others, any writings in damage of the King, or any person in the kingdom. This latter clause must have had reference to the many briefs of the Pope, who had proportioned the activity of his spiritual arms to the increasing peril of the King, his client. By the quick succession[3] of his threats, indeed, we learn the zeal of the pontiff, on the receipt of each additional alarm from England; and he soon afterwards sent a legate with fresh excommunications; but it would be idle to blame this busy meddling as unauthorized, for it was, most probably, invited by the royal emissaries.

The tide of war was, however, now setting in too strongly to heed such obstacles. The city of London seems never to have assented to the *mise* of Amiens, and, like the barons of the Cinque Ports and nearly all the middle classes[4], refused to obey the award. On the first Monday after Mid-Lent

---

statutis, provisionibus et ordinationibus regis Franciæ adquiescant."
[1] Dated March, 1264.—Rymer.
[2] MS. Bodl., in notes to Chr. W. de Rish. de bello Lew.
[3] By a Brief from Viterbo, 17 Kal. Apr. (March 16), 1264, the award was confirmed; by another, 12 Kal. Apr. (March 21), the Pope forbad the barons and clergy to conspire. By a third, 10 Kal. Apr. (March 23), he

again cancelled the Oxford Statutes, and absolved all from their oaths.—Rymer.
[4] "Et fere omnis communitas mediocris populi regni Angliæ, qui vero non posuerunt se super Regem Franciæ, prædictum arbitrium suum contradixerunt."—Lib. de Ant. Leg. [Mr Stapleton reads "penitus" instead of prædictum.]

(March 31), the citizens rose in tumultuous violence against the royal cause, and the anger caused by the tidings of this outbreak put an abrupt end to all negotiation. The King dismissed the bishops with a caution to depart quickly and never return to talk of peace unless they were sent for[1], announcing at once his resolve to maintain the award in all particulars to the best of his power.

There was indeed much to irritate the King and his party in the riots and ravages of the Londoners. The bell of St Paul's was rung as the concerted signal for their assembling in arms, and they were directed by two eminent citizens, Thomas de Puvelesdon[2] and Stephen Buckerell[3], under whom they proceeded to destroy the property of all opposed to them, not exempting even the private dwellings of the King and his brother. All was wantonly laid waste at the country-house of the latter in Isleworth, near the Thames, his fences levelled, his orchards uprooted, and the head of a large fishpond, lately made at a vast expense, cut through[4]. These private injuries naturally embittered the hostility of the parties, but the King had himself unhappily set the example of them long ago, having in 1233 caused the property of Gilbert Basset and Richard Siward, followers of Richard, the Earl Marshal, in his rebellion, to be so treated, ordering their houses to be pulled down, their parks, gardens, and woods to be destroyed, their fish-ponds to be filled, and their meadows ploughed up[5].

---

[1] Add. MSS. 5444.
[2] The name is Puvelesdon as witness to a grant.—Rot. Pat. 1265. It is Pilvesdon in W. Hem., Piluesdon in H. Knight, Pyweldon in Fabyan, Piulesdona in Househ. Exp. He will be mentioned again.
[3] The body of a person of the same name, of South Streatham, perhaps his father, was found by the King in his way to London, at Merton, Jan. 10, 1258, drowned in a ditch, owing to drunkenness.—Cal. Rot. Pat. 48 Hen. III.
[4] On this land, afterwards in possession of the Crown, Henry V. founded the monastery of S. Bridget, a community of English nuns, which is said to have survived to the present times, though often driven to residence in foreign countries.
[5] T. Wyke.

CHAPTER VII.

WAR RENEWED.

"Fright our native peace with self-born arms."—RICH. II.

BOTH armies appear from this time[1] to have been put into immediate action without further parley. While the royalists in one quarter were harassed, so that not even their wives[2] escaped captivity, de Montfort appointed a general meeting of the barons at Northampton, on the walls of which town, in order to display his alliance with the clergy[3], the banner of St Peter's keys[4] was displayed in conjunction with those of the barons. Before the assembly of the chiefs could be accomplished, the military spirit of Prince Edward led the

---

[1] Plac. de Quo Warr. fo. 766. In 8° Edw. I. an action was brought at the suit of the Crown against Reginald FitzPeter to recover some lands "extra civitatem Wintoniæ"—the defendant pleaded a grant from Henry III. in 48°—to this the King's attorney replied that the King was then under durance, and the grant therefore void. Proof however was given of the date being previous to April 4, 1264, when the war began, and it was therefore adjudged to be good.

[2] Those of R. de Leyburne, R. de Cliffort, and others, were thus seized at Gloucester.

[3] 1263, major pars cleri fuit cum Baronibus.—Contin. of Chr. Guil. Neubr. 1199 to 1299, by a monk of Furneux Abbey.—Hearne, III. p. 814.

[4] The arms of the Abbey of Peter-borough (gules, 2 keys saltireways between 4 crosses patée potencée) were displayed on the walls (*vexillum cum clavibus Santi Petri* cum vexillis Baronum) by the tenants and monks of the abbey, "licet quibusdam invitis," which made the King swear to destroy the abbot and monastery.—On the capture of the town, "mediante pecuniâ cum donis et amicis in curia regis procurantibus idem Abbas (Robertus de Sutton) fecit plures fines," paying 300 marcs for contempt of the King's summons. In return a letter of protection was given by the King, which seems to have been of no use, "nullus enim de parte regis deferre voluit literis suis, cum sibi fuissent porrectæ, sed unusquisque pro se deprædebatur et cepit redemptionem."—Chr. Walt. de Whittlesey.

King's army into the field, and such was the energy of his movements that on April 5, only a few days after that appointed for the muster of the royal lieges, he made a vigorous assault on Northampton, accompanied by Prince Richard, William de Valence, de Cliffort, de Mortimer, and the great Scotch chieftains. Young Simon de Montfort, no lukewarm descendant of his family, with the fresh honours of knighthood[1], was among the most eager defenders of the town. The careful training of such a father could scarcely fail to make good soldiers, and such accordingly we find all the sons of the Earl of Leicester, even the one who began as priest, turning to arms in his later life: "Quar jamès son travayl perdra, que pur prudhome[2] fra." Young de Montfort on this occasion advanced with such reckless impetuosity to repel the attack, that his horse becoming unruly under the excitement of his spurs, carried him into the outer ditch of the town, where the enemy took him prisoner without difficulty, and it required the interference of Prince Edward to prevent his being put to death.

Near the north gate, within the inclosure of the walls, bordering on a stream leading to the river, stood the Cluniac Priory of St Andrew, a cell to S. Marie de la Charité, on the Loire. Guy[3], the royalist prior, had, in 1258, succeeded one who had been promoted to the same office in the kindred priory of Lewes, where King Henry afterwards lodged at the time of the battle. Many of the monks, as well as the prior, were Frenchmen, and had sent information to the King while at Oxford that they had treacherously undermined the wall, and concealed by timber the outward opening of the passage they had prepared. While the attention of the garrison was called off by a deceitful parley, they now found

---

[1] "Recenter novo militiæ cingulo decoratus." "Non tepidus æmulator."—T. Wyke.
[2] Hist. de Fitzw., p. 17.
[3] Guy, prior from 1258 to 1270, was imprisoned by the barons after their success at Lewes.—Dugd. Monast. A convent of Carmelites is said by Dugdale to have been founded at Northampton in 1271, by Simon de Montfort, but it is not probable that the earl's son, then in exile in Italy, should have been the founder.

an opportunity of thus admitting Philip Basset[1] and forty knights, by whom the town was unexpectedly overpowered. The surrender of the castle two days afterwards added a great many important prisoners to the royal triumph, including fifteen bannerets and many other knights of less rank. Among the most distinguished was the veteran Peter de Montfort, the earl's kinsman, with his two sons, Peter and William. Peter was the head of a powerful branch of the family with large possessions, which had descended to him from an ancestor[2], who had earned them by his services at the Conquest; he had always sided with the barons.

"Et Sire Pere de Montfort
Si tint bien a leur acord
Si out grant seignurie."—Pol. Song from Roll 13th c.

He had served the state in embassies and war, having had the guard of the Welsh frontier in 1258 committed to him, and had been selected as one of the twenty-four councillors of the Oxford Statutes. His subsequent fate will hereafter come under our notice.

Another of the prisoners was Adam de Neumarket, whose ancestor had used a soldier's licence under the Conqueror to appropriate the territory of Brecknock. Adam was summoned to Parliament after the battle of Lewes, and fell a prisoner to Prince Edward in 1265, but was permitted ultimately to compound for his confiscated lands. Baldwin Wake, who, with his brother Nicholas, was included among

---

[1] H. Knight.
[2] Hugh de Bastenburgh, a Norman, had grants of 28 lordships in Kent, 10 in Essex (for which he refused to account, according to Domesday), 51 in Suffolk, and 19 in Norfolk. His grandson took the name of de Montfort.
Peter's father, Thurstan, held 12½ knights' fees (including Whitchurch, Wellesborne, Beldesert), and built the castle of Henly in Arden, d. 1216.
Peter had been ward to Peter de Cantilupe, and married, in 1229, Alice, daughter of Henry de Aldithely, by whom he had—
1. Peter, who recovered the estates by the Dict. Kenilworth from forfeiture, d. 1287. His son John was with Edward I. in his wars, but this branch was extinct in the next generation.
2. William, married Agnes Bertram de Mitfort, killed 1265.
3. Robert, married a daughter of the Earl of Warwick.—Dugd. Bar.

the most distinguished prisoners, was an active knight, twenty-six years of age, whose name occurs in all the great transactions of the war and treaties. His mother Joan de Stuteville[1], now married to Hugh le Bigot, had purchased of the King the wardship of her own son for 9000 marcs (£6000); indicating both the domestic miseries of feudalism and the honourable efforts of an anxious mother to avert them. Baldwin Wake is represented by some to have been at the battle of Lewes, but it may be doubted whether he had this additional opportunity of proving the readiness of his sword in the cause. He was again taken prisoner in 1265, but escaped to join in the last struggles of young Simon de Montfort at the close of the war: he was, however, pardoned for a fine of two years' value on his estate, and died 1282[2].

Others of the fifteen bannerets, William de Ferrers, Roger Bertram de Mitford[3], Simon FitzSimon, Reginald de Waterville, Hugh Gebyon, Philip de Drieby, Thomas Maunsel[4], Roger Boteville, Robert de Newington, and Grimbald Pauncefot[5], took part in the subsequent events of the civil war, the latter alone being distinguished by a treacherous surrender to the royalists of his trust, as will be seen hereafter.

All the chiefains[6] who had gathered together for the

[1] She died in 1276.
[2] "Wake, or two bars gules, in chief three roundles gules."—Rolls of Arms. His wife, Hawyse, was daughter of Robert de Quinci.—Dugd. Bar.
[3] His father had sided with the barons against King John, and died 1242. Roger had been employed in 1258 to rescue the King of Scotland from the thraldrom of his guardians. On his being now taken prisoner, Mitford Castle, Northumberland, was taken possession of on behalf of William de Valence. His son Roger died 1312, and as his only child Agnes died without issue, his four sisters became his heirs.

[4] Descended from Philip Mansel, a Norman, who accompanied William the Conqueror. He held lands in Glamorganshire; arms, argent, a chevron between three maunches sable. His descendant Thomas was in 1711 created Baron Mansel of Margam.
[5] W. Rish. Pauncefot has the addition of "serviens" to his name in MS. Bodl. 91 Bern.
[6] Among the names of inferior rank many are again met with in the course of the war. T. Wyke adds William de Furnival. The Bodl. MS., Bern. 91, names William de Warre, G. de Lewknor (" azure, three chevrons argent."—Rolls of Arms), John de Dykelynge, H. de

intended conference of the barons at Northampton, were thus seized at once, and strictly imprisoned[1]. Among those who shared the same misfortune were the scholars who had been driven from Oxford, and were here found fighting against the King with the utmost zeal. They are said to have had their own banner on this occasion, and to have done more damage with their bows, slings, and crossbows, than all the rest.

The appearance in arms of a class of such natural loyalty marks strongly the wide diffusion of discontent, and their conduct incensed Henry to such a degree, that he was at first bent upon putting them all to death, and was only restrained by the risk of offending irreparably the many powerful families to which these youths belonged; many of them in their alarm adopted a hasty tonsure to escape under privilege of clergy[2]. One of the earliest acts of the barons, after their success at Lewes, was to order the return of these scholars to Oxford[3].

Though there had been much animosity, and many acts of plunder and ravage before, yet this may be considered as the first great conflict of the civil war, and a fearful example of the barbarities of such a strife was exhibited. Northampton was sacked by the royal army with every circumstance of rapine and sacrilege, as if it had been in an enemy's country, and even a royalist chronicler looks upon the calamities, which soon fell upon those guilty of such

Pembrigge, W. Marshal, W. de Harecurte, W. de Gyleford, John Esturney, Rich. de Caleworth, Ralph Peroth, Ingram de Baillol, G. Russell, steward of the Bishop of Lincoln, Rich. de Hemyngton, Simon de Pateshyll, W. de Wheltoun, Eustace de Watford, Edm. de Arderne, Phil. Fitzrobert, Robert Maloree, Roger de Hyde, Andrew de. Jarpenville, Roger de Hakelington, W. de Preston, Simon, brother of Reginald Waterville, Hamo de Wycleston, Roger de Monteney, W. Awngcvin, Ralph de Diva, Philip de Daventre, Richard Everard, Ralph de Wodekyme, Roger de S. Philibert, I. de Rye, W. de Lymare, Hugh de Tywe, John de Boseville, Ralph de Brotton, John de Bracebridge.

[1] Those detained at Northampton were put under the custody of "Nicholas Hawresham."—Walt.Hemingford.

[2] Walt. Hemingford.

[3] St Paul's, May 30, 1264.—Rot. Pat.

K

excesses, as a just[1] retribution. On first hearing of the attack on Northampton, Simon de Montfort had advanced with his troops as far as St Alban's, intending to relieve those besieged in the castle, and when the news of their surrender met[2] him there, his comrades were loud in their desponding lamentations; firm, however, in his purpose, he calmly attributed the reverse to the usual fortune of war, and encouraged them by declaring that "the month of May should not pass over without all the joy of their enemies being turned to fear and confusion." The blow was felt indeed to be severe, and the earl, "raging like a lion deprived of his whelps[3]," resolved to countervail the disaster by striking in another quarter.

The unhappy example of outrage at Northampton was disgracefully followed at London under his influence. Besides a general plunder of the property of William de Valence and other aliens, the excited citizens did not even spare the deposits of money at the Temple, which then served as a substitute for a bank[4]; "in this," as a chronicler observes, "resembling fish, who snatch at all they can[5]." John FitzJohn is said to have been the leader of this rapine, and to have shared[6] its fruits with Simon de Montfort, though the latter would appear, as we shall see, to have been in Kent at the time. A suspicion of intended treachery fell upon the Jews, who being the principal makers of Greek fire, were accused of intending to set fire to the city, and of preparing false keys[7], in order to betray the city-gates. The first provocation may have been given by a Jew having wounded a citizen[8], but a fearful massacre was the result.

---

[1] "Justo Dei judicio sunt consecuti, non habentes jus querelæ."—T. Wyke.
[2] W. de Rish.
[3] "Ipse quasi leo in saltu raptis catulis sæviens."—Mat. Westm. W. Rish. de Bello Lew.
[4] In Madox's Exchequer is an order from the King from Portsmouth, July 6, 1253, to remove his money and jewels from the Temple to the Tower; in 1268 and 1271 fines, &c., were ordered to be paid into the Temple for safe custody.
[5] Chr. Mailros.   [6] T. Wyke.
[7] W. Rish. Chr. Cott. Vesp. B. xii. MS. Hosp. Linc.
[8] Lib. de Ant. Leg.

At Easter, a Christian festival too often disgraced by similar calumnies and persecutions, a number of Jews, variously stated at from forty-seven to two hundred[1], were barbarously murdered. Among these is particularly noticed Koe, the son of Abraham, one of the richest in the kingdom, who had, in 1256, paid the King 2000 marcs (£1333. 6s. 8d.) for the privilege of inheriting the chattels of his own father[2]. In Canterbury a similar massacre occurred by the orders of de Clare[3].

The Earl of Leicester in the meanwhile had undertaken the siege of Rochester, and for this purpose had carried with him all manner of military engines, of which the English were then wholly ignorant. The defence was gallantly conducted by the Earl de Warenne, assisted by Hugh de Percy, Roger de Leyburne, and John Fitzalan; but de Montfort forced his way across the river, by drifting against the bridge a vessel laden with combustibles[4], and, securing the gate of the city during the alarm, succeeded in confining the garrison within the walls of the castle adjoining. Much violence and licence ensued in additional retaliation on this seizure of Rochester. Churches were plundered, and fugitives pursued by horsemen even to the very altars; many parts of the cathedral buildings were occupied as stables[5]; and though soldiers are not apt to be rigid observers of church ceremonies, yet in an age of such outward reverence for religious forms, it startles us to find all these outrages

---

[1] MS. Cott. Vesp. A. II. In 7° Edw. I: "Furent touz les Jues d'Engeltere pris pur la monoye qe fut vilement rotondu et fause."— "Sistrent Justic. à le Gildhall pur faire la deliveraunce, c'est a savoir, Sire Estevene de Pevencestre, Sire Wauter de Helyon, et Johan de Cobham et ceux q'il voleient à eux assocyer, pur le quele fet *furent* 3 *Chrestiens et* 293 *Jues treinez et penduz pur retundre* del moneye."—Fr. Chr. London.

[2] Cal. Rot. Pat. 40° Hen. III.

[3] Chr. Dover.

[4] W. Rish de bello Lew. William de Brows (Braose) was also one of the defenders of Rochester Castle. Simon de Montfort made his third successful assault by loading a boat "cum pice, carbone, sulphure et adipe porcina. 12 Cal. Maii (April 21) die Parascewe."—Chr. Gervas. Lel. Coll. Vol. I. 256.

[5] The oratory, cloisters, chapter-house and hospital were thus treated.
—MS. Cott. Nero D. II. by a Rochester monk.

committed on the solemn fast of Good Friday (April 18), forming an unexpected precedent for those of Cromwell's time. De Clare had attacked Rochester from another quarter at the same time, and the siege of the castle[1] was now pressed forward during several days by the barons with so much vigour, that it was on the point of success, when the news of the rapid march of the King's army compelled its abrupt abandonment[2].

The Mayor of London became alarmed at the approach of the enemy and the treachery of some citizens; at his urgent request, accordingly, Simon de Montfort withdrew from the siege, and returned to London on the morrow of St Mark, April 23[3].

Prince Edward had been continuing his successes; the town of Leicester, undefended by its earl, had endured the horrors of war; and Nottingham was betrayed to him. Wherever the royal army advanced, "its three associates—plunder, fire, and slaughter—followed; there was no peace in the kingdom; all was destroyed; clamour, and woe, and horror arose on all sides[4]." Thinking to find London an easy prey, the Prince directed his forces there, and when baffled by the hasty return of de Montfort to its protection, he crossed the Thames unexpectedly at Kingston, and made so rapid a progress towards Rochester as to appear there for the relief of the garrison in five days after leaving Notting-

---

[1] The curious contrivance by which water could be supplied to each floor of the keep from a well below, is still visible in the ruins of this castle. "The well is commonly in the substance of the wall, through which its pipe, of from 2ft. to 2ft. 9in. diameter, ascends to the first and second stories, opening into each (as at Canterbury, Dover, Rochester, Kenilworth, Portchester, Carlisle). At Newcastle and Dover the pipe terminates in a small chamber and has no other aperture. In some castles a similar pipe seems to have been used for the passage of stores and ammunition to the battlements."—G. T. Clarke in Arch. Journ. I. 97.

[2] Earl Warenne and William de Braose came to Rochester on Wednesday after Palm Sunday, and were attacked in the castle the next day. The siege was raised on the Saturday after Easter, and Warenne left Tuesday following.

[3] Add. MSS. 5444.

[4] "Comitaverunt ei tres sociæ, prædatio combustio et occisio; pax in regno nulla: cædibus incendiis rapinis et deprædationibus omnia exterminantur, clamor et luctus et horror ubique."—Chr. Roff. MSS. Ad. 5444.

ham. The fatigue of this march indeed caused the death of many choice horses on the road. This triumph was unfortunately sullied by unnecessary cruelty, for the few baronial soldiers, left by de Montfort to carry on the blockade, were seized and barbarously maimed of their hands and feet[1].

The castle of Tunbridge, belonging to the Earl of Gloucester, next [May 1] fell[2] into the hands of the royalists, thus inflicting a double mortification on that great chief, by the loss of his castle and of his Countess Alicia. The King, however, who had accompanied the royal army, allowed the lady, who was his niece, to endure but a brief detention, and then freely released her.

A strong guard, under twenty knights banneret, was left here under the expectation of an early attack from de Clare[3], while the King repaired to the coast, "towards the havenes with gret poer enou[4]," marking his course, as before, by rapine at Battel and elsewhere. During a halt of three days at Winchelsea[5], he applied in vain to the Cinque Ports for assistance, wishing them to send a naval force up the Thames to attack London. The wardens, however, who had throughout acted in the interest of the barons, sternly forbade the use of their ships; and the King, after exacting hostages for the fidelity of the Cinque Ports, quitted them[6], in order to collect all his forces at Lewes[7], the stronghold of his de-

[1] "Manibus et pedibus mutilatos."—T. Wyke.
[2] Tunbridge was taken by the King "in die Philippi et Jacobi villâ prius combustâ per castellum."—Chr. Gervas. in Lel. Coll. Vol. I.
[3] W. Hemingf.
[4] Rob. Glouc.
[5] H. Knighton. W. Heming.
[6] Bodleian Lib. (Rawlinson MS. B. 150.) This account, apparently by a monk of Battel, reports details of the King's journey not elsewhere noticed. At Combwell his cook, Master Thomas, going incautiously in advance of the army, was slain by a countryman, which the King revenged by killing many of the country people assembled under John de la Hay at Flimwell. At Battel the monks met him in procession, but were nevertheless plundered. The King went to Winchelsea, "revelling in the abundance of wine there," then to Battel, and on hearing of the advance of the barons to Hurst, where a nobleman, Roger de Tourney, was killed in the park by a chance blow of an arrow, then to Lewes. — See Lower's Battel Chron. p. 200.
[7] The unsettled state of orthography may be amply illustrated by the name of this town, as it appears in various authors: Leus in the King's summons of the prior to Parliament, 1265, and in Chr. Lanerc.

voted brother-in-law, the Earl de Warenne. He arrived at Lewes on Sunday, May 11[1]; but it was no easy matter in those times to feed a large army, and great dearth was experienced on this occasion. A contemporary account observes of this march through Surrey, Kent, and Sussex, that, "from the deficiency of victuals in that barren province many persons wasted away from want of food, and the cattle were lowing and failing all around from scarcity of pasture[2]." The small quantity of productive land in these counties, since become so flourishing, may be estimated by the thinness of the population at that time. A few years later, in 1278, a poll-tax[3] of 4*d.* was levied on all persons, male and female, of fourteen years of age. The sum of £588. 15*s.* 4*d.* was thus collected from 35,326 lay persons in Sussex[4] and Surrey, then united in one county. In Chichester, at that time probably the largest in population, £14. 9*s.* 8*d.* was raised from 869 persons. Priests paid separately 12*d.* each, and mendicants and children were exempted. Doubling the above numbers[5] in order to include these classes omitted,

it is called Liewes, Liawes, and Linwes, almost in the same page of MS. Lib. de Ant. Leg.;. Lyans in Nangis ; Linus, and Leaus in Rob. Brune, and MS. Cott. Nero. A. IV.
[1] On the summons of the King, the barons of the Cinque Ports "venerunt apud Lewes VI. Idus Maii" (May 10).—Chr. Wigorn. MS. "Venit in sequenti Sabbato ad villam de Lewes."—W. Heming. "In crastino SS. Gordiani et Epimathii inventus est rex apud Lewes."—Add. MSS. 5444. The feast of these saints was May 10. The Oxenede Chr. however dates his arrival on May 6, "on the Tuesday before the Feast of SS. Nereus and Achilleus," which was on May 12.
[2] "Dum rex fuit in provinciâ illâ sterili, deficientibus victualibus multitudo non modica famis inediâ tabescebant, rugiebant jumenta, et passim per defectum pabuli defecerunt."
—T. Wyke.

[3] Subsidy Roll of 18° Edw. I. in Archæologia, Vol. VII. pp. 337-347.
[4] Sussex was required to supply brawn and other provisions for the King's household; and in 1253 a demand was made on the county for 1000 ells of linen, very fine and delicate in quality.—V. Madox Exch. It is not known where this manufacture existed.
[5] By the census of 1861 the number of persons under fifteen years of age is roughly as 19 in 52, or rather more than a third. The clergy in 1278 were about 1·5 per cent. of the population. The mendicants cannot have been much more numerous. Consequently, though the numbers of persons in mature life are, no doubt, swelled at present by the increased average of life, I cannot but think Mr Blaauw's estimate excessive, unless he has allowed largely for probable omissions. P.

would give 70,652 for the united county, and 1738 for the cathedral city. Contrasting these numbers with those of the census in 1841, we may observe that the population had increased 12½ fold, Sussex being then 299,770, and Surrey 582,613, making a total of 882,383 persons.

On the retreat of the barons from Rochester, Simon de Montfort had been met by the Londoners with an unanimous support, which greatly increased his power and the numbers of his army. The hostility to the royal cause throughout these transactions of the citizens of London, already rich and important, whose habits and permanent interests would have led them naturally to cherish peace, is very significant, and must be accounted for, not only by their common share of dislike to an unnational King, but also by a keen sense of their own peculiar wrongs. It has been stated by an historian[1] that the barons became unpopular after exercising power for three years, but there is abundant evidence of the reverse being the truth: their actual sway indeed continued with little interruption nearly seven years (1258 to 1265), and their popularity much longer. The Mayor of London was a principal among the twenty-five barons who received Magna Charta from King John[2], and the Londoners considered themselves as the pledged guardians of public liberty. Their affections had never been sought, however, by King Henry, who had reserved all his grace and bounty for court favourites. No Machiavelli[3] had yet pointed out to princes with acute simplicity that "the prince must necessarily live always among the same identical people, but may well do without the same identical nobles, having it in his power any day to make and unmake, raise and deject such at his pleasure." While the main object of the King's policy seemed the advancement of his courtiers, the city of London was often

[1] Hume.
[2] V. Lord Chatham's speech, May 4, 1770.
[3] "E necessitato ancora il principe vivere sempre con quel medesimo popolo, ma può ben fare senza quelli medesimi grandi, potendo farne e disfarne ogni dì, e torre e dare a sua posta riputazione loro." — Il Prince.

subjected to his insolence, encroachment, and injustice. Arbitrary tallages and capricious fines had been repeatedly extorted from them on frivolous occasions: in 1227, twelve years after their support of Prince Louis, a penalty of 5000 marcs (£3333. 6s. 8d.) was imposed for that remote offence; a fine of 3000 marcs (£2000) was laid upon the city, because a priest charged with murder had escaped to sanctuary, though he had been in fact the Bishop of London's prisoner, having been claimed as an ecclesiastic. Their petition, too, on this subject was not only rejected, but the petitioners were reviled by Henry as "slaves," and some of them even imprisoned[1]. The customary gifts which they had offered him on joyful occasions had been received ungraciously as debts, without even the courtesy of thanks being returned. Often[2] had they been heavily taxed to pay for the fortification of their city and the Tower, though obviously intended to be used against their own freedom: their military exercises had been discouraged and scoffed at as unfit for such mechanics, and when, in 1253, some of the young citizens resisted and beat off the courtiers, who had rudely interrupted their game of the Quintain, the city was immediately punished by a fine of 1000 marcs (£666. 13s. 4d.)[3], this mimic war[4] being claimed as exclusively by the nobles and gentry at that time as the aristocratical privilege of duels has since been.

The noble edifice of Westminster Abbey had risen under King Henry's liberality[5], and in order to bestow fresh marks

[1] Mat. Par. Queen Eleanor, when Lady Keeper, had rigorously enforced her dues at Queenhithe, and also claimed from London a large sum as "aurum Reginæ" owing; that is, every tenth mark paid to the King on renewal of leases, crown lands, or renewal of charters. On non-payment, she in a summary manner committed to the Marshalsea prison the sheriffs, Richard Picard and John de Northampton (1253).—Ld. Campbell's Chancellors, i. 142.

[2] In 1243, 1246, 1249, 1258.—Fabyan.

[3] Mat. Par.

[4] They could fight in earnest, however, at times. A quarrel having arisen between the Guilds of the Goldsmiths and the Tailors, they met to fight it out with 500 armed men on each side on an appointed night. Many were killed and wounded before the authorities of the city could interfere. This was in 1226.—S. M. 754.

[5] The amount of his expenses on

of his favour upon it, he did not scruple to infringe upon the rights of others, On an occasion of this sort, in 1250, the city of London had adroitly interested Simon de Montfort and other nobles to procure them redress by exciting a kindred alarm for the security of their own chartered rights. A fair of fifteen days at the feast of Edward the Confessor was held by royal proclamation in Tothill Fields, and to ensure its success all the shops in the city of London were compelled to be closed[1]. A rainy October made the bad roads of approach worse, while bridges were broken down and fords became impassable, so that no buyers arrived to console the involuntary booth-keepers, who remained exposed to cold and mud amidst a dearth of provisions[2]. Grievances such as these, coming home to every bosom, and directly interfering with the personal comfort and profit of every shopkeeper in London, were more calculated to exasperate them than even the arbitrary maxims of Government which might lessen their political power. Nor were their retail dealings only thus interfered with, for their commercial intercourse with France was often subjected to the plunder and violent forestalling[3] of the King's officers, while the rigid exaction by the Queen of every tenth marc on goods landed in London was also much complained of. The most recent and most daring wrong which the court had inflicted was in the preceding year, when Prince Edward

the building down to Michaelmas 1261, was £29,345. 19s. 8d.; among other marks of his zeal he adorned the forehead of the Virgin Mary's image with an emerald and ruby, taken out of rings bequeathed to him by Ralph de Neville, Bishop of Chichester.
[1] Mat. Par.
[2] The city subsequently bought off the fair by a payment of £200 to the abbey.—Dart's Westm.
[3] In Madox Hist. Exch. p. 690, reference is made to a suit against the citizens John Travers and Andrew Bukerell (v. pp. 106–277) by Ralph de Dicton, bailiff of Richard, Earl of Cornwall, because the citizens did not bring all their boats of fish to Queen Hithe (Ripa Reginæ), as they ought and used (sicut debent et solent), on which the citizens claimed the King's warrant, inasmuch as the King had granted leave for their fishboats to land where they pleased (quod naves piscem deferentes applicarent ubi vellent).—Mich.14° Henry III. [Andrew Bukerel was mayor from 1232 to 1238. John Travers had been sheriff with him in 1224 and 1225. Lib. de Ant. Leg. pp. 5, 6.]

had come suddenly with an armed force to the Temple, in the dusk of the evening, and, under pretence of wishing to see his mother's jewels, had broken open the chests of treasure in deposit there, and had carried off £10,000[1] to Windsor for the purpose of the coming war.

It is no wonder that these and similar insults had estranged their loyalty, and they had now for four successive years elected as their popular mayor Thomas Fitz-Thomas[2]; affronting the King on the last occasion by not even presenting him, as usual, for royal approval. So attached, indeed, were they to this chief, that they persevered in their choice of him, even when he was a prisoner under royal displeasure in 1266. A convention was now signed by him with the Earls of Leicester, Gloucester, and Derby, Hugh le Despenser and twelve barons[3]. Many thousands of eager partisans, specified by some[4] as 15,000, by Rob. Brune as "sixti thousand of London armed men full stoute," now answered the appeal of Simon de Montfort, and came forward ready to advance with him under the standard of the barons against the royal army,

---

[1] T. Wyke. Chr. Dover.
[2] Fabyan. Stowe. The arms of Fitz-Thomas were 5 eagles displayed argent, 2, 2 and 1, a canton ermine. —MS. Harl. 1049.
[3] "Tunc temporis Barones et Londonienses confederati sunt scripto cyrographato et juramento quilibet duodecim annorum et amplius, standi simul contra omnes salvâ tamen fide domini Regis."—Lib. de Ant. Leg. p. 62. P.
[4] W. Rish de bello Lew. Mat. Westm. Chr. Roff. MSS. Cott. Nero. D. II. T. Wyke calls them an innumerable troop of Londoners.

CHAPTER VIII.

NEGOTIATIONS WITH THE ROYALISTS AT LEWES.

"We see which way the stream of time doth run,
And are enforced from our most quiet sphere,
By the rough torrent of occasion."—HEN. IV. II.

BEFORE leaving London, the Earl of Leicester, "faithfully sweating in the cause, and zealous for justice," had called together the bishops, clergy, and other discreet men of his party, to consult on the crisis of affairs, and it was resolved by them that peace, and the observance of the Oxford Statutes, should be purchased, even by an offer of money if possible, but in case of such terms being rejected, that the decision should be left to arms[1]. In pursuance of this policy the army, now reinforced, began their march from London May 6[2], in order to arrest the King's progress in the south. It is not known by what route the barons reached Sussex, but it is probable that de Clare, who had been in Kent, proceeded by a concerted plan to meet them, and when they had ascertained that the King was at Lewes they pitched their camp about nine miles north from that town at the village of Fletching[3], then surrounded by a dense forest.

[1] W. Rish. de Bello Lew.
[2] On the feast of S. John Port. Latin.—W. Rish.
[3] "Barones cum suo exercitu ad dictam villam (Lewes) approperantes intra villam quæ vocatur Flechinge tentoria sua figebant."—Chr. Wigorn. MS. "Flexemge or Flexingge, about six miles from Lewes."—W. Rish. Chr. and de bello Lew. "Flexinge sexto circa mille a prioratu de Lewes."—Chr. Roff. Mat. Westm. T. Wyke

Before the final appeal to arms, the barons despatched from hence, on a mission of peace, two eminent prelates, who had steadily adhered to them—Richard de Sandwich, Bishop of London, and Walter de Cantilupe, Bishop of Worcester, both well qualified for their office.

Richard de Sandwich was a worthy successor to Fulk Basset, before noticed, in his zeal for ecclesiastical liberty. From a prebendary of St Paul's he had risen, in 1262, to his present rank, which he retained till 1273. Soon after his elevation he was successful with his present colleague in urging to a conclusion the hasty armistice of June 1263, at a desperate crisis of the King's affairs, and in the following month the uncharacteristic duty of the custody of Dover Castle was assigned to him and two other bishops, distinguishing them thereby as neutrals and mediators. He had been an attesting party to the recent *mise* in France, and retained his fortitude and love of his Church[1] during the disgrace and exile, which overtook him in consequence of the part he was now playing.

The birth, station, and character of Walter de Cantilupe added dignity to his experience and courage. He had already occupied the see of Worcester twenty-eight years, having been elected during the lifetime of his father[2], a nobleman who had borne the high office of steward to Kings John and Henry, and had been sheriff at various times of Warwickshire and Leicestershire. Early deaths in rapid succession had carried off three generations of the family chief: his brother had conveyed the protest of England to

---

says, "the earl pitched his camp at seven or eight miles from where the King's army was." "Barones in abditis sylvarum latentes cum exercitu." The letter of the barons is dated "in bosco juxta Lewes."—Chr. Dover.

[1] Besides bequeathing 40s. for an anniversary obit on Sept. 12 in St Paul's, "for the good of his soul," he gave several church ornaments and vestments: some of these were curiously embroidered, "with wheels, griffons, and elephants," a brocade cope "with knights templars riding about below, and birds above."— Dugd. St Paul's. The brass monument of this prelate remained in honour in old St Paul's, until involved in the common destruction of so many works of art by the fanaticism of Edward VI.'s time.

[2] He died 1239.

the Pope; his eldest nephew William, after a brief military career, had been followed to his untimely grave by sorrowing crowds of abbots and barons, among whom were Simon de Montfort and Humphrey de Bohun[1]; Walter himself, who had been employed on foreign embassies, was ever an active and zealous friend to the liberties of the Church and State. In one of the regulations made by him for his diocese, in 1240, he assumes a singularly paternal character, enjoining "all priests every Sunday to warn both mothers and nurses not to keep their tender infants too close to them, lest by chance they should be suffocated, but to let them lie firmly propped up in their cradles[2]." He was one of the twenty-four councillors elected to watch the execution of the Oxford Statutes, and more recently, after reconciling the hostile parties of the state to an armistice, he had promoted the *mise*, by which he might have hoped to end these ·civil broils. The manner in which Prince Edward had lately delivered himself from the thraldom of a blockade, by practising on his too easy faith, has been already adverted to.

The task of peace was now resumed by these prelates under discouraging circumstances, when they proceeded to Lewes, charged with the offer of 50,000 marcs[3] (£33,333. 6s. 8d.) to the King, in compensation for the damages done by the baronial party in their late outrages, but annexing the condition so constantly urged, of the Oxford Statutes being held valid and executed. Other accounts, indeed, represent the King of the Romans as making the demand of £30,000, but this may have arisen from his avarice being so popular a topic of reproach:—

"The Kyng of Alemaigne, bi me leaute,
Thritti thousent pound askede he
For to make the pees in the countre[4]."

---

[1] He was related to them by his marriage with Eve [de Braose, great granddaughter] of the great Earl of Pembroke.
[2] Wilkins' Conc. i. 668.
[3] T. Wyke.
[4] Pol. S., from MS. Harl. 2253. The Chr. Dunst. says there were three proposals of peace, the first sent by knights, the second and third by the two bishops.

The bishops were bearers of the following letter, in which the barons endeavoured to reconcile their loyalty to the King, with their war against his evil advisers:—

"To their most excellent Lord, Henry, by the Grace of God, the illustrious King of England, Lord of Ireland, Duke of Aquitaine, the barons and others his lieges, wishing to observe their oath and faith to God and him, send health, and due service with honour and reverence:

"Since it is apparent by many proofs that certain persons among those who surround you, have uttered many falsehoods against us to your Lordship, devising all the evil in their power, not only towards us, but towards yourself and the whole kingdom:

"May your Excellency know, that as we wish to preserve the health and safety of your person with all our might, and with the fidelity due to you, proposing only to resist by all means in our power those persons, who are not only our enemies, but yours, and those of the whole kingdom;

"May it please you not to believe their falsehoods.

"We shall always be found your liegemen, and we, the Earl of Leicester and Gilbert de Clare, at the request of others, have affixed our seals for ourselves. Given in the Weald, near Lewes, on the first Tuesday after the feast of St Pancras[1]." (May 13, 1264.)

This address has been termed[2] "submissive in the language, but exorbitant in the demands;" and undoubtedly the courteous obedience professed by it stands in contrast to its resolute menaces, the submission being somewhat akin to the humility of the Biscayans, whose fixed law it was, that, until their lord swore to keep their privileges, "any order of his should be obeyed only, and not executed[3]."

---

[1] Chr. Dover, "datum in bosco juxta Lewes die Martis primo post diem S. Pancratii." In Chr. Rish. it is "Datum apud Flexing." Sir J. Mackintosh dates this May 10. S. Pancras was on Monday, May 12.

[2] Hume.

[3] "Y que si su Senoria enbiare mandamientos o provisiones en el entre, tanto sean obedicidas y no cum-

The royal court had been established at Lewes two days, when the bishops now approached on their mission. Prince Edward had made himself the congenial guest[1] of his gallant kinsman at the castle, while the King had taken up his residence in the great priory of Cluniac monks, situated in the low grounds south of the town. The prior William de Neville[2], who had been lately removed here from the convent of the same order, and whose treachery had facilitated the capture of Northampton, was now engaged in rebuilding the great western towers of his church, a work he did not live to finish, but for which he bequeathed funds at his death, in 1268.

The priory, in conjunction with four French ones, constituted "the five chief daughters of Cluny," near Macon, in Burgundy, the prior of Lewes being always High Chamberlain of the order. Subject as they were to a foreign authority, the monks, as well as their head, may well have had a bias towards the alien courtiers of the King, and doubtless rejoiced at the honour of receiving such distinguished guests as their inmates. The young Christian martyr, Saint Pancras, to whom the priory was dedicated, displayed no such marvels on the occasion, as were believed by his devotees to have occurred at his tomb in Rome. There any false swearer, who came near, either became instantly possessed of the devil and went mad, or fell down dead on the pavement, and this occurred in some cases where the test had been tried in vain at the tomb of the more in-

plidas."—Fueros de Vizcaya. In Hungary similar orders were laid aside respectfully, "cum honore deponuntur."

[1] He was again at Lewes as King, Aug. 1289.

[2] The name is Neville in Willis' lists, and in Harl. MSS. e Regist. Arc. Giff., but in Regist. pr. S. Andr. and in Ann. de Lewes it is Fonville, probably corrupted from Nova Villa (Neville). His bequests to the priory were many: a gold cup enriched with five gems, a gilt sacramental cup and four others of his best for the choir, a silver pall, £100 to buy tunics in alternate years, 200 marcs (£133. 6s. 8d.) to complete the two towers of the front of his church, which were ninety feet high and the walls ten feet thick, 100 marcs (£66. 13s. 4d.) to the treasury, a gilt cup to the refectory, and a silver goblet to the infirmary.—Dugd. Monas. He is not noticed in Rowland's "Nevill family."

dulgent St Peter[1]. Neither king nor courtier were affected at Lewes by this touchstone of truth.

Having adopted the discipline and black habit of St Benedict, they were often familiarly designated as the Black Monks, and let us hope they did not deserve the character given them by a satirist soon after this time, who describes the "Moyne Neirs" as members of the order of Easy Living (Ordre de Bel Eyse), getting drunk every day from mere jollity:—

" E sont chescun jour ivre,	They must perforce get drunk each day,
Quar ne sevent autre vivre,	They know of life no other way;
Mès ils le font pur compagnie,	But they only drink for company,
E.ne mie pur glotonie[2]."	And not a jot for gluttony.

The tact of finding excellent reasons for doing what they liked was not peculiar to this fictitious Order. In a similar manner the monks of St Denis offered sound clerical arguments to Charlemagne in favour of their hunting: the flesh of hunted game was so medicinal to their sick, and the skins served so well for their gloves and girdles, and for binding their psalters. Hunting accordingly continued for many ages the orthodox practice of churchmen. Walter de Suffield, the Bishop of Norwich, in 1256, had bequeathed his pack of hounds to the King, and there were thirteen parks[3] well stocked with game belonging to that see at the Reformation. An interesting precedent was also furnished by the Archbishop of York in 1321, when he conducted his visitation with a train of 200 persons and a pack of hounds, which his clergy had to maintain, as he moved from place

---

[1] Legenda Aurea. Pancras having refused to worship idols at the command and entreaties of Diocletian, was beheaded A.D. 287, at Rome. His head "which sweated blood for three days, when the basilica of S. John Lateran was on fire," is to this day annually exhibited there on his feast-day, May 12, Diar. Rom.

[2] Pol. S. from MS. Harl.

[3] Strutt's Anc. Sp. Compare the case of St Edmund's Bury. "Plures enim parcos fecit, quos bestiis replevit, *venatorem cum canibus habens*, et superveniente aliquo hospite magni nominis, *sedebat cum monachis suis in aliquo saltu nemoris, et videbat canes currere;* sed de venatione nunquam vidi eam gustare."—Chr. Jocelin, p. 21.

to place. Many a monk, like Chaucer's, was "an outrider that loved venerie," and the luxurious living in some of their cloistered retreats is amusingly caricatured in an early satire :—

> "All of pasties beth the wall,
> Of flesh, of fish, and a rich meat,
> The like-fullest that man may eat:
> Flouren cakes beth the shingles all
> Of church, cloister, bowers, and hall:
> The pinnes beth fat puddings,
> Rich meat to Princes and Kings.
>
> Yet do I you mo to wit
> The geese yroasted on the spit,
> Flee to the Abbey, God it wot,
> And gredith "geese all hot, all hot.
>
> The young monkes each day
> After meat goeth to play[1]."

The present guests at the priory of Lewes had all celebrated the great feast of the patron saint, on Monday, May 12, doubtless with all due merriment, and we shall see with what excited spirits they received the offer of peace on the following day. On the morning of the battle also they were so little alert as to be nearly surprised in their beds—a circumstance which tallies somewhat suspiciously with the warning of the satirist, if any friend should come to visit the black monks in the evening :—

"Ce vus di je de veir,	I'll tell you true what he will do,
Yl dormira grant matinée,	He'll snooze away far into day,
Desque la male fumée	Nor leave his bed until his head
Seit de la teste issue	From the fumes be free of the night's
Pur grant peril de la vewe[2]."	revelry,
	And much I fear he won't see clear.

That the Cluniacs were not wholly absorbed in devotion, authentic evidence was given by some English brethren of the Order, who set forth their grievances to Edward III. in 1331, complaining: 1. That a few foreign brethren, their privileged masters (mestres per heritage) sent the revenues

[1] Likefullest, pleasantest; pinnes, pinnacles; gredith, cry.—Cockaigne in Hickes' Thes.
[2] Pol. S. from MS. Harl.

out of the kingdom: 2. That the Prior of Lewes evaded the Act of Parliament, and persisted in sending new monks abroad for admission: 3. That heads of houses were chosen who knew nothing of clerical matters except scraping up money and sending it abroad: 4. That if a monk should speak of discipline or religion he would be despatched a hundred leagues off on foot, and with a stinted allowance; and on that account the order of Cluny has fallen into shame, and no one dared to speak of religion[1]."

Among those assembled round the King at this crisis of his fate were nearly all those allied to him by blood or marriage: his gallant son Edward, the favourite and mainspring of the army, and a second titled monarch, Prince Richard, King of the Romans, who had with him his chivalrous son Henry, a fresh convert, and a zealous one from the opposite party, and his younger son Edmund, a mere youth. The royal half-brothers, Guy and William de Valence, objects of so much national jealousy, were eager to revenge the insults of their exile and confiscation. The neighbouring fortress of Pevensey was now in the custody of William, who, though there does not appear to have been any distinct grant of the title, was considered at this time as the Earl of Pembroke[2], in right of the inherited lands of his wife Joan de Monchensy. The head, however, of the Monchensy family was in the enemy's camp, and the kinsmen were soon to meet in conflict.

John, the seventh Earl of Warenne and Surrey, was among the most constant and resolute of all the King's friends, whose half-sister Alice he had married. The lady,

---

[1] Reyn. Apost. Bened. Dugd. Mon. "Le kart, ke si un moyne parle de ordre ou de religion, il serrà mandè cent lewes hors, e a pe, e a poy despenses, e par icy le ordre de Cluny e alle a hunte e pur ice nul ne ose parler de religiun." A bull of Pope Celestine III., 1197, rebukes the Prior of Lewes for promising benefices before they were vacant, "et de non solvendis pensionibus clericis nobilium." Rymer.—Tanner's Not. Prince Edward was the first who confiscated the revenues of Lewes Priory, as alien, in 1285, to help his own wars.

[2] The estates had been granted to him in 1250, and he was summoned to the great councils as representative of the property.

indeed, is unpolitely handed down to us as proud, ugly, and ill-tempered, and she died mad[1]; but this was by no means the only alliance of the family with royal blood. The first earl was a kinsman of the Conqueror, and married his daughter Gundred[2], whose well-known tomb, near the priory founded by him, has preserved her memory at Lewes. Isabella, the sole heiress in the fourth generation, carried the earldom by her marriage, first to William de Blois, a son of King Stephen, and after his death to Hameline Plantagenet, a brother of Henry II. By his father's marriage with Maud, one of the Pembroke heiresses, John was nearly related to some of the powerful chiefs now opposed to him[3], but he gave to the King, with unflinching loyalty, all the influence derived from his wide possessions in Sussex[4], and the strength of the castle, at Lewes, at this moment so peculiarly important to him. A hostile ballad[5] of the time thus alludes to his wealth and spirit, at a time when the barons had checked him by the truce of 1263 :—

"Mes de Warenne ly bon Quens,	Proud of his wealth and many lands,
Que tant ad richesses et biens,	The good Earl Warenne raised his
Si ad apris de guere,	hands,
	Skilled in war, and quick to fight;

[1] Mat. Westm.
[2] Duchesne (Hist. Norm. Script.) though naming five other daughters, makes no mention of Gundreda; nor does Thierry (Conq. d'Anglet.); nor M. Lafreneye in Nouvelle Hist. de Normandie, 1816; and Orderic Vit. says, "the King gave Surrey to William de Warenne, who had married Gundreda, sister of Gherbod." The tradition of her parentage might therefore have been doubted had not her husband in his charter founding the priory described her as the daughter of Queen Matilda: "Pro salute animæ meæ et animæ Gundredæ uxoris meæ * * * et pro salutæ dominæ meæ Matildis reginæ, matris uxoris meæ."—Dugd. Monast.

"Cestriam et comitatum ejus Gherbodo Flandrensi jamdudum Rex derat." After the Conquest William granted to this Flemish nobleman for his services the city and county of Chester; but, being in Flanders on business, Gherbod was there seized by his enemies, and imprisoned for life. Chester was therefore, on account of his absence, granted to Hugh Lupus.—V. Order. Vit. p. 250.
[3] With the Earls of Gloucester and Norfolk and with the family of the Earl of Derby. P.
[4] His father William held 30½ knights' fees in Pevensey Rape, and 62 in Lewes Rape.
[5] Pol. S. from MS. 13th cent. Sir J. Mackintosh erroneously names Warenne as one of the principal leaders of the barons with Gloucester and Derby.—Hist. Eng. Pevensey Castle was committed to his custody, 1263. (Pat. 47° H. III.)

En Norfolk en cel pensis	In Norfolk late his thoughts did swell,
Vint conquerrant ses enemis,	Intending all his foes to quell,
Mes ore ne ad que fere."	But idle now lies his might.

Of all those who fought at Lewes, he[1], with Prince Edward, was the only one who survived to be enrolled among the warriors at Carlaverock, in 1301, civil and foreign wars having swept away all the others. In the interim he had steadily maintained his independence of character: his bold answer to the enquiries of the royal commissioners in 1276, as to the title by which he held his lands, was more conclusive in that age than rolls of parchment. "By this sword did my ancestor win them, and by this sword will I keep them." It is interesting to find him as a veteran still fighting by the side of his King so many years afterwards, and bringing forward his grandson Henry, Lord Percy[2].

After holding the earldom for fifty-four years, he was on his death in 1304 so esteemed, that King Edward caused prayers to be publicly offered for him, and the clergy sanctioned a promised "remission of 3000 days from purgatory to those who should relieve his soul by prayer[3]." Of the

---

[1] "Johans li bon Quens de Warene
De l'autre eschele avoit la rene
A justicier e gouvorner
Com cil ki bien scavoit mener
Gen seignourie et honnouree.
De or et de azur eschequeree
Fu sa baniere noblement
Il ot en son assemblement
Henri de Percy son nevou,
De ki sembloit ke eust fait vou
De aler les Escos de Rampant.
Jaune o un bleu lyon rampant
Fu sa baniere bien vuable."

Good Earl de Warenne on his steed
Had of the other troop the lead,
To govern or to check at will,
As one who had the noble skill
Barons and honoured knights to guide,
When proudly flying they descried
His chequered banner blue and gold
In his squadron, young and bold
His grandson Henry Percy, came,
Seeming as if he vowed to tame
The Scots, and singly to attack,
While high in sight of all there flew
His golden banner's lion blue.

[2] He was the son of his third daughter Eleanor, and succeeded his father (a royalist prisoner at Lewes) in 1272. He married Eleanor, daughter of Richard, Earl of Arundel.

[3] He was buried before the high altar of Lewes Priory, "in pleno pavimento sub planâ tumbâ."—MSS. Vitell. XIV., 14 ex reg. Lew. The

Archbishop, the Bishops of Chichester, Rochester, and five others, authorized this indulgence, inscribed on his tomb:—

"Ky pur sa alme priera
Troiz mill jours de pardon avera."
For his soul whoever prays
Of pardon has 3000 days.

other principal royalists at Lewes, the kindred and fate of a few may be traced, to show by what various motives of interest or loyalty, and after what changes of opinion, they were there united in the same cause. John Fitzalan, Baron of Clun, in Wales, was in possession of Arundel Castle, as the representative of his mother, Isabella de Albini, heiress of her two brothers, the last earls of that name; but though in favour at court he never enjoyed, nor did his son after him, the title of earl, though this is contrary to a popular opinion of its tenure[1]. He had fought in the Welsh wars, and had mainly assisted in the recent defence of Rochester. The widow of his maternal uncle, Warenne's sister, whose spirited interview with the King has been related, was yet alive, and this connection naturally associated Fitzalan's banners with those of that chieftain. The advantage of all the great strongholds of Sussex, Lewes, Pevensey, Hastings, and Arundel, being in friendly hands, had probably determined the movement of the royal forces to this part of the kingdom, as affording a military position of great strength, increased by the facility of receiving fresh supplies of men and money from France.

[1] He died 1267. His grandson, Edmund, was the first of his name summoned to Parliament as Earl of Arundel, and by marriage with Alice, heiress of the last Earl de Warenne (who died 1347), introduced additional wealth and honours into the family. The "fair Brian de Fitzaleyn, full of courtesy and honour," at Carlaverock, had a seal, which, instead of any heraldic device, exhibited two birds, a stag, a rabbit, and a pig, with the motto, "Tot capita tot sentencie."—Cartwright's Rape Arund. Report of H. of Lords. The arms of Brian Fitzalan are barry, or and gules, in the east window of Bedall church. The pedigree of the Fitzalan family has been given by the Rev. R.W. Eyton, Arch. Journ. 1856, p. 333:—

William de Albini,   Hugh de Albini,   Isabella de Albini,
    4th Earl.   5th Earl, d. 1243,   m. John Fitzalan, Baron of Clun,
                      m. Isabella d^r. of   who d. 1177?
                      W^m. Earl de Warenne, |
                              d. 1282.   John m. Maud Verdon,
                                                d. 1267.
                                                |
                                            John m. Isabella de Mortimer,
                                                d. 1272.
                                            Edmund m. Alice de Warenne,
                                                d. 1326.

Others of the kindred of the Albinis were with Fitzalan: Roger de Someri[1], who had married his aunt, was a soldier of experienced service in Gascony and Wales. He had felt the rigour of the feudal bonds in a remarkable manner, soon after he had become the heir of his nephew, who died young, all his land being confiscated on account of his having neglected the royal summons to receive knighthood. By the same feudal supremacy he had been prohibited, in 1262—probably at the instigation of the barons, who may have mistrusted him—from continuing to build the castle of Dudley, and he had but recently obtained licence to do so, perhaps at a moment when the King was a more free agent.

Robert de Tattershall[2], a cousin of Fitzalan, was a gallant and powerful knight, holding twenty-five fees, who had already been engaged in the Welsh wars.

One of the most conspicuous royalists in rank was Humphrey de Bohun, known as the good Earl of Hereford. Descended from a kinsman of the Conqueror, his father had been one of the firmest upholders of Magna Charta, and he had himself, on many occasions, displayed the same independent spirit, when provoked by its infringement, the encroachments of the Pope, or the overbearing influence of the alien courtiers. His marriage with one of the Pembroke heiresses had increased his importance, and he had stood as one of the nine sponsors at Prince Edward's baptism, in 1239. His services when a crusader, and in Wales, had inured him to the ordinary aspect of war; but the greatest trial of his courage must have been now to see his eldest son[3], an able

---

[1] Arms of Someri: "Or two lions passant azure."—Rolls of Arms. He died in 1272.

[2] He died in 1274. Arms, "Chequy or and gules, a chief ermine."—Carlav. His son claimed, in 1297, the office of Hereditary Chief Butler in right of his grandmother, Mabella Albini. Dugdale says he fought against the King, at Evesham (Esc. 49° H. III.).

[3] The father was the second earl, but Dugdale appears to confuse him with his son, and represents him as always taking part with the barons, until he became a prisoner at Evesham. His son, Humphrey, undoubtedly fought against the King, and died before him; and the homage of the grandson was taken after the earl's death, 1274.—Cal. Inquis. p. mort. Dugd. Bar.

and restless soldier, leading on part of de Montfort's troops, and persevering throughout the war allied to the same party, as well as John de Haresfield[1], his son by a second wife.

In similar opposition to the head of his noble family stood Hugh le Bigot[2], a good soldier and a skilful lawyer. His early political tendencies having united him with the barons at Oxford, they had made him a Justiciary, and entrusted him with the command of Dover, from which the King had dismissed him as soon as he dared. He was, however, now ranged in support of the Crown, and after his flight from Lewes re-appeared at Evesham to fight for the same cause, recovering finally his confiscated estates.

The family influence of de Warenne may also have brought other knights to the royal side. William Bardolf[3], whose mother was a Warenne, had been selected by the King as one of the twelve councillors at Oxford, but being a good soldier, and having, in 1241, seized the notorious outlaw, William de Marisco, in Lundy Island, the barons had placed him in command of Nottingham, in 1258, and again in 1263. This trust, however, he had recently betrayed[4] into the King's hands, after the Northampton victory. The barons were, at this moment, encamped on his lands at Fletching, and he became their prisoner on the following day.

The large possessions of Henry de Percy gave him great influence, not only in the North[5], but in Sussex, where he

[1] The remainder of his elder brother's estates was secured to him and Milo, another brother, by grant, 1266.—Rot. Pat. 50° H. III., where Humphrey is misnamed Henry.
[2] Arms of le Bigot, "Or a cross gules."
[3] He was a ward of Hubert de Burgh, as a minor, had a grant of free warren at Fletching, in 1254, and died 1274. Arms, "Azure 3 quintefoilles de or."—Rolls of Arms. His son is honourably mentioned at Carlaverock, as "a rich and chivalrous knight of lordly presence."
[4] T. Wyke.
[5] The manor of Skelton, brought into his family by his grandmother, was held by a singular but easy tenure, the lord being bound, on every Christmas-day, to lead the lady of Skelton Castle from her chamber to mass and back. Percy died in 1272. His son has been already alluded to as accompanying de Warenne at Carlaverock. He was the direct ancestor of Hotspur, and, by females, of the late Earl of Egremont.—Dugd. Bar. Cartwr. Rape Arundel.

was Lord of Petworth. He had given £900 to the King for livery of his lands, and the liberty of marrying whom he pleased—a privilege certainly worth paying for, but which he did not abuse; for the lady whom he chose, Eleanor, the daughter of Earl de Warenne, would have had no difficulty in gaining the King's consent. After sharing in the Welsh campaigns with honour, he had been leagued with the barons up to the preceding year, when his estates were confiscated. De Warenne may be supposed to have induced his submission by their restoration, in consequence of which he had gathered the adherents of his noble banner to assist the King at the capture of Northampton, and was again prepared for the combat at Lewes.

Another knight was present, whose name has become more distinguished by modern genius than it was in his own times—Philip de Marmion[1]. He had been ward to William de Cantilupe, whose representative, the Bishop of Worcester, he now saw coming from the enemy's camp as ambassador. Having for many years followed the fortunes of the King in Gascony, where he had been taken prisoner, and in Wales, and having been one of the sureties for the King's observance of the Oxford Statutes, he was earnestly summoned by his Sovereign, when the attempted re-action began, to come to him, "with horses, and arms, and all his power, and with all the assemblage of his friends, not only on his due allegiance, but on his friendship." He had accordingly been made sheriff of Suffolk and Norfolk in 1263, and had aided the seizure of Northampton. At Lewes he had the mortification of seeing his two uncles, Robert and William de Marmion, fighting against him. In reward of his services he was appointed, for a time, governor of Kenilworth, on its surrender after the battle of Evesham, and received also the grant of Tamworth.

Philip Basset[2] deserves especial mention, as having so

---

[1] Arms, "Vair fess gules."—Rolls of Arms. Banks' Family of Marmion gives another, "three swords in pale, points down, chief vair."

[2] Baron of Wycomb, co. Berks. Arms, "Or, three piles gules, a quarter ermine."—Rolls of Arms. "Ermine, on chief indented gules

much distinguished himself by his valour at Lewes, near which, at Berwick, he possessed some lands, granted by King John to his grandfather Alan; and the priory had also received the grant of a church from his family. He had himself, in early life, together with his brothers, incurred forfeiture by rebellion, but had long been confidentially employed by the King both in peace and war. After having been on the mission to the Pope and Council at Lyons, and at home having several castles entrusted to his command, he had been named, in 1261, as Justiciary, and has been mentioned as forcing his way through the undermined wall of Northampton. Like Warenne, Fitzalan, Percy, and Bardolf, he not only had the local interest of property in Sussex, but like them too had the misery at Lewes to know—what must unhappily often be the case in civil war—that some of his own kindred were ranged as leaders in the opposite ranks[1].

One of the most eager and uncompromising royalists was Roger de Mortimer[2], grandfather of the well-known favourite of the name, deservedly executed by Edward III. His line of ancestry from the Conquest included the distinguished names of Longespée, de Ferrers, and a Welsh Princess; and he was himself married to Matilda, daughter of William de

three mullets or."—Carlav. 1. In the Deed confirming the Peace 1259, the large seal of Philip de Basset is still extant, and exhibits on an escutcheon 3 bars indented—cart. 629. 10, Archiv. du. roy.: and a small seal of his, bearing the same arms, is appended to the Deed of Reference to Louis IX. by the barons, 1263.— Arch. du roy., cart. 630. 20. A remarkable privilege of having mass performed in his presence at any church he might come to, even though it lay under interdict, was granted to Philip Basset, in 1245, by Pope Innocent IV. This favour is avowedly shewn because, from his rank and power, Basset was likely to be able to requite the Papacy on occasion.

[1] He died 1272. Of his daughters, Aliva married Hugh le Despenser, and afterwards Roger le Bigod, junior; Margery married John Fitz-John.—Dugd. Bar. [In saying that some of Philip Basset's kindred were ranged as leaders in the opposite ranks, Mr Blaauw probably alludes to his son-in-law, Hugh le Despenser, whom the barons nominated as Chief Justiciary in 1258, and who fell at Evesham; to Ralf Basset of Sapercote, whom the barons made castellan of Northampton; and to his cousin, Ralf Basset of Drayton. But the connection of the two latter with Basset of Wycomb is not ascertained, and was anyhow very remote.]

[2] "Mortimer, barré de or e de asure, od le chef palée, les corners geroune, a un escuchon de argent."—Rolls of Arms. Dugd. Bar.

Braose—an owner, like himself, of large estates in Wales. His desolating attacks, in 1263, on the bordering properties of the baronial partisans by plunder and fire, may be said to have begun the war, as they naturally provoked retaliation. He had been prominent at the storming of Northampton, and was doubtless of equal activity at Lewes.

Fulk FitzWarren[1], a veteran of high connections, who had been born on a Welsh mountain during his father's outlawry, and who was drowned in the Ouse during the battle, must have recently adopted the party, which proved fatal to him. He had been employed in 1245 by the malcontent knights and barons at the Dunstable tournament, on a service very characteristic of the manners of the age,—to warn the Pope's secretary, Martin, who had been plundering for his master with great diligence, instantly to leave the country. A clerical chronicler[2], speaking of this Martin, declares that out of respect to the Church he deems it safer and more honourable to be silent as to his wanton and wrongful rapacity. FitzWarren, though not silent, did not waste many words in executing the commission. The interview was short and decisive; the soldier went up to the secretary at the Temple with a stern look, and bluntly delivered his message at once: "Get out of England immediately." On Martin asking, "Who orders me this? do you, of your own authority?" he was answered, "The whole community; and if you will take good advice, you will not stay here three days longer, lest you and yours should be cut up into fragments," backing the threat with oaths. Martin made a vain appeal to King Henry for protection, who greeted his request of a safe conduct with, "May the devil conduct you into and through hell!" His fear during his hasty journey to Canterbury was so excessive, in consequence of these threats, that

---

[1] "Quartele argent et gules endente."—Rolls of Arms. His sister Eve married Prince Llewellyn.—W. Heming. His arms in the south aisle of Westminster Abbey are

"Quarterly per fess indented argent and gules." For the seal of Ivo Fitz-Waryn, see Arch. Journ., Sept. 1856, p. 279.

[2] M. Par.

the sight of some men, who had met to buy timber in a wood, induced him to offer his guide, Robert Norris, preferment in the Church for any of his relations if he would but save him from their attack. Norris despised the bribe; but, playing upon his alarm, made him skulk along byeways to Dover at full speed until he embarked.

A highly curious specimen of a baron's life in the thirteenth century is presented by the memoirs[1] of Fulk FitzWarren's father, of the same name; the narrative, though more romance than history, being evidently founded on facts. Henry II. had brought him up in the palace as a companion to his own sons and the Welsh Prince Llewellyn; but a boyish quarrel he had with Prince John, at a game of chess, was the means of affecting his way of life for years afterwards. With his four brothers he was knighted by King Richard, who loved them as fellow-crusaders, and he is praised as "without a rival in strength, courage, and goodness." He acted as Warden of the Welsh marches, but when the revengeful John, as King, cheated him out of Ludlow, and denied him any justice, he formally renounced his homage, and became an outlaw, in which capacity many of his wild and strange adventures are recorded. Though fifteen knights had promised John to capture him, he proved them to be "fools for their promise," and slew them by the help of his brothers. He made use of his own long spear to measure out for himself the rich stuffs and furs of the King's merchants, whom he plundered whenever he met them; and being the object of several proclamations yet extant (1203, 15, 16, 17,) he adopted sundry disguises. In the cowl of a monk he was married to Maud Vavasour by the

---

[1] M. Michel, the French editor of the MS. in the Br. Mus., is in error, when he identifies the subject of the memoirs with the Justiciary drowned, who in that case would have been 100 years old.—V. Hist. de Foulkes FitzWarin, Paris, 1840.
Fulk FitzWarren the 1st married Hawyse de Dinan, in Wales.
Fulk the 2nd, surnamed le Prudhomme, m. 1. Maud, daughter of Robert Vavasour; 2. Clarice de Auberville.
Fulk the 3rd, drowned at Lewes.— V. Inquis. p. mort. 1° Edw. I. [and Calend. Geneal. I. p. 203].

Archbishop Hubert Walter (1193-1205), an old fellow-crusader, who wished thus to rescue his brother's widow from the persecutions of John. When hemmed in on one occasion by his enemies, who cried out, "Now lords, all at Fulk," (Ore, Seigneurs, tous à Foulk), he answered them boldly by "Yes, and Fulk at all" (certes et Fulk à tous). After gaining distinctions in tournaments at Paris, he turned pirate, and had a singular discussion with Mador, an old sailor, on the comparative merits of dying at sea or in bed; the knight, having learnt that the sailor's forefathers for four generations had been drowned, remarked, "Surely you must be very foolish to dare go on the sea." Mador, however, on questioning the knight, and learning that his ancestors had all died in their beds, was enabled to retort, "Surely, Sir, I wonder then that you dare enter any bed." Landing on a Scotch island, he played at chess with a chief there, until a quarrel arose during the game, at which indeed he seems to have been unable to keep his temper; in the fight which ensued, he possessed himself of a hauberk, which he continued ever after to prize highly. After a marvellous adventure with a dragon near Carthage, and other feats at Tunis, he prowled about Windsor forest until he took King John prisoner, and finally extorted pardon and restoration of his property. He then settled down quietly in the country, founded the priory of Alberbury[1], in Shropshire, and after some years of blindness and decay, was buried there with his two wives[2]. Whatever degree of fiction may be mixed up with the story of his life, it is probably no inapt representative of the main features of many a baron of that period.

The absence of the twenty bannerets, whom the King had left to garrison Tunbridge, must have been deeply re-

[1] It is referred to as an existing foundation in 1233 (Cart. 17° H. III.), and was afterwards given, as being an alien couvent, to All Souls' College, which still retains it. The seat of the Fitz Warrens was Whittington Castle, Shropshire, a gateway and some towers of which remain.—See Arch. Journ. XII. 398.

[2] How M. Michel could prolong his life, and restore his sight, in order to drown him at Lewes, if he read his own book, is difficult to imagine.

gretted by him on the eve of a battle, and though the list of his friends at Lewes comprises some noble and many honourable names (besides those whom historians may not have pointed out to us), yet it is obvious that very few of the great barons of the kingdom were on his side. It was, indeed, as it has been popularly called, the Barons' War—for nearly all the strength of that class was embodied in de Montfort's army.

It must have been to supply this deficiency that the royal numbers were swelled by so many powerful Scotch chieftains, specially summoned as lieges of the crown, whom the Scotch King, Henry's son-in-law, had willingly despatched to assist the court in its distress. Of the competitors for the crown of Scotland a few years later, two in person, and the immediate ancestor of another, were now doing suit and service to the King of England at Lewes. [The son of] one of these great claimants, John Comyn[1], of Badenagh, was destined hereafter to become the prisoner of one of his [father's] present comrades, de Warenne, and the murdered victim of the grandson of another, Robert Brus[2].

John Baliol[3], Lord of Galloway, after being governor of Carlisle, had exercised so paramount a control for two years over the youthful King Alexander III., and his bride Margaret, daughter of Henry III., that he was obliged to pur-

[1] From Comine, a Norman family. "Gules, three garbs within a double tressure, or." John Comyn, the younger, was made prisoner at Dunbar, by de Warenne, and murdered by Brus, at Dumfries. He married Joan, daughter of W. de Valence.

[2] Robert de Brus was a lawyer, and sat as a Judge in Westminster in 1250. He married Isabella, daughter of Earl of Gloucester, and in 1268 became Chief Justice till the death of Henry III. He was buried at Guisborough, in Yorkshire, in 1295.

[3] Bailleul was the original Norman name. He was Baron of Biwell, in Northumberland, and died 1269.

"Or, an orle gules."—Carlav. From Guy Baliol, who had received the original grant of Bywell, descended Barnard, his son, who built Barnard's Castle on the R. Tees.
Guy.
|
Barnard.
|
Barnard took prisoner K. William of Scotland.
|
Hugh, sided with K. John.
|
John, succeeded 1278.
"Joune baniere avoit el champ Al rouge escu voidie du champ."— Carlav.

chase pardon by the payment of a considerable fine. He had already obeyed the summons of the English crown, to which he was liable, as holding thirty knights' fees, by serving against the Welsh, but on his refusal to acknowledge the authority of the Oxford Statutes, he had brought down confiscation upon his estates, the removal of which he had sent his son to negotiate. The personal intimacy, formed during the present campaign, may have influenced the subsequent alliances of his family; of his sons, who probably were with him at Lewes, the eldest, Hugh, married Anne, daughter of William de Valence, and the son of Alexander the younger, was the celebrated John Baliol, who was for a short period King of Scotland, and who married Isabella, the daughter of the Earl de Warenne.

Ambition not having yet severed the Baliol and the Bruce, their rival names were here linked to the same cause; —the prospect of a crown had not yet dawned upon them to create those feuds and strifes which so long convulsed two countries, united by nature within the same sea-girt bound; struggles within so narrow a sphere, that their Italian contemporary looked upon them with great contempt, as those of distant barbarians, forgetting for the moment the constant turmoil of almost every city in Italy at the time.

> " Lì si vedrà la superbia ch'asseta,
> Che fa lo Scotto e l'Inghilese folle,
> Sì che non può soffrir dentro a sua meta."—
>
> Dante, *Par.* xix. 121.

The services of the Norman ancestor of Robert Bruce had been rewarded by the Conqueror with lands, and the present Lord of Annandale, whose mother was the heiress, in whose right the crown was subsequently claimed, held ten knights' fees in England: from this lineage were the Stuarts descended. Robert's wife was Isabella, aunt to the young Earl of Gloucester, in the hostile camp: the treacherous murder [of the son] of his present fellow-soldier Comyn, by his grandson, cast a deep stain on his family in after-times.

VIII.] NEGOTIATIONS WITH THE ROYALISTS AT LEWES. 159

Reinforced with these succours from the hardy North, the royal army had the advantage of numbers[1] over the enemy, in addition to the King's authority being with them—always an important element of strength in an old monarchy. "Is not the King's name 40,000 names[2]?" Their haughty confidence in this superiority little inclined the chiefs to give much heed to the pacific embassy, which the two bishops were now bearing to them. When admitted into their presence in the great refectory[3] of the priory, which still retains some evidence of its former extent, they delivered their proposals.

Besides tendering compensation for damages, they reported de Montfort's offer to "abide by the decision of select churchmen, competent by their wisdom and sound theology, to determine what statutes should remain in force, and how far their previous oaths should be binding, the barons wishing by this device to keep their faith as Christians, and avoid the stain of perjury."

A violent clamour immediately arose on the statement of these terms to the assembled kings and royalists:—

"Vox in altum tollitur turbæ tumidorum	Then rose on high their haughty cry,
En jam miles subitur dictis clericorum	Shall churchman's word rule soldier's sword?
Viluit militia clericis subjecta[4]."	Knighthood's debased, 'neath priest low laid.

The very proffer to warriors of a peace, which appeared to make them subordinate to the clergy, was deemed an insult, and Prince Edward impetuously burst out: "They shall have no peace whatever, unless they put halters round their necks, and surrender themselves for us to hang them up or drag them down, as we please[5]." The bishops could

[1] "Rex quidem Angliæ confidens in multitudine complicum suorum, et paucitatem partis adversæ habens contemptui, æstimans eos adversus ipsum nihil ausuros."—T. Wyke.
[2] Rich. II., iii. 2.
[3] Its position is remarkable, as having a running stream beneath its floor. It has been used as a malt-house.
[4] Polit. S.
[5] "Edwardusque dicitur ita respondisse:
Pax illis præcluditur, nisi laqueis se

readily understand the temper of the party, when they heard their offers thus treated, and the formal answer given to them breathed the same scorn and defiance in the following letter[1]:—

"**Henry**, by the grace of God, King of England, Lord of Ireland, Duke of Aquitaine, to Simon de Montfort, Gilbert de Clare, and their accomplices;

"Since it manifestly appears by the war and general disturbance already raised by you in our kingdom, and also by conflagrations and other outrageous damages, that you do not observe your allegiance to us, nor have any regard to the security of our person, inasmuch as you have lawlessly oppressed those barons and others our lieges, who adhere with constancy to their truth towards us, and since you purpose, as you signify to us by your letters, to harass them as far as lies in your power,

"We, considering their grievance as our own, and their enemies as ours, more especially seeing that our aforesaid lieges, in observance of their truth, manfully assist us against your faithlessness;

"We, therefore, value not your faith or love, and defy you, as their enemies. Witness myself, at Lewes, on May the thirteenth, in the 48th year of our reign[2]."

Collis omnes alligent, et ad suspendendum
Semet nobis obligent, vel ad detrahendum."
* * * * * *
" Comitis devotio sero deridetur,
Cujus cras congressio victrix sentietur."—Pol. S., v. 249.

The last line proves the meeting and the royal answer to have occurred on May 13, the day before the battle. "His literis coram Rege lectis et intellectis, rex cum ingenti indignatione Baronibus sub hac forma rescripsit."— Chr. Wigorn. " Barones exulati et facultatibus nudati aut vincere cupiunt aut vinci. Regales vero, tam alienigenarum quam indigenarum copiositate con-

fisi, hos vero tanquam seductores aut *scismaticos* de terra tollere temptant. Salomone vero dicente quod bellum cum dispositionibus ut non tam de periculo capitis agitur quantum et animæ."—Chr. Lanercost.

[1] "Epistolam Baronum suorum contemnens Rex ad bellum totis affectibus exardescit, ac talem eis diffidationis responsalem misit."—Chr. Roff. MS.

[2] Rymer. Lib. de Ant. Leg. Chr. Dover. W. Rish. The original letters are in Latin. The date of May 12 appears in W. Rish, and another chronicle, but the barons' letter being dated with so much detail, "on the first Tuesday after S. Pancras," whose feast was Monday, May 12,

The King of the Romans was at this time full of resentment at the recent plunder of his private property, the loss of which naturally touched his parsimonious feelings; and, being extremely proud of his dignity, the disrespect they had presumed to show him excited his indignation. He had discouraged the King therefore from listening to any compromise, as he might otherwise have done[1]; and, in concert with Prince Edward and the other leaders, he now added another letter of haughty and uncourteous import to the refusal:—

"Richard, by the grace of God, King of the Romans, always august, and Edward, the first-born son of the illustrious King of England, and all the other barons and knights who firmly adhere to the said King of England, with sincere faith and force, to Simon de Montfort, Gilbert de Clare, and to all and each of the other accomplices in their treason;

"We have understood, by the letters you have sent to our Lord the illustrious King of England, that we are defied by you, although indeed this verbal defiance had been proved before by hostilities against us, by the burning of our goods, and the ravage of our possessions.

"We therefore let you know that you are all defied as public enemies by each and all of us your enemies, and that henceforth, whenever occasion offers, we will, with all our might, labour to damage your persons and property; and as to that which you falsely charge us with, that the advice we give the King is neither faithful nor good, you in no wise speak the truth; and if you Lord Simon de Montfort, or you Gilbert de Clare, are willing to assert the same in the court of our Lord the King, we are ready to procure you a safe-conduct to come to the said court, and to declare the truth of our innocence, and the lying of each of you as perfidious traitors, by some one our equal in nobility and birth. We

and the King's letter being evidently an answer to it, the proper date must be May 13.
[1] W. Rish. De Bell. Lew.

M

are all content with the seals of the said lords, the King of the Romans, and the Lord Edward. Dated at Lewes, 13th day of May, in the 48th year of King Henry, son of John."

This war of words was an apt prelude to the fiercer conflict approaching. The confidence of the royal party in their superior strength[1], now led the King "by rash advice[2]," to look only to the stern diplomacy of arms, rather than to the struggle of subtlety in a chamber. "The mutual contract of support and fidelity, which was the essential principle of feudal tenure[3]," was thus avowedly annulled and renounced by both parties. In the history of Fitz-Warren, before referred to, a similar renunciation of homage is thus detailed: "My Lord King, you are my liege Lord, and to you I have been bound by fealty, while I have been in your service, and while I held lands of you, and you ought to have maintained my right, and yet now you fail me in right and in common law, and never was there a good King who denied law in his court to his frank tenants; wherefore I renounce my homage to you[4]."

The bonds of social union being thus abruptly broken, the great questions of civil government now in dispute, all important as they were, were abandoned to the chance decision of force—a wayward arbiter between right and wrong; often indeed resorted to at once in such cases, without even the attempt, as in this instance, to find other means better adapted to the dignity of human reason.

---

[1] With the King were "60,000 pugnatorum et ad bella discretorum. Barones cum civibus Londinensibus 40,000 pugnatorum, *non tam ad pugnam discretorum.*"—Chr. Wigorn.

[2] "Rex minus sano fretus consilio."—T. Wyke.

[3] Hallam, Mid. Ages.

[4] Hist. de Foulques FitzWarin. "Pur quoi je vus renk vos hommages." In a similar manner the Abbot of Arbroath brought to K. Edward in 1297 at Berwick the formal renunciation of homage of the Scots who had sworn fealty, including Balliol's.

CHAPTER IX.

THE MARCH UPON LEWES.

> " An if we live, we live to tread on kings,
> If die, brave death, when princes die with us!
> Now for our consciences, the arms are fair,
> When the intent of bearing them is just."
> 1st Part HEN. IV. Act 5, Scene 2.

THE prelates returned to the camp of the barons at Fletching with the answer to their pacific mission, and on the same evening (Tuesday, May 13,) proclaimed at once to the expecting warriors that there remained no hope of peace to the church, or liberty to the state, unless won by the sword.

> " The Barons ne couthe other red, tho hii hurde this,
> Bote bidde Godes grace, and bataile abide iwis[1]."—ROB. GLOUC.

While nothing could be more impressive than the conduct of these bishops, a noble solemnity of purpose, combined with a vigour of action fitted to the emergency, was displayed by Simon de Montfort and his soldiers. A royalist chronicler[2], while calling the war monstrous and detestable, bears testimony to the barons "as having among them all but one faith, one will in all things, one love towards God and their neighbour; and so unanimous in brotherly affection,

---

[1] " The barons certainly could resolve on nothing else, when they heard this, but pray for the grace of God, and abide the battle." "His literis Barones graviter animo vulnerabantur."—Chr. Wigorn.
[2] Mat. Westm.

that they feared neither to offend the King, nor even to die for the sake of justice, rather than violate their oaths."

For the battle now acknowledged to be inevitable, the Earl of Leicester passed the whole night in anxious preparations, but did not omit amidst all his cares that prayer and attendance on religious services, which was remarked as his constant custom. He exhorted all his followers to repent and confess their sins, and the Bishop of Worcester[1] did not shrink from bestowing his episcopal absolution on the kneeling soldiers, or from promising admission into heaven to all who might now die fighting manfully for justice. One account[2], indeed, goes so far as to describe the bishop as now "putting off the peaceful priest, and putting on the warlike soldier, carrying a sword by his side instead of the crosier, and a helmet on his head instead of a mitre;" but these are probably figurative expressions to denote his zeal and courage in the cause. Cantilupe was not neglectful of the duties of a churchman, as then understood; he completed and endowed, in 1265, a chapel for four priests in his cathedral, and though his tomb lies there neglected near the screen of the choir, it is interesting to think that his mantle was caught and transmitted by some of the boldest defenders of civil and religious liberty; Latimer, Hooper, and Hough were worthy to follow him in the see.

After this solemn scene, they all put a white cross upon their dress[3], in token of the religious sanction stamped upon their efforts, and in order to recognize each other in the combat. A white cross had been always adopted in a like spirit by the English crusaders, in distinction from the red cross of the French; but there was, unhappily, a stronger necessity for such outward marks of party in the battle of

---

[1] Mat. Westm. erroneously ascribes this to the Bishop of Chichester. "Notable episcopal divinity to encourage rebels to fight against their king."—Prynne, Vol. II. 1022.

[2] Chr. Mailr.

[3] According to the chronicle of Lanercost, both the fronts and backs of the barons were marked by crosses.

IX.] THE MARCH UPON LEWES. 165

Lewes, where on each side the same banners and ensigns were to be raised by hostile members of the same families— a sad but ever-recurring calamity in civil war[1].

Although de Montfort has been reproached by a modern historian[2] as a religious hypocrite, there is no proof whatever of such a charge, nor was it ever made in his life-time; and there must have been much sincerity and consciousness of right to have admitted such a consecration of the war. Even had the great leader been justly liable to the accusation, his single example could not have so infected at once the bishop and the many thousand soldiers with the same vice, as to induce them thus to kneel in blasphemous mockery at so awful a moment of peril and enterprise.

Although the distance from Lewes did not admit of "each battle seeing the other's umbered face," yet, to 'this night-scene of solemn energy while "armourers were accomplishing the knights," and the soldiers were "inly ruminating the morning's danger," a striking contrast might be drawn in the unguardedness of the royalist camp, where more provision had been made for dissolute riot than for watching the enemy. We learn, on the authority of an eye-witness[3], that the song, the dance, and the wine-cup

[1] Henry III. had adopted the same white cross at the great battle of Lincoln, in 1217, the legate Gualo wishing to stamp the war with a religious feeling.—Chr. Mailr.

[2] Hume. Lingard says, "It was the peculiar talent of this leader to persuade his followers that the cause in which they fought was the cause of Heaven."

[3] "Protestante mihi uno nobili qui ibi fuerat." "Pars vero adversa negligentius agens noctem illam coreis et cantilenis occupans, potationibus et scortacionibus insistebat, adeo ut cœnobio solemni S. Pancratii Martyris non parcerent, quin coram altaribus sacris obscœna cum meretricibus cubilia fecerunt." Again in the flight after the battle, "tam viri quidem fugientes quam miserrimæ meretrices locatores sequentes."—Chr. Lanerc. "Quod tot fornicarias fœtidi lenones Ad se convocaverant, usque septingentas."—V. 152.

"Qui carnis luxuria fœda sorduerunt, Factis lupanaribus robur minuerunt Unde militaribus indigni fuerunt." —V. 164 Polit. S. from MS. Harl. 978.

Roger le Bigot, the marshal, was with the barons, and his absence may have contributed to the disordered licence in the Royal camp. Some of his duties are described in Rubro Libro de Scaccario Regis, f. 30.

"Doit apaisier les noises, et visiter tous ceulœ qui couchent font en la salle et per la verge douze leughes dehors d'environ, des choses qui appendent à la verge et la couronne.

made the priory of St Pancras, on that night, the scene of boisterous revelry. Neither the precincts of the church, nor even the very altars, were free from the profanation of their vices[1]. Among the armed inmates of the convent, buoyant with the excitement of the morning's discussions and surrounded by their wanton followers, no thought was allowed to intrude of the morrow's dangers, or of that eternity about to open upon so many of them in a few hours. The baronial and royalist parties, on the eve of battle, rise up before us as distinct in manners as the Cavaliers and Roundheads of later times.

After his cause had been so impressively sanctified, Simon de Montfort had to fulfil all the duties of a general, imposed upon him by the esteem of his friends and the confidence of his troops—a great and serious trust, but one congenial to his nature. The eloquent terms which have been applied to another founder of a free constitution might well describe him at this hour of decision : "What he loved in war, far above the heat of battle, was the great effort of intellect and will, armed with power to achieve some grand design, the mighty mixture of agency and fortune, which seizes and transports the highest as well as the humblest minds[2]." To de Montfort the approaching contest

---

Et si nul fait homage au Roy a camps armes à cheval, le Marescal avera le cheval et les armes.

Il gardera tous les huis ("doors," whence "huissier") ou le Roy conseille, fors huys de la chambre le Roy.

Et doit faire crier le baan de Roy as villes, ou le Roy doit gesir et à 12 leughes d'environ.

Et si soloit estre que le Marescal devoit avoir douze demoisellez à la Court le Roy, qui devioient faire seirement à son Bacheler qu'elles ne sauveroient aultres putains à la Court qu'elles memes, ne Ribaudes sans avowerie de assre; ne laron ne mesel qu'elles ne le monstreront au Marescal; et il doit pourveoir la Court de tout.—Spelman, in v. Marescallus.

[1] Compare Chron. Jocelin. p. 40.
[2] Washington, by Guizot. It is very probable that the ancestor of *General Washington* was present with the barons at the battle of Lewes. In the list of knights from Durham in the Boldon Buke (v. MS. note, p. 170) the 59th name is "Walter de Weshyngton à Weshyngton." In Bishop Pudsey's portion of the Boldon Buke (1183) William de Hertburn held the whole vill of Washyngton (in the deanery of Chester, south of Jarrow) except the church and churchlands, by free rent of £4 and by the service of attending the bishop's great hunt with two greyhounds, having exchanged his lands at Hertburn with the bishop. He or his

must have seemed, not a mere field to display his talents as a soldier, but a fearful throw on which the freedom and happiness of a whole nation were staked, and well fitted was he to "stand the hazard of the die." The rough verses[1] of the age thus fondly dwell upon his name and qualities:—

"Il est apelé de Montfort,	True to his name is he called de
Il est el Mond, et si est fort,	Montfort,
Si ad grand chevalerie,	Lofty and strong as a Mount and a
Ce voir et je m'acort,	Fort,
Il eime dreit, et het le tort,	A knight of mighty chivalry.
Si avera la mestrie.	I vouch it true and clear as light,
El Mond est veréement,	He hates the wrong and loves the right,
Là ou la comun a ly concent,	So shall he gain the mastery.
De la terre loée;	Truly the Mount of refuge he,
C'est ly Quens de Leycestre	To which the willing people flee,
Que bout et joius se puet estre	Extolled by all the land.
De cele renomée."	Of such a goodly name and fame
	The Earl of Leicester well may claim,
	Joyous and proud to stand.'

A less friendly hand[2] represents him at this time as "raising his horns of pride, devising great things, and pondering on sublimities." Proud indeed, he might justly feel, if in his loftiest visions he caught a shadowy glimpse of the future destinies of the people, in whose cause he was about to fight, if he could have foreseen that from his personal efforts there would ultimately arise a vital energy, by which the expanding form of English freedom would cast off the slough of ignorance, bigotry, and servility, until with unbounded power and dominion, physical and intellectual, the nation should present to the world a fresh model of happy government as yet unknown.

descendants assumed the local name of Washington in consequence. Wᵐ. de Washington appears as a witness to a charter of Bishop Stichill (1260-1274). In Bishop Hatfield's survey (1345-1381), "Wᵐ. de Wessyngton miles tenet maner: et villam de Wessyngton per servic: forin: redd: 1111 li:" The direct male line ended about 1400, but from younger branches of the family were probably descended the Washingtons of Aldwicke Street, co. York, whose pedigree is given by Dugdale (1666); and the Washingtons of Leicestershire, the ancestors of the American General.—V. Hutchinson's Durham, Vol. II. p. 489.— Surtees' Durham, Vol. II. p. 40.— Arms, arg. 2 bars and 3 mullets in chief gules.

[1] Polit. S. from MS. 13th century.
[2] T. Wyke.

Nearly fifty years had elapsed since English armies had met in open field on their own soil. Although the royal prerogative had been frequently resisted by denials of supply, by threats of war, and by actual restraint, yet the King's person had never, during that interval, been exposed to hostile attack. On the last occasion, at Lincoln, many chiefs, in disgust at King John's misgovernment, had adopted the dangerous expedient of supporting the pretensions of a foreign prince, but there was now no thought of such treason: the confidence of the barons was in their own strength, and though the conduct of the court had excited their indignation, yet respect to the King's person was not forgotten. No change of dynasty was aimed at: they renounced their allegiance to a misguided sovereign, but were ready to resume it when he should be again in a fit state to receive it.

In deference to the punctilious feelings of chivalry, which required a leader to be at least an equal, if not a superior in rank—a point of honour which no knight, however lavish of his life, would have surrendered—Simon de Montfort was careful to confer[1] knighthood on many of the young nobles of his army:—

"Hii hovede under boskes and new Knights made,
And armed and attired hom, and hor bedes gerne bade[2]."

ROB. GLOUC.

The belt and sword of knighthood could, at this time, be bestowed by any prince[3], bishop, or knight; and among

---

[1] W. Heming. makes this take place on the descent from the hill to Lewes, but the eve of the battle is more probably stated by others:—
"Comitis militia plurima novella
In armis novitia, parum novit bella.
Nunc accinctus gladio tener adolescens,
Mane stat in prœlio armis assuescens."—Polit.S.fromMS.Harl.978.

[2] "They hovered under woods, and made new knights, and armed them, and equipped them, and earnestly said their prayers."

[3] Even abbots, until 1102, exercised the privilege. Hereward had been knighted by the Abbot of Peterborough, previous to an intended attack, in order to command others. The new knight was required to be a freeman, but there was no limit as to age, and, like the Hungarian nobles

those thus enabled to command others, was Gilbert, the young Earl of Gloucester[1], surnamed Rufus, next to de Montfort the most important chief of the party. Two others also are mentioned, as now for the first time invested with the knightly belt—Robert de Vere, a young noble of twenty-three years, who had lately succeeded, as Earl of Oxford, to the hereditary possessions gained by his Norman ancestors, and to the principles which had led his father to oppose the arbitrary pretensions of the Pope and the King on all occasions. On his being taken prisoner at a later period of the war, his estates were confiscated, and he was glad to take advantage of the Kenilworth decree to recover them[2]. John de Burgh also now first made his public appearance, probably eager to resent the insults put upon his family[3].

Though the vigil of knighthood was usually passed in churches, on this occasion the busy camp was the necessary substitute; for a plan seems to have been contemplated of a night attack upon Lewes, which was, however, abandoned in favour of a more open one by daylight[4].

Before sunrise, accordingly, on the morning of Wednesday, May 14[5], the whole army of the barons was in motion

to this day, he was freed from all taxes by Henry I. Degradation was effected by taking away the belt.—V. Henry's Hist.

[1] "Rufus erat et pulcher aspectu."—Chr. Tewks. MS. Cotton. Cleop. C. III. f. 220, in Dugd. Monast. II. 61. Arms, de Clare, or, 3 chevrons gules.

[2] He died 1296; his daughter married William de Warenne.—Walt. Hem. Dugd. Bar. "Veer, quarterly or and gules, a mullet argent, bordure endente sable."—Rolls of Arms. [Robert de Vere, when Earl of Oxford, would hardly have borne his arms within a bordure. W. S. W.]

[3] Robert de Grenequer and Henry de Hastings were also among the knights made on this occasion.—Chr. Gervasii Monachi, Cantuar. Leland Coll. I.

[4] "Non de nocte subito surripit latenter,
Immo die redito pugnat evidenter."—Pol.S.from MS.Harl.978.

[5] The exact day is so variously indicated by authors as to cause some confusion. Stow names May 12; Lib. de Ant. Leg., Mat. Westm., and Rastell's Chr., May 23; but the greater number of authorities fix it on Wednesday May 14, as the feast of S. Victor, or S. Boniface, or the Wednesday after S. Pancras, or the Wednesday before S. Dunstan (May 19), or the day before the Ides of May; all different modes of marking May 14. —V. T. Wyke, MS. Harl. 978, Chr. Petrob. Chr. Wigorn.[Chr.Dunstaple], and others. "The fourtend day of May the batail of Leaus was."—Rob. Brune.

towards the town, about nine miles distant. A dense forest[1] occupied most of the country through which this march was to be conducted, but such exact orders had been issued by de Montfort to each banneret, how to direct his own forces and to meet at the appointed spot, that all parts of this military movement were combined with a regularity quite novel in England. After an encampment for several days on the lordship of William Bardolf, now at Lewes with the King, intelligence of this march could readily have been conveyed to their lord from Fletching, if there had been any hearty good will[2] in his tenants towards the cause he had lately adopted; and the same remark will also apply to the possessions of de Warenne at Newick and Hamsey, through which they necessarily passed to reach the foot of the Southdowns. No alarm, however, was given, and when about two miles from Lewes, the barons, continuing unobserved, ascended the great ridge of hills, probably up the hollow valley called the Combe, where the projecting shoulder of the Downs would cover their march from the town.

Though the King did not consider the barons to be so near, or bold enough to attack his superior force, he had, on the Tuesday, stationed a watch of several armed men upon the summit of the hill, in advance of his camp, to look out for the baronial troops. So lax, however, was the discipline, or so small the expectation of present danger, that the appointed sentinels, growing tired of their duty towards

[1] "Edicitur publice quatinus ante solis ortum ereptis armis exeant de boscis ubi magna pars exercitus pernoctabat, et conveniant extra villam de Flexinge, quæ distat de Lewes per sex milliaria."—W. Rish. de Bello Lew. The real distance is about nine miles.

[2] A letter of Neville, the fifth Earl of Westmoreland, 1557, well expresses the natural bond of tenants and landlord, when he desires that it may be so arranged in the distribution of troops, "that every man of worshipe may have the conduction and guyding of his owne friends and tenants, as I think the herts of the people is suche, that they will sooner be perswaded by their own natural lords and masters, and more willinglie serve under them for love, than with strangers for money."—Coll. Herald. Sentiments worthy of the family, whose standard boasted "a tenir promesse vient de noblesse."

morning, returned into Lewes, and abandoned their post to the vigilance of a single man, and he, naturally enough, when left to himself, had fallen asleep. In this condition he was found by the advancing soldiers of de Montfort, and compelled by fear to give all the information in his power as to the royal force[1]. Having thus gained the crest of the hill, their orderly march was continued with such caution, that the foremost troops nearly reached the town before any alarm was given.

It happened that the preceding evening the King had commanded some foragers to be sent in search of fresh supplies of hay and corn, a great scarcity of which was felt at Lewes[2]. These men, on leaving the town early in the morning, were now intercepted by the van of the barons. Though several were killed in the skirmish, yet the hurried flight and the return of the others was sufficient at once to arouse the royal party to a sense of their imminent danger.

The main army of the barons in the meanwhile continued to advance along the ridge of the Downs, until they came within sight of the bell-tower[3] of the Priory, when Simon de Montfort, dismounting from his horse, as did the other chiefs, once more addressed them and his soldiers: " O my beloved comrades and followers, we are about to enter upon a war to day for the sake of the government of the kingdom, to the honour of God, of the blessed Mary, of all the Saints, and of our mother Church, and at the same time for the observance of our faith. Let us pray to the King of all, that if what we now undertake pleases Him, He would grant us vigour and help, so that we may exhibit a grateful service by our knightly belt, overpowering the malice of all enemies. If we are His, to Him we commend our body and soul." This appeal was answered in a similar spirit, all falling prostrate

[1] Oxenede's Chr.
[2] W. Heming. H. Knight.
[3] "Cum accessissent ad montis descensum, qui est juxta Lewes, intuentes cænobii campanarium, descendit de dextrario." — Oxenede's Chr. [For a minute determination of the site of the battle, see Appendix A.]

on the turf, and imitating the form of a cross with their outstretched arms: "Grant us, O Lord (they exclaimed), our desire, with mighty victory, to the honour of Your name[1]."

On rising from this act of devotion, de Montfort proceeded to take up his position, and distribute his forces with his usual skill. While his flanks were defended by abrupt, almost precipitous ground on either side, a gradual slope of more than a mile in his front enabled him to overlook all the approaches of Lewes, and to observe in security the movements of his enemy. The town was greatly protected on the north, the east, and partly on the south by the windings of the river Ouse, up the course of which the waters of the sea were then allowed to flow freely, and to spread widely over the adjoining country at every tide[2]. This was, however, no impediment to the attack of de Montfort from his favourable position on the west of the town. A pious writer of the time, anxiously ascribes the advantage[3] of the ground to the King's party, in order to make more evident the assistance of Heaven in winning the victory; but this assumption is not consistent with the locality, unless it may refer to the strength of Lewes and other castles in Sussex being in the hands of the royalists.

A singular expedient was employed to deceive the enemy, which, though apparently trivial, proved, in the sequel, of considerable advantage. The accident has been already mentioned, which befell Simon de Montfort a few months before, when on his route to Amiens, by the stumbling of his horse[4],

[1] Oxenede's Chr. W. Rish. says: "Oratione pariter et admonitione persuasoriâ a duce eorum factâ."
[2] Doomsday represents the burgesses of Lewes supplying 16,000 herrings, and the salt-pans extended as far inland as Ripe. According to the same authority, rent was paid at other places in eels, herrings and salmon, and a manor in Essex paid the lord what is termed "Herring-silver."—Placit. Henry III. The small hills, now surrounded by meadows, near the Priory, were described as islands in the charters of the first and sixth Earls of Warenne, and at the surrender to Henry VIII. the Priory owned 2000 acres under water. — Horsefield's Lewes. Dugd. Mon.
[3] "Sic et locus hostibus fuit opportunus,
Ut hinc constet omnibus esse Dei munus."—V. 375, Polit. S. from MS. Harl. 978.
[4] Chr. Dunst.

and though he had quickly recovered from his lameness after his forced return to Kenilworth, he had used occasionally, while yet weak, a carriage which he had caused to be built for him in London. This vehicle, after having been for some days purposely employed for his own conveyance, so as to give the enemy reason to suppose him still disabled, was brought on the field of battle:—

> "The Erle did mak a chare at London thrugh gilery,
> Himself therin suld fare, and seke be wend to ly[1].—ROB. BRUNE.

It is not easy to determine the nature of the vehicle used by de Montfort on this occasion, as there is much obscurity on the earlier form of carriages in England. There was a "chær" used for the conveyance of distinguished persons in Anglo-Saxon times, which appears to have been a four-wheeled car, with a hammock slung on hooks between two poles, and occasionally carried four persons[2]. A royal officer is recognized in Doomsday as providing carriages for the King. At a later period there was an ornamental covered carriage, without springs[3], on two wheels, the form of which would admit of the addition of grating to the apertures, so as to resemble de Montfort's car. As nothing on wheels, however, could well have accompanied the march across the rough tract of forest to the Southdowns, or could be supposed to give ease to an invalid, it was more probably a species of

---

[1] "The earl had a car made at London through deceit, for himself to be carried in, and be considered to lie therein sick."—W. Rish. de Bello Lew.

[2] V. Strutt's Dresses. J. H. Markland in Archæol. v. 20, from MS. Cott. Claud. B. IV. of the eleventh century. At p. 37 of MS. are four such cars, with four persons within each.

[3] The body of William Rufus was carried in a "rheda caballaria"— W. Malms., or "lectica equestris"— —Mat. Westm. (Abbas Hugo æger) "reportatus est ad nos in feretro equitario." "Abbas dicebat, quod si oporteret eum feretro equitatorio portari, non remaneret."—Chr. Jocelin, pp. 5, 70. K. John is described by Mat. Par. as carrying about his prisoners, including Hugh de Brun, in carts in a novel manner, "vehiculis bigarum novo genere equitandi et inusitato." Such vehicles were only used by persons of dignity, and Philip le Bel, in 1294, passed a sumptuary law, restricting their use to such, "premierement nulle bourgeau náura char."—V. Archæol. Vol. xx. pl. 17, from MS. of Roman du Roy Meliadus, of the fourteenth century, formerly in Roxburgho Collection.

litter[1], borne between two horses, a conveyance which remained in use long afterwards on state occasions, for women, or for sick persons. The iron grating, which constituted its framework, served the purpose of a cage, with a door of entrance; and in this were shut up some unhappy Londoners, who had opposed Simon de Montfort and their fellow-citizens, on the day of his forcible entry across London Bridge, in the preceding autumn. These prisoners, Augustine de Hadestock, Richard Pycard, and Stephen de Chelmareford[2], were old men of considerable importance in the city.

This car, with his baggage, was purposely stationed by de Montfort on a conspicuous point of the hill, and was left surrounded by his own standard and pennons, with a competent guard under the charge of William de Blund[3], a gallant young warrior, who had been a party to the arbitration of the French King, and was attached to the service of de Montfort. The tents and baggage of the other barons were also arranged on the hill[4].

As the general use of armorial ensigns had not been established before the Crusaders, their first appearance dur-

[1] In Johnes' Monstrelet, pl. 7, the Queen of Francis I. makes her entry into Toulouse in a litter lashed on the back of two horses. Evelyn travelled in a litter from Bath to Wotton, in 1640, with his sick father. —V. Diary, I. 9. In 1680, when the wounded General Skippon was thus conveyed, "the horse-litter, borne between two horses, tossed the major-general like a dog in a blanket." —Harl. Misc.

[2] Authors differ as to the number of these prisoners. T. Wyke names the three as above, and calls the car a quadriga; W. de Heming puts two Londoners in the "currus, quem fieri fecit comes ad equitandum." H. Knighton also has two men, and describes the "currum quasi falcatum in quo equitaret ac si esset ægrotus, cum esset bellator robustus et fortis." Chr. Mailros speaks of "duos inclytos Londinenses senes," describing, also, the car as "currum subdolum quem foris fecit ferro per totum contegi—currus habebat quendam angustum egressum:—vas dolositatis—vas perfidum—vas inexpugnabile." W. Rish. and Mat. Westm. have four prisoners. Some houses in Queenhithe, forfeited by Simon de Hadestock, late citizen of London, were granted to Ottoninus de Graunam by Letters Patent, Westm., Oct. 15, 1265.—462 Chanc. Rec. 5th Rep. Simon was, in 1266, elected by the citizens as sheriff, but the Barons of the Exchequer refused to swear him into office.—Ant. Leg.

[3] He was related to the de Veres by his mother, and on his death in the battle his sisters became his heirs. W. le Blunde held a manor in Essex, and five lands in Norfolk. —Cal. Inq. p. mort.

[4] "Barones tentoria sua et sarcinas locaverunt super montem."— Mat. Westm.

ing a great battle in England was probably on this occasion; and to a good soldier they must have been an efficient help in the marshalling and directing the movements of an army. The scene must have been an animating one at this moment, when the barons, each under his own banner[1], were preparing themselves and their horses, on the broad expanse of the Downs, for the approaching combat:—

"Lá ont meinte riche garnement	Rich caparisons were there,
Brodé sur cendeaus et samis[2],	Silks and satins broidered fair,
Meint beau penon en lance mis,	On lances fixed gay pennons see,
Meint banière desploié :	Many a banner flowing free ;
E loing ostoit la noise oie	To distant ears his eager cry
Des henissement des chevaux ;	The neighing war-horse sends on high;
Par tote estoient mouns et vauls	On every hill and vale around
Pleins de summers e de charroi	The sumpter beasts and carts abound;
Que la vitaile e la courroi	Arms, forage, victuals, scattered lay,
De tentes et de pavillons."—CARLAV.	With huts and tents in close array.

It was probably from the nature of the ground, which here branches off into three projecting points separated from each other by deep hollows, and all more or less advancing towards Lewes, that de Montfort now separated his forces into four divisions, over three of which he appointed eminent leaders, keeping the other under his own command in reserve.

On his left, towards the north, along a declivity, which ends close under the castle walls, were placed the Londoners— zealous, but undisciplined partisans, who eagerly claimed the honour of the foremost station; and Nicholas de Segrave[3] was, at his own request, made their leader. The chequered fortunes of his grandfather, exposed to the capricious favour and persecution of the King, did not deter his father, Gilbert,

---

[1] "Barones in plena planicie descendebant et equos cingentes arma præparabant."—W. Heming. The plain may be understood as the open slope of the Downs, not the level at their feet. "Barones erectis vexillis in declivitatem cujusdam montis quæ oppidum Lewense finitimâ a civitate disterminat."—T. Wyke.

[2] Cendeaus, cendal, a taffety or satin — samis, samit, silk Sarrasinesche, sarsnet or Persian, These were probably Asiatic goods imported from the great mart of Bruges.

[3] "Segrave, sable, lion rampant argent crowned or."—Rolls of Arms.

from faithfully serving his sovereign abroad, where indeed he sacrificed his life by a detention in an unwholesome prison by the French. Nicholas had himself served in the Gascon wars, but at home, both at Oxford and subsequently, had adhered to the barons with such zeal, as to earn a special excommunication from Archbishop Boniface. Being fortunate enough to escape, almost singly, from the general rout and capture at Northampton, he had sought refuge in London, and had gone from thence to share in the siege of Rochester. His recent intercouse had made him known and acceptable to the citizens now placed under his guidance. His mother, Amabil, was the wife of one of the royalist chiefs, Roger de Someri, and this alliance may have assisted him, after he had been wounded and taken prisoner at Evesham, in recovering his lands which had been granted away to Prince Edmund. Before his death, in 1295[1], he had accompanied Prince Edward on his crusade.

With him were associated, as bannerets, Harvey de Boreham[2] and Henry de Hastings[3].

No one was throughout more active against the King than the latter, an enmity which may have arisen from his having been ward to Guy de Lusignan—the great abuses to which such a connection was liable, often giving rise to future hatred. Although yet young, he had numbered two Welsh campaigns, and having since joined in the plunder of aliens, he stood an excommunicated man. His marriage with Joan de Cantilupe[4] only confirmed his natural inclinations for the cause he adopted, and his zeal continued unquenched by

---

[1] He left five sons, of whom John and Nicholas were at Carlaverock:—

" Nicolas de Segrave o li
  Ke Nature avoit embeli
De corps et enrichi de cuer
  Vaillant parc et qui jeta puer."

Nicholas de Segrave was there,
Whom nature had embellished fair
With grace of form and richest heart,
Bold knight, in whom fear had no part.

[2] W. Rish. de Bello Lew. Harvey de Boreham was a Justice of the Common Pleas, fin. lev. Sept. 3, 1265.

[3] Hastings, or a manche gules.

[4] She was sister to the sainted Bishop Thomas, and heir of another brother William, Lord of Bergavenny, which title was subsequently merged in that of Hastings.—Banks' Dorm. Bar.

disasters to the last. De Montfort when in power, having assigned some castles to his trust, he withstood all threats and promises after the defeat of Evesham, and held out Kenilworth in defiance long afterwards, even maiming the hand of a royal herald who came to summon its surrender. This act procured him a special exemption from pardon, and a sentence of seven years' imprisonment, though by Prince Edward's mediation he only suffered two. His forfeited estates were divided between his enemies, Roger de Clifford and Roger de Leybourne, who preferred their claim from their alliances with his two daughters[1].

The centre of the barons' army, which must have occupied that branch of the hill descending with an uninterrupted slope into the town, was led on by de Clare, so freshly girded with the soldier's belt, together with John Fitz-John[2] and William de Monchensy—able and experienced soldiers, whose wealth and rank increased their importance.

The baron Fitz-John was now about twenty-six years of age, and even before coming to his majority had married Margery, the daughter of his present opponent Philip de Basset. Although Fitzpiers, Earl of Essex, his immediate ancestor, had been high in the confidence of the King, Fitz-John justified the trust reposed in him by the barons during these wars by great ability and a desperate fidelity to their cause, even when it had become hopeless. He had been a principal party in the London riots, and was among those summoned to Parliament after the battle of Lewes. After holding Ludlow and some castles of the royalist de Mortimer

[1] Henry de Hastings died 1269. His arms in the North aisle of Westminster Abbey are "or, a maunch gules." His son John appeared in good repute at Carlaverock:

" Au fait de armes fiers et estous
En ostel douz et debonnaires."

Restless and proud on war's alarm, At home all courteous, meek, and calm. Having married Isabel, the sister and co-heir of Aymer de Valence, the earldom of Pembroke came into the family in 1339. The abeyance of this ancient barony of Hastings was determined in 1841, in favour of Sir Jacob Astley.

[2] "Johannes Filius Johannis in bello strenue pugnavit, et multas galeas conquassavit, et multos ad-versariis cepit et incarceravit."— Chr. Wigorn. Dugd. Bar. Arms of Fitz-John, " Quarterly or and gules, a bordure vairy."

in his custody, he was nearly the only man of note taken prisoner at Evesham after a stout defence, but he wilfully forbore to make his peace or compound for his estates, and when he died, 1276, his brother succeeded him.

His comrade, William de Monchensy[1], about thirty years of age, was another determined partisan. On succeeding, in 1255, to his father, one of the most noble, wealthy, and prudent warriors of his age, and who had married one of the great Pembroke heiresses, he had been for a brief period the ward of William de Valence, who had married his sister. This did not attract his affections to the court, and he attached himself without reserve to the baronial party. On his subsequent capture at Kenilworth, his lands were given to his brother-in-law, but on the last day allowed by the terms of grace, his mother produced him in court when in a state of great sickness, and so procured their restoration. Some years afterwards he was fighting in Wales under Edward I., and at the siege of Drossellan castle was, with many others, crushed by the fall of its towers. De Valence then claimed to possess himself for the third time of his estates; and tried, though in vain, to bastardize his only child Dionysia. She afterwards married her guardian Hugh de Vere.

The right wing was commanded by Henry the eldest, and Guy the third son of de Montfort. Henry, with his father's spirit and principles, shared also his public labours, and was a partner in his triumph, defeat, and death. Humphrey de Bohun the younger[2], already referred to as confronted with his own father in this civil strife, and John de Burgh were also in this part of the field. The latter, who was the grandson[3] of the ill-used guardian of the King, might well distrust

---

[1] Mont Cenis, pronounced Mont Chency by the Normans. His ancestor, Guerin de Mont Chency, had seized and kept possession of Keymes, in Cardigan Bay. "Or, three escutcheons barry vert and gules."— Rolls of Arms, Dugd. Bar.

[2] He died in 1265, after being made prisoner at Evesham.

[3] John de Burgh was also with the barons at Evesham: his lands were thereupon seized.—See Dugd. Bar. p. 700. He married Hawyse, daughter and heir of W. de Lanvaley, and

the policy and intrigues of a court by which his family had been raised to official power and then persecuted with savage insult.

One of the most powerful and steady adherents of the barons, in spite of his kindred with de Warenne, was Roger le Bigot, Earl of Norfolk, who held the office of Earl Marshal by cession from his mother in 1247[1]. His name appears in all the deeds of peace and war among the firmest of the baronial party, and he was excommunicated in consequence.

The main spring of these moving powers, Simon de Montfort, placed himself at the head of a reserved force, in such a position as might best enable him to direct and aid the other divisions, while he watched the varying fortunes of the day. Thomas de Puvelesdon, an eminent merchant of London, already noted as conspicuous in the riots, was there with him.

Though particular stations in the battle have not been assigned to more than those now named, yet there were many other nobles of importance and historical name who were also fighting in the ranks of the barons' army.

The merits of Hugh le Despenser[2], who had formerly been in the service of the King of the Romans, and had accompanied him abroad in 1257, recommended him to the office of Justiciary of England after the Oxford Statutes, but from this the King had dismissed him. Though his wife, Aliva[3], was the daughter of an enemy, he testified his attach-

---

died 1280. Dugdale makes him the son of the Justiciary.
[1] Maud, the eldest daughter of the Earl of Pembroke, married: 1. Roger, Earl of Norfolk; 2. William, Earl de Warenne. She died 1248. The earl, who is confused by Sir J. Mackintosh and others with his nephew, the royalist, Roger le Bigot, was made governor of Orford Castle by the barons, and died 1270. His arms in the north aisle of Westminster Abbey are, "Or, a cross gules."

[2] "Quarterle de argent et gules, bende, sable, les quartiers de gules fretté de or."—Rolls of Arms. Despenser was made Justiciary of England by the barons 1260. Afterwards in the same year Philip Basset was appointed Justiciary by the King without the assent of the barons. Despenser was restored before the *mise*. His attestation was required to all the writs sealed with the Great Seal, as a check upon the King.
[3] Aliva, daughter of Philip Basset.

ment to de Montfort by dying with him at Evesham. His son and grandson became the mischievous favourites of Edward II., and have branded the name with historical infamy, but we find the former in his earlier and better days, attending Edward I. at Carlaverock, and thus praised:—

" Ki vassaument sur le cursier   A mounted knight who well did know
Savoit desrompre une mellee."   To charge and rout a marshalled foe.

Robert de Ferrers[1], Earl of Derby, destined to be the last of his race enjoying that title, seems to have imbibed his hatred of the court from having been long subject to its care and control. The death of his father in 1254, by the accidental overthrow of his vehicle on the bridge of St Neots, when[2] helpless from gout, threw him as child into the wardship of the Queen and Peter de Savoy, and at the age of nine they caused him[3] to espouse Mary, a half-sister of Henry III. On scarcely attaining manhood, he had distinguished himself in 1263, by taking more than his share in plundering convents and the property of the royalists, even against the wishes of de Montfort; and his subsequent conduct was of the same tenor—violent and capricious—so as to incur the distrust of all parties. There may, indeed, be some doubt of his presence at Lewes, though named as among those who authorized the barons' letter to the King; for one chronicler[4] states, that, being only verbally attached to the cause, he never met the enemy in open combat, and refused to obey the summons to Lewes, choosing to shelter himself by an imputation on de Montfort, of a treasonable collusion with the Welsh marchers.

The father of Richard de Grai, a man of unusual learning and moderation, had withdrawn into the retirement of his own estates, happy in his old age, to escape from "the labyrinthine intrigues of a court[5]." The two sons, Richard

[1] Henry de Ferrieres, was one of the commissioners for the Doomsday survey. Arms in Carlav., "Gules, seven mascles or voided."
[2] M. Par.
[3] His sisters, Agnes and Isabel, married William de Vesci and Gilbert Basset.
[4] W. Rish. de bello Lew. Holingshed Chr.
[5] M. Par.

and John, had pleased the King by their ready vows as crusaders[1] to such a degree, that "he kissed them like brothers;" but Richard had subsequently taken the command of Dover[2] for the barons, and had been vigilant in preventing the export of treasure to the banished aliens: he was, however, dismissed by Hugh le Bigot for remissness in allowing the Pope's envoy, Walascho[3], to land there. With his son John, in the following year, he became a prisoner at the surprise of Kenilworth, and his forfeited estate was only recovered by the conditions of the final act of grace[4]. His brother John, meanwhile, had continued stedfast to the King, and had with difficulty escaped across Fleet ditch during the London riots, while his house outside Ludgate, and his thirty-two horses, were plundered by the mob[5]:—

" Mès mi Sire Jon de Gray	Master John de Gray came proudly
Vint a Lundres, si ne sai quoy	down,
Que must une destance	But I wonder why from London town
Par entre Lundres et ly,	He fled at such a quick rate;
Que tot son hernois en perdi:	His house and his goods were rudely
Ce fu sa meschance [6]."	tost,
	His horse gear and horses all were lost;
	Such was his piteous fate.

Robert de Vipont[7], a warrior of an eminent family in

---

[1] This was on the preaching of the Cross by Bishop Cantilupe, of Worcester, and Bishop de la Wych (S. Richard), of Chichester, 1252.
[2] By Patent, July 20, 42° Hen. III.
[3] Walascho, a gray friar, had brought over the Pope's letters for the institution of Aymar to the see of Winchester.
[4] "Barry of six, argent and gules." He died 1271, when his son, born 1254, succeeded, who was at Carlaverock:—
" Henri de Grai vi je la
Ki bien e noblement ala."
There was seen Sir Henry de Grai
Who well and nobly kept his way.
John de Gray held various offices during his life, being Justice of Chester, 1249; Governor of Northampton Castle, 1253; and Steward of Gascony, 1254. Retiring from this office, he was Governor of Shrewsbury in 1257, and Constable of Dover Castle, 1258. He died 1266. Joane, widow of Pauline Peyvre, hearing that the King had given her in marriage to Stephen de Salines, an alien, by the advice of her friends, being then at London, matched herself to this John de Gray. The King was much offended, but ultimately accepted a fine of 500 marcs.—Dugdale, Bar. I. 712.
[5] Ann. Dunst.
[6] Polit. S. from MS., 13th century.
[7] "Vipont, argent 6 aneus or."— Rolls of Arms. The bishop died 1254.

Westmorland, had been educated as a ward under his uncle, Thomas, Bishop of Carlisle, and was, perhaps, induced to take the side he did by the influence of Fitz-John, whose relation, Isabella, he had married.

A similar motive may also have brought Robert de Ros, whose mother was another relative of Fitz-John. The name of his grandfather, who married a Scotch princess[1], stands as one of the chosen sureties of Magna Charta, and he received a grant of lands from Henry III. His father, after faithfully serving in the Gascon wars, had returned home without the King's sanction in 1242, on the singular plea of being disabled by poverty from staying longer, and all his estates were in consequence confiscated. This was, however, thought so unjust by the King's brother and many other nobles, that they immediately imitated his example.

Robert de Ros had himself, in 1244, purchased of the King, by a large fine, the marriage of a royal ward, Isabella de Albini, daughter of the Lord of Belvoir. He had been inured to war in Wales, and it was to his special custody that Prince Edward was subsequently consigned at Hereford. After the ruin of his party he redeemed his lands from forfeiture, and was succeeded on his death, 1285, by his son William, who was one of the competitors for the Scotch crown in 1291.

John de Vescie delighted as little as others in the recollection of the intercourse between his family and the court; for a resentful memory may well have been cherished of the licentious insult offered to his female ancestor by King John. Her husband, Eustace, of a proud Norman family, had stamped his principles on Magna Charta, and neither the alliance with the quasi-royal blood of a Longespee[2], his own wardship under Peter de Savoy, nor his marriage with

---

[1] Robert de Ros, whose monumental effigy still remains at the Temple church, married the daughter of William the Lion. Ros; "Gules three bougets arg."—Carlav.

[2] His father's second wife was a sister of Ferrers, Earl of Derby, a connection which may have influenced him. Eustace held 24 military fees and Alnwick Castle. Arms, Vesci; "Or a cross sable."

Mary, daughter of Guy de Lusignan, could win him to the royal cause, though he had commanded troops with honour in the public service during the campaigns of Gascony[1].

Another ward of the Queen, who felt no gratitude for such costly patronage—the profits of his estates having been assigned to her for the maintenance of Prince Edward—was John Gifford[2]. After several campaigns against the Welsh he earned the archbishop's excommunication by his adherence to the barons, and was generally esteemed as one of the bravest soldiers of the party:—

"Sire Jon Gifford deit bien nomé
   *   *   *   *
E si fu tous jors a devant
Prus e sages e pernant
E de grant renomée[3]."

One name renowned must needs be told,
John Gifford first and foremost ever,
Agile and daring, quick and bold.

The castle of Kenilworth had been provided by de Montfort with warlike engines of defence not then known in England, for his engineering skill was repeatedly acknowledged by his contemporaries; and John Gifford, having been appointed its governor, had lately sallied forth from it to make a successful attack on Warwick castle, where he captured its earl, William Mauduit[4], and his countess: their ransom amounted to 1900 marcs (£1266. 13s. 4d.). The subsequent conduct of John Gifford will be again referred to.

Some of the same names which have been already noticed among the royalists occur again on the opposite side. The two brothers, Robert and William Marmyon[5],

[1] After being a prisoner at Evesham, he compounded for his estates, and went with P. Edward to the crusade, from which he returned, 1274, and married, secondly, a Beaumont, kinswoman of Queen Eleanor: he died 1289.
[2] Of Brimsfield, co. Gloucester. Walter Gifford was one of the Doomsday commissioners. Hugh Gifford had been tutor to the sons of Henry III., and died suddenly of apoplexy, at Canterbury, in the King's presence.—M. Par.
[3] Polit. S. from MS. thirteenth century.
[4] The countess was Alice, daughter of Gilbert Segrave. William had become earl, 1263, through his mother. He died 1268. Dying without issue, his heiress was his sister Isabel, married to William de Beauchamp, Baron of Elmley in Worcestershire.—Dugd. Bar. W. Rish. de bello Lew.
[5] Robert had been governor of

stood, in this manner, opposed to their nephew; and Hugh and John Neville[1] to the royalists of the same name: Ralph Basset[2] of Drayton, likewise, disregarded the hostility of his kinsman[3] Philip, and rivalled his valour and perseverance in a different cause. He took some castles in Shropshire into his custody for the barons, and nobly refused to quit Simon de Montfort in a moment of extreme peril at Evesham, declaring that he did not wish to live if that chieftain were to perish. His wife, Margaret, being the daughter of a royalist, Roger de Someri, her influence was powerful enough to recover the estates from forfeiture after his death, previous to her taking the veil.

A few other baronial chiefs may be briefly noticed. The ancestors of Gilbert de Gaunt[4], descended from the illustrious family of the earls of Flanders, had married a de Montfort. Gilbert, who had been governor of Scarborough in 1257, before the civil troubles, became a prisoner to Prince Edward in 1265, but was again taken into royal favour afterwards:

Tamworth Castle; William held lands in Lincolnshire, Derbyshire, and at Berwick, near Lewes: he was summoned to Parliament by the barons.—Banks' Marmyon. Inquis. p. mort.

[1] Hugh de Neville, Chief Forester, of an Essex family, married Joan, daughter and heiress of Henry de Cornhill, a sheriff of London in 1289. Prince Edward took him prisoner, 1265.—Dugd. Bar. He forfeited lands in Essex, part only of which were restored to him on his giving up the remainder to Robert Waleran, 50° H. III. Pat. John was his brother, and married Margaret de la Warde, who afterwards married Sir John Gifford.—See Archæol. Journ. II. p. 370. In M. A. Wood's Letters of Royal and Illustrious Ladies, Vol. I. p. 42, is an interesting letter (written about 1258) from Lady Havisia de Neville to her son Hugh, then a crusader in Syria. She urges him to return in order to procure the restoration of his lands, procuring a letter from the Pope to the same effect if possible. William Fitz-Simon had brought her word that he was very destitute and in need of money, which she promises to raise if she can, and advises him to borrow in the meanwhile as much as he can. "For I hope, by the help of God, if you could well accomplish what you have to do about the acquisition of our lands, that you *will see such a change in England*, that never in our time could you have better accomplished your wish or more to your honor......Sir Walter de la Hide, Joanna your sister, and all our household salute you."

[2] His son, Ralph, was summoned to Parliament, 1295.—Banks' Dorm. Bar. Basset Arms, " Or, three piles gules, a canton ermine."

[3] See p. 153, note 1. P.

[4] "Sir Gilbert de Gaunt, barre of six, or and azure, a bend gules."—Rolls of Arms. He died 1274.

Robert, Baron de Tregoz[1], from his marriage with Juliana de Cantilupe, a niece of the Bishop of Worcester, naturally sided with the barons; in arms also on the same side was Henry Hussey[2], a knight who held property in Sussex, and whom we might have expected to find biassed to the royalists by his marriage with the niece of the wealthy pluralist, John Mansel, whose ward he had been. Jordan de Sackville[3] was taken prisoner while fighting at Evesham for the barons; Hugh Poinz[4] was a gallant warrior, who had served against the Welsh in the lifetime of his father; John Gynvile[5] and Robert de Tony[6] are mentioned as among the barons; the latter was, perhaps, connected with the lords of Trim in Ireland. John de Caston of Kent was one of the followers of de Clare, who pleaded in after years the King's pardon to all such who had been in the battle of Lewes[7].

[1] Tregoz, "Azure, two bars gemellée, in chief a leopard passant, guardant, or." — Rolls of Arms. Geoffry Tregoz had three manors in Norfolk, 1256.—Inquis. p. mort. He was slain at Evesham. John de Tregoz, who held the castle of Ewyas Harold (co. Hereford) by barony, died A.D. 1300. His elder daughter, Clarissa, married Roger de la Warr, and had a son, coheir to his grandfather. The other daughter, Sibil, married William de Grandison, and was buried at Abbey Dore.

[2] Henry Hoese (Hussey), of Wilts, and of Harting, co. Sussex,. married Joan, daughter of Alard le Fleming, who held the manor of Pulborough and other property: he died 1292. His son was summoned to Parliament, 1294. Arms, "Ermine, three bars gules."

[3] He was pardoned Oct. 6th, 1265. —Rot. Pat.

[4] "Poinz, barre, or, et gules."— Rolls of Arms. His male heirs failed in the third generation.

[5] Arms of Genevill, Simon de G., "noir a trois breys (barnacles for horse's nose) d'or, au chief d'argent ung demi lion de goules." Geoffry de G., "azure, 3 breys d'or, au chief ermine demi lion de goules."—Rolls of Arms. [Geoffry de Gynville was some time Justiciary of Ireland. Gilbert's Historic and Municipal Documents, p. xxv.]

[6] Tony, "Argent, a maunch, gules."—Carlav. His ancestor had been standard-bearer to the dukes of Normandy, and held thirty-seven lordships at the time of Doomsday. Roger de Tony, the head of the family, was a firm Royalist; and, in consequence, the barons, in July, 1264, gave Henry de Hastings a grant of his castle of Kirtling, co. Cambridge. Roger's son, Ralph de Tony, a baron by tenure, was succeeded in 1294 by Robert de Tony, then of full age, who formed part of the bodyguard of Prince Edward at Carlaverock in 1300. In a deed, 1301, he is styled "Robertus de Touny Dominus de Castro Matil." [Castle Maud in the Welsh Marches.] He died 1310.

[7] Placit. p. 168. Geoffry de Park, of Blakiston (from Old Park on the Wear), was also at the battle. — Archæol. Journ., June 1855, p. 150.

The long list may be broken off with the confession made by a contemporary[1]:—

Mout furent bons les Barons,	Many and good were the barons bold,
Mès touz ne sai nomer lur noms,	But the names of all cannot be told,
Tant est grant la some.	So vast their long array.

At the risk of weariness, the fortunes and alliances of the principal actors in the battle of Lewes have been thus purposely detailed: such facts may teach us a livelier sympathy with the historical characters of former days, whom we are too apt to consider only as so many bright names[2], instead of men having the same domestic ties, and passions, and motives as ourselves; they are interesting also as the remote ancestors of many families still existing among us, and as enabling us to note, from the frequency of their intermarriages, how few in number the great nobles then were, and how sternly they held themselves, as a class, apart from all such connection with the people at large; but a higher and more solemn duty would also seem to require the particulars of these opposing kinsmen, in order to bring home the evils of civil war more pointedly to the feelings of all who know how to value those links of kindred which were designed to "knit society into a willing harmony." According to the proverb of the clans, "Blood is warmer than water;" but even the genial warmth of family love is too readily overpowered by the feverish passions of civil discord, and it is but seldom that the glory of success can compensate on such occasions for the stifling of the earliest and best emotions of our nature.

---

[1] Polit. S. from Roll, thirteenth century. For a very curious list of the barons and knights of Durham who fought at Lewes, see Hutchinson's History of Durham, Vol. II. p. 219, ed. 1787, and MS. Bodl. Laud. I. 52, by Bishop Tunstall, temp. Hen. IV.

[2] This reflection is ably urged by Professor Creasy in his "Spirit of Historical Study;" and on this principle he recommends the detailed examination of a detached portion of history, rather than the hurried view of a wider sphere—a practical suggestion, of which the author of these pages has experienced the benefit.

CHAPTER X.

THE BATTLE OF LEWES.

Hæc Angli de prælio legite Lewensi,	Read, Britons, of the Lewes fight,
Cujus patrocinio vivitis defensi,	By which ye live in freedom's might;
Quia si victoria jam victis cessisset,	For if the conquered side had won,
Anglorum memoria victa viluisset.—	England's name and fame were done.
Polit. S. from MS. Harl. 978.	

AFTER these dispositions of the barons' forces were made, their march was continued towards Lewes, along the smooth declivity of the Downs; and, according to one account, some parties were sent forward, with the hope of driving the King out of the town by setting it on fire at several points. The royalists, however, although in haughty security their preparations had been loosely made, were not inactive as soon as their scouts had aroused[1] them from their beds to a knowledge of the impending crisis.

It was but two days before (May 12), that the King had sealed at Lewes letters patent[2] to confiscate the lands of John Cobham and William Say of Kent, for having opposed him at Rochester, and to grant them to Prince Edward, in the easy confidence of victory. Another remarkable document was now drawn up, on this morning of

---

[1] "Per castra expergefacti quantocius in arma colligunt."—Chr. Roff. MSS. Nero D. II.

[2] Rot. Pat. 48° H. III. It will be seen, however, that William de Say made his peace with the King, as he headed a body of Royalists in their retreat from the battle of Lewes.

approaching battle, bearing evident signs of haste and confusion; and, indeed, the parties who witnessed it never met again on that day or for a long time afterwards. It is endorsed, as having been drawn up irregularly, and was probably intended to be sent abroad by some one who was prevented by the issue of the battle. After reciting the 5th Article of the treaty with the French King, before referred to, by which the sum for the maintenance of 500 horsemen for two years was to be settled by commissioners, King Henry thus proceeds:—

"Whereas we, not caring to wait for the arbitration of others on this matter, came to this amicable conclusion, by the advice of worthy men, and by common consent, that the said Lord King should be held bound to us for 134,000 livres Tournois, to provide for the expence of 500 soldiers as before said; We have since received all the sum, and acknowledge that full satisfaction has been made to us by the said King concerning it, giving quittance for ever to the said Lord King of France, on behalf of ourselves and our heirs; but since we have already expended a great part of the said total sum of 134,000 L.T. for the advantage of the kingdom of England, we promise that we will expend the remainder of the same money in the service of God, or of the Church, or for the advantage of the kingdom of England, as we are bound to do, and as is more fully contained in the form of the treaty.

"In testimony of which matter, given at Lewes, on the 14th day of May, in the year of our Lord 1264, and in the 48th year of our reign, by the King himself, by the King of Alemain, by Roger de Leiburne, and by others of the King's council.

"And be it known that Master Arnulph, Chancellor of the King of Alemain, dictated and wrote the above letter with his own hands, without the advice and assent of any Clerk of the Chancery, and it was countersigned before the council of our Lord the King, at Lewes, on the day above stated[1]."

The clause in the original treaty, which put the expenditure of this money under the control of the twenty-four elected councillors, had been long disregarded by the King; and it would seem from this document that he still had in hand some portion of this dangerous supply from his brother King, although the two years of the treaty had been long passed; unless indeed, under cover of the stipulation, Louis

[1] Rymer.

had from political motives exceeded the promised sum thus formally acknowledged[1].

Prince Edward, issuing from the castle, was promptly[2] afield, and chose his position at once, on the nearest point to the right, or north, opposite the advancing Londoners, whom he marked out as his personal foes; while around him thronged de Warenne, de Valence, and all the more youthful and ardent spirits[3] of the camp, proud of such a leader.

Towards the south the King of the Romans with his gallant son[4] commanded the left wing, and prepared to meet the young de Montforts.

King Henry himself, though he had never shewn any talent for war, yet felt all the importance of the struggle, and took up his place as a central reserve; though no longer young, he had yet all the courage and strength fit for a king and soldier on this emergency, and never did he better prove them, or had greater need of them. The great[5] nobles of his court formed a body-guard near his person, and he flung a haughty defiance to the enemy, as his dragon standard was displayed before him:—

> "Ther the bataile suld be, to Leaus thai gan them aile,
> The Kyng and his meyne were in the pryorie:
> Symon cam to the feld, and put up his banere,
> The Kyng schewd forth his scheld, his dragon full austere;
> The Kyng said on hie, Simon je vous defie."—ROBT. BRUNE.

[1] By a letter, dated Westminster, May 13th, 1260, King Henry had sent to borrow 5000 marcs, to be reckoned for according to the treaty: by another, Westminster, Dec. 12, 1261, he acknowledged the receipt of 10,416 L.T.; and also 10,000 marcs in 1262.—Rymer, Rot. Pat.

[2] "Regalis exercitus occursurus eis declivium montis ascendit."—M. West. "Circa diei horam primam de villa Lewes exivit regius exercitus cum magno apparatu."—Chr. Wigorn.

[3] "Edwardus cui flos exercitus intendebat, cum tota sibi favente militia."—T. Wyke. The contemporary poem, also, speaks of them as:—

"De sua virtute Satis gloriantibus, ut putarent tutè Et sine periculo velut absorbere Quotquot adminiculo Comitis fuere."
—V. 109, Polit. S.

As some of those who afterwards fled are expressly mentioned as accompanying P. Edward (W. Heming.), it is important to their characters to remark that they could not have fled till the battle was over.

[4] T. Wyke, however, places P. Henry with P. Edward.

[5] "Posterior cohors 400 loricati." —M. West. The Worcester Chr. states the royal army to have been 60,000 men, and the barons' 40,000.

This royal banner of the dragon has been noticed by all the chroniclers[1], as an especial signal of Henry's resolution to give no quarter. Some[2] suppose that he adopted it as the device of the West Saxons (a golden dragon on a red shield), but it was more probably a mere personal cognizance rather than an heraldic bearing. The order for the creation of this "austere" beast is still extant. Edward FitzOdo, the King's goldsmith, was commanded in 1244 to make it "in the manner of a standard or ensign, of red samit, to be embroidered with gold, and his tongue to appear as though continually moving, and his eyes of sapphire, or other stones agreeable to him[3]:"—

> "Then was ther a dragon grete and grimme,
> Full of fyre and also venymme,
> With a wide throte and tuskes grete[4]."

It had been hoisted at Chester[5] in 1257, previous to an invasion of Wales, and again lately at Oxford :—

"With his ost he wende both, and arerde is Dragon[6]."—Rob. Glouc.

The dragon may fairly be presumed of heraldic kin to the griffon, of which it is said, that "having attained his full groweth, it will never be taken alive, wherein he doth adumbrate, or rather lively set forth the propertie of a valourous soldier, whose magnanimitie is such as hee had rather expose himselfe to all dangers, and even to death itselfe, than to become captive;" his being rampant being an "evident testimonie of his readiness for action[7]." In 1264, however, the dragon could be no peculiar attribute of kingly wrath, for it was in common use by other war-

---

[1] Oxenede's Chr.: "The dragon, which, when seen in the army, is the sign of death and mighty revenge." W. Rish.: "With outspread banners preceded by the royal standard, which they call the dragon, foretokening the judgment of death." [It had already been displayed on the royal march to Northampton. — Ann. de Dunstapliâ, p. 229.]
[2] Lingard's Hist.
[3] Walpole's Anecd. It was to be kept in Westminster Abbey till the King came there.
[4] Poem of Sir Degore, in Warton's Hist. Poetry, p. 180.
[5] M. Par.
[6] "With his army he turned about and reared his dragon."
[7] This lively adumbration is from Guillim's Heraldry.

riors; it is seen as a pennon to a lance, and on a shield in the Bayeux tapestry depicting the Conquest; it embellishes the seals of knights[1], and had been exhibited by de Montfort himself soon after the adverse award in January:—

"When Sir Simoun wist the dome ageyn them gone,
His felonie forth thrist, samned his men ilkon,
Displaied his banere, lift up his Dragoun."—ROB. BRUNE[2].

The armies being now face to face, and the trumpets[3] having given the signal, the first shock of battle was soon fiercely given by Prince Edward, whose impetuosity spurred him forward to revenge upon the citizens of London their late insults to the Queen, his mother:—

"And vor to awreke is moder, to hom vaste he drou."—ROB. GLOUC.

Although the practice had been introduced at this period of commuting by escuage the personal service of forty days required by feudal tenures[4], yet, on an occasion where all felt so deep an interest, the armies were principally composed of those who had come in answer to their summons, as vassals either to the crown or to the covenanted barons, leading with them long trains of inferior dependents. London alone had poured forth a willing host without compulsion, and her citizens may be considered as the only volunteers in either army. The rare occurrence of so many of them being thus found assembled in arms, estranged from their homes and usual occupations, proves how popular the cause was, and must have been peculiarly distasteful to the proud nobles of the court party, who had scoffed

---

[1] A dragon is frequently seen under the horse of the knight, on seals of this period.

[2] "When Sir Simon knew the judgment given against them, his wickedness burst forth, he gathered all his men, displayed his banner, and lift up his dragon."

[3] "Tubis terribiliter clangentibus."—T. Wyke. In the Histoire de Fitz-Warin, several musical instruments are named as heralding in a tournament. "Lors resonerent le tabours, trompes, buysnes, corns, sarazynes que les valeys rebonderent de le soun."—p. 11.

[4] The quantity of land constituting a knight's fee (feudum militis), varied considerably in different parts of the country. In King John's time, there are instances of six hides forming a fee in Berkshire, and twenty-seven hides constituting only one in Kent.—V. Abb. Placit. Joh.

at, and interrupted their practice of arms with contempt, "as not fit for bran-dealers, soap-boilers, and clowns[1]." Besides their want of habitual skill, other disadvantages should be remembered; the barons and knights of this period came into the field, not only taught to look upon the skilful use of arms as almost the only education worthy of their birth, but with their bodies protected by shields, and by coats and caps of ring-armour[2]. Always mounted on horseback, they could readily wield their far-reaching lances, or their heavy maces (martel de fer), their battle-axes (solid or bristling with six blades each), and their well-tempered swords for nearer combat. When thus furnished, it required no excess of courage to attack large bodies of inexperienced and ill-armed foot soldiers, whom the policy or careless inhumanity of these times and long afterwards sent to battle with weapons powerless to resist the close attack of a mounted enemy, however formidable bows and slings[3] may have been to a distant foe. "The bravest men have little appetite for receiving wounds and death without the hope of inflicting any in return[4];" and gunpowder, the great leveller of such distinctions in war, remained as yet a mysterious and pregnant secret in the cell of Roger Bacon[5],

[1] M. Par.
[2] Even every knight could not afford so expensive a suit as a hauberk of mail, the "consertam hamis auroque trilicem loricam," of Virgil. Out of 130 knights under Henry II. in Ireland, only 63 were thus provided. Edward I. made it obligatory on those who possessed land of £15 value, and goods of 40 marcs (£26. 6s. 8d.) to have an habergeon (coat of mail), an iron helm (chapel de fer), a sword, a knife, and a horse; those who had lands of 40s. were to have a sword, knife, bow and arrows.
[3] The sling in use consisted of a stick three or four feet long, with a loop of leather at one end to receive the stone. The stick was held in both hands, behind the head, in order to give greater force in throwing.—V. Strutt's Ant.
[4] Hallam's Mid. Ages, Vol. I.
[5] His purposely obscure receipt for gunpowder is well known.—De Sec. Oper. Nat. c. xi. But justice has even yet been scarcely done to his foreknowledge of other miracles of modern art, steam-boats, locomotives, telescopes, &c. The following passages, literally translated from his works, may surprise and interest some persons: "For vessels may be made for navigation without any men to navigate them so that ships, especially for the river, or for the sea, may be borne on under the guidance of a single man, with greater speed than if they had been full of sailors. Carriages also may be made so as to be moved without any animal force, with an incalculable impetus."—De Sec. Oper. c. iv. After describing glasses, by which all that an enemy

that mighty forerunner of English science, who was now living in suspicion and restraint as a penalty on his superior chemistry and philosophy.

The gallant troop of Prince Edward must have been brilliant like that described[1] afterwards at Carlaverock:—

"La maisnie au filz le Roy	With gallant train came the son of
Ki mult i vint de noble aray,	the King,
Car mainte targe freschement	A noble array did his meyne bring:
Peinte e garnie richement,	Many a knight with painted shield
Meinte heaume et mainte cha-	Richly decked on fresh blazoned field,
peau,	Many a burnished helm and cap,
Meinte riche gamboison garni	Many a linked hauberk wrap
De soie et de cadas et coton,	Their limbs, or quilted for the fray
En leur venue veist on	Many a silken wamboys gay;
De diverses tailes et forges."	In varying guise and colours bright
	The throng pressed onward into sight.

did might be discovered at any distance, he adds: "so also we might make the sun, moon and stars come down lower here (descendere inferius hic)."—Persp. p. 3, 2, 3. "Contrivances also may be made to walk at the bottom of the sea or rivers without danger to the body. Bridges also may be made across rivers, without piers or other support. Machines also for flying may be made, so that a man seated in the middle may turn round a certain mechanism by which artificial wings may beat the air, flying like a bird."—Epist. c. iv. Bacon, however, expresses some doubt as to the latter marvel. Though these prodigies were enough to startle any mind, Bacon was persecuted by the church, not by the state.

[1] At the period of the battle, the shield (targe) was heater-shaped; the head was guarded by a hood of ringarmour, or by a flat-topped helmet (heaume); the sword was broad and pointed; the hauberk, or coat of chain armour, had the rings placed edgewise, but many had a cheaper dress, a quilted tunic of leather, wadded with tow (cadas) or cotton, called gamboison, wambais, or haquetons; the emblazoned surcoat, a long loose sleeveless dress of linen, was worn over all: the spurs were of one strong single spike, called a "spur speare," justifying the phrase, "il brocha le cheval de eperons:" he spitted his horse with his spurs.—Hist. de Fitzw. [The shield was then longer than the heater-shaped, more kite-shaped, but straight at the top. Meyrick's notion of rings set edgewise has been abandoned: such representations are believed to have been one of the several modes of representing chainmail. Emblazoned surcoats were, I believe, then unknown, and for about fifty years later. A host was not in 1264 so gay in colours as at Carlaverock. W. S. W.]

Several suits of plate-armour in the Tower have been weighed, its gradual disuse being marked by the diminished weights. The weight of a coat of mail at the Tower is seventeen pounds.

Date.	Armour of	Weight of Armour.		Total, lbs.
		Man, lbs.	Horse, lbs.	
1516 } 1520 }	Henry VIII.	67 85	70 57	137 142
1555	Earl of Huntingdon	104	23	127
1570	Sir H. Lee	75	—	75
1618	Duke of Buckingham	50¾	—	50¾
1605	James I.	63	—	63

Though the Londoners had so zealously sought the foremost position, yet their want of discipline and practice little qualified them to withstand the charge of such a chivalry as now assailed them, and they were forced to give way to the onset, in spite of the efforts of their leaders, Hastings and Segrave. The Prince, who is said[1] to have "thirsted after their blood, as the hart pants for cooling streams," did not relax after his first success, but having broken their foremost ranks, continued to advance upon their rear, which soon became disordered by the retreat of others thrown back upon them. It is probable that, as an additional incentive to the Prince's eager wrath, the car and banners of de Montfort were visible[2] from this part of the battle-field. In spite of some personal defects, such as a slight hesitation of speech, and a drooping eyelid, inherited from his father, yet the Prince's fair handsome countenance, animated by such passionate excitement, and his tall stature giving him so firm a seat on horseback, "erect as a palm[3]," must have rendered him a conspicuous object of military admiration to his followers. Though his deadly grasp, and the flashing fury of his eye when angry, were compared to the leopards of his arms, he was, like them, all gentleness (douce debonaireté) when with friends.

Without regarding the distance he had already advanced from the King's army, and blinded by his rage, he led

---

[1] W. Rish. de Bello Lew.
[2] "Videntes sui in planicie currum quem fieri fecerat Comes."— W. Heming., H. Knight. The plain, "planicies," may have been any level part on the Downs. From the mention of 60 Londoners being drowned in the Ouse in their flight, the left wing may have been placed in the level near Hamsey; and while Montfort overlooked the whole from the Downs, the car may have been also in the same direction as the Londoners in the plain. See Appendix B.
[3] "Ut palma erectus in ascendendo equum."—Chr. Roff. "Elegantis erat formæ, procero staturæ, quâ ab humeris et supra communi populo præminebat.—His hair changed at different epochs, ab argenteo in flavum— in nigredinem, senectute in cygneam. —Frons lata, cætera facies pariliter disposita, eo excepto quod sinistri oculi palpebra demissior paterni aspectus similitudinem exprimebat. Lingua blæsa—tibiarum longa divisio."—Chr. Evesham, 1260. Lel. Coll. Vol. I. When his tomb was opened, 1774, Longshanks was found to measure 6 ft. 2 in., fully justifying his familiar name.—Neale's Westm. Ab., V. Carlav. His arms were "three leopards or with label azure."—Roll of Arms.

them onward, and forced back his enemy with such vigour that the citizens at length broke into a flight[1]—neither strange nor disgraceful under the circumstances, but fatal to all chance of their success. One account[2] even represents their leader, Hastings, as the first to fly for his own safety, but this seems very improbable considering his character; another statement[3], that this flight was a preconcerted stratagem of de Montfort, is as little credible, though indeed he may have expected such a result from the defective[4] nature of such troops. At any rate, the rout was complete; along the most northern slope of the Downs numerous bones and arms have been found, tracing the direction of their flight towards the West, where the abrupt steepness of the ground afforded fugitives on foot the best chance of escape from horsemen. For four[5] miles was the hot pursuit continued—whole crowds of citizens falling slaughtered under the Prince's unsparing sword, while others, to the number of sixty, were drowned in attempting to cross the Ouse.

By these movements, which seemed to promise victory to the royalists, one entire wing of each army was early cleared off the ground; and this vacancy rendered all the more conspicuous de Monfort's car and banners, which seemed to indicate his presence. In emulation of the Prince's triumph, and ignorant of the imprudent length of his pursuit, the King of the Romans was tempted by the prospect of securing the great rebel leader, and directed his forces to that distant point. While the most obstinate re-

[1] "In primo conflictu major pars et Londinensium et equitum et quidam milites et Barones posuerunt se in fugam versus London." Such is the honest avowal of the London chronicler.—Lib. de Ant. Leg.
[2] T. Wyke.
[3] Oxenede's Chr.
[4] "Londinenses ad bella verbis expediti, non tamen in arte bellicâ periti."—Chr. Wigorn.

[5] M. Par., M. Westm., Chr. Roff., say four miles; W. Heming., "for a considerable space;" H. Knight, "two or three miles;" Miss Strickland, in her agreeable "Queens of England," with a licence denied to geography, makes the Prince pursue to Croydon and back on the same day, some eighty miles: no wonder his party was tired on its return.

sistance, however, prevented him from penetrating so far, confusion arose in his own ranks from the storm of stones and arrows hurled at them from the upper ground.

The headlong impulse of Prince Edward, in the meanwhile, had not only driven off the field all opposed to him, but had brought him so far into the enemy's rear as also to encourage his soldiers to make an attack upon the car, with the hope of surprising the helpless invalid supposed to lie[1] within it, and of plundering the baggage. They fell upon it, therefore, with such fury, that during the obstinate struggle the standard-bearer, William le Blund, was overpowered and slain. No de Montfort, however, appeared in answer to the clamours of reproach and hate addressed to him: "Come forth, come forth, Simon, thou devil; come out of the car, thou worst of traitors!" The contemporary monk[2], on recording this taunt, breaks out into some bold words, which evidently came from the heart.: "It should, however, be declared that no one in his senses would call Simon a traitor; for he was no traitor, but the most devout and faithful worshipper of God's Church in England, the shield and defender of the kingdom, the enemy and expeller of aliens, although by birth he was one of them."

While every hand was eager to secure the prize during this fierce contest, the unhappy Londoners, imprisoned within their iron cage, fell victims to the confusion, being slain by their own friends without being recognized. One account makes them, indeed, perish by fire—the barons having placed combustibles around the car; and a deceitful message is also said to have been sent, informing the King that the Londoners were so distrustful of Simon de Montfort, that

---

[1] W. de Rish. de Bello Lew. W. Heming. places the car in the plain, without any guide or driver near it, as if deserted; but it is impossible to suppose it unguarded, when the standard-bearer was killed there.

[2] Chr. Mailr. Having taken up the narrative from 1262 in the same spirit, he is called a fool (satis ineptus) by the modern editor, W. Fulman, 1684.

they were ready to burn him alive should he play them false, as they expected, in the battle[1]. There does not, however, seem to have been time to lay so deep and improbable a plot.

This incident is fixed, by some authors, as occurring during the Prince's first advance; but by others[2], with more probability, on his return. The fact of his long and distant pursuit being certain, he would not then have halted for a merely passing assault on the car, though some of his friends may have then begun an attack, in which he joined on his return; and this seems necessary to account for his long absence from the main field of battle until the victory was lost.

De Montfort must have watched with exultation the success of his stratagem, in thus diverting the attention of the enemy—a success increased beyond his hopes by the rashness of the young Prince. With the decision of a masterly eye, he rapidly directed all his efforts against the weakened body of troops among whom King Henry had stationed himself. To the strength of his right wing, in which were his sons, he now added the fresh impulse of his own reserve, and while his princely foe was indulging a passion, and following a delusion, his single aim was to gain possession of the King's person, well knowing that "by the seizure of the shepherd, the sheep would be dispersed[3]," and the fortunes of the day decided, notwithstanding the defeat of his left wing and the pressure on his centre by the King of the Romans.

Though his numbers were less, they were firm in principle, and they fought with enthusiasm. In the glowing phrase of the chronicler[4], "now flashed forth the lightning

---

[1] Chr. Mailr.
[2] T. Wyke, Chr. Mailr., Robt. Brune on one side; W. Heming. and H. Knighton on the other.
[3] W. Rish. de Bello Lew. "Industria Comitis hoc docente, totum pondus prælii versum est in reges Angliæ et Alemanniæ."—T. Wyke.
[4] "Ibi apparuit virtus Baronum fulminea, inhiantius dimicantes pro patria."—W. Rish., copied verbatim by the royalist Mat. Westm.

valour of the barons, fighting for their country with more breathless zeal." After a long and violent attack, they succeeded, by the aid of their numerous slingers, in disordering the division under the King of the Romans, so as to compel him to seek refuge in flight; and several nobles, including de Bohun, Fitz-Alan, Bardolf, Tattishall, Somery, Percy, and the three great Scotch leaders—some of them confessedly panic-struck[1]—surrendered themselves as prisoners.

The King now unexpectedly found himself exposed to direct assault, when deprived of the greater part of the forces on which he had depended for support. His son had become entangled in the enemy's snare beyond the reach of immediate recall, and his brother was flying for his life. At no period had Henry shown any capacity for war, but, as far as personal courage can entitle him to our respect, the Plantagenet monarch evinced much manly resolution when his danger at Lewes excited him into activity. Mounted on his choicest warhorse[2], he gave by his own example the best encouragement to his friends; and though his horse was killed under him, he mounted another, which met with the same fate. Severely wounded in his own person by the swords and maces[3] of his foes—a proof of the close combat he must have engaged in—he saw also several of his most faithful friends falling around him, mortally wounded, after their utmost exertions. Among all the combatants

---

[1] Hoc ipsi ore proprio confitebantur, quorum unus erat Dominus Henricus de Perci unus de melioribus in regno."—Chr. Dover. W. Rish., W. Heming., Robert Pierpoint was among the prisoners.—Rot. Pat.

[2] In reference to the heavy armour of the riders, peculiar qualities were looked for in a war-horse, which made them unfit for ordinary use, and they were not mounted till actual battle. The crusaders had brought back horses from Syria, and Richard I. had two Arabians; King John had imported some from Flanders, and Henry III. had some horses sent him from Germany. The importation of Spanish horses afterwards improved the breed.

[3] "Dextrario suo sub se confosso."—W. Rish. "Dextrarius ejus occisus."—W. Heming. "Equo electissimo sub se confosso."—M. Westm. The Lewes chr. however says, "Rex bene verberatus gladiis et maciis, et duo equi sub eo mortui, ita quod vix evasit." "Equus Regis sub Rege a Gilberto Comite de Gloverniæ subnervatur, et rex cum reverentia custodiæ mancipatur."—Chr. Wigorn.

the last to retire or yield was Philip Basset[1], though gashed with twenty wounds :—

> "Sir Philip Basset the gode knight worst was to overcome,
> He adde mo then tuenti wounde as he were inome."—Rob. Glouc.

"Oh, wretched sight! (exclaims the chronicler with more feeling than usual) when the son strives to overpower the father, and the father the son: kinsman against kinsman, fellow-citizen against fellow-citizen, with their swords brandished on either side, drunk with the gore of the slain; felling, maiming, and trampling their foes under the horses' feet, or binding their prisoners alive in straitest bonds[2]."

So many of the royalists were now among the captives or the slain, that the remainder of their broken ranks[3] were at length obliged to consult the safety of their sovereign and themselves by a retreat into the Priory, from whence they had marched in the morning so full of hope and pride; and it gave a peculiar relish to the triumph of the conquerors, to observe that the same party which had so recently committed sacrilegious outrages on churches, at Northampton, Battle, and elsewhere, should now betake themselves to a church, as the best refuge in their distress[4].

Their only hope of retrieving the fortunes of the day now rested on Prince Edward, whose victorious advance they had witnessed in the morning; and while awaiting the issue of this last chance, strong guards were posted round all the approaches of the Priory[5], so as to increase its defence by all

---

[1] "Hugo le Despenser Philippum de Basset *studuit salvare*, et eum ab adversariis voluit liberare, sed ille quam diu stare potuit, militi se reddere noluit."—Chr. Wigorn.

[2] W. Rish. de Bello Lew.

[3] Perforataque est acies ipsius Regis."—W. Heming.

[4] * * "Dei sapientia Fortes fecit fugere, virosque virtutis In claustro se claudere * * * in ecclesiâ

Unicum refugium restabat, relictis Equis, hoc consilium occurrebat victis;
Et quam non timuerant prius prophanare,
Quam more debuerant matris honorare,
Ad ipsam refugiunt, licet minus digni."
—Polit. S. from MS. Harl. 978, Vol. XXXIII.

[5] T. Wyke erroneously makes the surrender of both Kings to occur in

the means in their power. Had they been near enough to reach the castle when forced to retreat, they would probably have fled there rather than relied on the imperfect security of the peace-adapted building of the monks; though even there the boundary wall, enclosing a space of thirty-two acres, could keep an enemy at bay for a time.

Lewes being a town of considerable antiquity, there appears to have been an imperfect inclosure of wall round it; for the repair of which, the earliest murage grant extant, dated two years after the battle, authorized the levy of tolls for three years. The activity of the now extinct iron trade of the neighbourhood is traced in the articles thus taxed on entering the town: "For every cart laden with iron for sale 1$d.$; for every horse-load of iron for sale, through the week, a half-penny;" and the extent of the adjoining forest is thus indicated: "For every tumbrel of squirrels for sale a half-penny[1]."

The Priory was at no period included within the walls; but the strong and extensive circuit of the castle, with its double keep[2], enclosed a royalist garrison in unimpaired confidence. It held also some important prisoners, who had been captured in the earliest successes of the day.

Among these, John Gifford, already referred to as one of the best soldiers in the barons' army, was the most conspicuous, and to effect his release[3] was a strong motive in their attack on the castle. No doubt of his good faith was

the Priory, before the Prince's return. "Ilecques fu la bataille dure et aspre, mais au drenier ne pot endurer li roys le fors dou Conte Symon, ainsois sen fui il et sez filz Edouars en l'abbaye devant dite, pource que il cuida eschapper."—Nangis.

[1] Rot. Pat., 50° H. III.; in Horsfield's Hist. of Lewes, I. 162. A payment was made, in 1290, for the iron-work of the monument of Hen. III. in Westminster Abbey, to Master Henry of Lewes.—Househ. Exp. from Rot. Mis. 56. 17.

[2] The mound to the N.E. may perhaps not have had any large tower upon it, but have been the mound often found in Norman Castles, as at Carisbrook, Clare, Cardiff, Pevensey, Tonbridge, &c., a mere tumulus of earth, intended to facilitate the inspection of the country and the interior of the castle. In later times of Edward I. a similar mound with tower was called a bailly.—See Archæol. Journal, I. p. 100.

[3] Walt. Heming.

at this time entertained, yet there was something suspicious in his conduct and early capture, which later events[1] seem to confirm. With his comrade, William de Maltravers[2], he had at the first onset taken two Royalist knights prisoners, Reginald FitzPiers and Alan de la Zouch. Both of these captives, however, either by negligence or treason, were so loosely guarded, that they were found at large afterwards, until taken for the second time, when FitzPiers was detected still retaining all his arms and fighting, and Zouch[3], disguised as a monk[4], in the Priory. This circumstance gave rise to a dispute as to ransom, which afforded Gifford subsequently a pretext for abandoning the barons.

In another part of the battle-field an important prize had gratified the baronial troops. They had so closely followed the flight of the King of the Romans, as to track him to a windmill, where he had secured the door, and delayed his

---

[1] See p. 101, note 3.

[2] Like Gifford he became a royalist, and at Evesham he was distinguished by his barbarity towards the earl he was now serving under; John de Maltravers held Childrey, co. Berks, by the service of one knight in the time of Henry III.; Lytchet-Maltravers, co. Dorset, was held by the service of five knights. Eleanor, the heiress, in a subsequent generation, carried the estates to the Fitz-Alan family. Arms, " Sable, a fret or, with a file of 3 points ermine."— V. Lysons' Berks., Hutchins' Dorset, Vol. III.

[3] Alan de la Zouch, of Ashby, of an illustrious descent from the Earls of Brittany, was much in the confidence of the King, and enjoyed large grants made to his father and himself (V. Calend. Rot. 45°, 48°, Hen. III.). He held two fees in Sussex under Henry de Percy (Cal. Inq. p.m.). After serving in the wars of Gascony he was made a Justice Itinerant in three counties [1261—1266, and Justice of all the King's Forests south of Trent 1261]; he is called Seneschal of the King (Rot. Pat. 47° Hen. III.), was surety for the King at Amiens,

and afterwards [c. 1267] was Constable of the Tower. He married Elena, daughter of Roger de Quincy, Earl of Winchester, and had interest, in 1267, to obtain the redemption of his niece's forfeited property. " Zouche, gules bezantée d'or."— Rolls of Arms.

[Having a lawsuit with Earl Warenne (c.1268—1270) he was attacked by that earl's retainers in Westminster Hall, and wounded so grievously, that he died of the injuries inflicted. The earl was pursued to his castle at Reigate by Prince Edward, and forced to surrender. He was mulcted in 10,000 mares, ultimately reduced to 7400, of which 2000 went to Alan's son and heir, Roger, who had also suffered in the scuffle. Excerpt. e. Rot. Fin. II. 525. Chron. Rishang. p. 58; Wyke, p. 234; Dugdale's Baronage, I. 78; Foss, Judges, II. 528.] The earl was also forced to walk from the Temple to Westminster Abbey, and there make oath that the assault did not arise from previous malice.

[4] Rob. Glouc., and Add. MSS. 5444, relate this anecdote, and the subsequent dispute as to his ransom.

surrender as long as possible. Even so frail a defence as a mill sufficed, for a time, against the imperfect weapons of attack then in use.

No precise spot on the Downs now retains the tradition of this mill, though it was pointed out long after by the name of "King Harry's mill[1]:" as it is distinctly described by two contemporaries[2] as a windmill with "sayles," it must have occupied the usual situation for such structures on the ridge of the hill[3]; and we may therefore consider Prince Richard to have advanced some distance from the town at the time of his rout, when, his retreat to the Priory being cut off, an escape towards the nearest point of the coast would have been his principal object.

While the King of the Romans remained thus blockaded in the mill, he was for some time exposed to the rude jests and reproaches of those with whom he had so often and so recently been leagued: "Come out, you bad miller," they shouted; "you forsooth to turn a wretched mill-master—you

[1] "Motus est exercitus Baronum versus quoddam molendinum circa Lewes," to which a more modern hand has added a marginal note, "called King Hary's mill to this day."—Add. MSS. 5444. Windmills are said to have been introduced into France and England, c. 1040. (Fosbroke, Encycl. of Antiquities.)

[2] "Molendinum quod vi ventorum dicebatur molere."—Chr. Mail. See also the ballad in the next page. "He wende that the sayles were mangonel." Doomsday notices two mills of 23*s.* at Lewes. The Lewes monk (MS. Tib. A. x.) says, "Hæc omnia facta fuerant apud Lewes ad molendinum suelligi." These latter words have been interpreted "the Mill of the Hide," on the authority of Spelman (Glossar.), who gives the meaning of "hide" to Swulinga, or rather Sulinga, from a Saxon word, signifying a plough, and considers two sulingæ to constitute one military fee. A deed of Isabella, Countess of Warren, widow of Hamelin, grants a lease of a mill near Lewes, at the rent of 22*s.* to Richard de Cumbes, where it is named "Sidelune mill," (quoddam mólendinum quod vocatur Sidelune melne).—See Hist. of Warren. This may possibly be the same. According to Mr W. Figg, of Lewes, there are about 32 acres of land called "the Hyde," formerly belonged to the Priory of St Pancras, situated at the west end of the town, on the south and west sides of the ancient church of St Mary, now St Peter and St Mary Westout, otherwise St Ann. In the northern part of this land, about where the Black Horse Inn now is, a windmill is shewn in an old map of the Wallands by John Deward, about 1618. There may have been an older mill on this "Hyde," molendinum suelligi, as the spot necesarily lay in the line of those retreating to the Castle. (March 1844.)

[3] A modern account, Horsfield's Sussex, describes the mill as in the low ground on the Winterbourne stream, but in that case it must have been a watermill.

who defied us all so proudly, and would have no meaner title than King of the Romans, and always August[1]!" The latter addition, though as invariably affixed to his German dignity, as "Defender of the Faith" to our own sovereign in after times, seemed strange and ludicrous to the ears of the English. His altered plight was ridiculed also in a popular ballad[2] of the day:—

> "The Kyng of Alemaigne wende do full wel,
> He saisede the mulne for a castel,
> With hare sharpe swerdes he ground the stel,
> He wende that the sayles were mangonel
>   To helpe Windesore.
> Richard, thah thou be ever trichard,
> Trichen shalt thou never more.
>
> The Kyng of Alemaigne gederede ys host,
> Takede him a castel of a mulne post,
> Wende with is prude and is muchele bost,
> Brohte from Alemayne mony sori gost
>   To store Windesore.
> Richard, thah thou be ever trichard,
> Trichen shalt thou never more[3]."

As evening[4] came on and no chance of escape appeared, King Richard was obliged to give himself up to his enemies, and was led away in custody, even loaded with chains, according to one account[5], and accompanied by his second son, Edmund, yet a youth. Though he yielded himself up to Gilbert de Clare, as the chief in command, it would appear that John Befs[6]—of a rank too inferior to receive the im-

---

[1] Chr. Mailr.
[2] It has been frequently printed, and lately in Polit. S. from Harl. MS. Percy in his "Ancient Reliques" not understanding the allusion, remarks that "the verses very humorously allude to some little fact which history has not condescended to record," and supposes it to refer to his large watermills at Isleworth where he might have lodged a party of soldiers.
[3] Glossary—*wende*, thought: *mangonel*, engine to throw stones: *thah*, though: *sori gost*, wicked spirits: *trichard*, trickster: *trichen*, trick.
[4] The Lewes chr. says the greater part of the royal army was entirely overthrown before midday. "Ita fuit quod maxima pars regis exercitus inter primam et meridiem funditus sternata." This, if correct, must mean the King's own division.
[5] Chr. Mailr. Another authority seems to intimate that the mill was only used to secure the prisoner in.—Ad bellum de Leaus.—ubi Dominus Simon—capto Comite in molendino ad custodiendum posuit.—Chr. Laudun. in MSS. Cott. Nero. A. IV. "Cum filio suo Edmundo adhuc impuberi captivatus."—T. Wyke.
[6] Perhaps the name was Bovis,

portant surrender of a King—was the principal agent in his capture, and was honoured with knighthood subsequently in reward for his services:—

"The King of Alemaine was in a windmulle inome,
Vor a yong knight ymad tho right,
Sir John de Befs ycleped, that was suith god knight,
That much prowesse dude a dai, and the King him yield in doute,
To the Erl of Gloucestre as to the hexte of the doute[1]."

ROB. GLOUC. p. 532.

At length, after the victory had been thus decided, about eight o'clock[2] in the evening Prince Edward returned from his reckless triumph over the Londoners and his bootless attack upon the car.

Many a great battle has been lost in the same manner, by the rash indulgence of private feelings of exultation or revenge. In modern times the advantages of self-control in the eager soldier, of strict obedience exacted by and yielded to one calm sagacious mind, have been generally recognized and adopted; but at this remote period, with a loose cluster of independent chieftains, each the jealous peer of the others hastily collected and soon to be dispersed, such discipline or prudence could not be looked for. The chief praise was then always given to individual courage and strength, rather than to the fulfilment of an appointed duty.

"To while Sir Edward was about the chare to take,
The Kynge's side, allas, Simon did doun schake,
Unto the Kynge's partie Edward turned tite, (speedily)
Then had the Erle the maistrie, the Kynge was discomfite;
The soth to say and chese, the chare's gilery
Did Sir Edward lese that day the maistrie."—ROB. BRUNE.

Beaufo or Boves. Nicholas de Beaufo, a knight of Norfolk, is mentioned.—Cal. Placit Henry III. Adam de Beyfin held five manors in Shropshire, 1261, 1263.—Cal. Inquis. p. mort. Hugh de Boves was sent to Bristol in 1213, and a ship for ten or twelve horses was ordered to be prepared for him. Rot. Claus. 159. He was drowned, with many others, near Yarmouth, Oct. 26, 1215.—Wendover, III. p. 333.

[1] "The King of Alemaine was taken in a windmill, for a young knight took him, then justly made knight, called by Sir John de Befs, who was truly a good knight, and did many exploits that day, and the King yielded himself in alarm to the Earl of Gloucester, as to the highest chief of the force."

[2] "Expensa est magna pars illius diei usque ad octavam horam."—Chr. Mailr. "Pugnaverunt usque ad noctem."—Lib. de Ant. Leg.

The Prince arrived with his horses jaded and his comrades weary, all "journey-bated" like himself[1] after their long service, which had now continued from early dawn to the evening of a long summer's day. He expected to find a triumphant welcome from his party as victorious as himself:

"With gret joye he turnde agen, ac lute[2] joye he founde."—ROB. GLOUC.

On the late busy field of battle none were to be seen but the dead and the dying, no remains of either army fighting, and nothing but the banner of de Warenne, still flying on the castle-keep, to assure him of the contest at all continuing. Mortified by so unexpected a scene, and uneasy for the safety of his father, though still eager to renew the fight, he made a circuit[3] of part of the town, in order to reach the castle, towards which point the tide of war had pressed onwards, when receding from the field.

A stern and desperate resistance had there repulsed all the efforts of the barons, and the Prince's presence inspirited the besieged; but, ignorant of the King's fate, and gloomy with apprehensions, he soon after forced his way to the Priory, in order there to learn the whole of the fatal truth.

At this crisis a great many nobles and knights, who had accompanied the Prince during the day, feeling their strength and hopes gone, resolved to take advantage of the shades of evening to effect their escape[4]. The number of these fugitives is variously stated as 300[5] or 400 well-armed chiefs, and among them were many whom King Henry might certainly have expected to share his fate. His own brothers, William de Valence, and Guy de Lusignan[6], and the Earl de

---

[1] "Lassitudine sic quassatus, quod ulterius dimicare non poterat. Tam ipse quam hi qui eum sequebantur etiam cum suis equis immoderato labore fuerunt sic fatigati, quod vix respirare potuerunt."—T. Wyke.

[2] Ac lute—and little.

[3] "Villam circuens pervenit ad castrum."—W. Rish. "Circumduxit villam usque ad castellum."—W. Heming.

[4] "Ecce omnes quasi qui cum eo steterant fugæ indulserunt."—Mat. Westm.

[5] "300 loricati."—W. Rish. "400 loricati sive culpâ sive non culpâ."—Mat. Westm. "The chiefs, and more than 70 choice armed soldiers, who belonged to their house and family."—Walt. Heming.

[6] Geoffry de Lusignan and Hugh are not mentioned as present at

Warenne, though in sight of his own castle, all bound by kindred and favours to their Sovereign, now abandoned him; Hugh le Bigot, and many of the highest chieftains, being their comrades in this flight:—

"Many on stilleliche hor armes a wei caste,
And chaungede hom vor herigaus, som del hii were agaste,
And mani flowe in to the water, and some towards the sea.
And manie passede over and ne come nerere aze[1]."—ROB. GLOUC.

This desertion was considered as reflecting disgrace on the parties at the time; "they fled (observes the chronicler) without a blow, though not without blame." If, however, the well-known reason[2] for running away can ever be made palatable to military critics, it might be so here; for these very runaways soon formed the nucleus of a force which was ultimately destined to retrieve the fortunes of the King, whom they were now leaving in such imminent peril.

They made their way through the town towards the bridge, where the mixed crowd of fugitives and pursuers became so great that many in their anxiety to escape leaped into the river, while others fled confusedly into the adjoining marshes, then a resort for sea-fowl. Numbers were there drowned and others suffocated in the pits of mud, while, from the swampy nature of the ground, many knights who perished there were discovered, after the battle, still sitting on their horses in complete armour, and with drawn swords in their lifeless hands. Quantities of arms were found in this quarter for many years afterwards[3].

Lewes, but W. Rish. refers to William and his other brothers flying with him from the battle. "Fugitque Comes de Warenna cum duobus Regis filiis (sic) Willielmo de Valence et Gwydone fratre ejus."—Walt. Heming. "Earl de Warenne" again fled ingloriously from his army when defeated by Wallace in 1297 at Stirling.

[1] "Many silently cast away their arms, and changed them for spurs, some of them were terrified, and many fled into the water, and some towards the sea, and many passed over, and never came back again."

[2] "Bellat prudenter qui fugit sapienter."—W. Rish. of the Londoners.

[3] Chr. Lanerc. gives these details on the authority of a noble eyewitness; the crowd at the bridge is, however, wrongly timed, as happening at the commencement of the battle. "Belli victoria eisdem *cœlitus donata*. Quidam autem de exercitu Regis per

Those fugitives who succeeded in crossing the bridge, at once hurried on to Pevensey Castle that very night; and, not content even with the shelter of that friendly fortress, got ready there some vessels in which they embarked the next day for France—the heralds to the Queen of the total discomfiture of their party. Their version of the battle represented King Henry as having been seized in bed by the barons without any previous warning; and, by these falsehoods to justify their own flight, they moved the French court to great anger[1]. Their escape, whether honourable or not, was undoubtedly a subject of vexation and anxiety to the triumphant de Montfort, as the ballad of the day clearly shows:—

"By God that is aboven us, he dude muche synne,
That lette passen over see the Erl of Warynne;
He hath robbed Engelond, the mores ont tho fenne,
The goldt ant the selver, ant y-boren henne,
    For love of Wyndesore.

Sir Simond de Mountford hath swore bi ys chin,
Havede he nou here the Erl of Waryn,
Shulde he never more come to his yn,
Ne with sheld, ne with spere, ne with other gyn,
    To help of Wyndesore."

Sire Simond de Montfort hath swore by his cop,
Havede he nou here Sire Hue le Bigot,
Al he shulde quite here a twelf-moneth scot,
Shulde he never more with his fot pot,
    To help of Wyndesore[2]."

The town being now in the utmost confusion, the flying royalists and the exulting barons were almost undistinguished in the entangled mass thronging the streets: crowds of wounded men lay there, while the loose horses of those who had been slain, or who had abandoned them in their retreat

---

pontem ex parte orientali villæ fugerunt, et nimio timore perterriti fugiendo se construxerunt et sic se in aquam submerserunt, et diem vitæ suæ clauserunt."—Chr. Wigorn.

[1] "Ad iram non modicam mendaciis nefandis."—Add. MSS. 5444.

[2] Polit. S. from MS. Harl. 2253. Glossary:—*ant y-boren henne*, and carried them away: *havede*, had : *his yn*, his house (Lewes): *gyn*, engine: *cop* (kopf), head: *al*, although: *quite*, pay: *pot*, trudge with his foot.

to the Priory, were now wandering about in the dark without riders[1]. Pillage was uppermost in the thoughts of one party, and flight in the other; but at the castle and the Priory an obstinate resistance was still maintained. The garrison of the former increased the tumult and horror of the scene by calling fire to their aid. The Greek fire was in common use at this time, and it is probable that something of this nature was employed. "Spryngelles of fyre[2]," that is, pellets of tow dipped in Greek fire, were thrown from a sort of mortar[3]; with these, or some similar contrivance, they succeeded in setting fire to several houses of the town, which were probably then built of wood from the neighbouring Weald. The Priory was soon, in retaliation, treated in a similar manner, and for a time the church was fearfully illuminated[4], though the flames were subdued before the destruction of the buildings.

Prince Edward was once more mustering his broken troops to rush out and renew the hazard of the battle, when de Montfort interfered to suggest an immediate truce[5], preparatory to negotiations on the morrow. On this timely proposal being accepted, the carnage and destruction of the conflict, which had been the terrible occupation of so many thousands during a long summer's day, at length ceased.

"Contrary to all expectation (observes a contemporary

---

[1] "Nec facile discerni poterat per longum spatium, præ multitudine vulneratorum, qui dicerentur Regales qui Baronales. Interim tumultuabat civitas per partes utrasque, vacabant enim spoliis et rapinis et equis occisorum stabiliendis nec adhuc se mutuo recognoscere potuerunt."—Walt. Heming.

[2] V. Romance of Richard Coeur de Lion, in Warton's H. Poet. i. 158. According to Anna Comnena, Greek fire was composed of bitumen, sulphur, and naphtha. "Emissis telis igneis magnam partem villæ incenderunt."—Walter Heming. A number of fire arrows were found in an old house near the high bridge of Lincoln and exhibited at the meeting of the Archæological Institute, July, 1848.

[3] "Can mortar be right? Was not throwing of fire then effected by means of tow attached to arrows steeped in turpentine and ignited? Whether 'spryngelles' were tufts of blazing tow, or pieces of wood like the shafts of an arrow, I am doubtful."—W. S. W.

[4] "Illuminata est ecclesia telis eorum."—Walt. Heming., H. Knighton. Joinville reports the camp of the crusaders to have been illuminated by such implements.

[5] "Nocte sequenti pax quædam reformata est."—Chr. Roff. M.S.

chronicler[1]), the barons had thus gained a wonderful victory, which they attributed with gratitude to Him alone by whose support they had passed through the mortal dangers of the struggle." The same spirit of devotional joy, and affectionate gratitude to the achievers of such a victory, pervades other accounts written at the time. Among the most remarkable is the long Latin rhymed poem before referred to, composed immediately after the battle, by one who, amidst much calm argument on regal power and civil liberty, evinces his feelings by such bursts as the following:—

"May the Lord bless Simon de Montfort, his sons and his comrades, who have so nobly and boldly fought, in compassion on the sad fate of the English, when they were so unspeakably trampled under foot, and nearly deprived of all their liberties, and even of life, languishing under their hard Princes.

"Blessed be the Lord God of Vengeance, who sits on His high throne in heaven, and by His own might treads upon the necks of the proud, making the great subject to the weak. He has subdued two kings and their two heirs into captivity, as transgressors of the laws, and has given over to ignominy all the pride of their warfare, with their numberless followers[2]."

That de Montfort was not only held in esteem as an able soldier, but was considered as "backed by the general favour of the people," is expressly asserted by a French chronicler[3] of the time. Although he only incidentally mentions the battle of "Lyaus," he praises de Montfort, as "noble, chivalrous, and the ablest man of the age," and anxiously claims him as a Frenchman. That he had the support of public opinion in England cannot indeed be

---

[1] W. Rish. de Bello Lew.
[2] Polit. S. from MS. Harl. 978. v. 65.—V. 383.
[3] Nangis; his history is both in French and Latin. "Erat in Angliâ non tamen de Angliâ sed de Franciâ ducens originem." "Noble, preus en armes, et moult sages bons du siecle." "Communi fretus favore populi." "Par l'asentement du peuple commun."

P

doubted, and among other proofs, it may be noticed that it had driven the King to rely upon the arms of foreigners in this battle. Edward had introduced Spaniards, and the northern barons had brought with them their Scotch vassals, who were as much aliens in blood, language, and nationality as those from the Peninsula.

Of these a great number perished, and their chiefs were taken prisoners. Few names have been recorded of those slain on either side. On the side of the conquerors, besides William le Blund already referred to, Ralph Heringot[1] is the only baron mentioned. Of the other party, twenty-three barons, who bore banners, were either taken or slain, and two justiciaries[2] perished—William de Wilton by the sword, and Fulk de Fitz-Warren drowned in the Ouse.

The blood of many others was of course shed; for, as is quaintly observed in the poem last quoted, "it certainly was not by smooth words, but by hard fighting, that de Montfort subdued the proud, and squeezed out the red juice[3]."

The number of the slain in this decisive battle, thus obstinately contested with all the gathered strength of each party, the first fought on English ground after the repose of half a century, was necessarily great, but has been left wholly uncertain by the conflicting records of the chroniclers, happily unused to such calculations. "It was there

---

[1] Stephen Heringod held a manor and lands in Kent in 1257. Inquis. p. mort. [Cf. Rot. Hund. 1. p. 227.] Ralph de Haryngot, was, in 1258, one of the four knights chosen by the county of Surrey.—Pat. 42° Hen. III. Mat. Westm. calls him "Heringander." W. Rish. "Heringaud." Nicolas Harengod (Haringot) was lord of the manor of Battle, co. Sussex, in right of his wife Sybilla, daughter of Ralph de Yclesham.—Battle Abbey Charters, p. 41. The seal of Harengot in green wax is to a charter of 1273, p. 48. An account of the family in Waldron, Sussex, is given in Sus. Arch. Coll. Vol. XIII. p. 90.

[2] W. Rish. pp. 33, 34—Lib. de Ant. Leg. p. 52. ["Fulco Fitz-Warine, who was a Shropshire baron, is never mentioned even as a Justice Itinerant."—Foss, Judges of England, I. p. 336.]

[3] "Quos quo modo reprimit? certe non ludendo
Sed rubrum jus exprimit dure confligendo."—
Polit. S. from MS. Harl. 978.

seen (says one[1]) that the life of man was as the grass of the earth; a great multitude, unknown to me, was slain." As the numbers stated by various authors[2] vary from 2700 to more than 20,000, we may turn aside from so distasteful an enquiry, glad to believe in the smallest amount of destruction, and may adopt at once the conclusions of Robert Brune:—

"Many faire ladie lese hir lord that day,
And many gode bodie slayn at Leaus lay.
The nombre none wrote, for telle tham mot no man,
But He thut alle wote, and alle thing ses and can."

The traces of the battle are deeply stamped on the history and constitution of the country, legible as those of Magna Charta, but the only local record of the vanquished monarch is the simple name of "Mount Harry," ever since popularly affixed to the lofty point of the Downs near the field of battle. This is so distant from Lewes (nearly two miles) that it was probably in the rear of de Montfort's army; but it may, indeed, have been where his car and standard were placed, or where the King had posted his negligent watch[3] overnight. The low mounds caused by the

[1] Oxenede's Chr.
[2] MS. Cleop. D. ix. says that 600 of the slain were buried by the monks, according to their account, but many others were killed and drowned; the Lewes Chr. 2700 slain, more or less; Waverley Chr., MS. Cleop. B. xiv. MS. Bodl., and Chr. Lanercost, more than 3000; Rob. Glouc. 4500; Chr. Winton MS. D. ix. makes 4514 in all, that is 2070 besides the Londoners; and with this number agree Worcest. Chr. and MS. Nero, Chr. P. de Ickham; Walt. Heming., W. Rish., Mat. Westm., 5000 slain: T. Wyke states nearly 5000 slain, "many of them fallen by the just judgment of God in retribution for the sack of Northampton" (non habentes jus querelæ). "Ex utraque parte numerati per manus sepelientum 2730," besides the drowned, the wounded, the citizens of London, and the fugitives.— Chr. Wigorn. "10,000 ex parte regis interfectis.—xv. barones interfecti." Cotton MS. Nero, A. iv. Fabyan and Rastall: "Over 20,000 slain, as sayth myn auctours."

[3] A beacon was established near this spot in the late war when a French invasion was expected. Two miles more to the westward, on the escarpment of the hill, there is a large cross cut out on the turf, which is now only visible under peculiar circumstances of light. This may, possibly, have been a pious device of the times to excite the prayers of distant travellers for the repose of the souls of those slain at Lewes, but it cannot be accepted as evidence of the barons having made their ascent at so distant a spot, contrary to the

heaps of bodies interrupting the smoothness of the turf, a decayed bone, or a broken weapon occasionally found, alone recall the memory of the angry thousands once assembled there.

express words of Will. Rishanger: "Cunctis igitur montem qui distat a Lewes duobus milliaribus summo mane ascensis."

CHAPTER XI.

THE MISE OF LEWES.

*"A proper title of a peace, and purchased
At a superfluous rate."*—HEN. VIII. Act I. Scene 1.

THERE was much of wise policy as well as forbearance in de Montfort's suspension of hostilities, proposed at the very moment when his sovereign lay a defenceless prey before him. As a mere soldier he might have pushed the issue to a violent extremity, but as a statesman his arm was arrested. Had the Priory—which the opinions of the age and the authority of a jealous Church invested with the privileges of sanctuary—been taken by storm that night, the horrors that might have ensued, the violence to the King's person, perhaps even his death, would have deeply perilled the cause of constitutional liberty. The inherent attachment to monarchy which has ever distinguished the English character—that loyalty, which has been truly described as "scarcely less refining and elevating in a moral point of view than patriotism, and exciting as disinterested energies[1]"—would have been outraged by so undisguised a collision. To obviate such feelings, the constitutional fiction, since so often and well employed, of casting blame and responsibility on others rather than the King, had even

[1] Hallam, Mid. Ages.

in these early times, been found expedient, and had throughout been put forward to justify the barons. While their war was directed against his bad advisers, they appeared to respect "the divinity that doth hedge a king," and were still able to vaunt themselves as his true liegemen. To carry on this convenient fiction was obviously the most politic course, and accordingly all the subsequent arrangements were founded on this basis, the appearance of free agency being studiously preserved to the King.

De Montfort, during the night, so strengthened the blockade of the Priory and castle as to render escape hopeless; and on the following day, Thursday, May 15, the commissioners of each side met to fix the terms on which the future government of the kingdom was to depend.

The King is said[1] to have appointed two monks of the order of preachers (Dominicans) to the office[2], but it is more probable that they were Cluniac monks of the Priory, the confusion easily arising from the similarity of dress and the common appellation of Black Monks. The barons were also represented by ecclesiastics, stated on the same authority to have been two Grey Friars (Franciscans); but it is much more probable that the two bishops of London and Worcester, already employed on such missions, should have resumed that duty. There was, indeed, an establishment of Grey Friars near the bridge at Lewes, but they are not at all likely to have been trusted by the barons with so important a charge. Prince Edward has even been represented as flying to them and being there taken, but this must have arisen from mistaking the Priory for a convent of that order:—

[1] Walt. Heming.
[2] It is possible that John Peckham, said to be a native of Lewes and educated by the monks of S. Pancras, was in the town and employed. He was a Franciscan, and rose by his own talents to the archbishopric of Canterbury, 1279 to

1294. Adam de Marisco, in one of his letters [speaks of John de Pescham as "a scholar honourably distinguished for correct habits and proficiency in learning, who kindled by a divine yearning has just entered the religious order of Minor Friars." A. de Mar. Epist. p. 256. Ed. Brewer.]

"And to the Frere Menors in to toun Sir Edward flew vaste,
And ther as he nede moste, yeld him at laste."—ROB. GLOUC.

Simon de Montfort is said[1] to have influenced the treaty by threatening to advance upon the Royalists with the heads of the King of the Romans, Basset, and his other prisoners fixed upon his pennons; but so needless an insult is not to be believed. When the natural terror of the one party and the confidence of the other are considered, there was plainly an unquestioned power of dictating terms, and under such circumstances the conditions of an agreement are soon discussed and settled. On the same Thursday, accordingly, the articles were drawn up and assented to of the treaty of peace, which has ever since been known as the *mise* of Lewes[2].

The deed itself, though frequently referred to in authentic documents, not being extant, its substance must be collected from the statements of the chroniclers, which, however, do not vary materially. The fullest account professes to sketch out the written form of the articles agreed upon, and appears consistent with known facts, though from a royalist bias it calls the barons "accomplices of the Earl of Leicester[3]," a term which certainly would not be used in a deed dictated by them.

The *mise* stipulated that "the King and his adherents on the one side, and the Earls of Leicester and Gloucester, with their adherents (accomplices) on the other side, should procure two Frenchmen to be chosen in the presence of the illustrious King of France, by means of three prelates and three nobles of France, to be named and summoned by the said King; and that the two, when chosen, should come to England, and associate with themselves a third per-

[1] Mat. Westm.
[2] "Tunc nullo renitente quidquid voluit potuit ordinare, extorto a Rege et Domino Edward quodam sacramento, quod et ipse Comes etiam cum suis præstitit, statutum quod-dam quod Misam Lewensem inusitato nomine nuncupabat."—T. Wyke. It was, however, not an unusual term at the time.
[3] Mat. Westm. following T. Wyke.

son[1], belonging to England, whom they should select; and whatever the said three should determine, both as to what the King should confirm or annul, and also as to all controversies which had arisen between the parties concerning the government of England, should remain thereby fixed, and ratified by the corporal oath of the parties, according to a deed drawn up on the subject, certified by the seals of the King, and of the aforesaid parties; and that Prince Edward and Prince Henry, the firstborn sons of the King and of the King of the Romans, should be given up as hostages for the fulfilment of the above on the part of the King.

These hostages, it is explained by another authority[2], were to be considered as substitutes for the lords Marchers and others, not then prisoners—referring to de Mortimer and those who had escaped from the battle.

An additional article is also given[3], which was certainly acted upon to some extent, namely, that the prisoners on both sides should be released without ransom.

Other writers refer the arbitration to two spiritual and two temporal nobles, French, according to one[4], or English, according to a second[5], with the Count d'Anjou and the Duke of Burgundy as umpires in case of disagreement.

Another chronicler[6]—who, although contemporary, does not use the word *mise*—states the articles of the agreement to have been seven:—1. Referring the disputed points to the Archbishop of Rouen, the Bishop of London, Peter le Chamberleyn, Hugh le Despenser, the Justiciary, and the Papal Legate, who were to settle everything, except the release of the hostages: the 2nd required the concurrence of three of the above: 3. That they should swear to choose only Englishmen for counsellors: 4. That the King was to be guided by them, and that Magna Charta and the Charter

---

[1] "Tertium de Angliâ."—Mat. Westm.
[2] "Pro Marchiensibus et aliis qui in ipso bello captivati non fuerant tanquam obsides tenerentur."—T.
[3] Wyke.
[4] H. Knighton.
[5] Fabyan.
[6] Lib. de Ant. Leg.
[7] W. Rish. de Bello Lew.

of the Forests should be observed; that the King should be moderate in his expenses and grants until his old debts were paid off, and he was enabled to live on his own means[1], without oppression to merchants or the poor: 5. That the award should be duly secured, and that then the royal hostages should be released, on giving pledges not only not again to excite discord in the kingdom, but to repress it in others: 6. That the Earls of Leicester and Gloucester should have ample security, as well as their adherents, not to suffer any damage on account of past deeds: 7. That the terms of the agreement should be debated in England, and settled finally by the next Easter at latest.

These slightly varying descriptions of the *mise* are substantially the same, all implying a reference to France, and the surrender of the two young Princes.

There can be little doubt that the latter important condition was mainly introduced by the voluntary generosity[2] and high spirit of Prince Edward, in order to avert the personal captivity of the King.

"Edward that was King, with his owen rede
For his fader the Kyng himself to prison bede[3]."—ROB. BRUNE.

A royal proclamation, referring to this event, in the following year describes the Prince as having at that time "totally lost, by his inconsiderate levity, the grace of public favour, which he had before acquired by becoming hostage of his own accord[4]."

In spite of the publicity of this event, one ancient authority chooses not only to make King Henry himself the prisoner, but actually depicts his arrest in a rude drawing on his manuscript[5], and, to complete the story, repre-

---

[1] "De suo."
[2] "Sponte sed invitus ab eâdem (ecclesiâ) exiens."—MSS. Add. 5444.
[3] "Edward, who was King, of his own accord offered himself as a prisoner for his father, the King."
[4] Rymer, July 7, 1265.

[5] Chr. Laudunense a Christo ad 1338, in MSS. Cotton, A. iv. 110. The feet of the figures have been clipped off at the bottom of the page in the original.—V. copy of MS. drawing, pl. 4, p. 254.

sents also the King with his own hand killing de Montfort at Evesham.

These conditions of peace, duly certified by oaths and seals, while they relaxed, as was natural, nothing of the previous demands of the victorious barons, and even despised more stringent security for their fulfilment, yet introduced no new pretensions even at this moment of power, and the constitutional maxim of respecting the person of the King was carefully upheld, at least in words, even when so much disgrace and ruin were attributed to his advisers. Whether there be just ground for supposing bad faith in either or both of the parties to this *mise*, and how far its provisions were faithfully executed, will be seen by following the course of events a little longer.

The reference of the national dispute (for it was nothing less) to the arbitration of France, the repetition of an expedient so recently tried without success, may certainly excite surprise and even suspicion; but it was, nevertheless, this condition which was considered so much the essence of the whole treaty, as to have obtained for it, then and since, the distinctive name of the *mise* of Lewes.

On the following day, Friday, May 16, the surrender of the royal Princes, as substitutes for their respective fathers, took place. Even after giving this bail; however, the King of the Romans does not appear to have been a free agent for some time, but was required to purchase his liberty by the payment of a large sum of money five months afterwards. As much as £17,000, and £5000 in gold, have been stated[1] as his ransom, and his estates were certainly put under sequestration to ensure payment.

Prince Edward, the more dangerous foe, and the more valuable pledge of submission, was almost immediately sent in custody to Dover, under the charge of his former friend, Henry, de Montfort's eldest son. This compulsory ride to Dover, under circumstances so altered from his former visits

[1] Chr. Mailr.

there, and his late attempt to surprise it, was a popular topic of ridicule in those days:—

> "Be the luef be the loht, Sire Edward,
> Thou shalt ride sporeless o thy lyard[1]
> Al the ryhte way to Dovere ward;
> Shalt thou never more breke fore-ward,
> And that roweth sore:
> Edward thou dudest ase a shreward,
> Forsook thy eme's lore[2]."

A royalist chronicler asserts that the Prince was treated "less honourably than was becoming[3];" and another even goes so far as to say,

> "In prison nere a yere was Edward in a cage."

But we must allow some licence even to such poetry as Robert Brune's, and we have, in disproof of such a charge, not only express testimony[4] that "he was treated with courtesy, not as a captive;" but the Prince's own feeling conduct towards his jailor, Henry de Montfort, whose burial he attended in person with every mark of regret and respect after the battle of Evesham.

All appearance of his former court was dismissed by the King on Saturday, May 17th, when the nobles and knights, who had devotedly fought for him, his ·familiar friends, and even his personal attendants, were all discharged. Many of the chiefs, who had come from the Marches, or the distant North, left Lewes at once for their

---

[1] In Warton's Hist. Poet., speaking of Richard Cœur de Lion's horse, an old poem says: "Favell of Sypres (Cyprus) ne Lyard of Prys (Paris), Ben not at ned as he ys."

[2] Polit. S. from MS. Harl. "Whether willing or unwilling, Sir Edward, you shall ride spurless on your horse, all the direct way towards Dover, you shall never more break your promise, and that is a sore trouble to you; Edward, you acted perversely when you forsook your uncle's instruction."

[3] "Minus honeste quam decebat fecerat custodiri."—T. Wyke, Chr. Roff.

[4] "Regem Angliæ licet ceperunt, tamen non quasi captivum sed curialiter tanquam dominum custodierunt." —Taxt. Chr. "Quos dominus Symon in deditionem postea suscipiens et tanquam dominis suis quandam reverentiam exhibens, eos honorabiliter captivavit."—Nangis. Gest. S. Lud. "Regem honore quo debuit in tali casu fideliter observavit."—Nang. Chr.

homes[1], not daring to trust themselves in de Montfort's power. Many, indeed, both lay and clergy, were plundered in their retreat[2], while one party, under William de Say[3], joined the garrison of Tunbridge Castle; and although the royal warrant for its surrender was soon received there[4], they nevertheless kept together as an armed body. While forcing their passage across the country, they gratified their angry revenge by slaughtering at Croydon[5] a party of the Londoners returning from the battle, and finally made good their way to Bristol, which they gallantly maintained in Prince Edward's interests until his escape.

After the royal household and party were thus broken up, de Montfort prepared to leave the scene of the battle, and to remove King Henry with him after his week's eventful sojourn at Lewes.

[1] It may be remarked, in reference to this dispersion and to the scarcity of provisions, that the King's army had been summoned to meet on March 30, so that the customary forty days of service had already expired; and this consideration may also account for the rapid movements and great enterprises of this army during the stipulated period.

[2] Mat. Westm.

[3] William de Say, of an ancient family, held forty-two knights' fees. He was governor of Dover, Canterbury and Rochester castles 44° H. III., and died 1272. Cal. Inq. p. m. Arms, "Quarterly or and gules, on the first a lion passant azure, armed gules."

[4] From an entry in the Hundred Rolls it seems probable that Tonbridge did not surrender at once, and that preparations were made to besiege it. "Item dicunt quod cum Hundredus de Stuting adisset per preceptum domini Regis ad obsidendum castrum de Tunebrigg, &c." Rot. Hund. I. p. 227. P.

[5] H. Knighton. This incident gave rise to the error of Prince Edward's continuing his pursuit of the Londoners to Croydon at the battle.

CHAPTER XII.

GOVERNMENT OF THE BARONS.

"It is to your ancestors, my Lords, it is to the English Barons, that we are indebted for the laws and constitution we possess; their virtues were rude and uncultivated, but they were great and sincere; their understandings were as little polished as their manners, but they had hearts to distinguish right from wrong, they had heads to distinguish truth from falsehood; they understood the rights of humanity, and they had spirit to maintain them."—
Lord Chatham's Speech, Jan. 9, 1770.

"HAIL to the Earl, inspirited and puffed up by success, glorying beyond measure in the prowess of himself and his sons whom he so tenderly loved, that in his anxiety to promote them he blushed not to attempt the most daring enterprises!" Thus ironically exclaims a royalist chronicler[1], whose indignation is particularly excited at the King being made to travel about with Simon de Montfort, crying out upon it as "unheard-of wantonness of guilt, exceeding in arrogance even the very pride of Lucifer."

That de Montfort exercised the power which his victory gave him, is certain; but as the proceedings subsequent to the *mise* have been much misrepresented, it will be worth while to note down with some detail the facts authenticated by public documents, and to watch how far he may be liable to the charge of self-aggrandisement. This appeal, indeed, to

[1] T. Wyke.

facts, is but a repetition of one made for him by a contemporary[1].

Provisions had been already failing in the King's army, it may be remembered, before the battle; and, as the providence of an extensive commissariat did not then accompany armies, de Montfort was probably as little prepared to support his own troops long at Lewes. A speedy removal, therefore, became a necessity to both; and the route chosen towards the east enabled him to secure the fortresses of the Cinque Ports, especially Dover, which a few days subsequently (May 28) the King ordered to be entrusted "to his beloved nephew, Henry de Montfort[2]," the jailor of his son.

On the day of leaving Lewes the King reached Battle, and dated from thence, May 17, the appointment of Drogo de Barantin, as Governor of Windsor Castle[3], and other orders for the immediate release of the Northampton prisoners, particularly the relations of the Earl of Leicester, his son Simon de Montfort, and Peter, a veteran ever active and stanch to the cause of his great kinsman, with his two sons Peter and Robert. Their discharge appears studiously disguised under the courteous pretext inserted in the royal order, which requires their advice, because "according to the form of peace, made between us and the barons, it is necessary that we should take counsel[4]."

Only a fortnight had elapsed since the King's troops had been at Battle, flushed with their recent successes, and committing ravages and extortions[5] at the Abbey there, and at

---

[1] " Seductorem nominant Simonem atque fallacem,
Facta sed examinant probantque veracem."—
Polit. S. from MS. Harl. 978.
[2] Rymer.
[3] Rot. Pat. 48° Hen. III.
[4] "Cum per formam pacis inter nos et barones initam et firmatam—deliberare debeamus."—Rymer.
[5] "Namque monasterium quod Bellum vocatur,

Turba sævientium, quæ nunc conturbatur,
Immisericorditer bonis spoliavit.
 *   *   *
Monachi Cistercii de Ponte Roberti
A furore gladii non fuissent certi,
Si quingentas Principi marcas non dedissent,
Quas Edwardus accipi jussit vel perissent."—
Polit. S. from MS. Harl. 978.

the neighbouring one of Robertsbridge. The monks must have relished the spectacle of speedy retribution, which now brought the wrong-doer humiliated and harmless again to their door.

Similar orders were now issued with the King's authority, transferring to the barons the custody of all the royal castles; and it must have forcibly evinced to distant counties the entire prostration of the royalists, when they received the royal proclamation, "forbidding all hostilities, and commanding the arrest of all disturbers of the peace, which had been made by the disposition of Divine grace[1];" and this was dated (May 25) from Rochester, the very point whose resistance had so lately baffled de Montfort. Like terms of contentment and pious gratitude appear in several other proclamations at this period: the King referring to the peace as "made by the inspiration of Divine grace;" "by the co-operation of Divine favour[2]." Strong words, not fit to be lightly used, but fearfully contrasting with his furious denunciations of the same transaction subsequently.

On the 28th of May we find the King in London[3]. The palace of Westminster had been accidentally burnt[4] two years before, in consequence of which he now became a guest under the roof of the bishop, whose proffer of peace he had rejected at Lewes.

The loss of his usual residence was an additional mortification to Henry, whose taste had induced him to adorn all

[1] Rymer. Latin proclam. to co. Derby.
[2] Rymer. St Paul's, June 2, 1264; St Paul's, June 4.
[3] He arrived on the day before the Ascension.—Fabyan. The fire at the palace was on Feb. 7, 1262.—Add. MSS. 5444. "Combusta sunt proprio igne suo parva aula Dom. Regis apud Westmonasterium camera et capella et receptorium et aliæ plures domus officinales."—MS. Harl. 690.
[4] There is a charge for scindulæ (shingles) for the King's Palace in Westminster in 1163; so that probably it was roofed with that combustible material. Brayley's Westm. p.19. The King immediately after the fire applied to the Bishop of London, then recently elected, for timber to repair his loss. The bishop in his reply, Feb. 19, 1262, regrets the calamity, but states that his woods had been so destroyed during the vacancy of the see, that little or nothing was left to repair his own houses. His steward should report thereon, before he made any promise to the King. No. 511 Chanc. Rec. 5th Rep.; Rymer, new edit. I. 424.

his palaces by every embellishment in his power. The best artists, including some Italians, were thus employed by his directions, and there seems some powerful evidence of oil colours being used by them in their paintings, though long before the acknowledged period of such an invention[1]. Green, sometimes with golden stars, seems to have been a favourite colour for the walls of his rooms; but besides the representations of "pretty[2] cherubim with cheerful and merry countenance," and of several saints, especially his royal predecessor, Edward the Confessor, there were also some series of scriptural and historical subjects, which must have called forth skill in art. A Florentine[3] painter, in 1256, was de-

[1] In 1239, Edward, the son of Odo, was paid £117. 10s. for oil, varnish, and colours bought, and for pictures in the Queen's chamber, made during fifteen days' work. Sir F. Palgrave, in his "Truths and Fictions," quotes from Liber Horne an order of the painters of the guild of St Luke, that "no craftsman shall employ other colours than such as shall be good and fine, good synople, good azure, good verdigrease, and good vermillion, or other good body colours mixed and tempered with oil (autres bonnes couleurs destemprés d'huile)." Odo, son of John, the Fusour in the Exchequer, granted to Edward, son of Odo the goldsmith, his office of Fusour for twelve marcs silver on going to the Holy Land, 24° Hen. III. 1240. In 1267 the King allowed Odo to depute Hamon de Wroxhull for two years to his office. It was finally surrendered to Edward I. in his 13°. Madox, Hist. Excheq. p. 201.

[2] "Duos cherubinos cum hilari vultu et jocoso," ordered to be painted in the tower of London, 1236.

[3] William, a monk of Westminster. He was also employed at Windsor, in 1260. [The following notices are probably taken from the Close Rolls. Sir T. Duffus Hardy has mentioned several of them in his Introduction, pp. xlv. xlvi:]—

1228. 20s. for painting the great Exchequer Chamber.

1232. June 3, Kidderminster. King's chamber wainscot in Winchester to be painted with the same pictures as formerly.

Woodstock chapel to be painted with the Saviour, four Evangelists, S. Edmund and S. Edward.

1236. Great chamber at Westminster to be painted of a fine green to resemble a curtain. Sides of St Stephen's chapel to be green with crucifix, Mary and John. Three glass windows in chapel of S. John, to represent the Virgin Mary, the Trinity, St John, and two images of S. Edward delivering ring to S. John. April 7. St Peter's church in Tower to be painted with the Virgin, SS. Peter, Nicholas, Catherine, St Peter as an archbishop; image also S.Christopher; histories of SS. Nicolas and Catherine to be painted at their altars with two cherubin.

1237. August, £4. 11s. to Odo for painting pictures in King's chamber at Westminster.

1238. Chamber at Winchester to be painted green with stars of gold and compartments containing Histories from the Old and New Testament.

1239. To Odo for oil, &c.

1241. Two windows in the hall to be filled with pictures.

1248. In Queen's chapel, Winchester, S. Christopher to be painted, and S. Edward.

sired to paint "in the wardrobe where the King washes his head," a man rescued from his enemies by his own dogs. A political enigma may lie hidden in this device[1], though occurring before the civil troubles began, and at any rate the subject harmonised with the King's situation on many occasions. Other subjects of a nature less congenial to his spirit, however, seem also to have been favourite ones, as the history of Alexander (taken probably from the romance written 1200), in the Queen's chamber at Nottingham, and the history of Antioch, with the single combat of his uncle Cœur de Lion, in Palestine[2]. The King's adopted motto, which was inscribed profusely in Latin and French on the walls, and even on his chess-board, seems characteristic enough of his prodigal bounty to favourites:—

"Ke ne dune ke ne tine ne pret ke desire."
"Qui non dat quod habet non accipit ille quod optat."
"He who gives not what he has,
His chief desire lets slip pass."

To have loved the fine arts, in the midst of ignorance and barbarism, is no mean honour to the English King, and by such encouragement he fulfilled a duty, which has been

1249. John de S. Omer to paint Wardrobe at Westminster.
1250. In S. Stephen's Chapel, be painted the Apostles round the wall, Day of Judgment on West, and Virgin on a panel.
1251. Exploits of Richard I. to be painted in Tower (as at Clarendon 1237), by Th'. Espernir.
1252. Queen's Chamber in Nottingham Castle to be painted with history of Alexander; window in Northampton Castle to be painted with Dives and Lazarus; five statues of Kings, carved in freestone, gift to St. Martin's ch., London.
1262. Windsor Castle paintings to be restored; paintings in Great Hall at Guildford to be repaired, and paintings to altar made.
1270. Twenty marcs to Master Walter for painting our chamber in Westminster.

[1] Rot. Claus. 40° Hen. III.
[2] "The Chamber of Antioch we wish it called," adds the King in his order for Westminster. The same subject was also painted at Clarendon, 1237, and in the Tower, 1251. John de S. Omer and Walter de Colchester, sacristan of S. Albans, eminent painters at this time.—See Walpole's Anec. and Mad. Exch. In 1292 appears the name of Walter, painter, and Thomas his son; and about the same time, *passim*, there occur among the payments of the King's household artists, John of Soningdon, John of Carlisle, Roger of Winchester, Thomas of Worcester, Roger of Ireland, John of Nottingham, William of Ross, William of Oxford, Godfrey of Norfolk, &c.—Brayley's Westm. 91.

neglected or ignobly perverted by many of his successors. A great impulse, contemporaneous with the rise of Strasburg (1277), Cologne (1240), Rheims (1215), Amiens (1220), and la Sainte Chapelle (1245), was given during his reign to church-building in England; besides 157 religious houses, the cathedrals of York, Salisbury, Lichfield, Worcester, Gloucester, Ely, St Paul's, Durham, Wells, and Winchester, were in progress for the future ornament of the country[1].

Contributions were sent to the royal menagerie from all quarters, proving how widely his zoological taste was known. An elephant, the first seen in England, was given him by France, 1255; a bear, by Norway; three leopards, in allusion to his arms, a camel and some buffaloes by the Emperor[2].

The Queen's chaplain, John de Hoveden, has left a very pleasing specimen of poetry[3], which may have been current at court, in his verses on the nightingale; and had Henry withheld his lavish grants from less worthy objects than such poetry and his other peaceful pursuits[4], these would

---

[1] A fact, interesting to the history of art in England, has been lately ascertained by Rot. Pat. Edw. I., in Househ. Exp. The shrine of Edward the Confessor, and the beautiful effigies of Hen. III. and Queen Eleanor of Castile, have been long attributed to Pietro Cavallini, who was not born till 1279. The shrine, however, was begun in 1241, and completed before King Henry's death, and the statues were in progress in 1290, payment of £113. 6s. 8d. being made to W. Torrelli for his work on them.

[2] M. Par.

[3] "Avis perdulcissima ad me quæso veni,
Veni, veni, mittam te quo non possum ire,
Ut amicum valeas cantu delinire
Ejus tollens tædia voce dulcis lyræ,
Quem heu! modo nequeo verbis convenire," &c.

(Ver. 4).— MSS. Cott. Cleop., A. xii., p. 67. Philomela per J. de Hoveden, capellanum Alionoræ Reginæ, matris Edwardi primi.

[4] Among these may be remembered his care to supply London with pure water, "for the poore to drink and the rich to dress their meate." In 1235 was begun the first cistern of lead, the great conduit in West-Cheap, castellated with stone; the pipes were enclosed within a large brick arch, so as to admit of workmen descending for the purpose of repairs. Henry Wales was the mason. The water-course from Paddington to Jameshead was 510 rods, on to Mewshead 102 rods, on to the Crosse in Cheape, 484 rods. Tyborne water was also conveyed in leaden pipes of six inch. diameter (in 1236) from the springs towards the city boundary by private subscriptions, and a grant from Gilbert de Sandford.— S. M. 758.

have caused no exhaustion of his finances and no jealousy among his own barons, to goad them into civil war, and reduce him to the dependent condition in which he now was. It has been, however, remarked in reference to the ultimate result, that "his vice of prodigality was the only part of his character useful to his country[1]."

Among the earliest measures to heal the wounds of the late struggle, the Jews were now allowed to share in the restored tranquillity. They had been farmed out in 1255 to the tender mercies of Prince Richard, for the sum of 5000 marcs (£3333. 6s. 8d.), and in 1256 and 1261 the King had granted him the dangerous permission to examine their strong chests[2]; they had been suspected also and plundered by the barons; but they were now permitted to return to their homes, and in London a royal proclamation commended them to the especial protection of the mayor[3].

The Northampton prisoners were required to be brought up to London for release, exchanging them, "man for man[4]," for those taken at Lewes; and as several of the prisoners are found at large soon afterwards, the writs to that effect seem to have been obeyed even by the firm royalists, including Roger de Mortimer, Roger de Clifford, and James de Alditheley[5], to whom they were addressed. The latter, James de Alditheley, of the ancient house of Verdon, was a great friend of the King of the Romans, whose coronation he had witnessed. He had been constable of Newcastle,

[1] Sir J. Mackintosh.
[2] Rymer. Cal. Rot. Westminster, Feb. 24, 1255. "De scrutando omnes archas Judæorum, ac de capiendo omnia sua bona in manus regis per totum regnum."—Tower, July 18, 1261, Rot. Pat. In 1265, Oct. 1, the King recalled his pardon of the debts of Jews, as having been made under constraint.—Rot. Pat. 49°. In 1270 a grant of 6000 marcs (£4000) was made towards Prince Edward's crusade (de Judaismo) from the profits on the Jews. They were worse treated afterwards, and in 1290 expelled by Edward I. from England. [The "archæ Judæorum," as Mr Walford points out in a letter to Mr Blaauw, were probably the public chests, in which were kept copies of the securities made to the Jews by their debtors.]
[3] Rymer, June 11, 1264.
[4] "Prisonem pro prisone."—Rymer. Thus Geoffry de Nevill, in the service of Prince Edward, a Lewes prisoner, was exchanged for Robert Newington, taken at Northampton.—Rot. Pat.
[5] The Alditheley or Awdley Arms, were gules, a fret or.

and being, like his father before him, sheriff of Shropshire and Staffordshire, was in that capacity repeatedly called upon to repel the attacks of the Welsh borderers. Though the prisoners[1] now in his power were released, yet he did not desist from raising forces to oppose the barons until their final overthrow[2].

The barons, in their anxiety to obtain possession of the royal castles at this time, caused the King to order his fair daughter-in-law, the Castilian princess, immediately to quit Windsor Castle, where she had awaited the chances of the war. The name of Eleanor, until rivalled in our own days, has long served as the noblest type of conjugal love on the English throne[3]. Her courage, as well as the refinement of her taste and manners, are well known; and when she closed a life of purity and affection at the age of forty-seven, all can sympathize with the chivalrous profuseness of her husband's regret. Stately crosses marked the thir-

---

[1] Robert de Sutton, Robert Fitzwalter, Philip de Covel, John de Wiavil, &c.—Rymer. "Robert de Sutton" was perhaps the Abbot of Peterborough who had sent his men under the banner of his convent to Northampton to resist the King; he was in office from 1262 to 1274.—Chr. W. de Whyttlesey.

[2] He afterwards went on pilgrimages, in 1268 to S. Jago di Compostella, and in 1270 to the Holy Land; and died by breaking his neck, 1272.—Banks' Dorm. Baron. Arms, gules, a fret or.

[3] The popular belief of the cross having given rise to the name of Charing (Chère Reine) is an error, as noted in Hasted's Kent (folio, 1790), Vol. II. p. 211. Domesday makes mention of "Cheringes" in Kent, called in other ancient records Cerringes and Cherring. In Dugdale's Monast. VI. 677, is a deed relating to the Hospital of Ronsivall (Plac. coram Rege apud Westm. de term. Mich. 7°, Ric. II., Rot. 21, Midd.), thus describing its situation and referring to its foundation by William, Earl of Pembroke; the elder Earl William died 1219, the son in 1231.

"Hospitale de Ronsivall juxta Charyng Crosse in Diœc. London., capella de Rounsyvall—cum ex parte Prioris Hospitalis beatæ Mariæ de Rounsyvall nobis sit supplicatum, ut, cum Willielmus Mareschallus, nuper Comes Pembrochiæ, per cartam suam, quam Dominus, Henricus quondam Rex Angliæ, progenitor noster per cartam suam confirmavit, unum messuagium et certa tenementa in Cherryng, ubi prædicta capella jam situata existit." Richard II. having granted the ground to Nicolas Sleke, recalls the grant, in order to restore it to the prior, "Westm. 24 Apr. anno regni nostri sexto." The jury affirm this, "Juratores dicunt super sacramentum suum quod Willielmus Marischallus, &c., &c., dedit et concessit Priori et conventui Hosp. B. M. de R. et successoribus suis in perpetuum unum mess, et certas terras et tenementa in Charryng." The hospital belonged to the foreign Priory de Rosida Valle of Pampeluna in Navarre, and was suppressed by Henry V. as alien. Northumberland House was built 1614 on the site. "Anno 1292," "Crux apud Cheringes incepta fuit."—Leland's Collect. II. 356.

teen[1] spots hallowed by her corpse on its passage to the tomb[2], on which the continuous light of waxen tapers[3] preserved the memory of her soft brilliance, even down to the days of the Reformation. The royal mandate for her removal sounds harsh and peremptory:—

"The King to Eleanor, consort of our first-born son Edward, health. Since we wish by all means that you should leave our castle of Windsor, where you now protract your stay[4], we command you to come forth from the same with your daughter, with John de Weston your steward, with William Charles your knight, with two damsels and the rest of your household, your furniture and goods, and to come to Westminster, there to dwell until we shall have ordained otherwise: and this, as you love our honour and yours, you will by no means omit, because we undertake to excuse you toward the said Edward your lord, and will preservè you harmless: We, therefore, by these present letters patent, receive you, your said daughter, John Weston, your damsels and household and chattels into safe and secure conduct. In witness whereof the King, June 18, St Paul's, London[5]."

This is said to have been the only occasion on which she was separated from her husband during her wedded life, and leaving England soon afterwards with her suite, she did not return until the close of the civil war.

[1] The five crosses of Northampton, Stratford, Woburn, Dunstable, and S. Albans, have been lately proved to have been built by John of Battle, and her statues were carved by Alexander of Abingdon and William of Ireland. In 1292—3—4 numerous payments, amounting to £394. 3s. 8d., were made to John of Battle (cementario), on account of his work, "Pro facturâ Crucis." "Pro Cruce facienda."—Rot. Pat. Ed. I., in Househ. Expen.

[2] She died Nov. 28, 1290, at Hardby in Lincolnshire [probably Harby near Lincoln, but in Nottinghamshire. Opus Chron. p. 49. Walsingham, I. p. 32. See, however, Taxter's Chronicle, p. 244. There is another Harby in the county of Leicester and the diocese of Lincoln, not far from Grantham, which the Osney Annals (p. 326) seem to indicate as the place]. Her heart was buried in the church of the Friars' Preachers of London. The entombment of her body in Westminster Abbey took place Dec. 17. An original letter of hers exists in the Tower MSS. No. 1111, dated Guildford, Oct. 14, to Robert Burnell, Lord Chancellor (1274–9), and has been translated in M. A. Wood's Letters of Roy. and Illus. Ladies, Vol. I. p. 46.

[3] Neale's Westm. Abb.

[4] "Ubi nunc moram trahitis."

[5] Rymer.

Joan, the wife of William de Valence, who was at Windsor at the time awaiting her confinement, was likewise ordered to retire to some convent or other fitting place[1].

Other orders of greater importance speedily followed. One strictly prohibited the bearing of arms without obtaining a license, on pain of death or loss of limbs; another, which is expressly stated to be, "by the advice of the barons according to the treaty[2]," assigned the care of each county to special wardens with paramount authority. The friends of de Montfort were of course among those appointed: his son Henry was appointed to Kent, Simon to Surrey and Sussex, Adam de Neumarket to Lincoln, John de Burg to Norfolk, Ralph Basset to Leicester; and this measure, while it strengthened much the influence of his party, tended also to repress the disorders incident to civil war. King Henry had established, in 1252, a good system of police over the country. A watch was to be kept up all night in every city by six men at each gate, in boroughs by twelve men, and in villages by from four to six stout and good men, armed with bows and arrows and other light weapons[3]. These precautions, had, however, failed to secure persons and property amidst the agitations of the war; it had become perilous to travel, and "the poor were plundered even of their straw beds," in order to furnish supplies for the chieftain's castle[4].

---

[1] Rot. Pat. 48° Hen. III.
[2] "De concilio baronum ut provisum sit," dated from S. Paul's, July 4, 1264.—Rymer.
[3] Henry's Hist.
[4] "Domus insuper pauperculorum ruricolarum usque ad stramentum lectorum rimabantur et expilabantur."—W. Rish. The great abbey of Peterborough, which had been punished by the Royalists (p. 125 note 4), suffered equally in turn from the barons after the battle of Lewes. "Barones per universam Angliam, magnalia facientes, de Ab-bate de Burgo *graves fines* ceperunt, ex eo quod Abbas tenuit cum rege et suis. Sed unum *multum valuit* abbati et abbatiæ, toto enim tempore guerrâ durante, idem Abbas panem et cervisiam cum aliis cibariis, in quantum potuit, semper parari fecit, ita quod omnes qui venerant sive ex parte regis, sive ex parte baronum, portis abbatiæ semper apertis, fertiliter erant refecti. Ob illam causam maneria abbatiæ Burgi in pluribus locis *salvata fuerunt ab incendiis et aliis malis;* tanto tamen populo superveniente, multoties contigit, quod

The mixed state of social order[1] and violence at this particular period may be exemplified by the adverse pleas of a curious lawsuit[2] which arose from it in more tranquil times. The Prior of Breamore[3] had obtained a grant of the manor of Lymington from Isabella Countess of Albemarle and Devon[4], but the lady afterwards repudiated it as having been made at an unfit time[5] between the battles of Lewes and Evesham: the prior, on the contrary, denied the time to have been unfit, inasmuch as the King's Court of Exchequer was then open to the sheriff, the justiciary, and all other officers of the King throughout the kingdom, and that pleas and all things concerning the King's peace were then carried on as usual. To this the countess rejoined that the King was in the custody of Simon de Montfort, the Prince a captive in prison, and that plunderers and disturbers of the peace were riding about armed[6]; and, because she refused to adhere to the barons, she was

quando conventus post servitium celebratum horâ nonâ more solito in refectorio pro se victum sperabat obtinuisse, non erat companagium in tota Abbatia nec in partibus propinquis, quousque de Stanforde abduceretur et aliquando in itinerando fuit deprædatum." The Abbot "fecit finem" to Simon de Montfort by £20 of silver, to Gilbert Earl of Gloucester £20, to Henry de Montfort £6. 13s. 4d., to Simon de Montfort junior £6. 13s. 4d., to John Fitzjohn £6. 13s. 4d., to Henry de Hastings £6. 13s. 4d. All the various fines thus paid [on different occasions to both parties] amounted to £4324. 18s. 5d., an enormous sum in those times. There is no other so detailed an account extant of the losses incidental to the civil war, but even in this instance the abbey was considered to have endured less evil than others, owing to the attempted neutrality of the abbot, and his keeping open house for both parties.

[1] Graystanes (c. 7) praises the prior, Hugh de Stichill of Durham, for having stopped the plunder of both parties by gifts. "Prior Hugo multa effudit pro salvatione patriæ; nam venientibus ex parte regis, vel ex adversâ parte ad deprædandum Episcopatum, semper occurrebat ipse muneribus placans eos."—Angl. Sacr.

[2] Cal. Placit. 172.

[3] The priory of Breamore in Hampshire, for Augustine canons. Lymington does not appear among the endowments of the house at its surrender to Henry VIII. It may, therefore, be presumed the lady's plea was held good.

[4] Isabella was the second wife of William Earl of Albemarle, who died at Amiens, 1260. In 1268 she had livery of the Isle of Wight, as heir to her brother, the Earl of Devon (v. her seal, pl. 5). Her only surviving child, Aveline, married (1269) Prince Edmund Crouchback, and lies in effigy in Westminster Abbey.

[5] "Tempore inopportuno."

[6] "Cum equis et armis deprædando equitabant."

traitorously sold by her enemies for 500 marcs to young
Simon de Montfort, to whom the prior had throughout
been a fast friend; and that Simon, wishing to take her,
had followed her about from place to place with horses
and arms, till in her alarm she fled into Wales and there
remained till peace was re-established.

A great council was summoned under the influence of
the barons, to meet in London on the Octaves of the Trinity
(June 23); and to this, besides the prelates and barons,
each county was to send four discreet and loyal knights
chosen by them[1]. As a similar summons had been on
previous occasions[2] sent to the counties, there was no revolutionary novelty in now doing so; and though it is not
the object of these pages to trace here the gradual progress of the representative system so ably investigated by
others, yet it may be remarked that no mention was as
yet made of consulting the towns at this crisis.

This assembly[3] accordingly met in June, and drew up
a confirmation of the barons'·proceedings. "This is the
form of peace," says the solemn preamble, "approved in
common and in concord by the Lord the King, the Lord
Edward his son, by all the prelates and lords, and by the
whole community of the realm of England, to continue
firm, stable and unshaken both during the reign of the King
and of Prince Edward after his death, until the treaty previously settled between the said King and the barons at
Lewes by the form of a certain *mise*, should be fulfilled[4]."
For the reform of the government three discreet and faith-

---

[1] "Quatuor de legalioribus et discretioribus militibus Comitatûs."—Rymer.
[2] By William I., to collect the actual laws; by John, in 1213; by Henry III., in 1258.
[3] There seems much variation in the parties summoned to the Great Council. In 1217 they were the archbishops, bishops, earls, barons, knights and freeholders; in 1235, the earls, barons, and all others who held of the King *in capite;* in 1237 the same as 1217, with the addition of abbots, priors and clergy. The first regular writ actually extant is dated 1292, 22° Ed. I.
[4] "Apud Lewes per formam cujusdam Misæ." Again, subsequently, "donec Misa apud Lewes facta et postea a partibus sigillata fuerit concorditer confirmata."—June 25, 1264. Rymer.

ful native-born subjects were to be named and authorized to choose nine others, by whose advice the King was to regulate the command of his castles, entrusting them to none but natives. These nine were liable to be dismissed on the advice of the three, who were themselves to be removable by Parliament only. Provision was made more forcibly to ensure the perpetual observance of the Great Charter, the Charter of the Forests, and the laudable long-approved customs of the realm. Aliens, both laymen and clergy, merchants and others, were allowed freely and peaceably to come, stay, or go, on condition of their not bearing arms or being in suspicious numbers.

To this act of pacification are affixed the seals of Richard Bishop of Lincoln[1], Hugh Bishop of Ely, Roger Earl of Norfolk the Marshal, Robert de Vere Earl of Oxford, Humphry de Bohun, William de Monchensy, and the Mayor of London.

The King, in pursuance of this deed, authorized the Bishop of Chichester[2], his "beloved and faithful" Simon Earl of Leicester and Gilbert Earl of Gloucester, to select the nine councillors who were to carry on the government according to the laws and customs, "until the *mise* lately made between us and our barons at Lewes, or some other form, if any better can be devised, should be fulfilled[3]."

The arrangement of church matters was at the same time committed to three bishops; and Archbishop Boniface was peremptorily required, on pain of confiscation, to return from

---

[1] Richard de Gravesend, bishop from 1258 to 1280. He had acted as a mediator in the truce of June, 1263.

[2] Stephen de Berkstead, Bishop of Chichester, to whom some historians attribute the actions of the Bishop of Worcester at Lewes, lived till 1288. The result of his present appointment was suspension and excommunication in 1265, on which he went abroad, and being suspected by Edward I. of connivance in the Viterbo murder hereafter referred to, never put himself in his power by a return to England.

[3] "Donec Misa per nos et barones nostros apud Lewes nuper facta, vel alia forma, si qua melior provideri possit, compleatur."—Rymer. Lingard substitutes the Bishop of Exeter for Chichester.

abroad and confirm some bishops who had been elected in his absence[1].

There seems nothing to object to in these securities which the Parliament thought proper to exact on this occasion for the complete execution of the *mise* of Lewes. There is a progress in them towards a final adjustment; and although the power of the King was put in abeyance by them, yet events rapidly arose which proved how necessary such restriction had become.

Affection and party zeal were again mustering their strength, and the Church of Rome once more raised its far-stretching arm to strike in aid of the royal cause. Even before the battle of Lewes an armed force of hired foreigners had been gathered from Brittany, Gascony, and Spain, by the Queen and her son Edmund, now no longer wearing the mockery of the Sicilian crown, and this had been swollen by the fugitive royalists to a formidable host. In July the archbishop, the Bishop of Hereford, Peter de Savoy, Hugh le Bigot, de Warenne, John Mansel, and many others, assembled round this most powerful amazon[2], at Damme, in Flanders.

The most energetic measures were required in England to repulse this threatened invasion, and the people were immediately summoned to assemble in the counties opposite the enemy's coast[3].

The royal writ, which de Montfort caused to be issued for the purpose of this general levy, is of the most urgent nature, allowing of no excuses for neglect, either on account of the short notice, the time of harvest, or any private incon-

---

[1] S. Paul's, June 25.—Rymer.
[2] W. Rish. de Bello Lew. T. Wyke. Add. MSS. 5444. According to the Chronicle of Worcester she summoned the "Magnates Hyberniæ et *Aquitaniæ*," and assembled her army "in portu de Swenesmuthe." Damme is a few miles inland towards Bruges, on a canal.

[3] The letter of King Henry to Charles, Count of Anjou (867 Chanc. Rec. 5th Rep.), seems to belong to this period. He therein begs him, now that peace had been made with his barons, to induce the King of the French to prevent the hostile ingress of foreigners into England.

venience; military tenants were to come not only with all their numbers due, but with all the horse and foot in their power, and every township was to provide from four to eight men armed with lances, bows and arrows, swords, darts, crossbows and bills[1]. The levy in Essex, Norfolk, and Suffolk[2], was by express command kept together even longer than the forty days of service, and the goodwill of the people was such that a large force was quickly gathered in Kent. This was encamped on Barham Downs, near Canterbury, and thither also the court repaired. Before leaving S. Paul's the King had granted[3] to his "dear and faithful" Simon de Montfort a special license to travel with arms and horsemen, notwithstanding the general prohibition, on account of the hostages and prisoners he had to convey with him. The motive alleged seems sufficient to exempt him from the charge of ambitious pride, however jealous some of his colleagues may have been. The danger was pressing, and unless all classes had zealously contributed their arms and money, it was thought at the time that the alien enemy would have conquered England[4]. The collision, however, after all these preparations, was unexpectedly averted by the prevalence of contrary winds for so many months that the spirit and resources of the invaders were ruined by the long compulsory inaction; and after selling their horses and clothes from very want, their threatening force was finally dispersed.

Another advance was made at this time in fulfilment of the *mise* of Lewes, which suffices to refute the assertion, that

---

[1] "Balistis et bachiis."—Aug. 3. Pat. 48° Hen. III. in Brady's App. [The priory of Dunstable contributed four horsemen and six foot-soldiers, and spent thirty marcs in all besides what was paid for horses and arms.—Annales de Dunstaplia, p. 233.]

[2] A year after the battle of Evesham this zeal of the Suffolk people was remembered to théir cost by the King, who, when he was at St. Edmund's Bury, fined the abbot of that monastery 80 marcs "ex eo quod homines dicti Abbatis et conventus S^{ti}. Edmundi erant ad custodiam maris ne regina cum suo exercitu intraret in Anglia post bellum de Lewes."—Chr. Walt. de Whittlesey, Abb. de Petriburg.

[3] July 15, 1264.—Rymer.

[4] Chr. Taxt. On Sept. 1 a demand was made upon 'the clergy for the payment of the tenth which had been voted.—Rymer.

"no farther mention was made of the reference to France[1]." The King's proclamation from Canterbury, September 4[2], commissioned "Prince Henry, though a hostage at Dover, to repair in person to the King of France, in order more fully to treat of and confirm the peace, previously swearing to be faithful to that single object, and to return by the Nativity of the Virgin," September 8. The chivalrous honour of the young Prince, which has been already noticed, merited this rare confidence of de Montfort in his prisoner, but the very selection of such a character stamps the treaty with sincerity, and appears as honourable to the barons as to the Prince. Every precaution was indeed taken: nine bishops gave bail for his return in 20,000 marcs (£13,333. 6s. 8d.), and three French envoys[3], who had perhaps suggested the mission, undertook that he should not be detained abroad. So strong was the animosity among the French against the English, excited probably by the refugee royalists, that when Prince Henry landed with this embassy, the townspeople of Boulogne made a violent attack upon his suite, in which nine Englishmen were killed[4].

By a document[5], dated on the Thursday after the appointed day of his return, we learn that the form of peace, unanimously assented to by the Parliament, had been actually presented to King Louis, and "though (King Henry observes) we think the terms well suited to God, to ourselves, and to our kingdom, yet, having learnt that some not well informed of the truth assert the said form to be insufficient and unsatisfactory, we, willing to labour for peace with all our might, as we are bound to do, in order that the justice and truth of the facts may be made manifest, commission the Bishop of London, and Hugh le Despenser the Justiciary, with Charles d'Anjou, the French King's brother, and the Abbot of Bec to examine the said form, enlarging or diminishing it, and to

[1] Hume.
[2] Rymer.
[3] P. de Chamberlent, de Nigell, and Henry de Verdell.
[4] Chr. Roff.
[5] Rymer.

arrange all unsettled matters, except as to aliens ; the Archbishop of Rouen to act as umpire in case of disagreement." The seals of the Earls of Leicester and Gloucester authenticate this *mise*. Charles d'Anjou[1] was considered favourable to the barons, and undoubtedly befriended the sons of de Montfort in their exile; the umpire also was probably well-known to de Montfort, there being extant a letter[2] recommending him to the archbishop's intimacy while in France; but the transaction seems to indicate an honest wish for an equitable peace. Nor was this all : another commission[3] of the same date appointed the Bishops of Worcester and Winchester[4] and Peter de Montfort to treat with the French King in person concerning the reform of the future government of the kingdom, the King promising to obey the award on pain of excommunication. The arrangement of the disputes with de Montfort on private matters, meaning, probably, an indemnity for the Norman property of his royal countess, was made a preliminary point expressly left to the decision of Louis[5].

The article as to aliens may be noticed as the only point withheld from this official reference ; and while the exception marks incontestably the sense of past evils endured, and the unbending resolution not again to submit to them, there is nothing in such terms contrary to or beyond the *mise* of Lewes. A conciliatory disposition to relax its rigour is indeed throughout transparent.

The Pope was unwilling to abandon so useful a client as King Henry had proved ; but, having already extracted all he

---

[1] W. Rish de Bello Lew.
[2] Ep. A. de Marisco, p. 86, ed. Brewer.
[3] Rymer. By a separate deed, the Bishop of London and Richard de Mepham, Archdeacon of Oxford, were added to this commission.
[4] John de Exon had been one of the negotiators at Brackley, in June 1268. He incurred disgrace by his present employment, and died abroad 1268.
[5] Nangis states that de Montfort himself went over to treat at Boulogne, and that Louis, finding him inflexible, allowed him to return. "Quant il ot parlé à lui, et il vit que il n'en vout riens fere, il l'en laissa aler empais, pource que li avoit donné sauf aler et sauf venir." The mission of Peter de Montfort probably caused him to be confounded with Simon.

could hope for on account of Sicily, he had obtained a formal renunciation[1] of that crown, in order to proffer it to a new purchaser. With an interference, now become habitual, he despatched in return the Cardinal Guido di Fulcodio to denounce the barons and to withdraw the clergy from their party. This able agent, who became Pope Clement IV.[2] a few months later, was by birth a Provençal, and had been the most eminent lawyer in France[3], until his wife's death induced him to take orders. It may be mentioned, as indicating his literary taste, that amidst the political intrigues he was sent to conduct at Boulogne, he wrote from thence to Roger Bacon, asking for his scientific works. The great Franciscan refused at the time, on the plea of being forbidden by the rules of his order, but his Opus Majus was soon after written expressly for this Pope, and sent to him in 1267.

While the barons refused to admit the legate, he vainly warned them (Aug. 12) to release the King and the Princes, "detained as hostages under an empty colour of words by reason of a certain *mise*[4] that had been made." With as little advantage did he summon the Bishops of London, Worcester, Winchester, and Chichester[5] to Boulogne. They went (Sept. 1) without powers to negotiate; and, emboldened by the consciousness of popular support, appealed to a general council of the clergy to be held at Reading. The barons sent indeed Peter de Montfort, "as a zealous lover of truth, peace, and tranquillity[6]," with credentials to treat with the

---

[1] By Bartolommeo Pignatelli, Archbishop of Cosenza. "Il offrit tout l'appui du pouvoir de l'Eglise contre ses sujets, et il recompensa la condescension de Henri III. et de Edmond, en se liguant avec eux contre les libertés Britanniques."—Sismondi, Hist. Rep. Ital.

[2] W. Rish erroneously says Clement VI. Clement IV. had been Archbishop of Narbonne, Cardinal-Bishop of Sabina. He was elected Pope Feb. 5, 1265, and died Nov. 29, 1268.

[3] "Senza alcun dubbio il primo giurista di tutta Francia."—Platina, Vite dei Pontèf.

[4] "Compromissi."—Rymer.

[5] Rymer. T. Wyke and W. Rish. state that the bishops went to Boulogne, Mat., Westm. that they did not go.

[6] Rymer, Sept. 24, 1264.

legate, but the principles of national independence and papal supremacy were too opposite to admit of agreement, and the legate finally, on Oct. 20[1], pronounced the barons contumacious, and in the name of the Pope "solemnly excommunicated them and their adherents as rebels, especially Simon de Montfort, Gilbert de Clare, Roger Earl of Norfolk, the City of London, and the Cinque Ports, exempting only the King and his chaplains, whom (says the legate plainly) we do not believe sincerely to adhere to their cause." To these spiritual penalties he added a temporal one, strictly forbidding the export of wine, wheat, or any other merchandize to England[2].

Whether the respect paid to these menaces would have been great or small was not destined to be put to proof. The four bishops who are said to have been the bearers of these curses may have given a hint of the nature of their burthen to the Cinque Ports, one of the parties denounced; and they, having vessels at this period ever ready for daring or even lawless action, intercepted them on the high seas, and seizing the document, left it to find its own weight and value by throwing it overboard. Another account supposes the parchment to have been detected at the usual custom-house search[3], when the messengers landed with it at Dover, when it was immediately torn to pieces and thrown into the sea. The barons certainly did not discontinue their religious services in consequence of this interdict.

The legate's prohibition of commerce was as idle a blow; for, in fact, the Cinque Ports were so rigorous in cutting off all intercourse with the continent, that the prices of various articles rose considerably: wine from £2 to £6. 8s. 5d.; wax from £2 to £5. 1s. 9d.; a pound of pepper from 6d. to 3s. The export of wool and the import of foreign cloth were

[1] Before a large assembly of clergy and laymen, at Hesdin, near St Pol. —Rymer, I. p. 447. P.
[2] W. Rish. de Bello Lew.
[3] "Scrutinio ex more in portu facto."—Chr. Roff.

equally prohibited, and the white English woollen cloths[1], which were usually sent to Flanders to be dyed, were now, with an ostentatious spirit of nationality, worn undyed[2]. With a wiser political economy than was then current, the chronicler Wyke remarks on this, that "the Earl of Leicester, in order to tickle plebeian ears, had given out that the English might be well supplied without the intercourse of foreigners, which, however, was impossible, for the interchange of goods from diverse realms furnishes all sorts of advantages[3]."

Although both armies which had watched each other on the opposite shores were now dissolved without striking a blow, there were some intrigues yet stirring among the malcontents around Queen Eleanor which excited the anxiety of the King, and in the apprehension of some undefined evil he sent her the following extraordinary letter[4], by the Dean of Wells, under a safe conduct:—

"Windsor, Nov. 18, 1264. The King to the Queen of England, health and sincerely affectionate love: know that we and our firstborn Edward are well and safe, which we heartily long to hear of you; signifying to you that the business which concerns ourself, you, and our said son, so proceeds to the honour of God, of ourselves, and of yourself, blessed be God, that we have a well-grounded hope of having a firm and good peace in our kingdom, on which account be cheerful and merry. Moreover we have heard that certain persons at this time propose to make a sale or alienation of our laws, and of the prerogative of ourself and our son in

---

[1] The early manufacture of these is noticed in the regulations of Richard I.

[2] "Statuerunt insuper, quod lanæ terræ operarentur in Anglia, nec alienigenis venderentur, et quod omnes uterentur pannis laneis infra limites terræ operatis, nec nimis pretiosas vestes quærerent."—Chr. Walt. Heming, 1258. The bailiffs of Yarmouth inform the King that by his command they had given up to certain merchants of Amiens 43 sacks of wool seized at Yarmouth, on security that the wool should not be carried to Flanders nor sold to Flemings. Chanc. Rec. 5th Rep.

[3] "Diversimoda commoda."—T. Wyke. H. Knighton.

[4] Rymer. The original is in Latin.

those parts, to the disinheritance of us and our heirs, against our will, which you ought by no means either to wish or permit, wherefore we send to command you that you suffer nothing to be done or attempted in such matters. On these and other concerns, give credence to what Master Edward de la Cnol[1], Dean of Wells, bearer of this present, shall say to you on our behalf. Witness the King at Windsor."

Another letter which the dean at the same time bare to Louis IX., in which Henry also urged him to refuse his consent, is more explanatory than the above vague allusions:—

"It has lately become known to us that certain persons, contrary to conscience and to our will, propose to make or to procure a sale or alienation of our rights and possessions, established under your dominion, for which we have done homage to you, to the perpetual disinheritance of ourselves and our heirs[2]."

There is no other evidence on the subject, but the tenor of the alarm expressed seems to point to an intention of the Queen to pledge or sell to France part of the English provinces in France, in order to raise supplies of men and money. Whether written with the privity of de Montfort or not, there seems no ground to justify any charge against him.

Another occurrence soon displayed again the activity of the defeated party. The hostage princes had been moved from Dover to Berkhampstead, and thence to the palace of Wallingford, which the King of the Romans had strengthened and embellished for his own residence. While there so slack a ward was kept upon them as to encourage the idea of their rescue, and about this time some of his devoted partisans at Bristol made a desperate attempt to effect it. Some of these knights were fugitives from Lewes, Hugh Turberville[3] and Hamo l'Estrange, led by Robert Waleran and Warren de

[1] He was dean from 1256 to 1284.
[2] Windsor, Nov. 17, 1264.—Rymer.
[3] Thomas de Turberville, a knight of Glamorganshire, having been taken prisoner by the French in K. Edward's reign, was released on the promise to betray one of the Cinque Ports, but was detected and hanged.

Bassingburne[1]. Waleran was a knight of importance, holding twenty-five military fees, and much employed both as governor of castles and on foreign embassies[2]. The barons confiscated his lands, but the King, for whom he fought at Evesham, rewarded him with grants of Hugh de Nevill's forfeited estate, and made him one of the four governors over London. Bassingburne was equally resolute and active: he had served in the Gascon wars, and had been one of the King's sureties in the *mise*. He too had grants of estates forfeited by the battle of Evesham, and was additionally rewarded by the pardon (1268) of his son Humphrey, who had sided with the barons. After a rapid march to Wallingford, these zealous knights surprised the garrison by a sudden attack at the dawn of day. They were obstinately resisted, however, and to their demand of releasing Prince Edward, the threat was returned that he should be fastened to a warlike engine, and so hurled off from the walls to the besiegers:—

"That hii wolde Sir Edward vawe out to hom sende,
Ilithered with a mangonel home with hom to lede[3]."—ROB. GLOUC.

[1] Of co. Cambridge.—Inq. post m.
[2] Robert Waleran was Sheriff of Gloucester, ambassador in 1253, 1260, and Sheriff of Kent, 1263. [Castellan of Dover in 1261. Abbrev. Rot. Orig. L p. 17.] He restored some of de Nevill's lands, 1266, but only on condition of retaining Stoke Curcy and other feoda militum.—Pat. 50 Hen. III. He was tried (47° H. III.) for opposing the Oxford Statutes and acquitted. He was at the battle of Evesham. He was the husband of the eldest co-heiress of Hugh de Kilpeck (descended from Wm. FitzNorman, the lord of Kilpeck co. of Hereford in Domesday). Two years before his death, which was in 1272, having no heirs and being then old, Waleran gave the reversion of Kilpeck to his nephew Alan de Plokenet, whose son Alan made grants to Dore Abbey in 1319, and was buried there, on whose tomb is inscribed:
"Ultimus Alanus de Plokenet hic tumulatur,

Nobilis urbanus vermibus esca datur."
As he died unmarried, the estates passed to his sister Joan de Bohun.
—Hist. of Kilpeck, by G. K. Lewis. 4to. 1842.
[Compare Foss's Judges of England, II. pp. 503—505, and] Dugdale's Baronage.
[3] "That they would fain send Sir Edward out to them, fastened with a mangonel to lead home with them." The mangonel (manga, manganum) was the most powerful engine in the wars of the middle ages, by which not only great stones, but even horses and men were thrown. "Obsides eorum machinis alligatos ad eorum tormenta, quæ mangas vulgo vocant, decrevit ojbiciendas."—Radivicus; Spelman's Gloss.
"Gyines he had of wonder wise
Mangenelles of great quyentise."
—Rom. of Richard Cœur de Lion; Warton's H. Poet.
"Warin de Basingeburne, familiaris Domini Edwardi, tenuit cas-

The prince therefore came forward on the ramparts to entreat his friends to retire.

This gallant enterprise, though a failure, gave occasion to the removal of the hostages to the stronger castle of Kenilworth. The Countess of Leicester received her nephews there with all the courtesy of a hostess, and

"Wat she mighte dude hom of solas."—ROB. GLOUC.

It throws some light on the easy restraint in which the princes lived under her roof, and on the sincerity of de Montfort's wish for a pacific settlement, that three of the most formidable Royalists who remained in arms, Mortimer, Clifford, and Leybourne, were allowed to meet the King at Pershore[1], on December 12th, and are noticed as on their way, under a safe conduct, to Kenilworth, December 15, to hold a parley with Prince Edward, for the promotion of peace[2]. We have no account of these dangerous interviews, but the subsequent events, the renewal of the war, and the escape of the Prince, may have been there concerted.

tellum de Benefeld, quia Dominus Winfridus prisonus erat." Chr. W. de Whittlesey, 1264, after taking of Northampton.
[1] Rot. Pat.
[2] " Qui certam formam pacis nobiscum inierint; gressus suos versus Kenilworth duxerint ad loquendum cum Edwardo primogenito nostro et ad pacem plenius firmandam." The King's letter to the Marchers, from Worcester, Dec. 15, 1264.—Rymer.

CHAPTER XIII.

PARLIAMENT.

"What Prince soever can hit of this GREAT SECRET (of governing all by all), needs know no more for his safety and happiness, and that of the people he governs; for no state or government can ever be much troubled or endangered by any private factions, which is grounded upon the general consent and satisfaction of the subjects."

Sir W. Temple, Heroic Virtue.

ENGLAND was now at rest within itself; "domestic treason, foreign levy," having ceased to agitate it, it breathed once more in freedom[1], and the season seemed ripe for conciliating all classes of the community into one great brotherhood. By summons, dated from Worcester[2], Dec. 14, a Parliament was accordingly ordered to meet in London on the octave of St Hilary, Jan. 20, 1265. To this were invited twenty-five bishops, priors and deans, and on Dec. 24 were added eighty-three[3] more heads of monasteries, besides the barons, and two

---

[1] "Jam respirat Anglia, sperans libertatem,
Cui Dei gratia det prosperitatem.
Comparati canibus Angli viluerunt,
Sed nunc victis hostibus caput extulerunt."
Polit. S. from MS. Harl. 978.

[2] See Archæol. Journal, 1862, p. 309, for the Articles made at Worcester by common consent of the King and magnates in 1264, referred to in Parliament held in London, March 1, 1265, and transmitted under the King's seal to all counties, to be observed inviolably for ever. They are the same as the provisions in the Statute of Marlborough (52° Henry III.).

[3] In aftertimes, out of 122 abbots, and 41 priors, who were occasionally summoned, only 25 abbots and 2 priors were constantly so. There was nothing unusual in the number of ecclesiastics summoned on this occasion.—V. Lingard. The Prior of Lewes, though now summoned, does not appear to have been so during the whole of Edward I.'s reign, nor until the beginning of Edward II.

representatives from each county[1]. The preamble in describing the occasion of meeting referred to the late serious disturbances, as then happily appeased, and required the advice of the prelates and barons, "in order to provide by wholesome deliberation for the security and completion of the peace, and for certain other business which the King was unwilling to settle without them[2]." Of similar summons to all these parties there had been previous instances, but now for the first time the cities and towns were also required "each to choose and send two discreet, loyal, and honest men;" and this remarkable innovation seems, by the date from Woodstock, Dec. 24, later by ten days than the first summons, to have been an afterthought, the result of more mature deliberation.

"After a long controversy, almost all judicious enquirers seem to have acquiesced in admitting this origin of popular representation." Such is the remark of the highest authority[3] on the subject, and it is more fitting to assent to this conclusion than to renew the discussion.

England had indeed been preceded by other nations in applying the representative system to towns. Aragon had

[1] In 1254 the Queen and Regents summoned the tenants in chief to sail to the King's assistance, and "besides these two lawful and discreet knights should be chosen by the men of every county, in the place of all and each of them, to assemble at Westminster, and to determine, with the knights of the other counties, what aid they would grant to their Sovereign in his present necessity, so that the same *knights might be able to answer in the matter of the said aid for their respective counties,*" p. 34.—[Report on the Dignity of a Peer, Appendix I. p. 13.]

[2] Rymer.

[3] Hallam, Mid. Ages, Vol. III. As all the proceedings of de Montfort's Parliament were cancelled a few months afterwards by the Great Council at Winchester, other dates have been adopted by writers for the commencement of Parliaments. In 1267 (52° Henry III.) the Statute of Marlborough, considered as the first regular Statute, was enacted by the "magnates, and discreet men as well of the higher as of the lower estate."—The Statute of Westminster in 1275 was sanctioned by the prelates, lords, "and all the commonalty of the realm." Hume points to the Parliament of Nov. 1295 as "the real and true epoch of the House of Commons." The summonses were directed to the nobles and prelates and knights as usual, and to the bailiffs of about 120 towns. The preamble is a noble acknowledgment of popular rights: "As the rule of justice teaches us that what concerns all should be by all approved."

thus supplied deputies to the Cortes in 1133, 1142, and 1162; and Castile[1] had done the same, perhaps in 1109, certainly in 1188, but the privilege was dealt out with a stinted measure, and fell on stony ground, flourishing for awhile, and making a goodly show, but gradually dwindling to a mere form.

The arms of the Hungarian nobles had in 1222 obtained from Andreas II. the Bulla Aurea[2], their great charter, which secured liberty of person, free descent of property, restriction on the admission of foreigners to place or power, and, above all, a right of resistance in case of non-observance, but it included no germ of representation.

After the great struggle with King John the English barons had appointed twenty-five guardians to watch over the execution of Magna Charta, in which were some few but important clauses for the benefit of the people, mixed up with several limitations of feudal burthens; a similar expedient had been adopted after the Oxford Statutes. After fifty years' experience of the perils to which their privileges were exposed by the encroachments of the Crown, a stronger and more enduring security was now devised, by committing the care of constitutional freedom thenceforth to the people themselves, whose interests they thus identified with their own. We cannot at this remote distance of time estimate all the motives that led to this measure. To these early statesmen such "matters may have seemed (in Chaucer's energetic phrase) great and glorious for all the people;" although few at the time, perhaps not even de Montfort, felt the full importance of this advancing step of British liberty. None could have foreseen, when they dropped the precious seed into the ready soil, the long succession of abundant harvests which were to spring from it, and bless the land with all the elements of power and plenty.

The King, who, by his prerogative, could claim tallages from the towns, had in some degree prepared the way, by

[1] Hallam, Mid. Ages. "Embiados de cada ciudad." In 1305 there were 192 deputies sent from 90 towns.
[2] Paget's Hungary.

accepting, as a substitute for this tax on personal property, a sum of money assessed by the payers themselves[1]. He had felt no need therefore of their representatives in the great council of the nation, but to de Montfort, at such a crisis of unusual restrictions on the Crown, the wish naturally presented itself of exhibiting in a combined strength[2] all the outward tokens of public opinion, which he felt to be favourable to his own party.

That England should be indebted to a Frenchman for this great experiment—by its results the most important in our national annals—and that the English populace, in their fondness for this French statesman, should even have attributed the honours of sainthood to him, may now sound strangely to our ears. It was not, however, the last occasion when the intervention of a foreigner was gladly invited on behalf of English liberty; and the people as readily adopted such guidance in 1688 as they did in 1264.

It has been remarked by an eloquent historian[3] that "the motives of opposition among the barons were personal and vulgar, but on that wild stock was engrafted the jealousy of foreigners, the impatience of irresponsible advisers, and the repugnance to high preferment flowing from the mere good will of the King, which afterwards bore excellent fruit." The best claim on our thankfulness, which might be preferred by the barons, who first admitted the extended interests of citizens to raise a voice in Parliament, arises from the reliance on the sympathy of the community on this occasion. On any other supposition this appeal to public opinion would have been ruinous to their own interests, and it should be an

---

[1] The lords of manors had about this time commuted many of the predial services of their tenants for money payments, as malt-silver, wood-silver, schap-silver (for water-carriage), larder-silver, ward-penny, 1d. or ½d. in lieu of a day's labour, never thinking of any future change in the value of money.—Archd. Hale, Domesday of St Paul, pp. lvi. lvii. lix.

[2] The number of burgesses varied: in 1295 they were 200; under Edward III. they were 190. The Commons, however, were not mentioned as an assenting party in the preambles of statutes before 1306.

[3] Sir J. Mackintosh.

honourable praise to them, and an honest pride to us in aftertimes, that English liberty thus owes its birth to the noblest parentage—confidence in the People[1].

It was while taking these measures to assemble a Parliament, that de Montfort repaired to his own castle of Kenilworth, and it is said that he there kept his Christmas with such exorbitant parade as to retain 160 knights[2] in his pay around him. These festivities[3] have been blamed, as an invidious contrast to the more restricted splendour of the King at Woodstock at the same period, but they may have been only so many additional courtesies to the royal hostages under his roof.

The mutual release of the Northampton and Lewes prisoners having taken effect, the great northern chieftains, Baliol, and others of the Royalist party, received a safe conduct[4] to attend Parliament[5].

The King being naturally anxious that his son should recover his liberty[6], addressed an earnest appeal to de Mont-

---

[1] A modern author has expressed a very different judgment: "It is not an illustrious nor auspicious origin for the House of Commons, that it should have been called into existence at the invitation, and to serve the purposes of a rebel."—Legal Review of Origin of Representation, by H. W. Tancred, Esq.

[2] W. Rish.

[3] Christmas seems to have been a permitted time for riots, like the Carnival of modern days. In 1230, when the inactive policy of the King prevented the English barons, quartered at Nantes, from fighting, "they betook themselves to gluttonous banquets and drinking, according to English custom, as if it had been Christmas."—M. Par.

[4] This was dated Westminster, Jan. 17, 1265, for "John de Baliol, Peter de Brus, Robert de Nevill, Eustache de Baliol, Stephen de Meinill, Gilbert Hamsard, Ralph Fitzralph, Adam de Gesein, Robert de Stotevill, knights."—Rymer. Eustache de Baliol's seal (in Plate VII. of Surtees' Durham, folio, 1816) represents him as a knight on horseback with a knotted wheel on his shield. There is also the seal of Hugh de Baliol, a knight in mail with flat-topped helmet. The foundations of the castle of the Baliols at Querundon (Quarrington) are still to be traced. The seal of Peter de Brus (in the same plate) represents him on horseback, with a tunic over his mail and a lion rampant on his shield.

[5] The Parliament met January 20, 1265, at Westminster, in the Great Hall, "coram omni populo in Magna Aula Westmonasteriensi." (Brayley's Westm. p. 70.) It was attended by 5 earls and 17 barons. In 1283 Parliament consisted of 11 earls, 99 barons, the knights of counties, and 2 representatives each from London and 20 other towns.

[6] The Chronicle of Mailros (p. 240) describes the strict manner in which Simon de Montfort at this period

fort and de Clare for that purpose, Feb. 16. What would have been very hazardous previously, had now become easy by the representation of so many powerful parties in Parliament. On the 10th of March, therefore, Prince Edward, with his cousin Henry[1], were formally delivered to the King, after subscribing their adhesion to the peace of June, 1264. Parliament embodied in an Act[2], March 31, the conditions of this confirmed pacification.

After referring to the hostages, as depending on the final confirmation of peace, and to the observance of Magna Charta, as secured by their sanction to the peace of June, it proceeds thus: " And since our Lord the King, before the battle of Lewes, had renounced and put out of his fealty several of his good people of this land[3], fresh homage is now accepted, save and except that, if the King is willed to go against the things aforesaid, the barons should not be bound by this homage to him, until the things be amended and redressed." Prince Edward was to have his body-guard (*mesnée*) of unsuspected natives[4], to remain in England three years (intending thereby to prevent his raising an army of aliens), and to give up for five years to the Council the castles[5] which had been given as sureties at Lewes. A still more important surrender was also exacted of him, in order to diminish his means of offence; the whole country and castle of Chester, as well as the fortresses of Pec and New-

watched his prisoner the Prince. When Oliver, abbot of Dryburgh, came to him from his sister the Queen of Scotland, Montfort conducted him up to the Prince seated in state, and remained close to him during the interview, and escorted him out so as to prevent any secret communication.

[1] They are thus described in the deed, March 10th, 1265: "Par notre volonté et la leur se fusent mis ostages a demorer en la garde de Munsir Henri de Montfort."—Rymer.

[2] Rymer, March 31, 1265. The preamble and enacting part are in French, but it quotes the entire Ordinance of June, 1264, in Latin.

[3] " E pur ceo que notre Seignor le Roi devant la bataille de Lewes avoit defié plosiers de ses bone gent de terre, e mis hors de sa foie."

[4] " Derechef Munsir Edward avera sa mesnée e ses conseillers de genz de la tere qui ne soient mie suspecenus."

[5] After noticing the release of the hostages, the King adds, " we now desire him to surrender, for five years, the castles of Dover, Scarborough, Bamburg, Nottingham, and Corfe, which had been given as sureties at Lewes." March 17, 1265.—Rymer.

castle-on-Line, were to be given up to Simon de Montfort in exchange for other lands of equal value[1].

The conclusion of this arrangement was announced by proclamation, and nine bishops threatened excommunication on all who should act contrary to it[2]. The mediation of the French ambassadors had probably assisted in preparing these terms, as the King's passport for their arrival, March 15, expressly states them as coming "to us and to our barons." During the progress of the pacification King Henry remained in London[3], held in all outward honour, but submitting without resistance to the party in power. With whatever reluctance he suppressed all tokens of the rancorous hate which he afterwards manifested, and permitted the victorious barons to

"Feed like oxen at a stall,
The better cherished, still the nearer death[4]."

Some of his former adherents may have pitied him as "the mere shadow of a King[5]," but the external attributes of royalty were carefully preserved around him.

The rapacity and ambition of the barons, and especially of Simon de Montfort, after the battle of Lewes, have been loudly denounced by many writers, both chroniclers and historians, and, as little has been mentioned here to justify such a charge, it deserves examination. To have conferred a political benefit on the nation will not acquit them of acts

---

[1] "Ce Munsir Edward vaudra al Conte de Leycestr en fie le chastel de Cestre, e la vile e le contee ove totes les apartenaunces, et le Nefchastel sur Leine ove les apartenaunces, et le chastel du Pek ove les apartenaunces, si come il les tint e tenir deust, sanz nul retenement, pur otres terres que le Conte lui vaudra en fie a la value des terres, quil tient d'autre part, e des autres teres que le Conte tient en Angleterre en divers luis, lui fra la value au plus pres du conte de Cestre qil poet." This Act was signed "by the King, Prince Edward, Henry, son of the King of the Romans; and at their request, for greater testimony, by the Bishops of London, Worcester, Winchester, Durham, Ely, Sarum, Coventry, Chichester, Bath, Llandaff, the Prior of the Hospitallers, the Master of the Temple, the Mayor and Commons of London. Done at the Parliament of London, last day of March."—Rymer.

[2] Add. MSS. 5444.

[3] 1 Hen. IV. Act v. Scene 2.

[4] He continued in London till April 2.

[5] W. Rish. de Bello Lew.

dictated by sordid self-interest. The imperfect records of the times may have transmitted to us facts, maimed of the circumstances, which would not only have explained, but made them imperative for the completion of the schemes of reform and liberty then in progress; in the absence, however, of stronger lights, let us not flinch from looking at the shades of the picture, as well as the prominence of the more sunny outlines.

It has been loosely asserted by an eminent historian[1], that the great leader of the barons, the Earl of Leicester, aspired to the throne itself. There is, however, no trace of such a scheme having been imputed to him, even by his enemies, during his life, and his conduct in pressing for the fulfilment of the *mise* of Lewes down to his death, would sufficiently prove that he was content to share with others the ascendancy acquired by his own talents. The 'more plausible accusation of greedy avarice deserves closer enquiry. A Royalist chronicler[2] of the times states, that at the general distribution of the estates of emigrant Royalists among the conquerors, de Montfort appropriated to himself eighteen baronies[3]; and yet so contradictory are the witnesses of history, that an undoubted contemporary[4], writing in the interval between his triumph and his fall, expressly picks out, as a peculiar characteristic, his disinterestedness and neglect of his private advantage; and it is even asserted by a chronicler, that "his habitual prayer to God was, that divine grace would preserve him unstained by avarice and the covetousness of worldly goods, which had ensnared so many in his day[5]."

---

[1] Hume.
[2] T. Wyke.
[3] [The ground of this accusation probably is, that he took King Richard's eighteen baronies (see p. 68, note 4) into his own hands for a time. It is less easy to explain his seizure of a tenement in Sprowton, which had been in the occupation of Norwich.—Calend. Geneal. I. p. 121.] As regards the King's grant to him of the manor of Lugwardine, Simon de Montfort held it for 5½ years as security for a debt.—Bp. Swinfield's Household Roll, p. clxv.
[4] Polit. Songs, from MS. Harl. 978, v. 325, &c.
[5] Will. Rish.

We learn incidentally[1] that all the vast landed estates of the King of the Romans had been committed to the care of Simon de Montfort, after the captivity of that prince. His tenure was confessedly temporary, and as the revenues may have been used for raising the amount of his ransom, or for the public service, it would not be safe to rely on this fact alone to convict him of rapacity.

His clear hereditary claim to the office of high steward is an ample justification of the royal grant, dated from Westminster, March 20, which restored it to him.

We have already seen, however, that the sanction of Parliament (March 31) was set upon the transfer to Simon de Montfort of the large possessions which the heir of the Crown had been compelled to strip himself of. The King, by a grant shortly previous[2], had conferred these on Simon de Montfort and his heirs for ever; and by thus accepting so lucrative a prize, he would certainly appear to have abused the privileges of his peculiar position. It is but fair, nevertheless, to remark, that there were reasons of state requiring that Cheshire should not remain in hands likely to confederate again with the Welsh Marchers, and this motive, as well as personal influence, must be supposed to have guided the parliamentary barons in their measure of exchange. The surrender of Cheshire to the more trusty guard of de Montfort was stipulated on the principle of exchange; and a large indemnity, professedly an equivalent, having been given up by him from his own estates in Leicestershire[3] and elsewhere, these lands were, on May 8, 1265, in due form given up, as

[1] By a proclamation of the King to the county of Devon, dated Worcester, Dec. 13, 1264. The estates were restored after the battle of Evesham to the King of the Romans, "pro constanti fidelitate."—Rot. Pat. 49° Hen. III.

[2] "Castella de Chester, Pek et Novumcastrum habenda et tenenda sibi et hæredibus suis de nobis et hæredibus nostris in perpetuum. Rex omnibus, Westm. Mar. 20."—Rymer.

[3] The manors of Melburn Gunthorp, Soke of Ludham, Esingward, Kingishee, Everlee, Colingburne, Cumpton, Sepwyk, Bere, Hungerford, and Chawton, were thus transferred.—Rot. Pat. 49° Hen. III., in Nichols's Leicestershire. Melburn and other lands to the value of 500 marcs had been granted to the earl and his countess jointly in 1259.—Rot. Pat. 43° H. III.

a compensation to Prince Edward. It may also be observed that after the death of Simon de Montfort, when the King eagerly granted away all his confiscated estates, there is no trace of his having died in possession of more than his own hereditary property, with the addition of this exchange in Cheshire.

The pride and presumption of de Montfort's sons at this crisis are generally noticed by chroniclers, and it is possible that their influence over him—for he was a fond and unreproving father—may have prevailed on his better nature to yield to the temptation of undue aggrandisement; though a more full knowledge of the transactions of the period might perhaps efface what appears to tarnish his chararacter. One authority states that his eldest son, Henry, seized for his own use all the wool which English or foreign merchants had brought to port, "thus from a bold knight becoming a wooldraper[1]." Whatever degree of truth there may be in this, there is extant but one grant[2] of estates to any of his sons, and that was prior to the battle of Lewes. Peter de Montfort, whose relationship was very remote, received also a grant of two manors, and the unimportant favour of permission "to live in the house of the late Edward of Westminster[3]."

The ransom of prisoners taken at Lewes had opened an extensive source of gain to the conquerors, and for the security of such payments their estates were probably taken possession of. So fruitful of jealousy had this subject proved among the victorious chiefs that it had by this time cooled the zeal and friendship of de Clare, Earl of Gloucester, towards his older and more conspicuous colleague. De Montfort, suspecting treachery in some of the barons, had taken

[1] T. Wyke.
[2] The property of John Mansell, deceased, given to Simon de Montfort, junior, in 1263.—Rot. Pat. 47° Hen. III.
[3] Westm. March 14, 1265. Rymer. This Edward has been already noticed as employed in the paintings ordered by the King. In 1248 he was commanded to fill Westminster Hall with poor people, and there feed them from Christmas to Circumcision.—Rot. Claus. 32°.

on himself the nomination[1] of trustworthy wardens to the castles, to which de Clare had reluctantly assented. There were not wanting ready whisperers to interpret this as done in derogation of his just influence, and to make the youthful earl feel himself overshadowed by the too luxuriant power of his partner in victory. He had claimed to himself the ransom of the King of the Romans, as having surrendered at Lewes, in that part of the field where he was commanding, the money paid to redeem those taken in war; if less than 10,000 crowns, being usually considered the prize of the captors. But in this case the excess of the sum and the state importance of the prisoner, made such an exception to the rule in de Montfort's opinion, that he peremptorily denied the demand[2], with a taunt, "that he ought to think it quite enough to have saved all his own property by the battle."

This rebuke, indeed, considerably understated the advantages which de Clare had in fact derived from the event: for besides saving all his own estates, those of Philip de Savoy, and William de Valence, and also all the lands of the Earl de Warenne (except Lewes and Ryegate) during the King's pleasure, had been made over to his custody[3].

Even when assembled in arms at Canterbury in the autumn after the battle, almost in presence of the enemy, such topics arose to weaken the union of the barons. The

---

[1] W. Rish de Bello Lew. According to Chr. Roff. Cott. MS. Nero D. II. the causes of jealousy in de Clare were because the Earl of Leicester held the King in his custody, and led him about at his pleasure, entrusting all his castles to his own dependents (suæ dicioni), and claiming for himself and his sons the revenue of the state (emolumentum reipublicæ), which ought to have been in common, and also the ransoms of the captives entirely more than was just (plus æquo totaliter).

[2] According to MS. Cott. Cleop. A. XII., Chr. H. de Silgrave, the dispute was between the Earl of Gloucester and Henry de Montfort. The impetuous refusal of Hotspur on a similar occasion readily occurs as a parallel to this dispute:—

"I'll keep them all;
By heaven he shall not have a Scot of them;
No, if a Scot would save his soul, he shall not.
I'll keep them by this hand."
  1 Hen. IV. Act i. Scene 3.

[3] June 18, 1264. Pat. Rot. 48° Hen. III. H. Knyghton. Add. MSS. 5444.

bold warrior, John de Gifford, who had belonged to the household of de Montfort, thought himself entitled to the ransom of Alan de la Zouch. This also being refused by de Montfort, owing to the suspicious circumstances under which his twofold capture at Lewes occurred, as before related, Gifford angrily transferred his services to de Clare, and under his powerful protection not only retained the ransom and released his Royalist prisoner, but soon after justified de Montfort's distrust of him by repairing to the Forest of Dean[1], and there raising troops in great numbers to oppose his former friends.

[1] Rob. Glouc. T. Wyke calls him " singulare militiæ decus."—Add. MSS. 5444.

CHAPTER XIV.

TREACHERY AND HOSTILITIES.

"To work in close design, by fraud or guile,
What force effected not."
                                PARADISE LOST.

OTHER causes of ill-will had been rankling in the breast of the Earl of Gloucester, and it was not long before he contemplated revenge by carrying his banner into the opposite camp. The sons of de Montfort had, without authority, proclaimed a tournament to be held at Dunstable, in February, and had addressed their challenge especially to the de Clares. The enmity between the two families was so bitter that the holiday-show might easily have become a real battle; and it is stated[1] that de Clare, even at this early period, had formed a plot to entrap de Montfort and his sons into his power at this meeting. The Earl of Leicester, however, either from suspicion, or more probably from the danger of an armed concourse to the peace of the country at such a time—for it was while the Parliament was assembled—strictly forbade the tournament by a royal proclamation, in which the King urged that the absence of the knights on such a pretence might retard the release of his son, then about to be arranged.

This prohibition, so reasonable in itself, bore all the outward marks of authority, with the signatures of the King,

[1] Westminster Feb. 16, 1265.— Rymer. Another tournament had been forbidden in 1255, in the same manner, on account of the danger of Prince Edward in Gascony at that time.—Rymer.

the Justiciary, le Despenser, the Bishop of London, and Thomas de Cantilupe[1].

The latter churchman, in himself remarkable, must not be confounded with his uncle the patriotic Bishop of Worcester, under whose patronage probably he was employed, as we have seen, to represent the barons at the award of Amiens. A few days after joining in the above deed he was raised by the barons to the dignity of Chancellor[2], Feb. 25, though displaced by the King immediately after the battle of Evesham, Aug. 10. His intrinsic merit, however, not only procured him a pardon[3] in 1266, but the bishopric of Hereford in 1275, and a few years after his death in 1282 the honours of a saint were conferred on him by Rome.

[1] Thomas de Cantilupe, son of William, Baron de Cantilupe, studied at Oxford and Paris, was Chancellor of Oxford in 1262, and Archdeacon of Stafford when made Lord Chancellor. " On Wednesday next after the Feast of St Peter in cathedrâ (Feb. 22) Master John de Chishull, Archdeacon of London, restored to the King his seal, and he on the same day committed the custody of it to Master Thomas de Cantilupe, who immediately sealed with it."—Claus. 49° Hen. III. m. 9. He had a grant of 500 marcs a-year, payable at four terms, for the support of himself and the clerks of the King's Chancery. There is a letter of Thomas Cantilupe, as Chancellor, to the King, concerning an order with which the Dean and Chapter of St Paul's declined complying.—603 Chanc. Rec. 5th Rep. He died at Civita Vecchia in Italy, Aug. 25, 1282, having travelled to Rome on business of his see. His body was buried at Florence, his heart at Ashridge, and his bones only at Hereford, and their translation to his tomb (still extant, with its fine effigies of warriors in their niches on the sides, and lower Gothic arcade above) was honoured by the presence of Edward II., April 6, 1287. According to Matt. Westm. the miracles performed there were 163, and Engl. Martyrology states 425, including restoration to life.—V.Life and Gests of Sir Thomas Cantelupe, Butler's Lives of the Fathers, in Britton's Hereford Cathedral.

[2] His patent was endorsed as having been folded by the King with his own hands, and sealed in his presence. " Rex omnibus, &c. salutem. Cum dilectus nobis in Christo magister Thomas de Cantilupo per nos et magnates nostros qui sunt de Concilio nostro electus sit in Cancellarium Regni nostri, et nos ipsum ad officium illud gratanter admisimus, nos sustentationi suæ, et clericorum Cancellariæ nostræ providere volentes, concessimus ei 500 marcas, singulis annis percipiendas ad Scaccarium nostrum, &c., ad sustentationem suam et clericorum Cancellariæ nostræ prædictæ quamdiu steterit in officio. Teste Rege apud Westmonast. 26 die Marcii. Et sciendum quod Dominus Rex manu suæ propriæ plicavit istud breve, et in presentia sua fecit consignari, præsentibus similiter H. le Despenser, Justiciario Angliæ," &c.—Pat. 49° Hen. III. m. 18. The Countess of Leicester sent him a present of four gallons of wine at Sarum on the occasion, March 1, and a messenger from him reached the Countess at Dover, July 8.—Househ. Exp.

[3] Rot. Pat. 50° Henry III.

The letter of Edward I. to Clement V. testifies to his long intimacy with the humility, justice, and mercy of the deceased prelate, stating that since his death he had "shone by sundry miracles, such as restoring sight to the blind, hearing to the deaf, and motion to the lame; besides many other benefits conferred by the hand of heaven on those who implored his patronage." On the faith of these marvels, to which the credulity of others added the restoration of forty persons to life, the King implores the Pope "not to suffer such a lanthorn to be hid under a bushel, but to place it on a candlestick, by deigning to number him in the catalogue of the saints[1]." His shrine still remains in Hereford cathedral, and was once in great local repute for cures and miracles, though decorated only with the mail-clad effigies of his noble ancestry, rather than the groups of saints we might have expected to associate with him[2]. It is said that with him ended the line of English saints canonized[3] by Rome; for though popular feeling afterwards disposed freely and frequently of the title in favour of its own heroes and martyrs, whose merits worked miracles in spite of royal prohibition, yet six centuries have since passed over our reprobate generations without one acknowledged saint.

De Clare and the other combatants, who had made every preparation for this Dunstable tournament, were much disposed to set at nought this prohibition; but de Montfort was resolute, and threatening to "cast those who should disobey into a place where they should enjoy neither sun nor moon," went himself with the justiciary and a strong force, so as effectually to preserve the public peace so endangered[4].

Indignation at this interference now hurried de Clare

---

[1] Letter dated Westminster, Nov. 2, 1305, in Wilkins' Concil. I. 283.

[2] Britton's Hereford Cath. The bishop died in Italy, 1282, and his bones only were brought to his cathedral, and transferred to the north transept in 1287. The bishopric adopted his family arms (gules, three leopards' heads reversed, jessant, as many fleur de lys, or) for those of the see.

[3] He was canonized in 1307. The saint was a pluralist, and held many other preferments in York, Lichfield, and London; he was also Chancellor of Oxford.

[4] W. Rish. de Bello Lew.

forward into a treacherous correspondence with Roger de
Mortimer in Wales. The stanch Royalist was at first not
unreasonably suspicious of his good faith, and even required
hostages[1] for his own security, before he consented to meet
the earl's brother, Thomas de Clare[2], who, as governor of
St Briavel's, was at the time conveniently situated to carry
on the treaty. The terms of the betrayal, however, were
speedily arranged (in April) between these parties, when
they met; and it was, perhaps, some suspicion of this that
induced de Montfort to require fresh pledges[3] of fidelity
from de Clare. The false earl, though not prepared then
to throw off his mask, withdrew secretly from these demands, and leaving London under pretence of providing for
the security of his own estates, began to collect his followers
at Gloucester, with a resolution to weaken the authority
of de Montfort by all the means in his power:—

"Tho wende the Erl from Londone priveliche and stille,
As to socori is land, age Sir Simonde's will."—ROB. GLOUC.

Although he still acted in apparent concert with the
barons for some time longer, he was evidently awaiting his
opportunity for completing his desertion.

Other symptoms of uneasiness at the gathering forces
of the malcontents had already appeared among the barons.
Formal summonses[4] required the presence in Parliament,
on June 1, of some of the great Royalists, who were known
to be abroad. These were proclaimed at Pevensey, Lewes,
and Bosham, as the respective residences of Peter de Savoy,
Earl de Warenne, and Roger le Bigod. Troubles had broken out in the North also, which induced de Montfort to
move in that direction to suppress them, after the breaking
up of the Parliament in Lent, and there was an apprehen-

[1] H. Knighton.
[2] He was made governor of Colchester in 1266; went on a crusade,
from which he returned in 1271, and
London was put under his command,
1273.
[3] Add. MSS. 5444.
[4] Dated Westminster, March 19,
1265. The summons to them required them to appear "justiciam
facturi et recepturi," to do and suffer
justice.—Rymer.

sion of the Royalists landing there from France. He was with the King at Northampton¹, April 11, and when he heard that John FitzAlan, one of the released Lewes prisoners, had joined the armed malcontents, he authorized his son Simon, then probably besieging Pevensey, to secure the person of FitzAlan's youthful son, or failing that, to possess himself of Arundel castle².

The marchers in the interest of Prince Edward, in concert with the attempted rescue at Wallingford in December, had advanced as far as Pershore, and had been followed in their retreat by de Montfort. Driven by him successively from Hay, Hereford, and Ludlow, they had submitted at Montgomery to terms of peace, intended to obtain at least a year's tranquillity for that frontier. They agreed to go into exile for that time—a condition, however, which they evaded by taking shelter on the territory of de Clare³. Their hostile intentions becoming more manifest, de Montfort returned rapidly from the North, in order to watch them at Gloucester, where he was April 30⁴, and afterwards, May 13, at Hereford. The threatened insurrection soon assumed a serious importance, requiring all the energies of de Montfort to meet. On May 10, William de Valence, accompanied by Earl de Warenne, and numerous other Royalists, landed in his own lordship of Pembroke, and was welcomed by the malcontent marchers already in arms⁵.

It was at this time and under these harassing circumstances that de Montfort again evinced his anxiety for the

¹ Rymer.
² Dated Winchcumbe, April 16.—Rymer.
³ W. Rish. de Bello Lew.—Chr. Roff.
⁴ Househ. Exp.
⁵ The seal was transferred temporarily about this time to Ralph de Sandwich, Keeper of the Wardrobe, only to be used under authority of de Montfort's adherents. "On the Thursday next after St John Port Latin (May 6) Master Thomas de Cantilupe, the King's Chancellor, delivered the King's seal to Ralph de Sandwich, Keeper of the Wardrobe, in the presence of the King and of Hugh le Despenser, Justiciary of England, and Peter de Montfort, to be kept by him until Thomas should return, to be used in this manner: Ralph to keep it in the Wardrobe under the seal of Peter de Montfort, Roger de St John, and Giles de Argentenn, or one of them; when taken out, Ralph to seal the writs of course in the presence of the person under whose seal it had been

final settlement, which the *mise* of Lewes had made dependent on the decision of the French arbitration. The letter despatched to Louis IX.[1] bears fair testimony to the moderation and sincerity of the barons:—

"To the King of France, health and sincerely affectionate love: concerning our business, for which we lately sent to your presence our nephew Henry, son of the illustrious King of the Romans, we ask and require, with all possible urgency, by our prayers and by our love, that your serenity will be pleased to deliver to speedy effect those matters which concern us; for we, who cordially desire the expedition of the said business, will always be prompt and ready for all things, relating to these matters, on our own behalf and on that of our dependents, as our nephew, who is more fully acquainted with our willingness on this point, may also report to you by word of mouth. Witness the King at Hereford, May 18. By the King, Simon de Montfort Earl of Leicester, Peter de Montfort, Roger de St John, Giles de Argentein[2]."

It is a further proof of fair dealing that this letter should have been conveyed by Prince Henry[3], the former negotiator, who had already laid the terms of peace before the French King.

We miss indeed the name of the Earl of Gloucester from this document, and already rumours of disunion had spread a cloud over the aspect of public affairs, although some mutual friends, such as the Bishop of Worcester, le Despenser,

then enclosed, or in his absence, if he was not minded to be there, but mandatory writs only in the presence of such person and with his assent; and when the writs of course or mandatory were sealed, then the King's seal was to be sealed up under the seal of one of the three persons above-named, and to be carried by Ralph into the Wardrobe, to be there kept in form aforesaid, until Thomas de Cantilupe should return."
—Rot. Pat. 49° Hen. III. m. 16, in Lord Campbell's Lives of Chancellors, Vol. I. p. 155. The Chronicle of Worcester mentions Ralph de Sandwich as one of several who left the King's party in 1264.

[1] Messengers had also been sent to him by King Henry, April 14, 1265.—Rot. Pat. May 17, two armed galleys were sent to Whitsand for the French ambassadors. June 14, a safe conduct was granted for them to proceed to Hereford, and on June 21 the Countess of Leicester, at Dover, sent them a present of two sextaries of wine.—Househ. Exp.

[2] Rymer, in Latin.

[3] Rot. Pat. 49°.

Monchensy, and Fitz-John[1], had interfered with temporary success to reconcile chiefs whose union was so important to their cause.

While the King and de Montfort were at Gloucester, de Clare and Gifford had kept aloof with their forces in the neighbouring Forest of Dean, but when the two great chiefs had sworn[2] to abide by the arbitration of the above-mentioned four mediators in all things relating to the Oxford Statutes, a royal proclamation[3] hastened to re-assure the public. "It denounced all reports of discord between the two earls, which had alarmed the minds of men as vain, false, and invented by fraud, the more especially as in fact they were unanimous and of one accord in all things." Amidst all these smooth words, however, the announcement was necessarily made of the actual invasion of the enemy at Pembroke.

Some attempts at peace appear to have been made at this time. A safe conduct was granted, May 22, to enable Leybourne and Clifford to meet Prince Edward; and on de Warenne and de Valence forwarding, through the Prior of Monmouth, a demand for the restitution of their estates, they too were summoned to appear immediately before the King[4]. There scarcely remained, however, a hope of avoiding more bloodshed. The threads of intrigue were so perilously entangled around the barons, that the sword alone could cut a solution of them; and events now hurried on.

Prince Edward, who had been treated as a prisoner on parole since March, had accompanied the court to Hereford, and companions already known to him were appointed to attend him with the utmost respect. These were Thomas de Clare, his familiar friend and bedfellow[5], in whom de

---

[1] W. Rish. Rob. Glouc. Lib. de Ant. Leg.
[2] Lib. de Ant. Leg.
[3] Hereford, May 20, 1265. —Rymer.
[4] Rot. Pat. Hereford, May 24. The King at this period is described as wholly submissive to the Earl of Leicester: "Comes una cum rege sibi supplici et acclivi, cui necessarium erat de necessitate faciens virtutem."—Chr. Roff.
[5] "Tanquam familiaris et cubicularius Domini Edwardi."—T. Wyke. Thomas de Clare was included in the express pardon granted by the King to the Earl of Gloucester and John

Montfort, ignorant of his treachery, reposed great confidence; Robert de Ros, a gallant knight of his own age; and Henry de Montfort, his cousin and associate of many years:—

> "Sir Simon de Montfort out of warde nom
> Sir Edward him to solace, that to lute thank him com:
> He bitoke him Sir Henri is sone to be is companion,
> With him to wende aboute, to sywe him up and doun[1]."
>
> ROB. GLOUC.

A leader, with a spirit so able and a hand so ready as the Prince, was of the greatest importance to de Mortimer and the other malcontents, and every preparation was accordingly made in secret to favour his escape. This was effected, as is well known, by stratagem:—

> "Sir Edward bed Sir Simon, that he him geve
> To a prikie stedes withouten toun leve[2]."—ROB. GLOUC.

His friends having sent him an excellent horse[3], so spirited that few dared to mount him, he affected a wish of trying its paces and speed against the choicest horses of his escort; to judge of its fitness for a tournament, if such an occasion should arise[4]; and for this purpose repaired with them to a convenient spot to the north of the town, called Widmarsh. Here he mounted in succession all the others, and galloped them until their strength was exhausted:—

> "He asayed tham bi and bi and retreied them ilkone,
> And stoned tham all wery, standand stille as stone."
>
> ROB. BRUNE[5].

As soon as he had thus disabled them from pursuit, he rode off rapidly on his own fresh horse, with a parting taunt to de Ros, who had especial charge of him:—

> "Lordlings, now good day and greet my father and say,
> I shall soon see him and out of ward, if ich mai."
>
> ROB. GLOUC.

Gifford for having fought against him at Lewes, in consideration of their services at Evesham, Oct. 6, 1265.—Rymer.

[1] *Nom*, took; *lute*, little; *wende*, turn; *sywe*, follow.

[2] Sir Edward asked Sir Simon to give him leave for a horse-race out of the town.

[3] H. Knyghton. MS. Nero D. X. 201. Nangis says that de Clare had sent this horse under a feigned name.

[4] W. Heming.

[5] He tried and retried each of them one after the other, and stunned them all weary, standing still as stone.

Two knights (one of them probably Thomas de Clare) and four squires[1] attached to him, accompanied his adventurous flight, and a party of friendly horsemen, appointed to lie in wait, soon fell in with him, and conducted him in safety to de Mortimer's castle of Wigmore, about twenty-four miles distant.

This escape, occurring on the evening of Thursday, May 28[2], was announced by a proclamation of the King two days afterwards, and troops were summoned to meet at Worcester, in order to crush de Warenne and de Valence, whom it was supposed the Prince intended to join.

A few more days, however, brought fresh desertion and anxiety, for the Earl of Gloucester[3] now openly joined the Royalists, after first exacting an oath from Prince Edward that he would obey the laws.

Simon de Montfort could not fail to understand fully the increased danger of his position, from the union of such powerful leaders, and the shock given to the cause of the barons:—

"Schent is ilk Baroun, now Gilbert turnes grim,
The Montfort Sir Simoun most affied on him.
Alas, Sir Gilbert, thou turned thin oth,
At Stryvelyn men it herd how God therfor was wroth[4]."
ROB. BRUNE.

The public were again frankly made acquainted with this fresh defection. The proclamation[5] denounced the Earl of Gloucester as "having now fled to assist the rebellion of de Warenne, in contempt of his oath to abide by the written agreement, which had lately appeased the discord between

---

[1] Rymer. "Transito flumine quod dicitur Wey cum duobus militibus." —Chr. Rish.
[2] "Pentecost," "Vigil of Trinity." —Rymer, W. Rish., W. Heming.
[3] Stephen de Herewell, de Montfort's private secretary, was violently taken from a church by his orders, and beheaded.—Add. MSS. 5444. Lingard supposes the earl to have raised his standard on April 19, but the open rupture was not till the beginning of June.
[4] *Schent*, troubled; *affied*, relied. At the battle of Bannockburn, near Stirling (Stryvelyn), his son, Gilbert de Clare, by the Princess Joan of Acre, (his second wife (1290), after he had divorced Alicia de March in 1285,) was killed in 1316. It is curious to find so distant a calamity considered as a retribution on his present treachery.
[5] Rymer, June 7, 1265.

him and the Earl of Leicester, while Prince Edward by his inconsiderate levity had wholly lost the grace of public favour, which he had acquired by voluntarily becoming hostage." On the next day the King signed an order[1] to the Bishop of London, desiring him to excommunicate the Prince, "whom the rebels had unhappily found light to believe and easy to circumvent." The castle of Bristol[2] was also required to be immediately surrendered into de Montfort's hands, but to this order the knights who garrisoned it for the Prince, Warren de Bassingbourne, Robert Tipetot[3], John Mussegros (Musgrave), Patrick and Pain Chaworth, steadily refused obedience[4].

The bridges near Worcester having been broken down by the enemy in order to impede the arrival of the fresh levies, on their march to recruit de Montfort, he changed the appointed rendezvous to Gloucester, and then moved upon Monmouth[5] and Newport, in order to reach his enemy in South Wales. The difficulty of supplying an army with food at this period was strikingly illustrated by the King in May prohibiting any fairs to be held in Herefordshire, Shropshire, or Staffordshire, "that all provisions might be brought to the King alone[6];" and when the baronial troops were in Wales on this expedition, the English soldiers complained of their food among that rude people, who lived habitually on milk and meat. They regretted their accustomed bread, and longed to return to London[7].

---

[1] Hereford, June 8, 1265, signed by the King, Peter de Montfort, Giles de Argentenn and Roger St John.—Rymer.
[2] Hereford, June 9, 1265.—Rymer.
[3] "Tipetot." His arms in Richmond church, Yorkshire, are, argent, a saltire engrailed gules, with a crescent for difference.
[4] Rob. Glouc. [This, to say the least, is doubtful. A royal writ, dated June 9, at Hereford, speaks of the castle and town as having been committed with the consent of Prince Edward to the charge of Simon de Montfort, and directs that none of Edward's par- tisans be admitted into it. New Rymer, Vol. I. p. 457. Compare a paper by Mr Lucas in the Proceedings of the Archæol. Institute, 1853.]
[5] There was another proclamation against Prince Edward, dated Monmouth, June 28.—Rymer.
[6] Rot. Claus. 49° Hen. III.
[7] "Verum Anglici, panibus assueti, cum essent in terrâ Wallensium, solo carnium edulio vel lactis, quibus illa gens effera vivere consuevit, sine panibus vivere nesciebant, quamobrem illas provincias saltuosas et sylvarum devia non sine periculo transmeantes."—T. Wyke.

> "But since the King remained in puissant Lei'ster's power,
> The remnant of his friends, whom death did not devoure
> At Lewes Battell late, and durst his parte partake,
> The Prince excites again an army up to make;
> Whom Roger Bigod, Earle of Norfolke doth assist,
> England's High Marshal then, and that great martialist
> Old Henry Bohun, Earle of Her'ford, in this warre,
> Gray, Basset, Saint John, Lisle, Percie, Latimer(?),
> All Barons, which to him their utmost strength doe lay,
> With many a knight, for power their equals every way."
> DRAYTON'S Polyolbion, II. p. 33.

De Montfort, indeed, was recalled from his enterprise, by the apprehension of his communications in the rear being intercepted, the enemy having made more rapid progress in another quarter than he had expected.

Prince Edward, being joined by de Clare at Ludlow, had lost no time in raising troops within his own county of Chester, which, as well as Shropshire, was quickly overrun. The energetic Prince then directed his march by Worcester upon Gloucester[1], where de Ros had been left in garrison, but with a force insufficient to prevent its capture after fifteen days' siege. This result was made yet easier by the treachery of Grimbald Pancefot, who gained knighthood in reward from his new party. Though he fought against his former friends at Evesham, he was despised even by those who profited by his baseness[2]:—

> "Ac ther was never eft of him so god word as er."—ROB. GLOUC.

De Ros surrendered on June 29[3], at a time when the Earl of Leicester was on his distant expedition with the

---

[1] A letter from G. de Morle to H. de Mauley (725 Chanc. Rec. 5th Report) represents the Earl of Gloucester, Prince Edward, and William de Valence as besieging the castle of Gloucester; the King and the Earl of Montfort at Hereford, and expected at Gloucester, where Simon junior was also to come with his forces. H. de Mauley is advised to send a man to take care of his property.

[2] Grimbald Pancefot held lands in Herefordshire [as also in Gloucestershire, Worcestershire, and Kent. Rot. Hund. I. pp. 284, 416; II. pp. 181, 186].

He married, 1253, Constantia, daughter of John de Lingayn, whose dower from her father was to be six score and ten marcs, twelve oxen, and one hundred sheep. Being made a prisoner at Tunis in after-life, it is said he was redeemed by his wife maiming herself of her left hand, when she heard that his release could only be procured by the limb of another person. Their effigies, representing this, were formerly in the church of Cowarne Magna.—Duncumb's Herefordshire. Vol. II. pp. 97, 98.

[3] W. Rish.

King. From Monmouth all the wardens of the counties were commanded to attack the adherents of the rebels in all directions, and Simon de Montfort, junior, who had been besieging Pevensey castle, was at the same time[1] summoned to the immediate help of his father, now confessedly in danger. The order was readily obeyed by the son, and he led all his troops in reinforcement. Meeting with some resistance at Winchester on his march, he not only took, but plundered the city (July 14), and proceeded onward to the family castle of Kenilworth[2].

All de Montfort's sons are spoken of by several chroniclers as full of pride and addicted to riotous living. Some knight remonstrated with their father on his blindness in suffering their conduct:—

"For thou has ille sonnes foles and vnwise,
 Ther dedes thou not mones, ne nouht wille tham chastise:
 I rede thou gyue gode tent, and chastise tham sone,
 For tham ye may be schent, for vengeance is granted bone[3]."

ROB. BRUNE.

Young Simon certainly acted with little heed of the quick and bold enemy he had to deal with, after his arrival at Kenilworth[4]. Despising the security of the castle enclosure, he lodged with many of his soldier-nobles in the neighbouring village, either for the convenience of bathing early in the morning, or from motives of pride or "riotrie," for all these reasons[5] are variously assigned:—

[1] "Rex custodi Simoni de Monteforti juniori, Custodi pacis Comitatuum de Surreyæ et Sussexiæ, Monemue, June 28, 1265."—Rymer. A messenger was paid 8d. for going from Odiham to young Simon at Pevensey, May 1.—Househ. Exp.—T. Wyke. It appears from two letters (Add. MSS. 6166, Nov. 27, 28, pp. 388, 389) that the Bishop of Winchester was ordered, Nov. 24, 1264, to pay over 700 marcs, the surplus of a fine due to the Crown, to young Simon de Montfort, towards the expenses of the siege of Pevensey. De Montfort gave a quittance for 300 marcs of this sum at Winchester, July 16, 1265.

[2] Fabian. W. Rish. Simon de Montfort summoned also the northern chiefs (Magnates Boreales) on this occasion to bring their forces to Evesham.—Walt. Hem.

[3] For thou hast wicked sons, foolish and unwise; you do not reprove their deeds, nor will you at all chastise them. I warn you to give good heed, and correct them soon; you may be blamed for them, for vengeance is a granted boon.

[4] "Kellingiswurthe."—Chr. Mailr.

[5] "Forte minus sobrius dormiebat."—T. Wyke. "Dormientes in villa et abbatiâ, et erant multi mu-

"And ther it fel, alas, his heie hert him sende,.
Vor so muche he told of him sulf, and of his grete mighte,
That him ne deinde nogt to ligge in the castel by nigte.
And ther the sojourned eft, then rioterie tham schant,
Suilk ribaudie thei led, thei gaf no tale of wham[1]."

Rob. Glouc.

The Earl of Leicester had advanced from Hereford to meet his son, and his tactics were skilfully arranged, with the view of thus surrounding Prince Edward at Worcester, but his plan was entirely marred by the careless conduct of his son. After six days' negligence, a woman of the name of Margoth[2], employed as a spy in male disguise, transmitted to the Prince information of the unguarded state of the barons, by which he resolved immediately to profit. Making a rapid march by night[3], accompanied by William de Valence and the Earl de Warenne[4], the Prince entered Kenilworth in the early morning of August 2[5], before any alarm of his approach arose. The first notice of danger to the barons were the outcries in the streets; "Come out, traitors! by the death of God, you shall all be killed." Though many were seized in their beds, others were roused and betook themselves to a dishonoured flight from the backs of their houses. "Some were seen to fly with only their hose on, some with only a shirt or drawers, while others ran off with their clothes under their arms; few or none had time to put on all their garments, and young Simon de Montfort himself escaped with difficulty, almost naked, by a boat across the lake to the castle[6]."

"Of soft awakunge hii toke lute gome,
Vor to wel clothi hom, hii ne geve hom no tome,

niti sanguine vineæ."—Walt. Heming.
"Ut mane diluculo de lectis suis bene balneati—ut leviores efficerentur ad bellandum die posterâ."—Chr. Mailr. "Extra castrum decubantes videlicet in prioratu."—Chr. Roff.

[1] *Heie*, pride; *deinde*, condescended; *gaf no tale*, took no account.
[2] Walt. Heming.; Ann. Waverl.
[3] Margoth placed Prince Edward in ambush in a "vallis profunda et prope locum castri:" here, while arming, the Royalists heard the tramp of the enemy's foragers (longæ quadrigæ), and immediately seized them, and distributed the horses to the weary.—Walt. Heming.
[4] Lib. de Ant. Leg.
[5] Prince Edward left Worcester in the evening of the Feast of St Peter ad Vincula.—MS. Chr. Roff.
[6] Chr. Mailr.

> Ac Sir Symond him sulf among alle is fon,
> In to the castel of scapede an naked man vnnethe[1]."
>
> ROB. GLOUC.

Among the prisoners were twenty bannerets, including Robert de Vere, Earl of Oxford, William de Monchensy, Richard de Gray, Baldwin Wake, and Hugh Neville[2], who had all fought at Lewes. Adam de Neumarket, after a similar calamity at Northampton, was now a second time a captive. So much rich baggage and so many horses were taken by this surprise, that the very foot-boys of the Royalists rode back in triumph on the choice horses they found deserted by the routed knights. The prisoners were sent in custody to Gloucester, while the young conqueror prepared at once without any relaxation to follow up his advantage by a still more decisive blow[3].

---

[1] They took little care to awaken them softly, for they gave them no time to clothe themselves well, and Sir Simon himself scarcely escaped through all his enemies, a naked man, into the castle.

[2] Hugh Neville received his pardon in 1266 for his adherence to Simon de Montfort, and to Simon, junior.—Rot. Pat. Walter Colville was either killed or taken here.— W. Knighton, W. Rish., Rob. Glouc., Rob. Brune. "Johannes de Gray, filius Ricardi de Gray," is added to the list by Harl. MS. 542, p. 49. This was more probably the *son* of Richard II. (see pp. 180, 181) than the brother, who was a Royalist. William Montgomery (Monchensy?) was also a prisoner, according to Lansd. MS. 255, p.507.

[3] A charge of cowardice was afterwards brought against Edward which seems to refer to this surprise. "These are the words that Sir Wm. de Vescy said to Sir John Fitz-Thomas concerning our Lord the King of England." "And he told of a good chance that happened to him, and how it was despite himself, that he came to Kenilworth where he took many of the hostages and great people, and slew of the host of Sir Simon de Montfort the young and discomfited all beside. But before he came to Kenilworth he sent out people to know what company was with Sir Simon de Montfort. And when he had heard how many were there he said he would turn back, for all the host of England would have enough to do to encounter them. And then said Sir Roger de Clifford that if he turned back it would be great shame and blame to him and all the rest of his army, and might ruin England. And then the King that now is said that all the blame should be upon himself and he would turn back. 'Indeed,' said Sir Roger de Clifford, 'you will reap more shame and blame from this matter and this business than the rest of England.' And then said Sir Roger, 'however it be we will go on;' and he said, 'Banners forward!' And he rode ahead, and the King could not but go on for shame, and they carried it out well, as has before been said."—Rolls of Parliament, Vol. I. p. 127. P.

CHAPTER XV.

BATTLE OF EVESHAM.

"Des blutes heldenröthe
Jubelt von der Freyheit morgen-
roth."   KÖRNER.

On the reddened flood of martyrs'
blood
Glows the ruddy dawn of freedom's
morn."

THIS disaster, in itself important, was still more so in its consequences; for de Montfort was now hemmed in by the forces of de Clare and de Mortimer in different directions on the Welsh frontier, while he was anxiously awaiting the re-inforcement of his son. Llewellyn[1], Prince of Wales, had, indeed, sent some troops to his aid, having held a conference at Hawarden Castle with de Montfort, when a treaty of alliance had been established, by which that castle was ceded to the Welsh Prince; a condition reluctantly assented to by the King[2]. Before the news of the rout at Kenilworth could be known to the Earl of Leicester, the very expectation of young Simon de Montfort's arrival was skilfully taken advantage of to deceive and ruin him. The earl, in order to hasten the junction of his son, had advanced from Hereford, and crossed the Severn at Kempsey[3] (four miles south of

---

[1] How differently this Prince was valued by friends and foes appears by his two epitaphs. The Welsh one extols him as—
"Gemma coævorum, flos regum præteritorum,
Forma futurorum, dux, laus, lex, lux populorum."
While to English eyes he seemed

"Errorum princeps et prædo virorum,
Proditor Anglorum — trux, dux homicida piorum,
——Stirps mendax causa malorum."
V. Yorke's Royal Tribes.

[2] Dated Hereford, June 22, 1265.—Rot. Pat. T. Wyke.

[3] W. Rish.

Worcester), from whence, on Monday, August 3, he marched towards Evesham, proposing on the following morning to continue his approach towards his expected friends.

Prince Edward had watched his enemy's movements by the help of Ralph de Ardern[1], a traitorous spy in the earl's camp; and conscious also of having some spies among his own companions[2], he resolved to mislead them by commencing his march from Worcester at sunset towards Shrewsbury[3], until after a few miles he suddenly turned round and made a rapid march during the night in the opposite direction after the enemy.

At daybreak on Tuesday, August 4[4], after mass had

[1] One of the oldest families in Warwickshire, whose name still designates a district there. Thomas de Ardern, the head of the family, was on the barons' side, and, being taken prisoner at Evesham, was compelled to surrender all his lands to a Royalist kinsman, the father of Ralph. Arms, chequy, or and azure, a chevron gules.—H. Knighton; Dugd. Warw.
[2] "In sua comitivâ."—Walter Heming.
[3] Dies Martii.—Osney Annals, p. 168. Annals of Dunstable, p. 239. Mardi la veille de Saint Oswald.—

French Chronicle of London, p. 7. The day after the third day of August.— Wykes, p. 171. The day after the Invention of St Stephen.—Trivet, p. 266. The day before the Nones of August (Chron. de Lanercost, p. 76), which was Tuesday.—Rishanger, p. 47. P.
[4] There is a slight difficulty in understanding Prince Edward's march; and Mr Blaauw had evidently intended to go minutely into the question, from the number of parallel passages he had transcribed. An itinerary will shew what I mean:

Earl of Leicester.
Saturday, St Peter ad Vincula, Aug. 1, at Hereford.
Sunday, St Stephen, Martyr, Aug. 2, to Kempsey.

Monday, Invention of St Stephen, Aug. 3, by night to Evesham.

Tuesday, St Dominic, or Vigil of St Oswald, is marching upon Kenilworth.

The question is, where was the town Clive. Mr Blaauw and Dr Pauli have not offered a conjecture. Dr Lingard (Vol. III. p. 148) says Clains

Prince Edward.
At Kenilworth, to or towards Worcester.
In the latter part of the day at or near Worcester.—Matt. West., p. 395.
Goes on the North road as if towards Shrewsbury, Bridgenorth, or Stafford. (Wykes, p. 172.) Crosses the river near the town called Clive, taking up a position between Kenilworth and Evesham. (Chron. Rishang., p. 25. Trivet, p. 266.)
Marches upon Evesham.

(quasi Clino pro Clivo), a village about three miles north of Worcester. The difficulty is, that we must not only change the spelling but

been celebrated[1], absolution was again freely dispensed among the baronial soldiers, as on the eve of the battle of Lewes, by the same bold prelate:—

> "The Bissop Walter of Wurcestre asoiled him alle there,
> And prechede hom, that hii adde of deth the lasse fere[2]."
>
> ROB. GLOUC.

The barons were preparing to mount their horses and leave Evesham, in pursuance of their plan, when there came into view, issuing from the folds of the hill in the very quarter where they looked for young de Montfort, a large army advancing towards them in battle array, divided into orderly squadrons, and bearing in their van the emblazoned banners of their expected friends. The sight gladdened their eyes and hearts for a time, but it was to Prince Edward they gave this fatal welcome. The heraldic ensigns were his trophies snatched from the Kenilworth captives[3], and his approach had been purposely so contrived as to cut off all communication between the father and the son, and thus to appear in the direction most likely to give effect to the delusion.

It is remarkable that in the first two battles fought in England after the general usage[4] of heraldic distinctions, they should have been converted into successful engines of stratagem, and they have probably never done so much mischief since.

In modern times a telescope would have revealed the

create a river to satisfy this identification; as Prince Edward, marching S.E. from Clains, would not strike even an important stream for nearly eight miles. I incline to think, therefore, that the place meant is Prior's Cleeve on Avon, and that Prince Edward expected his enemy to strike the road from Chipping Camden to Stratford-on-Avon and Kenilworth, and was resolved to bar him from the castle at all risks. Meanwhile the roads from Evesham on Worcester and Alcester were occupied respectively by Mortimer and de Clare, the former of whom is described by Hemingburgh (p. 323) as coming up from behind. P.

[1] "Audito officio et accepto viatico."—Chr. Lanerc.

[2] "The Bishop Walter of Worcester absolved them all there and preached to them, so that they had the less fear of death."—V. Chr. Lanerc.

[3] W. Heming.

[4] The custom was not universal when the battle of Lincoln was fought in 1216.

fraud afar off, but in the absence of such instruments, the detection, when too late, was left to be made by de Montfort's barber Nicolas[1], who happened to be expert in the cognizance of arms, and who, without even a surname for himself, was the earliest amateur herald on record[2]. Observing the banners while yet distant, Nicolas remarked to de Montfort that they appeared to be those of his friends, and the earl confidently answered, "It is my son, fear not; but nevertheless go and look out, lest by chance we should be deceived." Ascending the clock-tower of the Abbey[3], Nicolas recognized at length, among the banners of the host advancing on Evesham, the triple lions of Prince Edward, and the ensigns of Roger de Mortimer, and other notorious enemies. He spread the alarm, but the error had continued long enough to be fatal, and little time then remained for the barons to prepare their defence.

The example of the skilful tactics of Simon de Montfort on former occasions had been watched with profit by Prince Edward; and his army, though superior in numbers[4], was no longer conducted in its rapid march with headlong rashness, as at Lewes, but with all the precautionary discipline which had been then employed against him. He had interposed between the two bodies of his enemies' forces, so as to be able to defeat them separately, and now, though fresh with

[1] "Simonis speculator Nicolas barbitonsor ejus, qui homo expertus erat in cognitione armorum."— Walt. Heming. "Venit ille in altum in cloccario Abbatiæ." Could this have been the same Nicolas mentioned by Roger Bacon as the tutor of Almeric de Montfort? (See p. 79, note 2, ante.) If so, he was so skilled a mathematician, according to Bacon, that he may have used some optical instrument to detect the enemy before others. Cap. xi. Opus Tertium, p. 35. [There was, however, a brother Nicholas, a Franciscan, who learned letters in England and became confessor to Pope Innocent IV. (1251-1261), and

Bishop of Assisi.—Brewer's Mon. Francisc. pp. 61, 551.]
[2] A few years later a Franciscan monk, Walter of Exeter, wrote of the siege of Carlaverock in 1300, from which numerous heraldic notices have been extracted in these pages.
[3] "Summitas clocherii ecclesiæ Evesham conflagravit fulgure, 1261." —Chr. Wigorn., p. 446. "7° Edw.I. (1279) reparatum est campanile de Evesham."—Chr. Evesh. Leland, Collect. Vol. I.
[4] "Habuit autem Edwardus sex homines vel septem ubi Simon vix habuit duos."—Chron. de Mailros, Gale, Vol. I. p. 231.

T

the pride of his victory, did not neglect to increase the power of his army, by arranging it methodically in divisions, that there might be no confusion in its advance.

When de Montfort, in order to reconnoitre the Royalists, ascended a hill, or as some[1] say the tower of Evesham Abbey, where he had been hospitably entertained, he was so struck with admiration of their improved discipline, that the natural pride of a soldier led him to exclaim with his usual oath (alluding to a relic of the chivalrous champion of Spain recently brought to England), "By the arm of S. James[2], they come on skilfully, but it is from me they have learnt that method, not from themselves."

At first only one division of his enemy, that led on by the Prince, had been seen by de Montfort, a small hill intervening to conceal the Earl of Gloucester's advance by a different line[3]. When the whole danger was revealed to him, it seemed at once so overwhelming, that he gave free permission for his friends to take flight, venting his prophetic apprehensions: "May the Lord have mercy on our souls, for our bodies are in the enemy's power." While escape was still possible, a generous rivalry led each leader to persuade others to adopt that means of safety which he rejected for himself. Hugh le Despenser and Ralph Bassett[4], when urged to fly, refused to survive de Montfort, and the great leader himself, when his son Henry[5] affectionately offered to bear the brunt of the battle alone, while his father should preserve his life by flight, steadily answered: "Far from me be the thought of such a course, my dear son! I have grown old in wars, and my life hastens to an end; the noble parentage of my blood has been always notoriously eminent in this one point—never to fly or wish to fly[6] from

---

[1] Dugd. Warw.; W. Rish.; W. Heming.
[2] He had used the same oath at the Oxford Parliament.—Chr. Lanerc. S. Jago held the rank and even the pay of general in the Spanish service down to modern times.
[3] T. Wykes.
[4] W. Rish. de Bello Lew. et Evesh.
[5] "Li dit doucement, 'Sire, alez vous ent.'"—Nangis.
[6] "Sui de si noble parente descendus, qui onques en bataille ne fui ne vou fuir."

battle. Nay, my son, do you rather retire from this fearful contest lest you perish in the flower of youth; you, who are now about to succeed (so may God grant!) to me and our illustrious race in the glories of war[1]."

Love and honour are ever deaf to such arguments, and all remained to perish. Though facing danger boldly in what he believed to be the cause of God and justice, de Montfort did not expect victory:—

> " Or ever he lift his scheld, he wist it sed amys;
> He was on his stede, displaied his banere,
> He sauh that treasoun sede, ' doun went his pouvere.' "
>
> ROB. BRUNE.

The enemy came rushing on, and though the surprise of the attack made the defence disordered and desperate, the barons gathered their forces into a dense body, and the contest during the two hours it lasted was obstinately fought. The emergency soon separated the zealous from the indifferent, and the Welsh auxiliaries[2] were the first to shrink from the barons' ranks, and to seek concealment among the corn-fields and gardens, where many were afterwards discovered and slain. The veteran de Montfort, though the circumstances gave him no opportunity to display his talents as a general, yet fought with all the vigour and courage of a young soldier. Undaunted by the superior numbers of his foes, he met and trampled under his horse's hoofs all those opposed to him, so as to carry dismay and wonder among the Royalists. One of the knights of that party, Warren de Bassingbourne, was obliged to rouse his faltering troops by reproaching them with their defeat at Lewes:—

---

[1] Nangis.
[2] W. Rish. de Bello Lew. Wallenses qui ad quinque millia æstimabantur.—Chr. Roff. Fugerunt Wallenses et in transeundo flumine See [? Dee, see Eng. Hist. Soc. ed, and Knighton, c. 2453] multi submersi sunt.—Walt. Heming. Humfridus de Boun cum omnibus peditibus qui ductor eorum in acie posteriori cum sex millibus ac Wallensibus cum plurimis armatis in primo conflictu juxta locum qui dicitur Syndelston propter timorem conversi sunt in fugam. Effugerunt plures de parte Simonis et in aquâ quæ dicitur Avona submerserunt. — Harl. MS. 542, p. 49.

> "Agen, traitors, agen, and habben ower thogt
> How villiche at Lewes ye werde to grounde ibrogt:
> Turneth agen and thenceth that that power all ower is,
> And we solle, as vor nogt, overcome ur for iwis[1]."
>
> Rob. Glouc.

Simon de Montfort (says one account) "fought stoutly like a giant for the liberties of England[2];" and even when all the weight of the enemy's force was made to press upon him personally, he resisted their assaults "like an impregnable tower[3]," with his dearest friends crowding around as if to defend him with the ramparts of their bodies[4]. One by one they dropped in death. Basset and le Despenser, the most faithful of all his friends, at length sank to the earth near him:—

> "Sir Hue le fer, ly Despenser,   Despenser true, the good Sir Hugh,
> Tres noble justice,   Our justice and our friend,
> Ore est à tort lyvrè a mort,   Borne down with wrong amidst the throng,
> A trop mal guise[5]."   Has met his wretched end.

"Never will I surrender to dogs and perjurers, but to God alone," cried de Montfort, when summoned to do so[6]. His horse had been killed under him, but though weakened by his wounds he yet fought on with so much spirit, wielding his sword with both hands against twelve knights, his assailants, and dealing his blows with so vigorous an old age, that, if there had been but eight followers like him, he would, according to an eye-witness[7], have put the enemy to shame. It is said that Prince Edward, before the battle, had been desirous of taking the earl and his sons prisoners, but the barons of his suite were resolved on their death[8], and an angry

---

[1] "Again, traitors, again, and remember how vilely ye were brought to the ground at Lewes. Turn again, and think that the power is now all ours, and we shall, as if they were nought, overcome them to a certainty."

[2] Chr. de Shepis.

[3] "Il se deffondoit de ses anemies aussi comme une tour qui ne peut estre domagiée."—Nangis.

[4] T. Wyke. "Paucorum militum vallo circumdatus."—Nangis.

[5] Pol. Song from MS. Cott., translated by G. Ellis in Ritson's Anc. Songs.

[6] Chr. Oxenede.

[7] "Tanta vi canitiei ictus vibrabat."—Chr. Lanerc. "Annosus sed animosus."—Chr. Evesham, Bodl. MS. Laud, 529, f. 64.

[8] Chr. Lanerc. "Cum staret pedes

multitude now pressed on de Montfort so fiercely, that, though fighting on to the last, sword in hand with a cheerful countenance, he at length fell when wounded by a blow from behind, overwhelmed by numbers rather than conquered[1].

"Thus ended by an honourable death the inbred chivalry and prowess which had been ennobled by so many deeds in so many lands[2]." "Thus lamentably fell the flower of all knighthood, leaving an example of steadfastness to others; but who can prevent familiar treachery? they who had eaten his bread, had now raised their heels against him; they who loved him by word of mouth lied in their throats, not having their hearts right with him, but betraying him in his necessity[3]." Such are the earnest comments of a French and an English chronicler on the event.

Had the victory been before doubtful, the death of de Montfort would have decided it, though his son Henry continued the hopeless resistance. Goaded to madness by the loss of his father[4], in whose sight he had been himself wounded, he sought only for a similar fate :—

> "Tarry, good *father!*
> My soul shall thine keep company to heaven.
> Tarry, sweet soul, for mine, then fly abreast,
> As in this glorious and well-foughten field,
> We kept together in our chivalry."
>
> HEN. V. Act III.

Nor was their re-union long delayed. Henry was soon overpowered and taken, and though a warm partisan[5] praises him as innocent and beautiful like Jonathan, and resembling David in faith and devotion, yet the ferocious Royalists mas-

---

pugnans gladio et occiso dextrario."
—H. Knighton; W. Rish.; Chr. de Shepis. "Multis perfossum vulneribus."—Nangis.

[1] "Where the battle and murther was is now a well, and grete elmes stande about the well; there is over the well an hovel of stone, and a crucifix and Mary and John."—Chron. of Richard Fox in Duke of Bedford's MS.

[2] Nangis.

[3] W. Rish. de Bello Lew.

[4] "D'autre part ses fils qui se combattoit aussi comme hors du sens pour la mort de son pere."—Nangis. According to Chr. Lanerc. his death preceded his father's. "Cecidit autem ibi ante patrem suum impubes miles et innocens virgo Henricus."—Chr. Lanerc. Chr. Mailr. also makes Henry the first to die.

[5] Chr. Lanerc.

sacred their helpless prisoner[1], resolved to glut their revenge with his blood. His younger brother Guy fell nearly lifeless among the heaps of the dead and dying, where he lay until picked up by the enemy and imprisoned. He recovered, however, from his wounds[2], and lived to play an active part afterwards in another country. The veteran Peter de Montfort shared the fate of his beloved leader, and of so many other comrades.

> " More murdre are nas in so lute stunde[3],
> Vor ther was werst Simon de Montfort aslawe, alas!
> And Sir Henry his sone, that so gentil knight was,
> And Sir Pers de Montfort[4] that stronge were and wise."
> Rob. Glouc.

Many chiefs of distinguished name are recorded among the slain :—

> " Sir Rauf the gode Basset did ther his ending,
> Sir Guy Baliel died there, a yong knight and hardy,
> He was pleyned more than other twenty."
> Rob. Brune.

The last named knight, a spirited Scotchman, had borne the standard[5] of Simon de Montfort at this battle, and refusing to fly or save himself, was found afterwards so mangled with wounds that his body could not be stripped even for burial. His companion, Roger de Rivle[6], was also among the bravest who fell. Thomas de Astley[7], who, at an earlier period of the civil war had eagerly seized upon the King's revenues in

---

[1] Nangis.
[2] "Guy li plus joes des freres chei entre les morts et les navrés ausi comme demi-mors, liquel fu recuellis et garis en bries temps."—Nangis.
[3] " Never was in so short a time." "*Werst*," first; "*aslawe*," slain.
[4] Hume inaccurately makes Peter the son of the Earl of Leicester, and seems to represent him attacking Worcester, 1264, as the younger brother of Richard, who was then a boy too young to bear arms.
[5] Gwydo autem, cujus ante memini, miles acerrimus, natione Scotus, cum tunc potuisset salvari morte temporali, noluit; occubuit igitur cum multis ex Magnatibus Angliæ, qui venerant ad bellum, ut decertarent pro justitia Angliæ.—Chr. Mailr. W. Rish.
[6] Chr. Mailr.
[7] Hostelee, Estley. His ancestor held three knights' fees under the Earl of Warwick, on the tenure of holding his stirrup. Thomas was knighted in 1242, and had served in Gascony. Warwickshire had been put into his custody by the barons in 1264.

his neighbourhood, and who had been in attendance on the Countess of Leicester at Odiham, a few months before, now fell a victim to his zeal for the earl, and his estates were soon granted away to one of the triumphant party[1]. The loss which made the most impression on others, as the untimely fate of youth could not fail to do, was that of two nobles, cut off in their early bloom, William de Mandeville[2] and John de Beauchamp[3], the latter on the first day of warlike service. A Royalist chronicler[4] here relents, and observes that "even stony hearts must grieve for the deaths of these two ingenuous youths, who excelled all their contemporaries in elegance of person, and whose tender age might have excused their treason." It would appear that they were butchered in cold blood after being taken prisoners[5].

[1] Warren de Bassingbourne had a grant of £151. 16s. 11d. from the estates of Astley, reserving a pension of £34. 18s. 1d. for life to his widow Edith, daughter of Peter Constable, of Melton, co. Norfolk. Andrew, the eldest son, however, recovered the lands, by the Dict. Kenilworth, for 320 marcs.

[2] John, the brother of William de Mandeville, had been also killed in his sight.

[3] There had been double marriages between the sons and daughters of Peter de Montfort and William de Beauchamp, to whom, as also to his wife Ida, there are letters extant of Adam de Marisco.—Cal. Rot. Pat. Mon. Franc. ed. Brewer, pp. 286, 301. [Mr Blaauw appears to identify this William and John de Beauchamp with the sons of William Beauchamp, of Elmley, to whom Dugdale refers the double marriage-contract with Peter de Montfort. Dugdale, however, says, on the authority of an old chronicle quoted in Leland (Itin. Vol. VI. f. 71), that Beauchamp of Elmley sent his sons in the Royalist ranks of Evesham; and the younger, John Beauchamp (of Holt), was alive late in the reign of Edward I. The John killed at Evesham was almost certainly (as Dugdale makes him) a Beauchamp of Bedford, and had inherited from a brother William only a short time before the battle.—Excerpt. e Rot. Fin. II. p. 427. Dugdale's Baronage, Vol. I. pp. 224, 227, 228, 250.]

[4] T. Wykes.

[5] Among the barons slain were also Robert de Tregoz, Walter de Creppinge, William Devereux, Roger Roulee, Hugh de Hopville, Robert de Sepinges, William de Burmugham (the three latter mentioned in Simon Mirac.), Robert de Hadreshill (Rot. Pat. 50° Hen. III.) Leland's Collect. adds a bishop, Roger de Soules, to the number. The Habyngdon MS. (in Libris Antiq. Soc.) adds Sir Gilbert Einefyeld, Sir John de Ind (? de la Lind), and Sir William Trossell. Harl. MS. 542, p. 40, adds Richard Trussell and William Devereux. Letters patent dated Westminster, Oct. 12, 1265, grant the lands of William de Ebroicis, killed at Evesham, to his widow Matilda for her life, she being sister of Walter de Gifford, Bishop of Bath, 1264–1267, then Chancellor.—No. 460 Chanc. Rec., 5th Report. [Walter de Crepping had been executor of the will of Hugh de Vere, Earl of Oxford, in 1263, and was probably son or grandson of a Walter de Crepping, a

Among the few illustrious captives rescued from the general slaughter, were some who had been the associates of Simon de Montfort during the whole of the political struggle, and were found true to the cause up to the complete triumph of the Royalists—these were Baldwin Wake, John Fitz-John, Humphrey de Bohun, jun.[1], Henry Hastings, John de Vesci, Nicholas Segrave, and Peter de Montfort's two sons. King Henry during the battle had unwillingly run some risk of being included among the sufferers, and had, when assailed by his own zealous friends, vainly exerted his voice with loud protestations, "By the head of God that he was the King; by the mercy of God that he was too old to fight:" until after a slight wound on his shoulder[2], the fall of his helmet caused him to be recognized, and placed in safety by his son[3].

Many of the baronial leaders were allowed to be buried by the monks of Evesham, and Prince Edward himself attended as a sincere mourner on the funeral of Henry de Montfort. The King had been his godfather, and the Prince esteeming him as his boyish playmate and foster-brother, as well as the comrade and friend of his manhood, with the chivalrous emotions so often noted in him, would not suffer him, even as an enemy, to pass to a dishonoured grave. The

judge in John's reign. The name was probably derived from Crepping, a manor of the earls of Oxford in Essex.—Foss, Judges, II. pp. 54, 55. William de Hardreshill, or Hardredeshull, had lands in Lincolnshire and Northamptonshire, was about five-and-twenty at the time of his death, and was stepson by his mother's second marriage of William de Arden, a member apparently of the Warwickshire family. See p. 271. Excerpta e Rot. Fin. Vol. II. pp. 368, 371, 376, 392. Cal. Inq. p. mortem, p. 59.]

[1] The title of Earl of Hereford is given him by Simon Mirac., and MS. Cott. Cleop. A. XII., but as his father lived till 1275 the title never came to him. According to the latter authority indeed he was killed at Evesham. Drayton mentions him:

"Young Humphrey Bohun still doth with great Le'ster goe,
Who for his country's cause becomes his father's foe:
FitzJohn, Gray, Spencer, Strange, Rosse, Segrave, Vessey, Gifford,
Wake, Lucy, Viscount, Vaux, Clare, Marmion, Hastings, Clifford."
DRAYTON's Polyolb. Vol. II. p. 33.

[2] Chr. Mail., "Rex percussus in scapula clamavit fortiter; erat enim vir summopere pacificus non bellicosus."—Walt. Heming. "Rex remedialiter vulneratus."—Mat. Westm.

[3] "Rex vero salvatus est per quemdam Baronem de Marchia Rogerum de Leyburne nomine."—Chr. Lanerc.

treatment of the aged Simon de Montfort's body was far different, and will be mentioned presently.

The atmosphere had been disturbed during the battle by a violent storm of thunder and hail, accompanied by an earthquake; and the darkness was so dense in many parts of the country, that the priests could not see to read prayers in their churches. These were so many signs to the ready superstition of the people that heaven sympathised with their grief at the destruction of their champions, "while (in the phrase of the times) the people of the Lord were in torment[1]."

With a similar feeling an ominous interpretation was now given to the appearance of a great comet, which spread its light across half the heavens during several months this year. No phenomenon of this nature was remembered, and all manner of calamities were attributed to it by various parties. One chronicler supposes it to have presaged the battle of Evesham[2], another observes with much simplicity that, "though it may have tokened many things in other parts of the world, this one at any rate is certain, that during its three months' duration Pope Urban began to be ill exactly at its appearance, and died the very night the comet disappeared[3]." Even the strong intellect of Roger Bacon was led astray by this natural wonder, and he reasoned of it in a strain not superior to the tone of his contemporaries: "Whence in the year 1264, in the month of July, when there was the apparition of a terrible comet, it is proved to have been generated by the virtue of Mars; for as Mars was then in Taurus, and the comet arose in Cancer, it ceased not

---

[1] "Et motum terræ dedit hora ferissima guerre,
Dum sic bellatur, Domini gens dum cruciatur."
—W. Rish. de Bello Lew. et Evesh. MS. Cott. Otho D. vii. "Pro justitiâ et juramento suo servando legitime, agonizantes migraverunt ad dominum."—Cott.MS. Faustina B. xiv.

[2] "Quæ fortassis tam inopinati eventus præsagium portendebat."— T. Wyke. Compare Robert of Gloucester's reference to it:
" Vor thretti mile thanne this I sai Roberd,
That verst this boc made, and was wel sore afcrd."
[3] W. Rish.

to run towards its cause, that is to say, Mars, as steel runs to a magnet; therefore since it moved towards Mars, and there lay hid, it must have been caused by Mars. Since, therefore, the nature of Mars is to excite men to anger, discord and wars, so it happened that the comet also signified the angers, discords and wars of men, as wise astronomers teach, but more truly the experience of the whole Church, proved by the wars of England, Spain, Italy, and other regions, which occurred then and afterwards. Oh, how much advantage might have been procured to the Church of God, if the quality of the heavens at that time had been foreseen by wise men, and made known to prelates and princes, so as to calm them by the desire for peace; for there would not then have been so great a slaughter of Christians, nor so many souls placed in hell[1]."

This remarkable comet is described as "a sterre with a launce—red and clear inou," appearing from St Margaret's day till near Michaelmas, and is supposed by astronomers to have re-appeared in 1556[2]. Should this identity be true, it may be again expected to recur in 1848[3], after completing its destined course of 292 years; and let those who may be curious in such omens then observe what illness of princes, what bloodshed in war, or what downfall of political chiefs may then result.

The victory of the King's party at Evesham was so complete, that the disproportionate loss[4] on the other side beto-

---

[1] Opus M. p. 4, pag. 243, ed. 1733. In some verses of later date Prince Edmund of Lancaster is called "Cometa Comitum," probably in allusion to the recent comet of 1305 (Halley's).—V. Polit. Songs, p. 258.

[2] For descriptions of it see Trivet. p. 262. Chr. Lanercost, Vol. I. p. 73, and Taxter's Chron. A. 1264.

[3] It did not appear in 1848. P.

[4] "Numerus militum occisorum nonies viginti—numerus servientum bene armatorum undecies viginti—numerus peditum de Wallia v. millia —de peditibus prædicti Simonis duo millia—in universo occubuerunt x. millia hominum."—Chr. Lanercost. "Ex parte D¹. Edwardi Principis cecidit Hugo Stragmiles et Adam de Kidmallis et pauci alteri. In villa, in cœnobii curia, in monasterio et capellis eorum et atriis, populi more pecudum obtruncati jacuerunt."— Harl. MS. 542, p. 49. [Ex parte domini Eadwardi uno tantum milite modica probitate notando et duobus armigeris interfectis. Matt. West. p. 395.]

kening more a surprise than a battle, caused it to be thus characterised:—

"Such was the morthre of Eivesham, vor bataile non it was."
                                                    ROB. GLOUC.

The Royalists had distinguished themselves by red crosses on their arms, and the few who fell in the action owed their death to neglect of this precaution, being killed by their own comrades in mistake[1].

The physical power of the barons, whether for good or evil, was shattered to pieces by this shock, but though the chance of war had decided so far, yet the moral effects of their brief government were destined to be more permanent. While preparing to mourn over the violent suppression of this attempted reform in Church and State, at the cost of blood and misery, the historical observer may perceive the principles of liberty which the barons had asserted, surviving their manly struggle, and springing up afresh with the quick germ of life. The representative system, whose expansion they had encouraged, had taken too stout a hold to be extirpated, and, from this root remaining unharmed, the branches of national freedom throve henceforth with vigorous enlargement, strong in its own vital influence, upheld by the will and nourished by the love of the people. Within thirty years (in 1297) even a successful warrior, Edward I., was obliged formally to renounce the claim of tallage without the consent of Parliament. The help of the principal churchmen and nobles mainly influenced this progress, although there were indeed many of all classes at the time anxious for civil liberty—the liberty of person and property—which was the only species then sought for or secured. No one had yet raised their thoughts to the entertainment of religious liberty—the free communion of the mind with its spiritual source—and no such claim had therefore been preferred.

Many of the privileges subsequently acquired by Parliament were purchased from the Crown in return for money,

[1] Chr. Roff. MS.

when its ambition or prodigality required such aid; the very vices of royalty being thus converted into national benefits: but, be it remembered, that the first and most important was a free-will offering from the barons, unbought and unstained.

The barons and their leader have been upbraided with having neglected in their days of power the provisions of the *mise* of Lewes. The time, place, and manner of reference to the King of France have therefore been pointed out, as well as the urgent importunity with which his decision was called for. The reproach is not only unjust, but may be fitly retorted by the fact that the King, when his power became again free from control, never made the smallest allusion or advance to the settlement of the government promised by the *mise*[1].

When William the Conqueror was told that one of his followers had cut King Harold's thigh after he lay dead, he degraded him from knighthood[2]. In sad contrast with this nobler feeling was the treatment of Simon de Montfort's corpse at Evesham, forming with chroniclers of all parties a topic of indignant outcry, even in that rough state of society. The earl's prostrate body was not only pierced with idle wounds, but mangled piecemeal[3], and the limbs separated and dispersed. The hands were cut off, and with the head fixed on a spear's point, were sent as a worthy present to the wife of Roger de Mortimer at her castle of Wigmore. "May that precursor of the Lord, whose head was served up at a banquet by a dancer, help the sender's soul!" bitterly remarks a chronicler[4].

---

[1] "Princeps Edwardus nec fidem nec spem datam pluribus observavit."—Nangis Chr.

[2] "Turpitudine notatus militiâ pulsus fuit."—M. Par.; H. Hunt; W. Malms. The incident seems depicted at the end of the Bayeux tapestry.

[3] "Vilissimo sæviendi genere furiens—minutatim in frusta."—T. Wyke. "In cumulum sui dedecoris amputatis eidem virilibus et membratim laceratum acephalum reddiderunt."—Nangis. The folio MS. in Cott. Nero D. II., by a Rochester monk, contains a rude drawing, at the bottom of p. 176, of the mutilation of the Earl of Leicester's body, and represents the Justiciary le Despenser lying near him.

[4] W. Rish.

"And among alle othere mest reuthe it was ido,
That Sir Simon the olde man demembered was so,
Vor Sir Maitravers (thonk habbe non)
Carf him of feet and honde, and his limes many on,
And his heved hii smitten of and to Wigemore it ssende
To Dam Maud de Mortimer that wel foule it ssende[1]."

Rob. Glouc.

By one chronicler[2], while recording with disgust the foul mutilation of his body, the incident is improved (in the preacher's sense of the word) as an appropriate judgment of God upon Simon de Montford after his marriage with a professed nun. Besides the more common indignities of brutal triumph, other atrocities were perpetrated on "the olde man" not fit for description, and it was the memory of this outrage which exasperated his surviving sons long afterwards to a bloody retaliation.

Some attribute this insult to Roger de Mortimer; others, as has been seen, to William Maltravers, who had probably deserted the cause of the barons, like Gifford, from personal motives. One of the chroniclers[3], however, studiously avoids polluting his page with any name, referring to him as "a certain person accursed of the devil," "a certain son of Belial;" and he records with evident satisfaction that, on being drowned near Perth two years after, his corpse likewise was found mangled by two enormous crabs which had fastened upon it.

Though the offering of the head to Matilda de Mortimer seems only worthy of a Scythian Tomyris, yet the lady had some of the noblest blood in her veins. Being one of the coheiresses[4] of William de Braose, who had wide estates in

[1] *Reuthe*, pity; *thonk*, thanks; *carf*, carved; *heved*, head; *hii*, they.
[2] Chr. Lanerc. "Testiculi abscissi fuerunt et appensi ex utraque parte nasi, et ita missum fuit caput suum uxori Domini Rogeri de Mortuo Mari apud castrum de Wiggemore."—Lib. de Ant. Leg.
[3] Chr. Mailr. "Quidam alius anathema diaboli"—"quidam ex filiis Belial." He was accidentally pushed into the Tay by a lady in sport at Kinclaven castle, in presence of the Queen Margaret.
[4] Matilda, Eleanor wife of H. de Bohun, junior, and Eva, widow of William de Cantilupe, divided the inheritance, 1259.—See p.101. Through Eva William de Cantilupe became lord of Abergavenny. She was probably buried at Abbey Dore.—See Archæol. Journ. for 1862, p. 27.

Sussex and Brecknock, the re-marriage of her grandfather to Gladuse, a Welsh Princess, afterwards married to Ralph de Mortimer[1], had probably caused her to spend most of her life among the savage borderers of Wales, and qualified her in the opinion of others for the reception of so unfeminine an offering[2].

Some portions of the mutilated body of de Montfort appear to have been sent for exhibition at different towns, "not for reverence, but for disgrace[3]," and some fragments, with the trunk, were collected by the monks of Evesham, with as much respect as they dared to exhibit, carrying them on a hurdle wrapped in an old cloth to their abbey; they were buried with his comrade le Despenser in front of the high altar[4]. The pious care of his burial by these monks[5], whose

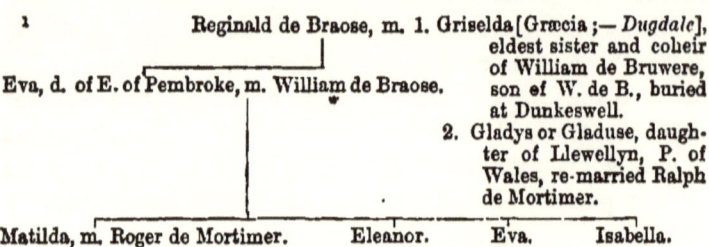

[1] Reginald de Braose, m. 1. Griselda [Græcia ;— *Dugdale*], eldest sister and coheir of William de Bruwere, son of W. de B., buried at Dunkeswell.

Eva, d. of E. of Pembroke, m. William de Braose.

2. Gladys or Gladuse, daughter of Llewellyn, P. of Wales, re-married Ralph de Mortimer.

Matilda, m. Roger de Mortimer. Eleanor. Eva. Isabella.

Mem. Braose arms, cross, crosslets *not* fitchée.

[2] On her husband's death in 1283, her lands were seized by the King, and not restored until she swore not to marry again without license. She died 1301.

[3] "Membra principalia a tanto viro amputata missa sunt loco exennii ad majores emulos *tam viros quam mulieres*, non osculanda sed opprobio ostendenda; sed cito signis terribilibus per ea ostensis venerationi sunt habita, perseverant enim huc usque carne integra odore aromatico."— Chr. Lanerc.

[4] "Truncus autem corporis sui tantummodo datum est sepulturæ in ecclesiâ de Evesham."—Lib. de Ant. Leg. "Sed dicunt quidam universa membra ejus taliter sparsa mirabiliter in brevi coadunata esse ad invicem, et condita esse in loco ubi nunc habetur honorifice sepultus, scilicet apud Abbatiam de Evesham."—Chr. Anon. MS. Cott. Cleop. A. 190. According to Ann. Waverl. de Montfort and le Despenser were buried, "ante magnum altare ante gradum inferiorem." The Chr. Evesham states the burial to have been conducted without outward marks of honour, from fear of the King.

[5] There was no abbot at the time, the vacancy after the death of Henry of Worcester (Nov. 1263) not having been filled up.—Dugd. Monast. "Reliquum corporis quod sub divo derelictum fuerat super scalam debilem et veterem collocaverunt, et vili et debili collobio et dilacerato cooperuerunt et ad ecclesiam conventualem de Evesham deportaverunt, et in lintheamine mundo involventes in monumento novo reposuerunt."— Chr. Abingd. MS. Bodl. 712.

guest he had been the night before his death[1], was soon rewarded by the lustre and profit of the many miracles worked by the relics of the sainted martyr; for such he was regarded by the people. "As the news of his death spread over the land there was a suspension of mirth, and an universal lamentation arose, until the sighs were turned into hymns of praise and gladness by the numerous miracles announced to have been effected by his unconquerable firmness and patience and purity of faith, and these gave hopes of hereafter recovering from the oppression of the wicked[2]." Such were the excited feelings of the time; and it is not improbable that his enemies afterwards removed and concealed his remains in order to check the veneration they were held in[3].

The first alleged miracle occurring immediately after his death is highly characteristic of the current manners and opinions. The bearer of the fearful trophy to Wigmore[4] had not found the lady Matilda in the castle. She was at mass in the neighbouring abbey, founded by the de Mortimers,

[1] Chron. Petroburg. (publ. by Camden Society) relates the severe punishment which the monks of Evesham brought upon themselves by favouring S. de Montfort. All their manors were seized, some by the King, others by Pr. Edward, the Earl de Warenne, the Earl of Gloucester and others (pro eo quod Abbas ex edicto Comitis misit apud Kenelwirthe servicium suum et alibi contra dominum regem). Fines exceeding 3000 marcs were exacted (sine dilacione) so that the abbey was long after loaded with debt. 1265°. p. 18.
[2] W. Rish. de Bello Lew. et Evesh.
[3] Chr. Abingd. states this expressly. Extensive excavations were lately made on the site of the abbey church, but nothing was found to identify the place of burial of the Earl of Leicester. [Mr Luard has referred me to an interesting passage in the Osney Annals (pp. 176, 177), which says that after a short time "quidam nostrates" murmured at

the earl's body having Christian burial, inasmuch as he was excommunicated and a traitor. They obtained leave to have the body dug up, and thrown into a farther place, which at the time of the writer was only known to a few. This was no doubt Dugdale's authority for saying in a passage Mr Blaauw had marked for reprehension that "the common people out of high indignation towards him who had been the chief instrument of mischief to the whole realm digged it up," &c.—Short View of the late Troubles.]
[4] Wigmore had been conquered from Edric Earl of Shrewsbury by the de Mortimer who accompanied William I. Two wooden bottles filled with wine were long kept there, which had been sent to Roger by the Queen of Navarre, 1279, in compliment of his valour at a tournament, and he added a carbuncle to his arms in her honour.—See Banks' Dorm. Baron.

and thither the messenger followed her, still bearing the head, and thrusting into his bosom the maimed hands sewn up in a cloth. As he rushed into the church in the eagerness of his zeal, and whispered the tidings of victory into the ears of the devout lady, at the moment of the elevation of the Host, the hands of Simon de Montfort, as if from the force of long habit during life, they were now irresistibly attracted to their accustomed duties at so solemn a service, were seen by the whole congregation to be raised up over the messenger's head, clasped together in prayer, although they were afterwards found within the bag, with its stitches undisturbed as before. The Lady Matilda, herself a witness of this scene, is said to have refused the hands admittance to the castle, and sent them back to Evesham[1].

As this marvel was enacted among his enemies only, it naturally became the forerunner of many among his friends; and, in spite of the discouragement of the court[2], the odour of his supposed sanctity diffused its efficacy over the land. The particulars of 212 miracles[3] have been noted down as they occurred, comprising all manner of cures effected, not only on men, but on horses, oxen, and hawks; fevers, fits blindness, dumbness, even death itself, all gave way when the patients were true believers, while distant revilers were struck dumb. Of the prayers directly addressed to the political saint, one hymn has been preserved to us:—

"Salve Symon Montis Fortis,	Hail, Simon de Montfort, hail,
Totius flos militiæ.	Knighthood's fairest flower!
Duras pœnas passus mortis	England does thy death bewail,
Protector gentis Angliæ.	Whom thou didst shield with power.
* * *	* * *
Sis pro nobis intercessor	Never did saint such tortures rend,
Apud Deum, qui defensor	As thee of martyr race:
In terrâ extiteras[4]."	Thou who on earth didst God defend,
	Now gain for us God's grace.

[1] "Sic se habet vera relatio."— Chr. Mailr.
[2] The celebrated "Défense à Dieu de faire miracle ici," in the Jansenist controversy, was here anticipated.
[3] Lately printed by the Camd. Soc. with W. Rishanger's Chr. from MSS. Cott. Vesp. A. VI.
[4] Mirac. Sim. de Montfort.

BATTLE OF EVESHAM.

But besides prayer, other curious modes of obtaining relief by his intercession were in common use, such as bending money in his honour[1], and the process of "mensuration," which consisted of the application to the sufferer of some fillet or string which had been previously put round the saint's body. Several priests certify to such miracles as the following specimen: "A certain man at Hawkesbury, dumb and convulsed for seven years, being measured by the earl, immediately recovered from all his infirmities. The Abbot of Pershore and many others bear witness to this." The priors of Gloucester, Oxford, and Waltham testify to others. The Countess of Gloucester, the Countess of Albemarle, and many noble ladies also appear as witnesses. Persons drowned and burnt to death recovered. "Avicia, daughter of Alan of Derby, after being unquestionably dead[2], roused herself and got well on being measured by Earl Simon." "Gregory de Grandun, rector of the church of Sapecot, reports of his ox, which would not eat for fifteen days, on a piece of money being bent in honour of the Earl, immediately ate greedily and recovered." Whole parishes and towns testify to some instances, among which some are dated as late as 1278, proving how long the memory of Simon de Montfort continued to exercise influence: pilgrims came to his tomb from afar, and though persons of all ranks readily attested the miracles performed there, yet none dared to talk openly of them, from fear of the King and Prince Edward.

These wonders have been justly scoffed at by a Roman Catholic historian[3] in modern times, as "a number of ridiculous miracles," but they were not so considered at the time; and the faith of political partisans even attributed similar miraculous power to Henry de Montfort and others of the nobles, whom they considered to have earned the crown of martyrdom at Evesham[4]. However little such claims of

[1] "Denario plicato ad Comitem."
[2] "Certissime mortua."
[3] Lingard, Hist. Engl.
[4] "Martirii corona laureati."—

Chr. H. de Silgrave, MSS. Cott. Cleop. A. XII. "Cujus postmodum justiciæ infallibile signum fuit crebra miraculorum exhibitio divinitus exhibita

supernatural agency may be adapted to the credulity of the present age, an age supplying humble followers to Mormonism, and educated crowds to Mesmerism, they mark, at any rate, the prevalent temper of a distant period, and strongly denote the affectionate regard in which the memory of Simon de Montfort was held.

"And so finished his labours, that glorious man Earl Simon (observes his contemporary[1]), who devoted not only his property, but his own self in behalf of the oppressed poor, in the assertion of justice and of the rights of the kingdom; he was commendable also for his literary knowledge, rejoiced always to be present at divine services, was frugal, and accustomed to watch at nights more than to sleep. He was stedfast to his word, grave in countenance, especially trustworthy, and respectful towards churchmen; endeavouring to follow the blessed Robert Grethead, Bishop of Lincoln, he committed to him the education of his children. By his advice he dealt with difficulties, and attempted and accomplished what he undertook, particularly those matters which he considered most useful. It is said, indeed, that the great enterprise, for which he strove unto death, was imposed on him for the remission of his sins, by the injunction of the bishop, who declared that the peace of the English Church could not be secured without the sword, and that all who died for it should be crowned with martyrdom. The bishop is also said to have foreseen the deaths of the father and son on the same day, and to have assured young Henry, with his hand on his head, that they should die in the cause of truth and justice."

The people had already made a saint of the bishop, whose principles he had imbibed and put into action, looking now on de Montfort as "the perfect pupil of a perfect master."

In the skill of arms and the art of war he was acknow-

circa Hugonem Dispensatorem, summum Justiciarium Angliæ, virum justissimum et æquissimum in omni judicio circa divites et pauperes et circa Symonem et nonnullos alios qui fidem Domino servantes usque ad mortem creduntur regnare cum Deo in gloriâ."—Chr. Mailros.

[1] W. Rishanger.

ledged to excel all of his time, while his stedfastness of purpose and composure amidst the greatest difficulties were equally remarkable. Many of his private habits befitted his character as a soldier. It is stated, on the authority of intimate eye-witnesses, that he was abstemious in eating and drinking, slept little, and was of a jocund and cheerful discourse[1]. Though his dress in public was of blue or crimson, as suitable to his rank, yet in private his plain russet tunic constantly covered a penitential haircloth[2].

The intimacy he maintained with two of the greatest scholars of the age, Bishop Grethead and Adam de Marisco, allows us to infer the character of his intellect and the inclination of his tastes in private life[3]. Both these are selected for especial praise by their friend Roger Bacon, as "most famous men, who by the power of mathematics knew how to explain the causes of all things, and to expound satisfactorily both human and divine matters[4]."

The Franciscan friar, Adam de Marisco[5], was frequently an inmate in de Montfort's family, and his curious and in-

[1] W. Rish. de Bello Lew. et Evesh.
[2] Chr. Mailr.
[3] "Litteraturæ scientia commendabiliter præditus."—W. Rish.
[4] Roger Bacon, Opus Magnum, p. 64. ed. 1733. It is curious to find two such great names linked together, as the Bishop's and R. Bacon's, in Hudibras, speaking of the conjurer, P. II. c. 3. 223:
"Yet none a deeper knowledge boasted
Since old Hodge Bacon, and Bob Grosted."
[5] "Wherever there was a marsh," says Professor Brewer, "there also would be found a De Marisco." Nevertheless he has himself done so much toward disentangling the pedigree of Adam de Marisco, that I do not hesitate to substitute his results with some of my own for a note of Mr Blaauw's. Adam de Marisco is said by Leland (de Script. Brit. p. 268) to have been a native of Somersetshire, probably to connect him with the family of the Justiciary of Ireland. It is at least equally probable that he was connected with Adam de Marisco of Andover, who is mentioned in official records of King John's reign (Chancellor's Roll, pp. 249, 254, Rot. de Fin. p. 447). Relatives of the famous Adam were Robert, probably a brother, who was made Archdeacon of Oxford about 1248; Thomas *consanguineus*; and William, *germanus*, bailiff of Bugden, and seemingly in Bishop Grossetête's service (Mon. Fran. pp. LXXVI—LXXVIII). Of the Somersetshire family the first known is probably W. de Marisco, who held the island of Lundy about 1200, besides land in Somersetshire (Rot. de Oblatis, pp. 101, 228, 291, &c.). A Geoffrey de Marisco was Justiciary of Ireland 1215—1228, and held lands in Munster (Leland, I. p. 195), and he or another Geoffrey joined in the Earl Marshal's rebellion against Henry III. In October 1234, William de Marisco,

teresting correspondence, still extant in manuscript[1], proves his cordial sympathy with him on all occasions, public and private. The King had appointed him, in 1257, in conjunction with the Bishop of Worcester and Hugh le Bigod, to negociate a treaty with France, under the direction of Simon de Montfort and Peter de Savoy, whose assent to their arrangements was made necessary[2]. During the campaigns in Gascony de Marisco was an anxious observer of the court intrigues, which affected his absent friend the Earl of Leicester, reporting frequent interviews with the King and Queen on his behalf, warning him of the enmity or the occasional courtesy of the Queen towards him; and though listening to the King's avowed confidence in the earl's integrity, yet leading him to expect the evasion of the sworn stipulations in his favour, and at times not daring even to approach the King when exasperated. Frequently did de Marisco send his messengers, Gregory de Losell and John de la Haye, with tidings of public affairs, as well as of the good progress and health of the young de Montforts, then pupils "of excellent disposition and of great hope," "advancing day by day in age, piety, and grace," under the Bishop of Lincoln's tuition. Amidst all his devotion to the Earl's interests, however, the good friar did not refrain from bold reproaches when the

son and heir of Jordan de Marisco, fined to recover the King's grace for complicity in that rebellion, and in Aug. 1235, another William de Marisco was formally excepted from the king's grace granted to his father Geoffrey (Excerpta e Rot. Fin. I. pp. 267, 286). It was probably this William who lived afterwards as a pirate on Lundy Island, and was hanged in 1242. Besides these, it is not improbable that Richard de Marisco, Chancellor 1214—1226, and Bishop of Durham 1216, "one of the household and manners of king John," (Wendover, IV. p. 46,) may have been of the Somersetshire family. Other noticeable de Mariscos of this period are (1) Adam de Marisco, convicted of robbery, and banished the kingdom (Mon. Fran. p. 613), (2) Richard de Marisco, hanged for killing Matilda Halfkarl his mother (Calend. Geneal. I. p. 27), and (3) Robert de Marisco of Wilts, outlawed for killing Jordan de Doniton (Exc. e Rot. Fin. I. p. 277) P.

[1] MSS. Cott. Vitel C. VIII. On one occasion Adam de Marisco went at the Queen's request to Reading and Odiham to treat about business concerning the king and his heirs; and soon afterwards to Brumhale (near Sunninghill in Berks and about four miles from Windsor), to meet the Earl and Countess of Leicester. Ep. A. de Marisco, p. 152, ed. Brewer.

[2] Westm., June 22, 1257.—Rymer.

interests of religion were in question; and one of his letters thus rebuked the Earl for having widowed the church of Odiham by taking abroad with him the Chancellor of Sarum from the duty of serving it:—"My mind has not been a little troubled by these thoughts, and I cannot think why you thus acted so evidently wrong; my grief is increased by what I hear, that you entertain certain follies[1] in this particular, which must be reproved, not defended. May heavenly light enable your eyes to see divine truth! lest seduced by the fallacies of the age, which God forbid, you fall into the pit with your blind leaders. By the honour of God, by your own salvation, by the dignity of the Church, I implore your pious discretion to study the correction of this transgression, and send back their shepherd to his own sheep[2]." Simon de Montfort's temper little welcomed reproof, even from so sincere a friend, and his anger on this occasion is referred to in a subsequent letter by de Marisco as excessive, but the friar replied with the honest consciousness of right: "As my own heart has not yet reproached me, I neither fear your judgment nor your accusation in this matter." In other letters de Marisco saluted the Earl by wishing him "the spirit of wholesome counsel, joined with the spirit of holy fortitude," exhorting him to "fear not, for the Lord is with you;" and hailed him as destined "to purge and enlighten the Church of God, as well as to establish a fitting government in the state, by his unwearied anxieties." Admitted to all the secrets of the Earl's designs, the cautious friar is found repeatedly urging restraint of tongue on his great leader, "for the heart of fools is in their mouth, but the mouth of the wise is in their heart." On one occasion he appears to refer to some daring enterprise of the Earl with similar prudence. "On the business, indeed, which you know of[3], it seems to me that nothing should at present be written, especially as it

[1] "Quasdam habetis ineptias."
[2] Epist. A. de Marisco, pp. 262, 266, 270—276, ed. Brewer. [Mr Blaauw, has, I think, mistaken the purport of Simon de Montfort's answer. The "immodica littera" to which he objected was one of extravagant commendation.]
[3] "Super negocio quod nostis."

concerns the most important matters, and on one side the greatest salvation is hoped for, while on the other the greatest dangers are not shunned. The voice alone, and not the mute writing, can fully answer the many questions. I therefore entreat your Serenity not to be displeased if I do not write back as you wished concerning that deed of such doubt and alarm[1], for I perceive how inexpedient it would be to introduce the peril of irreparable damage by any carelessness." By profession and character a man of peace, de Marisco excused himself even from the service of the Earl, when his duty called him to read lectures at Oxford, and he appears to have contemplated with horror the unbridled license of the civil war, and the sad spectacle of wickedness resulting from the gathering of armies and their contests.

The attachment of so eminent a man as de Marisco seems to reflect honour upon the Earl of Leicester, and there can be no doubt that the fall of this great political chief was widely lamented, not only by the barons of his party, but by the great body of the people, and by those who most sympathised with their feelings, the clergy. Most of the chronicles and poems of the times are by clerical hands, and they are nearly unanimous in regretting his overthrow, as that of a champion of the Church and people. There is something very solemn and plaintive in the poem called the Lament of Simon de Montfort, every stanza of which concludes with this burthen:

"Ore est ocys la flur de pris,	Ah! low now lies our flower of price,
Qe taunt savoit de guere,	Who led the war so well:
Ly Quens Montfort, sa dure mort	Earl Montfort's death shall England's
Molt emplorra la terre[2]."	breath
	Bewail with woe and knell.

[1] "De illo facto tam ambiguæ formidinis." The letters not being dated, it is not possible to ascertain what is thus alluded to by de Marisco. Some of the events referred to, however, sufficiently denote the dates of several: one speaking of Anian, as bishop-elect of St Asaph, was probably written in 1249; another, addressed to Henry de Lexington, Dean of Lincoln, between 1245 and 1254; others refer to the disastrous crusade of Louis IX. Epist. A. de Marisco, ed. Brewer, pp. 254, 326, 405.

[2] MSS. Harl. 2253, printed in Ritson's Ancient Songs, Political Songs, and elsewhere.

With a prophetic spirit, however, the author considered de Montfort, even by his death, to have gained the victory for his cause, in the same manner as Thomas à Becket had done:—

"Més par sa mort le Cuens Mountfort,
Conquist la victorie
Come ly martyr de Caunterbyr
Finist sa vie;
Ne voleit pas li bon Thomas
Qe perist Seinte Eglise,
Ly Cuens ausi se combati,
E morust sauntz feyntise.
Ore est ocys, &c.

* * *

Qe voleint moryr e mentenir
La pees e la dreyture,
Le seint martir lur fra joyr,
Sa conscience pure,
Qe velt moryr e sustenir
Les honmes de la terre
Son bon desir acomplir
Quar bien le quidom fere.
Ore est ocys," &c.

Yet by the blow that laid thee low,
Brave Earl, one palm was given,
Nor less at thine, than Becket's shrine,
Shall rise our vows to heaven.
Our church and laws, your common cause,
'Twas his the church to save;
Our rights restored, thou, generous Lord,
Shall triumph in the grave,

* * *

Each righteous Lord who braved the sword,
And for our safety died,
With conscience pure shall aye endure
Our martyred saint beside.
That martyred saint was never faint
To ease the poor man's care,
With gracious will he shall fulfil
Our just and earnest prayer[1].

A modern historian has remarked with great eloquence, that "he died unconscious of the imperishable name which he acquired, and which he probably considered as of very small importance. He thus unknowingly determined that England was to be a free country, and he was the blind instrument of disclosing to the world that great institution of representation, which was to introduce into popular governments a regularity of order far more perfect than had heretofore been purchased by submission to absolute power, and to draw forth liberty from confinement in single cities, to a fitness for being spread over territories, which experience

[1] The author has gladly availed himself of the translation of these two stanzas by G. Ellis, in Ritson's Anc. Songs, ed. 1829.

does not forbid to hope may be as vast as have ever been grasped by the iron gripe of a despotic conqueror[1]."

Such eulogies, and the affection of his contemporaries, must be fairly weighed against the charges of other authors. If Simon de Montfort were, indeed, as Hume terms him, a bold and artful conspirator with hypocritical pretensions to sanctity, of unbounded ambition, barefaced avarice, violence, ingratitude, tyranny, rapacity, and treachery, then, without dispute, his death was "the most fortunate event that could have occurred;" but in that case, the unexplained love of the nobles, clergy, and people, for his memory, after his life and power had ceased, will constitute a greater marvel than any of the two hundred and twelve miracles imputed to him.

[1] Sir J. Mackintosh, Hist. Engl.

CHAPTER XVI.

THE DISINHERITED.

"These disturbers were not so much like men usurping power, as asserting their natural place in society."—BURKE.

AFTER being alternately confirmed and annulled during seven years, the Oxford Statutes were now finally declared void, and the *mise* ceased to be thought of; but as those who had taken part in the battles of Lewes and Evesham had all their future lives influenced by their results, the personal fate of some of the survivors of the overthrow may be followed with interest a little longer.

By neither party was the scaffold resorted to for additional bloodshed after their respective triumphs; a moderation which contrasts remarkably with the ferocity of manners then general, and the practice of later times which may be considered more civilized. A stern and ample measure of vindictive retribution, however, was exacted in other respects by the King's party. Commissioners were quickly despatched into the different counties to seize on the lands and goods of all who had been concerned in those proceedings, which were now termed rebellious, though they had so recently borne the outward aspect, and exercised the influence of the united power, of King, Barons and Commons. No order or dignity was spared during the extortion of plunder on this occasion; some religious communities were even punished, not for their actual help or intercourse with Simon de Montfort, but for their presumed inclination towards his cause[1].

These severities were sanctioned by a Parliament held at Winchester, September 8, 1265, to which it does not appear that any representatives of the Commons were summoned. By legalising the confiscation of all the estates of de Montfort and the other defeated chiefs, the royalists provided a fund for their own reward, which was profusely distributed among themselves. The property, not only of the prisoners and survivors, but even of those slain, while fighting on the same side as the King, and under his royal banner, was included in this wide confiscation, for the Parliament considered them as traitors to have so acted, while the King was in subjection to the Earl of Leicester, who dealt with the King's seal as he pleased[2]. By this retrospective vengeance the sons and families of the defeated party became a large and distinct class of destitute sufferers, who were often referred to for several years under the name of the Disinherited[3].

A return of all the lands of rebels was required to be made to the King by October 13[4]. In the single county of Leicester a long list of landholders[5] was returned as rebels.

[1] W. Rish.
[2] " Sub virga et potestate Comitis Leicestriæ qui fecit quicquid voluit de Sigillo Regis."—Lib. de Ant. Leg. The King alleges the same reason in a Proclamation from Windsor, Oct. 1, for revoking his former letters, which excused from payment of debts to Jews " certain debtors, especially those who were openly opposing him and his first-born son, which he had signed while in the power and custody of Simon de Montfort, his enemy, who used his seal at his pleasure."—Rymer.
[3] Their number may be learnt by a solution of the following enigmatical lines in MSS. Cott. Otho. D. viii.—V. W. Rish., p. 145:
" Exhæredati si fiant connumerati
Millia cum binis deca bis sunt
acta ruinis."

One instance of restoration occurs of property seized unjustly or by mistake. The king's writ, dated Winchester, Sept. 14, 1265, to the Sheriff of Hertfordshire, orders him to restore the goods and chattels of John de Holemore, parson of the church of Hampton in "Wathamstede," if it be true that he never interfered in the disturbances of the kingdom. No. 441 Chanc. Rec. 5th Report.
[4] Rot. Pat. 49° Henry III., Sept. 21.
[5] Thomas de Cronesley, Robert Motun de Peyclinton, Ralph Basset, Peter de Montfort, all killed in battle; Nicolas Segrave, Henry de Hastings, John le Despenser, Richard de Grey, Robert de Wyvile, Saer de Harcourt, Geoffrey de Skeffington, as prisoners; William de Preston, John de Reygate, Brian de Gorva, William Mar-

The value of Simon de Montfort's own estates in the county is thus given: the Burgh of Leicester, £154. 0s. 4d.; Hinckley, £29; Lywalton, £20; Bogworth and Torington, £20. 8s. 9d.; Dersford, £19. 10s.; and in the royal grants disposing of them they are spoken of as having devolved on the King as escheats by his forfeiture[1].

The King's second son, Edmund, afterwards surnamed Crouchback from his habit of stooping[2], profited most of all by the grants arising from these events. His father gave him[3] all the estates, and the office of High Steward lately belonging to "our enemy and felon, Simon de Montfort, by whom war was excited in our kingdom," and to these were added also the Earldom of Derby, and the estates of Nicolas Segrave. The Queen, in 1291, enriched him further with the palace of Savoy; and these ample grants ultimately so raised the family importance of this prince[4], afterwards Earl of Lancaster, that in the fourth generation the inheritor of his wealth and title was enabled to depose Richard II. and to usurp the throne[5].

By another grant of the same date[6] Prince Henry received the estates of de Furnivall[7], and all the other chieftains were freely admitted to the division of the spoil. Roger

tell; also Robert Burdett, as having fought at Evesham, and Richard de Vernon, as having held Pec Castle for Henry de Montfort.

[1] "Ad nos tanquam escaeta nostra per prædictam forisfacturam suam devenerunt."—Rot. Pat. See Nichols's Leicest. Vol. I.

[2] On his tomb, however, in Westminster Abbey, he sits erect on his horse fully armed. His first wife, Aveline de Fortibus, has her effigy near him.

[3] By a grant dated Canterbury, Oct. 29, 1265, and witnessed by Hugh le Bigot, Philip Basset, &c.

[4] It is remarkable that the existence of this Prince at the death of Henry III. should have been overlooked in Hallam's Mid. Ag. III. 274, and that an argument should have been founded on "Edward, Earl of Cornwall, though nearest Prince of the blood," not enjoying any superior title to the regency on that account. Edmund (not Edward), Earl of Cornwall, was the only surviving son of the King of the Romans, but Edmund Crouchback was the nearest Prince of the blood.

[5] Henry IV. inherited the property from his mother, Blanche of Lancaster."

[6] Rymer.

[7] Prince Henry had a grant of the manor of Gringley (Oct. 29, 1265, Canterbury) which had belonged to William de Furnivall, of the county of Nottingham, who had adhered to Simon de Montfort down to the battle of Evesham.—Rymer.

de Mortimer had the estates of Robert de Vere, Earl of Oxford, given him (Oct. 27, 1265), and Gilbert de Clare received the lands of Henry de Hastings[1]. From the Rolls[2] containing the grants made to the conquerors, some names may be extracted as illustrating the history of the individuals, and also the confusion and arbitrary transfer of property incidental to civil war :—

Roger de Clifford had the grant of thirteen lands in Leicestershire and Warwickshire, and was made Justiciary of the Forests within Trent.

Roger de Leybourne had the thirteen manors of Henry Fitz-Aucher, and the house of Peter de Montfort in Westminster. He was also Warden of the Cinque Ports[3].

Thomas de Clare had a manor of Peter de Montfort, "our enemy[4]."

The Princess Eleanor of Castile, received the lands of Richard de Vernon and Richard de Gray, "rebels."

Hamo l'Estrange[5] had grants of several houses of the attainted Londoners.

Warren de Bassingbourne had three manors in Warwickshire.

Nicolas de Lewknor, the lands of Guy de Balliol, "rebel."

Alan Plugneth[6] a manor of William Marescall, "rebel."

---

[1] W. Rish. Rot. Pat. 49° Hen. III.
[2] Calend. Rot. Pat. 49° Hen. III.
[3] Letters Patent, dated Canterbury, Oct. 28, 49°, grant a pardon for treasons to R. de Leyburn. No. 461 Chanc. Rec. 5th Rep. He took the Cross to accompany Prince Edward on his Crusade, but died without going.
[4] The manor of Greatham, co. Durham, the forfeited estate of Peter de Montfort, "inimici nostri," was granted to Thomas de Clare by the king, at Stratford, May 23, 1267. It was recovered apparently under the Kenilworth Dictum, but finally ceded by Peter de Montfort (before 1274) to Robert Stichill, Bishop of Durham. A different owner to Greatham is assigned by the list of knights in Randall's MSS., "Sir Robert Bertram de Gretham."
[5] Of this family, descended from the Dukes of Brittany, some members took different sides in the civil war. Hamo had been ordered by his party to take the command of Bruges [Bridgenorth] Castle from his brother John, the sheriff of Shropshire and Staffordshire, to whom it was restored after the battle of Lewes. Hamo's bold attempt to rescue Prince Edward at Wallingford, before referred to, had earned his present reward. His brother John also, having supported the king at Evesham, received the lands of Richard de Mucegros in grant. Dugd. Warw. Arms, Gules, two lions passant argent armed gules.
[6] See p. 242 ante. The manor of Hasselbergh was thus given 1265, and confirmed 1267. Arms, "Sire Aleyn Plokenot, de ermyn a une bende engrele de goules." Rolls of Arms. Kal. and Invent. Each. Eustachia, the widow of Nicolas de Cantilupe, having married William de Ros, although the king had promised her to Alan Plunkenet, W. de Ros was decreed to pay reasonable amends (rationabiles emendas), and 200 marcs was accordingly paid as the value of the lady. Placit. p. 171.

Walter de Merton, lands of Robert Fitz-Nigel, "our enemy."
Richard de Tany[1], those of Robert de Sutton, "our enemy."
Ralph de Botiller, the manor of Nicolas de Segrave.
Robert de Stutevill, a manor restored, which the rebel Giles d'Argentin had seized.
William de la Valence, a manor of the late Henry de la Mare[2].

When policy afterwards sanctioned the restoration of some of these tokens of triumph, it will be seen with what reluctance and heartburnings such an unwelcome process was submitted to. If the barons after the battle of Lewes fed their pride and covetousness with the property of the vanquished, it is also clear that the royalists were not slow to reap the natural harvest of victory in their season.

The bishops, who had supported the fallen party, now became objects of persecution. The pope, or rather popes (for there was a quick succession of them), had throughout these troubles the instinctive sagacity to feel that the advance of civil liberty would be dangerous to their own pretensions, and they uniformly opposed the barons by all the means at their disposal. The legate who had been irritated by the resistance he had met with at Boulogne in 1264, had now become Pope Clement IV., and in that higher station had renewed his solemn excommunications in the church of Perugia, declaring void the oaths of the King and Prince, annulling all the grants made by the barons, and prefacing the act with an osentatious meekness peculiar to papal phraseology: "Since the Lord has appointed our Humility over nations and kingdoms, and has committed to us, although unworthy, the care of all kingdoms and kings, we declare these oaths void[3]."

As soon as the Pope learnt the Prince's escape, he wrote to authorise him to govern in the King's name: "Fulfil manfully, my son, the duties of your royal blood, and exert

---

[1] Arms, "Argent a maunch gules."
[2] Arms, de la Mare, "Gules, a maunch argent."—Carlav.
[3] Dated Perugia, Sept. 13.—Rymer. The language of Boniface VIII. a few years later was of the same haughty tenor: "The sword is in the hands of kings and soldiers, but at the nod and under the sufferance of the Priest."

the vigour of your noble mind to these purposes with becoming constancy and prudence[1]." When the triumph of the King was at length made known—and it seems that the news took two months to reach Perugia—the Pope's joy was heartily expressed: "Blessed be the Father of all mercies and the God of all consolation, who, comforting you in such straits, has snatched your life from the hunter's snare, bursting your bonds, and restoring you mercifully to your own people. To him, whose finger has worked all this, ascribe the glory. Exult therefore, oh illustrious Prince! exult and rejoice in the Lord." Mercy upon the fallen is then urged by the Pope from political motives, excellent and remarkable for their rare wisdom: "The humanity of forgiveness (he observes) will attract more people to love you and your son, than the severity of punishment will chastise; the fury of vengeance may suppress the hate of a few, but it will excite that of many[2]." The shrewd policy of these maxims, however, bore no fruit: the Legate Cardinal Ottoboni, in a Council held at Northampton[3], suspended from their functions and solemnly excommunicated the four bishops of London, Chichester, Winchester and Worcester. The two first unwillingly obeyed his orders to repair to Rome within three months: John de Exon, Bishop of Winchester, who had paid 12,000 marcs (£8,000) to the Pope for his investiture four years previously, followed them with a melancholy mind[4], and died at Rome in 1268; the Bishop of Worcester also, in a few weeks, ended his consistent career in poverty and disgrace[5]. "He was snatched away lest he should see evil days (observes a royalist chronicler); for so much did he excel other bishops in holiness, that he would not undeservedly have been enrolled among the catalogue of saints, if he had not acted against his duty to the King and the

---

[1] Rymer.
[2] Rymer.—Perugia, Oct. 4, 1265.
[3] Council at Northampton, according to Chr. Dunstable, on the Feast of S. Nicholas, 1265; according to Ann. Evesham, on the Quinzaine of Easter 1266.
[4] T. Wyke.—See p. 237, note 4.
[5] "Viliter."—W. Rish.

Apostolical Seat, by adhering strongly and firmly to Simon de Montfort[1]."

At a later period (from Viterbo, September 15, 1266) the Pope, " anxious for the pacific state of England," renewed his former excommunication of all the adherents of Simon de Montfort, forbidding even his legate to absolve them from it on any account, " except perhaps at the point of death[2]," and even in that case, should they recover, the curse was to be again binding on them.

Besides the spiritual penalties of excommunication, we must remember that persons under the ban of the Church were shunned as lepers, to whom no one could give food or burial. Well might Chaucer declare of his Sumpnour, " For curse will slay right as assoiling saveth[3]."

On thus meeting with these repeated curses, then of such fearful import in a worldly view, solemnly pronounced by mortal men against their fellow-Christians, it is pleasant to read the manly appeal from them to a higher judgment-seat, made by their great Italian contemporary, who, confident in the words of the Psalmist that " the goodness of God endureth yet daily," gives the sentiment to King Manfredi, a victim of this same Pope, Clement IV. :—

" Per lor maledizion sì non si perde, Chè non possa tornar l'eterno amore, Mentrechè la speranza a fior del verde."—DANTE, Purgat. 3.	Yet by their curse we are not so destroyed But that the eternal love may turn, while hope Retains her verdant blossom. Cary's transl.

The fate of young Simon de Montfort, so suddenly be-

---

[1] T. Wyke: according to whom he died about All Saints', 1265; according to others, Feb. 5, 1266. The Annals of Worcester say (p. 453) that he died Feb. 12 at his manor of Blockley, and was buried in his cathedral "juxta magnum altare." One of Adam de Marisco's letters to the Earl speaks of the bishops of Lincoln and Worcester as "of all others the most favourable in special friendship to me." "In articulo mortis positus, se dicebat errasse fovendo partem Symonis de Monteforti, et super hoc literas ad legatum direxit, petens beneficium absolutionis, quod obtinuit et decessit." Anglia Sacra, p. 496.

[2] " Nisi forsan in articulo mortis."—Rymer.

[3] Cant. Tales.

come the head, though no longer the heir of his family, by the deaths of his father and brother, was full of eventful changes. It does not appear that he had advanced a step from Kenilworth[1], after he had allowed himself to be there surprised, though his immediate junction with his father might have averted the fatal disaster at Evesham. Both shame and the want of the necessaries he had then lost[2] checked his movements, until the tidings of ruin overwhelmed him. For many days did he refuse all food and drink in the anguish of his heart[3], but his grief did not mislead him into acts of cruelty, when urged upon him by his partisans. Within the castle of Kenilworth, which had been fortified with the utmost skill by the Earl of Leicester, the King of the Romans and his youngest son, Edmund[4], were still detained in custody. Some angry zealots were eager to take a summary vengeance on them for the barbarous treatment of the great Earl, but young Simon, with equal policy and generosity, not only resisted this, but in September gave them their liberty[5].

The powerful friend thus secured to him did not fail openly to avow his obligation and to intercede for him at court, in spite of the hostility of de Clare, who, with the bigotry of a convert, protested against any mercy towards the son of his former colleague. Young de Montfort was allowed however to approach the King at Northampton, and was offered a pension of 500 marcs (£333. 6s. 8d.), during the continuance of tranquillity, after surrendering Kenil-

---

[1] According to T. Wyke, however, Symon saw the rout of his party at Evesham from a distant height, and then returned. Simon junior "volens ad patrem suum accedere quosdam obviam habuit qui venerant de campo et nuntiabant ei quid acciderat; ipse vero dolore effectus vehementi in castrum de quo exierat reversus est." Ann. de Wigorn.

[2] "Tam pudore quam rerum ablatarum inopiâ ad patrem redire differens."—Nangis.

[3] T. Wyke.

[4] "Cum filio postumo."—T.Wyke.

[5] The widow of Hugh le Despenser also released the royalist nobles in her custody at this time, and retired to her father Philip Basset. "Luctuosa se transferens mortem mariti sui inconsolabiliter deplorabat."—T. Wyke. Almeric de Montfort wrote to her from Dover, July 13, 1265. She afterwards married Roger le Bigot.

worth and retiring abroad. The garrison at Kenilworth, however, would take no orders but from the widowed countess, who held a grant of it for her life, and Simon, with a spirit too proud to submit to his humbled condition, and indignant at the severity shewn to his mother, suspected treachery on being compelled to accompany the King to London, and suddenly withdrew from the court, in Feb. 1266. Repairing to Winchelsea, he soon made himself formidable by his bold piracies at sea, and by gathering troops on the opposite coast[1]. His threatened invasion was denounced in a royal proclamation from Northampton, May 18, 1266[2].

It is unnecessary to detail all the scattered hostilities that ensued[3]. The resistance to the King's authority was obstinate and prolonged, though limited to a few points where the partisans of the barons still held a lofty language in claim of public rights and state reform. The "mountain nymph, sweet liberty," has often betaken herself to swamps without any detriment to her healthy complexion, as Venice and Holland and Athelney may witness. It was from the fens of Lincolnshire and Cambridgeshire, the isles of Axholme and Ely (so often the stronghold of refuge to the malcontent Saxons after the conquest, and fortified by their brave chief Hereward), that the disinherited under young de Montfort now spread terror far and wide for two years.

It is said that many of the barons then repented that they had not submitted to the Award of Amiens[4], but at any

[1] Ann. Waverl.
[2] Rymer.
[3] One of the greatest defeats of the barons was at Chesterfield, 1266, when they were suddenly attacked by the Royalists, "quasi dormientes." The Earl of Ferrers and "*Johannes Sayville* (*al. Dayville*) *homo quidem callidus et bellator fortis*" were among the chiefs of the barons. "*Sayville confestim armatus, dum exiret ut fugeret, percussit Dominum Gilbertum Hanusard* (see p. 248) *et eum cum ictu lanceæ dejecit in terram et aufugit cum paucis qui eum sequi poterant.*" Ferrers fled to the church, but was taken in his concealment, "*prodente eum quadam muliere.*" Sayville afterwards collected forces in Axholme (Haxailylum), captured Lincoln 1267, plundering and killing *the Jews*, and burning "*omnes cartas et obligaciones quascumque invenire potuerunt.*" —Chr. Walt. Hemingford, p. 587, ed. Gale.

[4] G. Daniel, Hist. de Fr. Vol. III.

rate their reply to the excommunications and reproaches of their enemy was fearless and dignified. "They professed, unreservedly, the same unshaken faith in religious matters which St Edmund and St Robert (Grethead) the church-reformers had held, and they complained of the irreverent banishment of the four popular bishops; when charged with plunder, they justified their living upon the goods of their enemies, who had unjustly disinherited them from the estates which their ancestors had won by the sword; and when reproached with treason, they asserted that they were but fighting, as they had sworn to do, for the good of the Kingdom and of the Church, anxious only to obey the Oxford Statutes, and averse from any crusade being preached which might lure away the natives of England, in order to make more room for favoured aliens[1]." This last objection, while it marks the waning popularity of the Crusades, had never been thought of under any other King than Henry III.

It was not until the cities of Norwich, Ely, and Cambridge had been taken by these desperate men, that the energy of Prince Edward overpowered them, July 27, 1267[2]. For this service the King had required the Abbey of St Alban's, among others, to send their quota of soldiers, who were accordingly conducted to the place of meeting by their archdeacon. Either this clerical troop[3] did not look military enough, or the King chose to punish their supposed inclination to the other side, for we are told that after they had been kept for twenty days at the place appointed, he exacted sixty marcs (£40), in lieu of the service of each knight, and so dismissed them[4].

---

[1] W. Rish. de Bello Lew. et Ev.
[2] Chr. Mailr.
[3] A discharge was given by the King to the *Bishop of Durham* (Robert de Stichill), Peter de Brus, Ralph Fitzltanulph (summoned to Parl. 1264), William Baron de Graistock and Nicholas de Bolteby, for their military service "of 40 days" per præceptum Edwardi primogeniti nostri fecerunt servitium quod nobis debent cum dilectis et fidelibus nostris *Henrico de Alemania*, Johanne de Balliolo, et cæteris, from Friday after St George to Monday the morrow of the Trinity, dated Northampton, May 23, 50° (1266).—Hutchinson's Durham, Vol. I. 216.—(See Rymer, Vol. I. 835).
[4] Will. Rish.

A similar outbreak in the North under the disinherited Earl of Derby was also suppressed by Prince Henry. Kenilworth, however, though blockaded by a large army, required a siege of sixteen months to reduce it.

Some of the incidents of the siege, the alternation of savage vengeance with chivalrous courtesy, are characteristic of the then usages of war. The besieged, on one occasion, cut off the hand of the royal herald who had come to summon them to surrender, and sent it to the King as a present from the disinherited; while at another time a wounded Royalist having died a prisoner in the castle, his enemies carried him forth in honourable procession with lighted tapers, and placed the corpse outside, so that his friends might bury him in peace. The garrison of 1200 men, besides whom there were fifty-three of their wives with their handmaidens, were so confident in their strength, that during many months the castle gates were left open all day in defiance, and a sallying party even took Tickhill Castle, belonging to Prince Edward. Trenches were cut to hem them in, and huge wooden towers holding slingers and bowmen, one especially called a Bear from its size, were advanced forward; barges were transported overland from Chester to assist in the assault across the castle lake; but the besieged resisted these efforts with success by mangonels and other engines, until hunger, which reduced them to eat horseflesh, and its follower, disease, obliged them to accept the terms of surrender offered them[1].

A species of compromise, relaxing the severity of their fate, was on this occasion arranged in favour of the disinherited; and the terms, though drawn up by a committee of Royalists at Coventry, caused much dissatisfaction among those of their partisans who disliked to give up their share of confiscated property. De Clare and De Mortimer retired from

[1] 1267. "51º mesme l'an, après la Trinité [June 12], comensa le siege de Kilingworth, et se tint jesk le jour Scinte Lucye prochein [Dec. 13] suiant qe le chastel fu rendu. Mesme l'an, entour la Scint Mychel, conquirent les desheritez l'Ille de Ely." —Fr. Chr. London.

court in disgust at such a process, though the former had been associated with the archbishop and others to consider the conditions on which the civil war might be brought to an end.

The Kenilworth decree[1], as it was commonly named, permitted the disinherited to obtain pardon for their treason, and restoration of their estates by payment to the Royalist grantees of fines varying from one to five years' value. Those whose guilt consisted in having accepted office under Simon de Montfort were required to pay one or two years' value, and those who had drawn their swords against the King, five years. Even from this composition, however, the de Montforts were in express terms altogether excluded; and special penalties, in fines of seven years' value, were imposed on Henry de Hastings for his personal assault on the King's herald, and on Robert Ferrers, Earl of Derby, whose violent outrages previous to the battle of Lewes were remembered now in bar of his pardon, even though he had not been present at Evesham. This nobleman had indeed lost the favour of both parties, for he had even been imprisoned by the Earl of Leicester the year before on account of his unsteady conduct; and after now making his peace with the Royalists, he again took up arms, and when defeated by Prince Henry was kept in custody for three years. Ultimately the ransom of his lands was fixed so high, £50,000, that they were never redeemed from Prince Edmund who held them, and the attainted earl was never able to recover his title[2].

Many of the disinherited took advantage of this decree of Kenilworth to compound for their lost estates[3], though

---

[1] Dated Oct. 31, 1267. The Royalists who devised it were the Archbishop, Nicholas de Ely Bishop of Worcester, Gilbert de Clare, Humphry de Bohun Earl of Hereford, Philip Basset, John Baliol, Roger Someri, with the Papal Legate Cardinal Ottoboni, and Prince Henry to act as umpire.—W. Rish.

[2] V. Abbrev. Placit. p. 187.

[3] Thus W. de Berwick claimed his lands from Ancellinus Basset; Brian de Guwiz from Robert de Briwes; Henry de Penebrigg from Hugh de Mortimer; W. de Tracy from Walter de Caple. Widows and heirs in a

the reluctance with which the new grantees submitted to their restoration gave rise to many disputes and lawsuits. Evidence of the King's lingering partiality for foreigners, the bane of his long government, had been visible by his grant of the earldom of Norfolk to his son-in-law, the Duke de St Pol[1], son of the Duke of Brittany. It is recorded indeed that the young Prince never ventured upon a seizin of the lands thus given him, knowing well that Roger le Bigot was too dangerous a competitor to meet with on such an errand with impunity.

The pleas by which the claims for restoration were met in the records of the King's courts were various, and some explain the manner in which this final pacification was carried into effect. Some claims were resisted on the plea that the original holder continued in rebellion after the battle of Evesham, or did not submit within the appointed time; others that the claimant was a London citizen, and as such not entitled to any indulgence. Some, as Geoffry de Herietesham, thought a boast of their own unshaken loyalty to the King during the whole war[2] a sufficient

similar manner advanced claims to the lands of those slain, as W. de la Puxle, Thomas Corbet, Lawrence Trelloske, Ralph de Normanville, W. de Eyet, W. de Byrmingham.—See Placit. Hen. III. and Ed. I. *passim.* ["Robert de Briwes appears to have held lands in Norfolk and Lincoln, and the manor of Staples in Somersetshire. There was a Justice Itinerant of this name between 1266 and 1271." Exc. e Rot. Fin. II. pp. 446—545.] "Hugh de Mortimer" was son of Robert de Mortimer of Ricards Castle, who held 23 knights fees, 12° Hen. II., and was related to the Mortimers of Wigmore. Hugh was ordered in 1260 to repair to Ricards Castle in order to oppose Llewellyn, and again in 1263. After the battle of Lewes, Hugh was obliged to surrender the castle to Simon de Montfort, after seeing the lands of de Mortimer ravaged: he recovered it

after Evesham; his seal bore "barry of six, charged with fleur de luces." He died 1275.—Dugd. Mon.
[1] John (son of John I., Duke of Brittany), afterwards John II., born 1238, married, in 1259, Beatrix, the daughter of Henry III., and died 1306. Peter de Dreux, Earl of Brittany, Earl of Richmond, died 1250. His son *John* bore the same arms as his father, chequy or and azure, a canton ermine, with the addition of a bordure gules bearing 10 lions of England.—Gell's Regist. Hon. de Richmond.

John d. 1286,
|
John d. 1333,
|
John IV. d. 1399,
|
John V. d. 1442.

[2] "Ante guerram et in principio medio et fine nunc et semper parti Domini Regis adhesit."

reason for keeping what they had got; and John de Bolemar, when accused of stealing three horses valued at 30*s.*, four oxen at 48*s.*, fourteen cows at £5, three bullocks at 21*s.*, eleven sheep at 21 marcs and 5*s.* (£14. 5*s*), boldly pleaded that he took them purposely, because he knew their owner, John de Gurney, had fought against the King at Lewes[1].

With the surrender at Kenilworth, December 1267, the civil war ended. The sagacity and enterprise of Prince Edward, more than supplying the defects of the incompetent monarch, enabled the royal cause to enjoy henceforth an almost undisturbed triumph. The great influence and popularity of the young Prince caused his persevering revenge again to weigh heavily on the unfortunate Londoners, whom, from the moment of their insult to his mother, he seems to have regarded as personal enemies. He could now gratify to the full the same vindictive spirit which had nerved his arm and blinded his judgment, when, "like an eagle in a dove-cot, he fluttered" them from the field of Lewes. By a royal grant (from Northampton, May 12, 1266[2]) the goods of all the citizens of London who had taken part with the barons were given over to his disposal. In spite of the safe conduct which had encouraged him to approach the King, Thomas Fitzthomas, who had

---

[1] Placit., Hen. III. Rex pro laudabili servicio quod Robertus filius Pagani et Will de Gouiz impenderunt, et pro dampnis quæ sustinuerunt in servicio Regis apud Lewes in conflictu ibidem habito, perdonavit eis pro hac vice de gracia speciali relevium suum quod Regi debent de terris et tenementis ipsos jure hereditario contingentibus de terris et tenementis que fuerunt Albredi de Lincoln nuper defuncti avunculi sui, et mandatum est Henrico de Monte Forti clerico escaetarum citra Trent, quod ipsos inde quietos esse permittat. T. Rege apud S. Paulum, Lond. xxi die Julii. Excerpta e Rot. Finium Henrici III. 1216—72. Vol.

ii. p. 412.

[2] Rymer. "Dominus igitur Rex domos et possessiones eorum (civium Londinensium) *et uxores dedit* alienigenis, et non solum, sed et aliorum exhæreditatorum, prout libuit dignitati suæ." Chr. Wigorn. Something of the same personal feeling may be seen in the fine of 500 marcs paid by the citizens of Hereford for their share of rebellion.—Rot. Pat. 49° Hen. III. On the other hand Prince Edward writes to the Chancellor, from Dover, Oct. 26, 1265, stating that he had received into his grace and favour certain "familiares" of the Countess of Leicester.—MS. Letter in Tower, No. 399.

for several successive years been the popular mayor of the city, was now seized at Windsor by the Prince's orders. His fellow-citizens would have manfully re-elected him even in 1266, had not the rival candidate, William FitzRichard, secured his own preference by means, which it is hoped are unknown in quieter times—the compulsory removal of the opposing electors[1]. Some of the other leaders of the city, Michael Tony, Stephen Buckerell, and John de la Flete[2], were imprisoned with him for a long time in the Tower, and among these sufferers we also recognize Thomas Puvelesdon, who had accompanied Simon de Montfort during the battle of Lewes. He appears to have been a wealthy mercer[3], and had been employed while the barons were in power, April 1265, to receive the oath of a suspected Royalist[4]. His forfeited estate was divided between the King of the Romans and Prince Edward, but he was again in 1286 entangled in treasonable acts[5].

A fine of 20,000 marcs (£13,333. 6s. 8d.) was exacted from the city by the Prince, in order to repay the loans raised abroad to equip the Royalist armaments, and when the citizens of London attempted to redeem their lands by virtue of the Kenilworth decree, they were met in the King's courts of law by the plea that the act of grace did not

---

[1] Fabyan. FitzRichard was elected only by the aldermen, not the people; but Roger de Leyborne was employed by the King to imprison the opponents. Fr. Chr. The liberties of the city were thus suspended for 5 years.

[2] "Michael Tony, orfeverer. Johan le chapeler de Flete."—Fr. Chr. Lond.

[3] In the Roll of the Countess of Leicester's expenses, July 1265, is an entry of 34 ells of rosett purchased from him: "Pro 34 ulnis rosetti emptis Londineæ per Dominum Thomas de Piulesdon, 113s. 4d."—See Househ. Expenses. Thomas de Piwelesdona had been elected their Constabularius by the citizens of London, and Stephen Bukerel their Marshal; their standards led them to the plunder of the King of Romans' palace at Isleworth. Lib. de Ant. Leg. p. 61. He is said to have devised a riotous meeting of the citizens two days after the battle of Evesham (Thursday), intending to murder forty of the principal Royalists, but the rumour of the battle prevented him (p. 114). He heads the list of culprits, p. 120, and Roger de P. is also on the same list, and Richard his brother.

[4] See a letter of the King, from Northampton, April 11, 1265.—Rymer.

[5] Fabyan.

include them, and that all their movables and immovables had been placed at the will and pleasure of the King alone[1]. In their present helplessness they might have been taunted by the Prince's comrades with the same bitter derision as the Scots at a later period:—

"Tprot, Scot, for thy strif!
Hang up thyn hachet ant thi knyf,
Whil him lasteth the lyf
With the longe shonkes[2].

[1] "Non comprehenduntur, sed omnino remanserunt ad gratiam et voluntatem Domini Regis."—Placit. p. 175. Thus William de St Omer refused to surrender the lands of Thomas Bax.—Placit. p. 171. Stephen Buckerel met with a similar denial. "William de St Omer" by a writ of the King to the Sheriff of Norfolk (dated Westminster, Oct. 10, 1265) had a grant of the goods and chattels of Richard de Gosesend, and John Hardel, forfeited for rebellion. —No. 407 Chanc. Rec., 5th Report. In 1269, Nov. 30, he had £40 yearly, so long as he should attend the business of the King's Bench. Chron. Jurid. [Compare Foss's Judges, Vol. III. p. 147.]

[2] Polit. Songs, p. 223, from MS. Harl. 2253, dated 1306. "Pshaw, Scot, for thy strife! hang up thy hatchet and thy knife while the life lasts of him with the Long Shanks."

CHAPTER XVII.

ELEANOR DE MONTFORT AND HER SONS.

And tho heo hadde al clene ir joye al verlore,
Me flemde ir out of Engleond without age coming.
Alas! ir tueie brethren, that either of hom was King,
And nadde bote ir one soster, and hir wolde so fleme,
Alas! were was love tho, sucche domes to deme?[1]—

ROBERT GLOUC.

THE quaint versifier quoted above almost warms into poetry with indignation at the treatment of the widowed Countess of Leicester by her own royal kindred. On so feeble a sufferer, now advanced in years[2], and one whose feminine virtues had earned from her chronicler the emphatic eulogy of being "gode woman thoru' al," the vengeance of the victorious party fell with a severity we should not have expected. Bereaved at once of her husband and her eldest son, her broken spirit had needed no additional pressure. Laying aside her purple dress she would wear nothing henceforth but woollen nearest her skin, and again assumed those garments of widowhood[3], which she had been so blamed for abandoning, when she married Simon de Montfort. For a long time did she indulge her domestic sorrow in abstinence from fish or flesh, but the King her brother relaxed nothing of his stern resolve in mercy to her private feelings, and sentenced her to perpetual banishment from England, as if

[1] "And tho' sho had utterly lost all her joy, they banished her from England never to return. Alas! her two brothers, each of whom was a King, and had but her an only sister, and yet would so banish her! Alas! where was then their love to pronounce such a sentence on her."

[2] She was probably about fifty-three years of age at this time.

[3] T. Wyke.

he considered her a fit partner in the guilt and punishment of her husband's treason.

From many of the interesting letters of Adam de Marisco being addressed to her, we learn that the Royal Countess had accompanied Simon de Montfort to Gascony, during the time of his government there amid the turmoils of civil war. The worthy friar seems to have valued her correspondence, and to have anxiously watched the course of events around her, often when absent expressing his regret, and when present reporting to the earl even her throes of coming childbirth with scrupulous anxiety. He cautioned her while abroad against the prevailing fashion of costly dress, "for too wanton ornament (he observes) leads matronly modesty into suspicion; who does not execrate this madness, which daily increases the wild desire of superfluous ornament, causing so much expense, and the employment of so many administering hands, offending the divine majesty and honesty of countenance?" He implored her even with tears to exhibit before God and man the example of praiseworthy matrons in all things. In one of his letters to the Queen of England[1], Adam de Marisco refers to the Queen's wish of conversing attentively with the Countess of Leicester at Easter "concerning the salvation of souls, and hopes that the grace of God may lead her to the way of eternal salvation;" seeming thereby to imply that the religious principles of the Princess were of a superior character, and looked up to with respect by the Queen and himself.

A very curious detail of the private habits of Princess Eleanor has been lately brought to light[2], which enables us to trace her movements, her guests, and her every meal daily during six months of this eventful year, 1265; and the parti-

[1] The preface of the letter is in Latin, the rest in French.—Ad. de Marisco, Epist. p. 290, ed. Brewer.
[2] Manners and Household Expenses, &c. The Roll of the Depenses pour la Comtesse de Leicester (Add. MSS. 8877) recovered from the wreck of the Montargis nunnery during the French revolution, consists of many narrow slips of parchment, several yards in length: every item of her housekeeping from Feb. 19 to August 29, 1265, is entered in it day by day in a clear small writing,

culars throw so much light on the state of society as to deserve our attention.

According to the entries of her household expenses by her steward, we learn that the luxury of the rich then consisted in supplying the table, amid some scanty dainties, with articles of food such as would now be rejected from the meanest hovel. What Roger Bacon then prophetically said of science holds good in meaner matters: "Wise men are now ignorant of many things which hereafter shall be known to the very mob of scholars[1]." The art of multiplying food has happily so advanced with the demands of an increasing population, that nobody is now reduced to feed on grampus or whale, which were then served up to princes. The tail and tongue of whale[2] were then prized as choice delicacies, to be dressed with peas, or roasted; and the porpoise[3] was served up with furmenty, almond-milk, sugar and saffron; but there would be little temptation in either dish at modern tables.

apparently her steward Christopher's, though some entries are scrawled in by another hand, Eudo, from April 15 to 28; the beginning and end of the Roll are missing. It is the earliest document extant of a private individual's expenses.

[1] "Multa enim modo ignorant sapientes, quæ vulgus studientium sciet in temporibus futuris."—Rog. Bac. De Secr. Oper. Art. et Nat. C. VII.

[2] Two hundred pieces of whale cost 34s. The whale fishery was carried on in the third century, as mentioned by Oppian, Liv. v., and the Flemish fishers used harpoons in the eleventh century (Life of S. Arnoud, Bishop of Soissons). The whales seem to have frequented the coasts of Europe in these early times, and the flesh was sold in slices in the market-places on the coast. Indeed the supply of food seems to have been the only motive for this adventurous fishery, the method of extracting oil being unknown till long afterwards.—See Vie privée des François, par le Grand d'Aussy, p. 84.

[3] Even in 1425 this formed an article in the city feasts of London, the prices were then as follows: "Porpeys, 10d.; oysters and muscles 6d.; salmon and herring with fresh ling, 15d.; a salmon, 21d.; codling's head, 8d.; 5 pykes, 6s. 8d.; lampreys, 6s. 8d.; turbot, 3s. 4d.; eels, 2s. 4d.; 800 herrings, 10s. 6d."—S.M.754. In the l'Estrange accounts in 1519 are the following entries: "Item paid to Mr Wm. Dadymond for a conger that my Master gaffe parte to my Lord of Norwiche, and parte spent in the house:" 1520, "18th weke. Item paid to William Inglond for a porpes, that my Master gaffe Sir Thomas Bedyngfeld the Pryor of Walsingham, Sir John Shelton and Sir Roger Townsend."— Archæologia, xxv. p. 425. At a later period Judge Walmysly at Dorchester had dolphin; at Launceston, porpoise; at Winchester, poor John (hake), muscles, whelks, razorfish; gull, puffin, kite, sparrows.—Expenses of Judges of Assize, 1596-1601.

Sea-wolves (*lupi aquatici*), which were perhaps the dog-fish still eaten in France, were also used as food. Four to six hundred salt herrings were daily consumed in the Princess' household, and the abundant use of other fish may appear from the bill of fare displayed in some of her fish-dinners now put on record:—

Sunday, March 1, 700 herrings. Monday, 2nd, 400. Tuesday, 3rd, 500. Wednesday, 4th, 400. Thursday, 5th, 600. Friday, 6th, 400.
Wednesday, June 17, plaice, breams, soles, and other fish, 35*s*. 1*d*.; with eggs for two dories to be put in bread, 4*d*.; pepper, 1*d*.; strawberries (frasæ), 4*d*.
Saturday, July 4, cherries, 4*d*.; conger eel, 3*s*.; herrings, 2*s*. 6*d*.; soles, 12*d*.; whelks, 9*d*.; crabs, 2*d*.; bass, 13*d*.; beans, 4*d*.; eggs, 18*d*.; milk, 3*d*.
On February 26, two carts arrived from Bristol at Wallingford, laden with 108 cods and lings, thirty-two congers, and five hakes. " Stokfis[1]" eighteen for three days; lobsters and shrimps 6*d*.

There was indeed a supply of fine flour (*panis de froille, boletella*) and wastel cakes (*gastelli*) for the countess and her few guests, but the common bread[2] for the many was a coarse mixture of wheat and rye (*mystelon*), which is still in use under the name of maslin in the North of England[3]. Large quantities of wine[4] from Guienne and Gascony were required, and were often made more palatable by being boiled with cloves or mixed with honey. When the countess was at Dover, the regular daily consumption for the knights of her high table seems to have been a quarter of a tun of Gascon wine, and half-a-tun of "bastard wine[5]" for the in-

---

[1] "Stocficz" is also mentioned by Rabelais, l. 4, ch. 59. The name appears to indicate that the cod fishery was principally carried on from the coasts of Flanders.

[2] When at Wallingford two and-half quarters of bread were brought there from Abingdon.

[3] For twenty-two gallons 9*s*. 2*d*. was paid; two tuns of red wine cost 66*s*. 8*d*. There are thirty-eight notices of English vineyards in Domesday, but the Countess of Leicester's Roll does not allude to any wine of English growth.

[4] See the household accounts of Sir Thomas L'Estrange of Hunstanton, Norfolk, in 1519—1520. In Archæologia, Vol. xxv. p. 425, in which "myxtelyn of store" is mentioned. The rye and wheat were ground together, and made an inferior brown bread.

[5] "A petell of bastard viii*d*.; muscatel sweet *wine*."—L'Estrange Accts. "Your brown bastard is your only drink."—Shakespeare, Henry IV. Part I. Act II. Scene 4.

feriors (*pro familiâ*). The beer in use[1] was made indifferently from any grain, barley, wheat, or oats, and was seasoned with pepper in ignorance of hops[2]. As the wife of Simon de Montfort was necessarily attended by many armed followers, and as she appears also to have had as guests[3] several hostages of distinction, the consumption of beer, as well as of wine, seems to have been rapid.

On April 18, five quarters of barley and four of oats were brewed into beer by women[4].
April 25, 188 gallons of beer were bought.
April 29, seven quarters of barley and two of oats were brewed.

Wheat was 5s. to 5s. 8d. a quarter; oats, 2s. to 2s. 4d.; peas and beans, both fresh and dried, onions, parsley, fennel, radishes, and a few other herbs, with apples and pears[5], were the home produce of our gardens; and it is pleasant also to

---

[1] We have a remarkable proof of beer not being the usual drink of persons of high degree, in the anecdote of Robert de Insula, the Bishop of Durham (1274—1283), who had risen from a humble origin. When he was at Norham, some country ale was sent him as a present by the Lord of Scremerston, the castle of the Swinnows. He drank it "*et non sustinens, statim a mensa surgens evomuit;*" on which he remarked, "see the force of custom; you all know my origin; neither from my parents nor my country do I derive the taste for wine, and yet now from being disused to my country liquor it is distasteful."

[2] Hops were grown in Flanders at an early period, and were imported into England from thence in the fifteenth century. An English physician of that time, Gilbert Kymer, speaks of beer when well hopped (*bene lupulata*), being a wholesome drink.—MS. Sloane 4, 166. In the sixteenth century, Harrison (Descr. Brit.) observes of hops that "the Flemings used corruption and forgerie in this kind of ware, and gave us occasion to plant at home, so that now we may spare and send manie over unto them."

[3] At Odiham she entertained Ralph, the Abbot of Waverley, Everard de Marisco, Reginald Foliot; to the Cistercian nuns of Wintency (in the parish of Hartley, Hants) she sent wine, and the Prioress visited her for several days. The wife of Thomas Alix, a gentleman of Hants, Margery de Crek, Katherine Lovell, Joan de Maule (daughter of Peter Brus, of Skelton, widow of Peter de Maule, who died 1242), were among her guests at Odiham. One of the Foliots, however, was a Royalist. A letter of Prince Edward, Oct. 7, 1265, to the Bishop of Bath, requests a writ addressed to the sheriff of Oxford in order to enforce payment of the ransom of William Foliot, taken prisoner by Fulk de Rycote.—Chancery MSS. in Tower, 5th Report Pub. Rec. No. 404.

[4] There is but one entry for yeast (pro gesta) 6d.; beer when bought seems to have cost from ½d. to ¾d. a gallon.

[5] When at Dover the countess sent to Canterbury for 300 pears, and paid 10d. for them, July 22.

recognize the ancient popularity of cheesecakes and gingerbread[1].

Whether foreign fruits, besides dates and almonds, were then imported does not appear; but a few years later (1290) the Castilian Queen of Edward I. purchased from a Spanish vessel at Portsmouth, raisins, dates, 230 pomegranates, fifteen citrons, and seven oranges (*poma de orenge*)[2], being the earliest notice of the latter fruit in Europe. Some Asiatic condiments, probably from Alexandria, were certainly added; spices, rice at 1½d. a lb.; almonds at 2¼d. to 3¼d. a lb., and of these 9 lbs. were consumed in a week; sugar at 1s. to more than 2s. a lb.[3] The latter article, which had been already praised by an historian as "most precious to the uses and most necessary to the health of mortals[4]," was at this time grown in Syria extensively, and from thence distributed to Europe.

How highly these foreign delicacies were esteemed appears by the present of them graciously sent by the Princess Eleanor (March 29), from Odiham in Hampshire, to her brother the King of the Romans, then a prisoner at Kenilworth. The royal gift[5] is thus noted in the detail of her accounts:—" 20 lbs. almonds[6] 6s.; 5 lbs. rice, 9d.; 2lbs. pepper,

---

[1] "In caseo ad tartas, 5d.," a frequent entry. "Pro una buxa gingibrade, 2s. 4d.;" and for 4 lbs. of gingerbread, 12s. "Pro cremio et butiro 8d.;" 100 eggs, 3½d. to 4½d.

[2] Househ. Exp. from MS. in Tower 18° Edw. I. In 1278 the same Queen sent to Paris for 100 cheeses of Brie, often the subject of praise in those times, and still in vogue, for which she paid 35s. to Thomas le Gaunter. —Rot. Mix. Turr. Lond.

[3] Four pounds of white powder, that is, pounded sugar, are charged at 8s.; at Easter 13 lbs. of sugar cost 28s.; the sugar sent to the King of the Romans seems to be valued at 1s. a lb.

[4] "Et canamellas, unde preciocissima usibus et saluti mortalium necessaria maximè conficitur zachara, unde per institores ad ultimas orbis partes deportatur."—W. of Tyre, who wrote 1182—4. Sugar was cultivated on the coast near Tripoli, and south of Tyre, and on the plains of Jordan. —See Dr. Robinson's Bibl. Researches.

[5] The present was conveyed by William de Wortham, who held lands in Suffolk, and was slain at Evesham.—Placit. 54°. Twenty pieces of whale were also sent to the King of the Romans, and on another day (May 24) twelve yards of scarlet cloth for his robe at Pentecost, at the rate of 7s. a yard, besides hoods of miniver and other garments for his son Edmund.

[6] In Chr. Lanerc. there is an anecdote of the Bishop of Durham amusing himself by letting his pet apes eat up a whole dish of blanched almonds.

XVII.]   ELEANOR DE MONTFORT AND HER SONS.   319

20d.[1]; 2 lbs. cinnamon, 20d.; ½ lb. cloves, 9d.; 1 lb. ginger, 18d.; 2 lbs. sugar (zucari), 2s."

The price of meat may be judged of by the purchase of two oxen, four sheep, and three calves, for £1. 2s. 10d.; of two calves for 1s. 6d.; of a calf and sheep for 3s. 3d., and sheep from Romney Marsh were supplied to the garrison at Dover for 22d. each[2]; ten geese cost 2s. 3d. Salt, which must have been much needed to prepare their store of winter food, seems very dear, ten quarts costing 44s. 6d.; but though the prices of these times may generally be multiplied by fifteen to represent the modern value of money, it is probable that the confusion of the civil war had raised the prices of the year 1265 beyond the usual average.

The Countess of Leicester had moved from Wallingford Feb. 22, 1265, to her husband's castle of Odiham, then under the governorship of Henry le Fornun[3], and she continued there, with a short visit to Reading, for more than three months, before the alarms of the civil war had begun to shake Simôn de Montfort's power. The royal hostages, the Princes Edward and Henry, passed a fortnight here with their aunt, accompanied by their huntsman and hounds, and 128 horses. They arrived March 17, under the care of Henry de Montfort, her eldest son, and were then probably on their return from London, where on March 10 their custody had been formally relaxed. Their preparations for sport at Odiham betray no symptom of rigorous confinement.

The earl, her husband, also spent a fortnight at Odiham with her at this time, bringing with him 162 more horses; so that with the forty-four of the countess the stables had to

---

[1] The Pepperers were amerced in the reign of Henry II. as an adulterine Guild, set up without the King's licence. Half a century later they filled the first civic offices. They were incorporated by Edward II. and changed their name to Grocers.—Introd. French Chron., London. p. xviii. Compare Introd. Munim. Gildhallæ, and Arch. Journal, 1857, p. 345.

[2] "Pro 13 multonibus emptis in marisco, 23s. 10d." In the Household Expenses of Robert de Swinfield, Bishop of Hereford (Camden Society, 4to. 1854), pp. 40, 42, &c., are entered the prices of numerous articles of food.

[3] He surrendered it to the King after the battle of Evesham.—Placit. p. 175.

provide for 334 horses[1]. Simon de Montfort quitted her April 1, and they then parted never to meet again.

The bounty of her table was not confined to the rich. During Lent eighteen quarters of wheat were given to the poor, and many other gifts at other times on ordinary occasions; the total expense was moderate. On a Wednesday in Lent, Feb. 25 for example, when the chief of the neighbouring abbey of Waverley[2] was her only guest, it was 16s. 5d., including some fresh fish to the value of 10s. 6d., and vegetables, 4s. 10d. Besides this, however, 400 herrings, the wine, beer, and bread, as well as the hay and two quarters of oats for thirty-two horses, were brought out from the castle stores, and are not included in the daily expense. A freer distribution of wine and beer is made at the feast of Easter, when Isabella, the widow of the Earl of Albemarle, was with her; the articles then purchased appear in the Roll as follows, the price not being added to those things which were brought out from the castle stores:—

"April 5, Easter-day—bread brought, 7s., also 2½ qu. froille (flour ground fine); wine, 11½ sextaries, one sext. sent to the attendants of the countess; beer before reckoned. Kitchen—meat bought in carcase, 29s. 11d.; fat (sagimen), 20d.; pullets, 6s. 8d.; kids, 5s. 3d.; eggs, 4s. 1d.; mustard, 2s.6d. Stables, hay for fifty-seven horses, oats five bush.; two bush. froille; sum, 57s. 1d."

The large purchase of eggs was probably for the usual Easter gifts of them, and a present of 12d. was also given to the nurse of Eleanor de Montfort.

---

[1] The number at other times varied from sixteen to sixty-nine according to her guests; her son Amauri, the treasurer of York, came with thirteen horses. The expenses of housekeeping during the earl's visit were set down in his Roll, not charged to the countess.

[2] This was the first Cistercian monastery founded in England, 1128. In 1245 the Princess Eleanor, Simon de Montfort, and their two oldest sons, had paid a visit there, and made a present of 50 marcs to the monks, and eighteen marcs to the fabric. Eleanor enabled them to buy 150 acres of land at Netham.—Ann. Waver. Ralph, the abbot, from 1251 till he resigned from ill-health in 1266, was summoned to Parliament in 1265.—Dugd. Mon. Eleanor was born about Michaelmas, 1252, while her father was absent in Gascony.

Among other striking illustrations of the manners of the times we must conclude that linen was little in use, for the only charge for washing during five months appears to be 1s. 3d.[1] There is presumptive proof that the countess encouraged reading in her family; for, after twenty dozen of vellum were bought for 10s., a payment of 14s. is made for writing a Breviary on them at Oxford for her daughter Eleanor's use[2]; and the damsel, though young, enjoyed also the rarer accomplishment of writing, for her letters to Prince Edward were sent at Easter by a messenger for 6d. The purchase of twenty-five gilt stars for the young lady's hat, costing 2s. 1d., is duly registered, as well as "fourteen long pins for her head-dress, 2d." A supply of needles was provided for the use of the drawing-room, and for the tailor[3]; their knives were kept in sheaths, worth 2d. or 3d.; the repair of four spoons was effected by devoting eight silver pennies to that purpose; and there were also some forks[4], though long before their use became general. While the young Eleanor was at Odiham the barber at Reading was twice sent for to bleed her[5].

Judging from what was paid to the servants and huntsmen of her sons and of her other guests, as well as to Jacke the keeper of her own harriers, the rate of wages seems to have been about 1½d.[6] and 2d. a day; the huntsmen received

---

[1] "Item pro lavanderia a Festo Nativitatis Domini, xv.d." This is an entry on Sunday, May 31. There was, however, a payment of 3d. for baths in May (pro balneis apud Odiham), which may be added to the cost of cleanliness.

[2] "Pro 20 doz. parchameni abortivi—ad portiforium Domisellæ Alionoræ." "Pro scriptura Breviarii Domisellæ Alionoræ de Montfort per visum fratris G. Bayun, 14s." Eleanor was born about Michaelmas 1252, while her father was absent in Gascony.

[3] "Pro acubus ad cameram et ad tailleriam, 4d." There are other charges for fresh shearing the cloth dresses of the countess, which were sent to London for that purpose. Some Paris rayed cloth was bought for young Simon at 4s. 8d. a yard; and some scarlet cloth for the countess and her son, bought of an Italian, cost £8. 6s. 8d. Two pair of boots for Eleanor cost 2s. 4d.

[4] "Pro uno forcario reparando ad cameram, 7d." Small trunks of stamped leather (de corio punctato) were made to hold the silver vessels.

[5] "Pro domisella fleobotomizandâ."

[6] Three servants (garciones) for ten days are paid 3s. 9d.; another servant for nine days, 13d. Henry III. granted

Y

the higher wages of 2*d*. by the especial desire of the royal countess. All the menials in her employ bear Saxon names, such as Ralph and Hande, bakers; Hicque, the tailor; Dobbe, the shepherd; the carriers, Diquon, Gobithesty and Treubodi; while we can picture to ourselves the very gait of Slingawai, the courier.

There being no other means of communication, a special messenger was necessarily sent with any letters, and for this there are frequent payments in the Roll, though even for long distances the rate of postage was wonderfully small[1]. Thus a servant bringing letters to the countess at Bramber from Porchester is paid 4*d*.; Slingawai earned but 2*s*. for going to the earl, then at Monmouth, from Dover; Gobithesty 3*s*. from Lewes to Hereford; 12*d*. from Dover to Windsor, and 6*d*. to Pevensey; Picard for carrying letters from the countess to Kenilworth in July, 16*d*.; Treubodi, 2*s*. and a pair of shoes for journey from Dover to Kenilworth, September 2; and to the messenger of Prince Edward in August, with letters—probably the announcement of the events at Evesham, 2*s*.

The countess had been living at Odiham some time, when the escape of Prince Edward from Hereford became the token of increasing troubles in the land, and accordingly on the evening of June 1 she moved for greater security to Porchester Castle, where her son was the governor[2]. It was

1*d*. a day in 1221 to his carpenter at Westminster, John of Canterbury.—Brayley's Westm. p. 31.

[1] Apparently a payment was made both by the sender and receiver of letters.

[2] "Sero recedentibus usque Porcestriam."—Househ. Exp. Simon, junior, had the grant of the castle, December 24, 1264. A payment was made of 8*d*. for letters to the earl sent by night just previous to the journey to Porchester, probably announcing that movement. In the Appendix to the Report of the secret Committee on the Post Office, 1844 (582), at p. 28, are some extracts from Records of the Queen's Remembrancer, "Rotulus Roberti de Chaury contra Walterum de Brading de expensis nunciorum post compotum factum," 1252—3. Among many others:

Jordano, *cokino* (coquin?) eunt London ad D^m J. Mansellum, 9*d*.

Simoni, nuncio fratris de Marisco 6*d*. de dono.

Simoni nuncio eunti apud Boloniam precepto Reginæ cum mensura filii Dominæ Matildæ de Lacy, 7*d*.

Petro barbatori Comitis Leycestriæ, deferenti rumores de partu ejusdem Comitissæ, 40*s*.

Rogero de Capella deferenti rumo-

probably by the advice of him or the earl that she soon afterwards made a rapid journey to Dover. There were with her at Porchester forty-five horses belonging to herself, nine to Simon, junior, eight to Almeric de Montfort, and four to the parson of Kempsing[1]; but a great many more, as well as carts, were hired[2] for the journey to Dover, and duly sent back. The purchase of a horse was from 30s. to 40s., both Simon and Almeric paying that sum (*pro uno roncino*). Her removal required eighty-four horses, besides a vessel for her goods sent round by sea. She was four days on the road; and on the first day, June 12, she dined at Chichester, and reached Bramber Castle, her expenses being £2. 11s. An extract indeed from her accounts during her journey may be interesting:—

June 12, Friday, Brembre.—For the countess, the Lords Ingeram de Balliol[3], Richard Corbet, Almeric and the men at arms of the Lord Simon and others, bread, 6s. 4d.; wine from the stores of the manor; beer, 2s. 11d.; fish, 10s. 6d. For dinner (pro dinerio) at Chichester, 1s. 2d. Stables, grass from the manor; oats for eighty-four horses, seven quarters being bought at 14s. Porterage, 3d. Also plaice and conger by William de Lake, 9s.; mackerel, 3s.; breams, 2s. 4d.; eggs, 1s. 2d.; pawria (?) 4d. Saturday, Wilmington, at the cost of the Lord Simon de Montfort. Sunday, Winchelsey, for the countess, the Lord Simon de Montfort, with all

res de partu Dominæ Mabillæ de Insula, 20s. de dono.
Simoni, cokino eunti ad D^m Rob. Waleran, 3d.
Waltero de Cofton, *valleto* Reginæ Scociæ, 13s. 4d. de dono.
From a Roll of 27° Ed. III. letter-carriers are paid from Windsor to London. 6d.; from Stratford to Chertsey, 12d.: from Mortlake to Thistleworth [? Isleworth], 12d.; from London to Sarum, 6s. 6d.
[1] Kemsing was part of the dowry of the Countess of Leicester, and had been given to Henry her son, March 14, 1265.—Rot. Pat. 90°. John de Kemsing accompanied her to Dover; he is mentioned in letters to the countess by A. de Marisco, describing a conference he had with the Archbishop of Canterbury.
[2] At Dover the countess had thirty-one horses, and lent nine to her son

Simon when leaving to re-inforce the earl; one of them, a liard, was valued at 24s. The expense of farriery for eighty-four horses on the journey was 8s. 4d., 1000 nails costing 13d. At Dover a meadow of four acres was rented for the horses at 40s. 1d. In one of Henry III.'s confirmations of Magna Charta, the rate of hire for the King's use had been fixed, for a cart with two horses, 10d. a day; with three horses, 14d. The Countess of Gloucester travelled from Chippenham to Odiham in April, and the Countess of Arundel from Porchester to Dover in some vehicle, payments being made to a driver (currutario).
[3] He is mentioned as an adherent of Simon de Montfort in the summons for the surrender of a castle, and had been taken prisoner at Northampton. —Rot. Pat. 49°. [See the Dunstaple Annals, p. 229.]

their suite, the burghers of Winchelsey and many others, bread, 20s. 4d.; wine, thirteen sextaries (of four gallons each), and one gallon, 18s. 10d.; beer, 10s. 10d.; boats, 10d.; porterage, 6d. Kitchen, for two oxen and thirteen sheep, 36s. 6d.; for thirty-five geese, 19s. 10d.; poultry, 6s. 2d.; eggs, 2s. 4d.; salad, 8d.; faggots (*busca*), 22d.; charcoal, 8d.; dishes (*disci*), 13d.; salt and spits (*brochiæ* or jugs from *broc.*), 5d.; water, 4d. For dinner for the same at Battle and for their horses, 17s. 2d. Stables, grass for nineteen score and fifteen horses (these 395 horses must have been partly for her escort), 12s. 10d.; oats, 12 qrs. 1 bush., 26s. 3d.; litter, 3s. 9d.; farriery (*forgia*), 7d.; water, 12d.; a horse hired for the small cart, 6d.; porterage, 6d.; dinners of twenty-one grooms (*garcionum*), 10d.;—sum total, £9. 4s. 8d.

Monday, Dover, Feast of S. Botolph, for the countess, and all the aforesaid, except when the countess eats in the castle with her women, one ox, seven sheep, and seven calves. For dinner at Romney, 27s. 5d. Hay bought for two nights, 14d.; grass for 107 horses, 5s. 9d.; oats, 6 qrs. 1 bush., 14s. 3d.

This route, which makes no mention of Lewes, though lying in the direct line, and which appears to avoid Pevensey and Hastings, all which towns were in the hands of her enemies, was naturally chosen as the safest from interruption, even though it may have been less perfectly provided with bridges, as the mention of boats and porterage would seem to imply. Her son, Simon de Montfort, left the siege of Pevensey to meet the countess with an escort at Wilmington[1], where the Benedictine Priory probably received them for the night. The countess having been a benefactor to Battle Abbey by the grant of a manor, had some claim on its hospitality; and the aged Prior, Reginald[2], who had the year before endured the plunder of the Royalists, and had witnessed the subsequent arrival of the King when no longer a free agent, and of Simon de Montfort fresh with triumph, now probably welcomed his royal wife in her flight to a place of safety. When at Winchelsea she feasted the burghers, who had always been devoted friends to the barons'

[1] This alien Priory, of which there are now few remains, was subject to the Abbey of Grestein, in Normandy.—Dugd. Mon. Its situation was pointed out to distant wayfarers by a gigantic figure of a man holding a staff in each hand, cut out on the turf of the chalk hill rising behind it.

[2] Reginald was Prior of Brecknock in 1248, and had become Abbot of Battle in 1260, dying at an advanced age in 1280.—Dugd. Mon. Gleanings Battle Abb.

party, and they were again twice (July 12, 30) feasted by her at Dover. The burgesses of Sandwich were treated in the same manner, on one occasion being so numerous that the guests were divided at dinner into two rooms, and additional wine and beer were bought for them. On Monday, June 15, she arrived at Dover, still accompanied by her son Simon, and in that castle, then under the command of her eldest son Henry, she awaited the result of the civil commotions in security.

Her two sons, Henry and Simon, left her[1] during the progress of the war to join their father, and her own horses were lent them for the occasion, but the garrison retained many distinguished knights for her defence. Among these were John de la Warre[2], with his twenty-nine archers, who, after sixty-three days' service at Dover, seem to have required clothing, cloth to the value of £6. 6s. being ordered for them, August 11; he afterwards assisted in the defence of Kenilworth[3], and by some is said to have been there slain by an arrow, but a free conduct to go abroad appears to have been granted to him, December 13, 1266. Richard Corbet[4], another of the knights who had formed the escort to Dover, had profited by the confusion of the civil war to seize upon the property of the head of his own family, a Royalist, who had repeatedly borne the office of sheriff in Shropshire. There were some others of note: John de la Haye, who had been made constable of Winchelsea and Rye, August, 1264, and had been active previously at the siege of Rochester, was a confidential friend

---

[1] Simon went from Porchester to Tunbridge, June 24; but Fulk Constable and others were sent by the countess, July 8, to join him in London.

[2] Roger, the first baron of the name, was at Carlaverock, and died 1320:—
" Ky les armes ot vermeillectes
O blanc lyon et crosselettes."
The Wests, who now bear his title, are descended from his female heir in the fourth generation. William de la Warre, who was among the Northampton prisoners in 1264, held ten lands in Herefordshire.—See Inq. p. Mort. 1269. [The name is there spelled " de la Were."]

[3] Rob. Glouc.

[4] His lands at Chawton, worth 100s., were seized by Henry Hnseee, as belonging to "an enemy of the King."

of the Earl of Leicester, and was frequently employed in carrying messages to him when in Gascony from Adam de Marisco[1]. His intimacy with the family appears also by some entries in the countess' Roll. Eleanor de Montfort bought a gold clasp for 15s. to give his son, August 3, and Almeric also gave him one worth £2. 4s. 8d., perhaps birthday presents. John de Mucegas, the constable of Salisbury[2] under the barons, had several soldiers with him here; Gilbert de Gaunt [descended from the old Earls of Lincoln], who paid 3000 marcs to redeem his estates; Matthew de Hastings, who appears to have been instrumental in surrendering Dover afterwards to Prince Edward, and was pardoned 1266[3]; Seman de Stokes[4], Waleran de Monceaux, both of whom were similarly pardoned[5]. Many of these had their wives with them at Dover, and besides Alice[6], wife of the Earl of Oxford, who had been taken prisoner at Kenilworth, there was one constant female companion of the countess in her journeys, Isabella, Countess of Albemarle; whether her presence was voluntary or constrained must be considered with reference to her subsequent lawsuit already described; but certainly

---

[1] Epist. Ad. de Marisco [ed. Brewer, pp. 268, 298. Professor Brewer notes that John de la Haye was son of a Ralph holding lands in Lincolnshire.—Exc. e Rot. Fin. Vol. II. p. 191].

[2] He was appointed December, 1264, and superseded by Walter de Dunstanvil, May 31, 1265; he died 1266. Walter de Dunstanville's father of the same name (d. A.D. 1240) had joined the barons against K. John at Runnymede. His son held 2 knight's fees and 2 hides at Broughton (Wilts); (see Wilkinson's Hist. Br. Gifford, p. 18), and died 1269.

[3] His pardon (Rot. Pat. 50°) states that he quitted Dover castle with his family in obedience to the royal command, and that he continued afterwards faithful.

[4] By a letter of Prince Edward to William the Bishop of Bath, dated Winchester, Sept. 23, 1265, his protection is given to Semannus de Stoke, Richard and John de Havering and W. de Tureville, who had given up the castles of Wallingford and Berkhampstead.—Records of Chancery in Tower, No. 403 in 5th Report Public Records.

[5] There were also at Dover, Ralph D'Arcy (who held lands of the value of 22s. in co. Lincoln.—Inquis. Rebell.), I. de Snaves, Peter de Bourton, I. de Dover, Ralph Haquet, Hugh de Coleworth, knight.—49° Rot. Pat. Th. de Sandwich, clerk, perhaps some relation of the Bishop of London, was pardoned at the instance of Prince Edward, Canterbury, Oct. 30, 1266.

[6] Alice was daughter of Gilbert de Sandford; Hugh de Vere, her husband's father, had paid 1000 marcs for her wardship and marriage.—33° Hen. III. Her family and 21 horses formed her suite.

her husband, while living, had always supported the barons[1]. Robert de Brus, or Bruys, also accompanied the Princess Eleanor throughout; whether freely as a guest and partisan, or compulsorily as a prisoner, is uncertain[2].

The fatal tidings of Evesham appear to have reached Dover on the 15th of August, and left the widowed Princess no hope of political eminence, or enjoyment of private luxuries. Some authorities represent her as endeavouring to appease the King by a surrender of Pevensey Castle, but this seems inconsistent with the long and fruitless siege of that fortress[3] by young de Montfort. It never was in the power of the barons, and certainly Kenilworth[4] and Dover, which were more immediately under the authority of the countess, were the only two castles in England which continued to resist the King after the battle of Evesham.

The stern sentence of banishment on his sister may have been the result of the King's anger on this very account; for harshness to his own kindred was not among his usual vices. The remembrance of the active zeal of his own Queen in dangerous times ought to have excited some more generous sympathy with the political firmness of the widowed princess. When it suited his own schemes, Henry III. had learnt how to value the devotion of an affectionate woman. As soon as his defeat at Lewes compelled him to dissemble, his main

[1] See p. 231. "Ad appellum Comitissæ de Insula (Walter de Scotenay) comprehenditur, judicatur et trahitur."—Walt. Heming, 1258°. Arms, gules, a cross potence vair. Her seal as Countess of Albemarle and Devon, and Isle of Wight, represents her arms dimidiated with those of her husband, and circumscribed: "Non caret effectu quod voluere duo."—Sandford's Gen. Hist. p. 101.

[2] In March 3s. 4d. was paid for 1½ fur of squirrel for the use of W. de Breose; and in July 7d. for two pairs of shoes. On July 12, 6d. was paid for guarding W. de Breose and his young son Simon. Among other attendants were Master Ralph de Coudray, who bought provisions for the countess, Neirnuyt (Nigræ Noctis), a servant, Thomas Salekin and his wife, who were pardoned Oct. 30, 1266. John Neirnuyt appears as a witness to the charter of Edmund, Earl of Cornwall, founding the Augustine College of Bons Hommes at Ashridge, Herts, 1286.—See Dugd. Monast. 6. 516.

[3] Simon was at Pevensey, April 30, on which day the countess sent letters to him there from Odiham.

[4] Treubodi was paid 2s., Sept. 2, for going as messenger from Dover to Kenilworth; and two grooms received 2s. 6d. for the same journey, Oct. 1.

reliance for help had been on his Queen's energy, and he had secretly enabled her to assume his own lost prerogative, and to receive from the French King the remainder of the sum due to him by treaty. Early in June, 1264, a few days only after she had heard of his overthrow, she gave a quittance[1] for 58,000 livres Touraine in the King's name; and the deed expressly mentions she was authorised by him so to act[2]. This large sum of money, the balance of the 134,000 livres Touraine previously mentioned, King Henry had often and solemnly pledged himself to employ in the service of God and the Church, and for the good of his kingdom; but in fact it purchased an army of foreigners to threaten England with invasion. This act of double dealing, so much in unison with his character, if discovered at the time by the angry barons might have cost him dear, had not his secret been safe in the bosom of his Queen, faithful to him in difficulties as Eleanor de Montfort to her lord.

The supplies of provision to the garrison of Dover were probably soon impeded by the Royalists, for there are several entries in the countess' Roll of oxen and sheep consumed there, avowedly obtained by plunder[3]. Her younger sons Almeric, a priest, and Richard, had been with her during the

---

[1] The Queen raised money also from the mayor and inhabitants of Oleron (see p. 40, note 1) at this time avowedly for the purpose of helping the King, and gave them a quittance for the gift, as having been voluntary, in order to secure them from future demands by the King founded on this precedent. She writes from S. Macaire, 13 Feb. 1265, 49°, acknowledging the receipt in warderobâ nostrâ from the mayor and others of Oleron of six score and four Pounds of Poictou, by the hand of a burgher for the relief of the King and Prince Edward (pro succursu faciendo Domino Regi et Edwardo); and on Feb. 14 it is put on record that Oleron had given 390 Pounds of Poictou money from their spontaneous will, not at all being bound to do so as a due (voluntate spontanea concesserunt, cum hoc ex debito minime tenerentur), so that no heavier aids could be demanded by the King in consequence hereafter. —Rymer.

[2] This document, in Latin, in the Archives du Royaume, at Paris, J. 630, has never been published; and, with some others relating to English history, has been inserted in an Appendix. It bears the seals of the Queen, Peter of Savoy, and Thomas Mansel, and is dated on the Sunday after the Ascension (May 29), in the month of June, 1264.—See pp. 85, 188.

[3] Aug. 23, by booty, half an ox. Aug. 24, by booty, half an ox and three sheep. Aug. 25, by booty, half an ox. Aug. 26, by booty, half an ox.

summer and at Dover. Richard had arrived, August 12, in a ship with about 100 sailors from Winchelsea, intended probably for the defence of Dover, and 100s. were paid to them. To twenty-nine archers of Pevensey also were paid 1s. each. The concluding part of her steward's Roll contains some entries significant of the great calamity which had fallen upon the countess. The purchase is recorded of ten ells of black serge (*nigræ saiæ*) for the hose and robe of her son Richard, 17s.; and twenty-four-and-a-half ells of grey serge (*pers*) for Wilequin, his attendant; for Gullot, clerk of the chapel, and for others of the household; while masses for the repose of the earl's soul are paid for, 12s. 9d. on August 19, and 7s. on September 3[1].

Almeric and Richard crossed over to Gravelines, September 18, in charge of 11,000 marcs (£7666. 13s. 4d.), despatched probably by their mother for safety. This so irritated the King that he urged King Louis to arrest the treasure in its passage and to take it in compensation for the damage done to foreign merchants in England during the late troubles[2].

That the commerce of the country would be seriously interrupted by the late disturbances is certain, independent of the prohibitions imposed by the barons; but it does not appear that foreign merchants had received any other intentional loss, unless in common with others at the time of general pillage. At some previous time, perhaps during the interval between 1258 and 1264, one of the King's friends had presented him with some advice on commerce[3], which might lead us to suppose the King was not unwilling to encourage it, as a means of procuring money for himself.

[1] In April a payment is entered of 7s. 4d. for oblations of the countess by Fulk Constable: he was afterwards taken prisoner at Kenilworth, on which Richard Tweng took possession of his lands, worth five marcs a year. Extracts from this Roll of the countess have been here given more copiously, as the printed book, excellently edited by Mr Turner for the Roxburghe Club, is unfortunately not published.
[2] By letter dated Oct. 10, 1265. —Rot. Pat. Hen. III.
[3] See Appendix C.

The writer, who expresses himself in a provincial *patois* of French, recommends himself to the King as having, in his continual desire to serve him, already suggested to his council the means of recovering his authority, and of supplying his need of gold and silver. "God and right are with you" (he writes to the King), "and may it please God that you follow them, for the greater part of good Christian people wish to help you, if you can but aid them with money." He is anxious for some sumptuary restrictions in a very contrary spirit, wishing to limit the prices of cloth for the clergy, allowing them but one garment a year "and nothing more" (*et nient plus*); he advises the English ladies to keep to what gowns they had got (*se tiegnent à leur reubes ke eles ont*), allowing them but one of 3s. the yard, "and nothing more;" he restricts even the archbishop's dinner to two dishes of meat, one boiled and the other roast, and his supper to one roast, "and nothing more," confining him to beer without wine at the latter meal, and forbidding him, as well as all others, to offer any manner of hospitality to those not of the same household. The most urgent recommendation, however, is to permit the export of wool (*laine de l'euvre*) to Holland and Brabant at a duty of five marcs the sack, which he says foreign merchants would not only willingly pay, but that no time should be lost in so pleasing them, and that they would in return respite the payment of debts due to them from the English knights as long as their services were required in warfare. It serves to show the great extent of this trade, when we find the writer of this curious paper calculating the proposed duty as certain of yielding 110,000 marcs (£66,333. 13s. 4d.) in six months, implying an export of 22,000 sacks in that time, which would enable the King to pay his levies of men, and become again independent[1].

The unhappy Princess, Eleanor de Montfort, on witness-

---

[1] This paper, without date or name, not having been published, is copied in the Appendix from the Archives du Roy., J. 1034.

ing the ruin of her husband's high fortunes, prepared to yield to her fate, and while she yet retained a remnant of power at Dover and Kenilworth, procured the mediation and good offices of her better brother, the King of the Romans, in behalf of herself and family, at the time of his politic release from the custody of her son Simon, before referred to. This Prince, early in September, signed a deed at Kenilworth, engaging himself to stand a true friend and help to his sister and her sons, and to assist them in claiming their rights and property, so far as his loyalty to the King would permit; and he seems honourably, though without success, to have fulfilled this pledge. The zealous Royalist, Warren de Bassingburne, appears to have been the agent in arranging this release, and was, in conjunction with Walter, Bishop of Worcester, and Roger de Meyland, Bishop of Chester, one of the sureties for the performance of the terms[1]. Eleanor, after thus doing all in her power, at length retired to France in October, though she left her son Simon at the time in imminent peril, and Guy a wounded prisoner. It may have been at this period[2] that Prince Edward regained possession of Dover, by the help of fourteen Royalist prisoners confined there, who had boldly seized a tower of the castle, after securing the treacherous connivance of two of their guards. The Prince, on hearing of this attempt, is reported to have instantly repaired there with his usual energy, travelling without even taking any rest, and soon to have forced the garrison to surrender[3].

---

[1] The document, being new to English history, is added to the Appendix (D), from the Archives du Roy., J. 1024. It is dated from the Priory of Kenilworth on the Sunday before the Nativity of the Virgin (Sept. 8), 1264.

[2] It was probably before the 29th of October when the Queen landed at Dover, and signalized her return by hanging some burgesses of the Cinque Ports who were practising piracy under cover of civil war.

An expedition from the Cinque Ports revenged this (Nov. 22) by setting fire to Portsmouth and routing its garrison with some loss.—Wykes, p. 179; Ann. de Wig. p. 456; Liber de Ant. Legibus, p. 82.. P.

[3] T. Wyke. "Egressa est de castro Comitissa, infaustis sauciata successibus." Winchelsea was afterwards taken with much bloodshed by the Prince.—Chr. Roff. MS. Audientes quoque quidam nobiles, qui in castro Dovorre in carcere tenebantur, quæ

The remainder of her days was passed by the Princess Eleanor in religious retirement at the Dominican Nunnery of Montargis, founded by her husband's sister. An ineffectual attempt at reconciliation was made in her behalf by the King of France the following year; but King Henry in his reply, though he nominally accepted his proffered mediation[1], pressed him urgently to "consider the enormity of the wrongs done to him by the late Simon de Montfort, his sons and their mother (it is thus only he designates his sister), both before the Award of Amiens and afterwards[2]." No alteration ensued, and it was reserved for the more generous spirit of Edward I. in 1273 to restore her dower as Countess of Pembroke, and to allude to her after her death, which occurred in 1274, in more gracious terms[3].

At Montargis she educated her daughter Eleanor, whom the earl had already betrothed to his friend and ally Llewellyn, Prince of Wales, and when of sufficient age she

domino suo Regi prospera contingebant, spiritu hausto fortitudinis, turrim castri viriliter occupabant suis custodibus resistentes. Quod cum Regis primogenito suo Edwardo innotuit, ad castrum Dovorre illud in manu valida obsidentes. Custodes quidem castri adversarios circumspecti miserunt legationem Regi, ea quæ sunt pacis rogantes, salvis quidem singulis vita, immo equis, armis, et ceteris nocivis castrum Regis primogenito reddiderunt.—MS. Chr. Roff.

[1] "Ordinationi vestræ et dicto de alto et basso totaliter duximus committendum."—Househ. Exp.

[2] Rot. Pat. 50 Hen. III., dated Kenilworth, Sept. 25, 1266.

[3] "Alionora quondam Comitissa Leicestriæ, amita nostra, quam dudum admisimus in gratiam et pacem nostram."—West. Jul. 1; Lib. 13. Edw. I. m. 3. Her heart was buried in the Abbaye de S. Antoine des Champs at Paris, founded for Bernardine nuns of the Cistercian order, in consequence of the vehement preaching of Foulques de Neuilly against matrimony. In the church,

begun in 1198 and finished under Louis IX., who was at the dedication with his mother, Q. Blanche de Castille, a mural monument was placed to Eleanor de Montfort, a print of which is at p. 168 of Le Père Menestrier's Veritable Art du Blason, 12mo. Paris, 1673. She is dressed as a nun, holding her heart in her hand, without any inscription, but with the arms of Montfort and her Royal alliances. In an old inventory of the furniture of the church is mentioned: "Upon the heart of the Countess de Leicester, a cloth for every day, one upon Feasts, one for Lent." The arms above are by Menestrier said to be, 1. Sicily, i.e. France with the label; 2. France; 3. Emperor of the West; 4. Emperor of the East, a cross with 4 bezants charged with a crosslet; 5. England; 6. Castille and Leon. Of the four coats of Montfort the two upper are for her eldest son Henry and Almeric the priest, both without difference; the third, Simon (?) has a label of four points for difference and the fourth is semé of crosslets, Guy (?)

sent her to Wales in fulfilment of the contract. The ship, however, in which the fair bride and her brother Almeric were sailing, being unfortunately captured near the Scilly Isles (1276)[1], they were brought to King Edward as prisoners. The lady was honourably treated at court as the King's cousin, and after some years' delay was married[2] to her espoused husband at Worcester (Oct. 13, 1278), in presence of King Edward and his Queen.

Almeric was treated with greater rigour, and had been previously one of the earliest to feel the active vengeance of the court against his family. Three days only after the battle of Evesham, Henry III. had written to countermand his former appointment of Almeric, as Treasurer of York[3], declaring to the Chapter of York that "since the war at Lewes he had been in custody, and that his seal had been used arbitrarily by Simon de Montfort against his will, but that now by God's grace he had resumed his powers[4]." Almeric, with his brother Richard, had left Dover in 1265, when they both repaired either to their cousin Eskivat, Count de Bigorre, or to Laura de Montfort, daughter of their uncle Almeric, with whom they had previously corresponded[5].

[1] By ships from the Cinque Ports. Walt. Heming. By ships from Bristol.—Chron. Rishang.
[2] Eleanor de Montfort left at her death, June 21, 1282, in childbirth, an only daughter, who died a nun at Sempringham.
[3] In the Liberate Roll (6° Edw. I. mem. 1) is an order for payment for the conveyance of the luggage of "Eleonora wife of our beloved and faithful Llewellyn, Prince of Wales," from Worcester to Whitchurch. A letter from her to Edward, from Llanmaes, July 8 (1279), professes anxiety to know and do his pleasure. She styles herself "Princess of Wales, Lady of Snowdon." In 1280, Oct. 18, she writes from St Anneir to the King very earnestly imploring his pity upon her captive brother Amalric. "For if your Excellency, as we have often known, mercifully condescends to strangers, with much more reason, as we think, ought you to hold out the hand of pity to one so near to you by the ties of nature." —See M. A. Wood's Letters of Royal and Ill. Ladies, Vol. I. p. 51, and in Rymer's Fœdera. He had been appointed Treasurer Feb. 2, 1265, succeeding John Mansell.—Rot. Pat.
[4] Aug. 7, Worcester.—Rymer.
[5] Eskivat was grandson of Guy de Montfort, their father's elder brother, who had married Petronilla, Countess of Bigorre in her own right. Laura was the second daughter of the head of the family, and died 1270. "April 6, Nuntio Dominæ Lorettæ de Monteforti venienti de Franciâ, 2s." The voyage of the two brothers to Gravelines cost £26. 8s., and they had also £13. 6s. 8d. given them for their journey.—Househ. Exp.

The friendly protection of the Count de Bigorre to his banished relations had been probably secured by their mother, the widowed Countess of Leicester, who, with her eldest son, in October, 1265, made an unreserved surrender of their rights to Bigorre, which had accrued to them from its grant to the late Earl, in 1256, when his nephew, the young count, had been unable to defend it from the hostile attacks of Gaston de Bearn[1]. This, at the time when civil war was ravaging the country, was a marked proof of the respect in which the military skill of de Montfort was universally held; but, under altered circumstances, his widow and his son now relinquished Bigorre to the protection of Thiebault, King of Navarre[2].

The privity of Almeric to the Viterbo murder, presently related, being suspected by Edward I., he did not venture to return to England, though he acted as executor to his mother, and had come to Paris in company with the Bishop of Chichester, intending to return. King Edward was an implacable foe, and paid a galley £1. 6s. 8d. for watching him and the bishop, besides employing a paid spy at Paris[3]. When at length he was captured in his voyage to Wales (1276), Almeric was detained in custody at Corfe and elsewhere for many years. Pope after pope applied for his release in vain; the brief of Martin IV.[4] (Viterbo, Sept. 20, 1280), appealed to the King "by the memory of the blood by which he was connected with our dear son, Almeric de Montfort, our

---

[1] Extraits des Registres de Champagne, Vols. IV. and v., pp. 474, 476, art. 8. Tresor des Chartres, p. 294. Eschivat de Chabannes, Count de Bigorre and Jourdain, his brother, by deed dated Tarbes, 1256, gave all the county of Bigorre to "their dearest uncle," Simon de Montfort, Earl of Leicester, "bono animo et spontanea voluntate quia magis volumus quod vos habeatis et vestri quam extranei."—This grant was confirmed at Paris, 1258, with a clause to preclude any future claim of restoration. The deed of surrender by the younger Simon de Montfort, not having been previously published, will be found in Appendix E.

[2] Thiebault (Theobald), King of Navarre from 1253 to 1270, had married Isabella, daughter of Louis IX.

[3] "20s. ad insidiandum."—Rot. Pip. 2° Edw. I.

[4] Martin IV., by name Simon de Brie, was elected Feb. 22, 1281, crowned March 23, died March 28, 1285.

chaplain[1]," and engaged that he should swear to leave England for ever. Edward finally delivered Almeric into the custody of the bishops in Convocation, and referred the question of his release to Parliament, Feb. 14, 1281. Archbishop Peckham interested himself in his behalf, and wrote to the King[2] that "we hear from your cousin, Sir Amorri, that he never intended to live in Wales, or blemish your honour in any manner; and as to the words you told us he had spoken in prison against us and others, we cannot find by the wardens that he ever said anything against your lordship;—if he were plotting, he would not be so desirous of your favour as he is." Some of the barons even to the last refused their assent; but the King, "mild and devoted to God," as the archbishop informs the Pope[3], granted it; and Almeric being solemnly pronounced free in the presence of many witnesses, was delivered to the Pope's agent at London to be conducted to France. At Rome he subsequently abandoned the priesthood and became a knight, dying soon afterwards.

Of his brother Richard nothing is known after his journey to Lourde, and it is probable that he died young abroad without leaving issue. The tradition that he was allowed to return to England subsequently under the assumed name of Wellysborne, seems unfounded[4]. The bearers of that name more probably were connected with the entirely distinct family of Peter de Montfort, if not altogether strangers.

[1] Wilkins' Conc.
[2] In a French letter, dated Slydone (Slindon), Eve of Trinity.
[3] London, Feb. 21, 1282.—Wilkins' Conc.
[4] "Richard se refugia en France avec sa mère."—Moreri, Dict.
[5] See Stothard's Mon. Eff., Dugd. Warw. There are charters extant purporting to be his, in which he names himself as "Wellysborne, son of the Count Simon Earl of Leicester, and one of the sons of the Lady Elenor, the King's sister:" his seal is inscribed "Bellator' filii Simonis de Montfort," and exhibits a knight in full armour, with the rampant lion on his shield, and a cross on his banner; but these are justly considered by Camden as spurious. Richard Wellysborne (of Wellysborne Montfort, in Warwickshire, which had long been possessed by Peter de Montfort's family), married Maria de la Rokhulles of that parish.

CHAPTER XVIII.

THE MURDER AT VITERBO.

"It will have blood; they say, blood will have blood."—MACB.

ONE more incident of a public nature, which connects the de Montforts for the last time with British history, and avowedly resulted from the events of the Barons' War, may fitly conclude these pages, and may be examined more circumstantially, as having attracted little notice, owing to its occurrence in a distant country.

The active spirit of Prince Edward after all resistance had been crushed at home, sought indulgence in the interprise of the distant Crusade; and, with his brother Edmund and cousin Henry, he took the cross from the hands of Cardinal Ottoboni (1270). When to the congenial allurements of distant adventure, and the unbridled license of war, the piety of the times added release from debts and remission from sins, we must not wonder at the Prince being able to gather a party of enterprising companions[1] for this Crusade, though the now cooler judgment of others on this point has been already noticed. A century before, the popular chants of

---

[1] "Earl of Gloucester." For a list of the crusading knights, who accompanied P. Edward, see Mr Hudson Turner's paper in Arch. Journ. Vol. VIII. p. 46. It includes Roger de Leyburn, and 9 knights, Brian de Brampton, and 1 knight; Roger de Clifford, and 9 knights; Robert de Mounteny, and 2 knights; William FitzWarin, and 2 knights; Adam de Gesemuth, and 5 knights; Thomas de Clare, and 9 knights; Alan de MonteAlto and 1 knight; William de Huntercombe, and 2 knights; Walter de Percy, and 3 knights; William de Valence, and 19 knights; Richard de la Rokele, and 2 knights; Payne de Chaworth, and 5 knights; Robert Tipetot, and 5 knights; Hamon l'Estrange; Pr. Edmund, and Gilbert de Clare, E. of Gloucester, were to follow.

the Crusades breathed more of religious than even military enthusiasm :—

"Ad portandum onus Tyri
Nunc deberent fortes viri
Suas vires experiri,
Qui certant quotidie
Laudibus militiæ
Gratis insigniri;
	Now let the strong in zealous throng,
	While yet they may, their strength
	    essay,
	And Sion's burthen bear;
	Advance with unbought chivalry,
	And spur on all in rivalry,
	    Fit warrior's fame to share.

"Sed ad pugnam congressuris
Est athletis opus duris
Non mollitis Epicuris:
Non enim qui pluribus
Cutem curant sumptibus
Emunt Deum precibus.
	No dastard cold of softened mould,
	But hardy knight in vigorous might,
	    This holy work must dare:
	They who at home in sensual ease
	Lavish their wealth the flesh to please,
	    Buy not Heaven by prayer.

"Lignum crucis signum ducis
Sequitur exercitus,
Quod non cessit, sed præcessit
In vi Sancti Spiritus.
   *   *   *
	The sainted wood,
	The Cross has stood,
	    To our host a shining light;
	It shrinks not back,
	It guides our track
	    In the holy Spirit's might.
	   * * * *

"Quibus minus est argenti
Si fideles sint inventi,
Purâ fide sint contenti:
Satis est Dominicum
Corpus ad viaticum
Crucem defendenti.
	Who money lack, need not turn
	    back,
	Nor scrip prepare, if faith be there,
	    The faithful feel no loss:
	The Lord's own body leads the way,
	Enough of food and cheer and stay
	    To those who guard the Cross.

"Lignum crucis, &c.[1]"	The sainted wood, The Cross has stood, &c.

Among those who now found this vent for their private restlessness, was one too powerful and vacillating to be safely left at home, the Earl of Gloucester. He had mainly contributed both to the rise and ruin of de Montfort, but, dissatisfied either with his share of reward, or with the utter

---

[1] Song of Master Berther, of Orleans, in 1187.—See Roger Hoveden, p. 639. In the same year, at Dunstable, "on the Vigil of St Lawrence the heavens opened, and in sight of many clergy and laymen a very long cross of a wonderful size appeared, on which our Saviour was seen to be nailed, crowned with thorns, and with outstretched hands the five wounds bleeding, but the blood, though it flowed, fell not upon earth."

disregard of all previous promises of constitutional reform, he had again resorted to arms against the King. He had even taken London[1], although too unstable to persist in any fixed line of conduct; he had afterwards submitted to the indignity of having the terms of his reconciliation referred to the Pope. His eldest son was accordingly required to be delivered up for three years to the Queen, or his castle of Tunbridge to Prince Henry, but by the wiser mediation of Prince Edward both these conditions had been remitted[2].

Before the return of Prince Edward from this expedition he was preceded by his cousin Prince Henry, who, in his journey through Italy, found himself at Viterbo at the same time with his two cousins, the disinherited exiles, Simon and Guy de Montfort.

The narrow escape of Guy from sharing the fate of his father and brother at Evesham has been noticed, and the circumstance, as vaguely transmitted by the tradition of three centuries, seems to have given rise to the fine old ballad of "the Beggar of Bethnal Green," the noble father of "pretty Bessee." The rescue of "young Montfort, of courage so free," from the heaps of slain after a battle is there effected by a fair lady:—

> "Who seing young Montfort there gasping to lie,
> She saved his life through charitie."

He was not long, however, in recovering from his wounds; and after an imprisonment, first at Windsor and then at Dover, had succeeded in escaping to the Continent by bribing his keeper and deceiving his guards[3]. On his arrival in Italy as a soldier of fortune, he was seized by the Pope's orders as an excommunicated fugitive[4]. Guy, however, possessed his father's military talent; and much as the Pope

---

[1] On this occasion the mob attacked the King's palace, which must have been rebuilt since the fire of 1263, and is described thus, "quod in diversis regnis comparationem recipere dedignatur."—Wyke.

[2] Woodstock, July 16, 1268.—Rymer. He married afterwards the Princess Joan, born at Acre during this Crusade.

[3] T. Wyke.

[4] Landino, Comment. Dante.

hated the de Montforts, this advantage, urged by a powerful Prince, more than compensated for his ecclesiastical demerits. The French Prince, Charles d'Anjou, who had accepted the Sicilian crown[1] from the Pope's gift after Prince Edmund's resignation, procured the release of Guy de Montfort, in order to put under his command 800 French knights. With these Guy took possession of Florence on Easter-day, 1267[2], and was appointed his deputy-governor, when the Prince became Imperial Vicar in Tuscany. After this important service Guy greatly distinguished himself by his zeal[3] for his master, contributing to his great victory over the rival king Corradino at Tagliacozzo, August 24, 1268, and was sent to reduce Sicily to his power[4]. In this the French were successful, but they had introduced "worse evils than greater luxury" among the Italians; their military strength might have long enabled them to retain the island in their grasp, had not the cruelties of the army, unchecked by King or Pope, at length roused the people by their excess to the vengeance of the memorable Vespers :—

"Se mala signoria, che sempre ac-
cuora
Li popoli soggetti, non avesse
Mosso Palermo a gridar, Mora,
Mora.—Par. 8. 73.

Had not ill lording, which doth
spirit up
The people ever, in Palermo raised
The shout of "death," re-echo'd
loud and long.—Cary's Transl.

[1] His wife Beatrice is said to have urged his acceptance of it, ambitious of thus placing herself on a par with the three Queens her sisters. She entered Naples in great pomp as Queen "with magnificent gilded carriages and plenty of richly dressed damsels, to which spectacle the people there were quite unaccustomed."—Ann. Muratori, 1266°. She died in 1267.
[2] G. Villani.
[3] Dante (Inf. 32. 116) alludes to his bribing Buoso da Duera, the General of the Ghibellines, in order to facilitate the passage of the French troops.
[4] Philip Count de Montfort, described as "a bold knight and ex-

perienced in arms," had been entrusted with the government of Bigorre, in 1258, as deputy for the Earl of Leicester, who invited his people there to obey him "tam fideliter quam amicabiliter tanquam nobis." See Trésor des Chartes, p. 292. He was also actively employed under King Charles, and was in Sicily. He was the son of Philip, Lord of Ferte, Aleps and Castries in France, and Lord of Tyre in Syria, who was a first cousin of Simon, the great Earl of Leicester, and was among those who had invited him to supreme power at Jerusalem.—See p. 45, ante. Nangis, Muratori.
[5] "Il lusso e qualche cosa di peggio."—Muratori.

He was rewarded, as others of his comrades were, with liberal grants of lands and baronies[1], and thus becoming Count of Nola, was high in trust and favour with King Charles.

His brother Simon, as the elder son, had been looked up to by the partisans of his father as his successor in the guidance of the popular impulses; and, as has been seen, made some attempts to retrieve the fortunes of the party. A contemporary poet thus earnestly expresses his anxiety for him immediately after the battle of Evesham:—

"Priez tous, mes amis doux,
le fitz Seinte Marie,
Que l'enfant, her puissant
meigne en bonne vie:
Ore est oces, &c.[1]"

Now all draw near, companions dear,
To Jesus let us pray,
That Montfort's heir his grace may share,
And learn to heaven the way[2].

After the final overthrow of his house and party, Simon had joined his brother Guy in Italy, and they were both together at Viterbo in March, 1271[3].

For two years after the death of Clement IV. (Nov. 29, 1269), a conclave of fifteen cardinals had been sitting in that city; and, as their tedious incubation had not yet produced a Pope, the interest attached to this election[4] happened to attract there at the same time Philip, who had lately succeeded to the crown of France, Charles, King of Sicily, and the English Prince Henry, passing through Italy on their separate journeys.

It adds to our interest in the untimely fate of Prince Henry to know that he had been recently married (March 6,

[1] "Hebbe da lui molti stati nel regno."—L'historia di Casa Orsini da Fr. Sansovino, Ven. 1565, p. 62. Filiberto Campanile specifies Cicala, Atripalda, Furino, as given to Guy.—See Dell' Armi dei Nobili, 2 edit. Napoli, 1618.

[2] Lament de S. de Montfort, from MS. Cott. in W. Rish. Polit. Songs. The translation from Ellis' Anc. S.

[3] Duchesne, Hist. Script. Norman Chr. Norm. dates this event 1257, and the battle of Lewes 1251.

[4] Teobaldo de' Visconti of Piacenza, then Archdeacon of Liège, was ultimately chosen; he was, at the time, absent at Acre, with Prince Edward, who on his return visited his former comrade as Gregory X., at Rome, with a great suite (magnâ comitivâ).—Lansd. MSS. 397, 3. Gregory was elected Sept. 1, 1271, crowned Jan. 27, 1272, and died Jan. 10, 1276.—Nicholas' Chronol.

1269), with the zealous approval of the King and Prince Edward, to Constance, the daughter and expected heiress of Gaston de Moncade, the wealthy and powerful Count of Bearn[1]. This alliance shortly preceded the journey towards Syria, from which, or rather from Tunis, Henry was now returning.

He was performing his devotions in a chapel opposite his lodgings on Friday, March 13, when the vindictive passions of the past barons' war selected him as a fresh and last victim. The two de Montforts, from the time of their cousin's arrival, had watched him night and day, resolved "with all intent of mind," to revenge the ruin of their family on one whose royal blood seemed to identify him with the authors of their father's death and their own expulsion.

The solemn description of the event which Pope Gregory afterwards put on record[2], represents Prince Henry's visit to Viterbo as commanded by Prince Edward, and encouraged by the King of Sicily, with the express object of restoring the de Montforts to the favour of the English Prince. This intention, however, if really entertained, could not have been made known to his angry cousins, and circumstances soon put an end to any such idea. The exclusion of the de Montforts from England was never revoked, yet the royal enmity of Edward did not extend, as in meaner instances of later date, to carved stone; and there still remains the armorial

[1] This marriage, which is not noticed in the usual pedigrees of the royal family, is dated by T. Wyke in May. Constance is mentioned as possessing Tickhill for her dower, when a widow in 1272.—Rot. Pat. 53°, 56° Hen. III. She was the eldest daughter of Gaston VII., Viscount of Bearn, and was married first to Alfonso, son of James I. of Aragon. There being no brothers, she was considered her father's heiress. It is to be hoped the lady did not inherit her grandmother's personal peculiarities, "a woman remarkably monstrous, and a prodigy of fatness."—M. Par. Edward I. wished her, on her return to her own country as a widow, to marry Aymon Count of Geneva (c. 1279), and Gaston promised to do this at the King's request. (Tower MS. No. 1456.) Constance urges the payment of the arrears of her dower from the King, and wishes to come to England to speak face to face with him, there being some coldness between them. She calls herself "Constance, relict of the late noble man Henry of Germany."

[2] Processus, in Thesaur. Cur. Recept. Scacc.—Rymer.

shield of the great Simon de Montfort on the walls of Westminster Abbey, the only public record of his high alliance and of his place in British history[1].

It was the time of Lent, so that Simon and Guy easily tracked the unfortunate Henry to the church at high mass[2], when, knowing that the two Kings of France and Sicily were also engaged at their devotions in the Franciscan church[3], at a distance, the opportunity of accomplishing their revenge presented itself. At first they intended to pluck him out from amidst his attendants, but the crowd being too great for this, the brothers rushed in upon him with drawn swords while the unsuspecting Prince was kneeling before the altar. From the very threshold of the church Guy fiercely re-

[1] Under the same window of the north aisle of the nave is also the shield of his enemy, John de Warenne; these are copied in the title-page, as are also those of Henry III., and the King of the Romans, from the Abbey. In the "Rolls of Arms," 1308-14, those of the Earl of Leicester, "gules, a lion or, tail fourchée," are among the extinct arms, "armes abattues." The descendants of Peter de Montfort at that time bore, "in Sussex and Surrey, Sir William de Montfort, bende or and azure," "John Montfort, bende of 10, or and azure." Under the 1st window East, are the shields of the Emperor Frederic II. and Louis IX.; under 2nd those of Clare and Bigot; under 3rd those of Montfort, the straps of the shield supported on the right by a projecting head of an aged bearded man wearing a coronet, on the left by a smiling head with curly hair. The supporter on the right of De Warenne is the head of a noble female with linen bands across her forehead and under her chin, that on the left has been cut away to make room for a modern monument; under the 4th is the shield of Albemarle. On the South side under the 1st window East are the arms of Henry III.; under the 2nd those of Alexander III. and Raymond Count of Provence (or, 4 pallets, gules); under 4th the shield of Richardus Comes Cornubiæ, supported on the right by a man's head, bare at top with curls at sides. Many of the shields exhibit the heraldic colours and the names inscribed on the small cornice over them.

[2] G. Villani. T. Wyke says it was early in the morning; Chr. Lanercost, that it was at vespers.

[3] There is the most singular discrepancy among different authorities as to the church in which the murder took place. According to Nangis, Trivet and W. Rish., it was S. Lorenzo, which is in fact the cathedral in the south of the town, and with this Platina (Vite de Pontefici) agrees. T. Wyke and Walsingham name the chapel of the confraternity of S. Blaise (S. Biagio). Ann. Wav., Chr. Oxenede and two Italians, Landino and Vellutello, call it S. Sylvestro, a parish-church in the middle of the town near the market-place; and this must have been really the scene of the murder, being the only one named fulfilling the Pope's description of its occurrence, "in a certain parish-church." The convent of S. Francisco, where King Philip represents himself as being at the time, is much farther to the North, near the Porta S. Lucia, according to the plan of Tarquinio Ligusti, Viterbese, 1596. Compare Gebauer's Leben des Kaiser Richards, s. 274.

proached him, "Thou traitor Henry of Almaigne, thou shalt not escape;" and without respect for the sanctity of the place or of the ceremony, they stabbed him repeatedly with their daggers, even while he clung so closely to the altar that four fingers of his left hand were nearly severed in the struggle to tear him from it[1]. Supposing him to be dead when he fell under their blows, the de Montforts retreated to the door and joined the troop of horse- and foot-soldiers whom they had placed there to secure their flight. One of his party asking what had been done, Guy answered, "I have had my revenge[2];" but when taunted with the worse usage his father had met with—"How was your father dragged about?"—he hurried back to fulfil every detail of the bloody retribution in his power, and dragged his expiring victim by the hair out of the church, venting his fury again and again upon him in spite of his clasped hands and cries for mercy. Every part of his body was mutilated with wounds; his side, loins, and face were savagely cut, as if the brothers exulted in acting over again the bloody tragedy of Evesham. "You had no mercy on my father or my brothers[3]," were the last insults heard by the Prince in his agony of death.

The audacity of the attack, and the armed force at the door, seem to have paralysed the Prince's attendants; while of the two priests then celebrating mass, and who interposed, one was killed and the other severely wounded[4]. The murderers mounted their horses at the church-doors and fled in safety to the Maremma, where Count Ildribaldino Rosso dell' Anguillara[5] (whose daughter Margaret was

[1] T. Wyke. Processus, Rymer.
[2] G. Villani, 7, 40, introduces the French words into his Italian text, "Je a fet ma vengeance." "Comment vostre père fut trane?"—thus giving an air of much authenticity to his account, for Guy would naturally use that language to his French comrades, independent of its being then in habitual use at the English court.
[3] "Puis le traina hors du mous-

trier. Henri le cria merci jointes mains, pour Dieu qu'il ne l'occeist, et Guy li rispondi, 'Tu n'eus pas pitié de mon père et de mes frères.'"
—Nangis; Processus in Rymer; G. Villani.
[4] T. Wyke; Processus in Rymer.
[5] Anguillara was a noble castle near the lake formerly called Angulare, now Lago di Bracciano. Hume represents them as taking refuge in the church of S. Francis, which they

the wife of Guy) had power to shelter them from pursuit:—

> "Vor in a Friday, the morwe up Sein Gregorie's day,
> As he stod at is masse, as that folc isay,
> Before the weved in his bedes at the secre rigt,
> Com Sir Gui de Mountford that was stalwarde knigt,
> And is aunte sone, alas! iarmed wel inou,
> And communes with him and to him even drou,
> And s(mote) im thoru out is suerd and villiche him slou."
>
> Rob. Glouc.[1]

Such is the account by the rough poet of "this hideous and abominable thing," as the Italian historian[2] justly calls it; and that it should have been done so publicly and within reach of the protection of the French Princess[3], naturally cast some reproach even upon them.

The letters of the two Kings, written upon the spot immediately after the event, are full of phrases of horror, and professions of pursuing the culprits, but so slack was the pursuit, that they were never forgiven by Prince Edward[4] to whom the letter of Charles was addressed:—

"In sorrow and grief of mind we acquaint you, that lately, when we and King Phillip were at the Roman court, Simon and Guy de Montfort, children of perdition, with no respect to the Roman Church, to the King, or to ourselves,

certainly did not do. Some consider Count Rosso as more expressly implicated in the murder, "cum consilio et auxilio Comitis Rufi."—Lansd. MS. 229. T. Wyke also involves Almeric de Montfort: "Simon cum Guidone necnon Comite Rufo, cujus filiam duxerat, non sine assensu, ut credi poterat Emmerici fratris eorundem," &c.

[1] *Weved*, altar; *bedes*, prayers; *rigt*, rite. The feast of S. Gregory was on March 12.

[2] G. Villani.

[3] "Rege Franciæ et rege Siciliæ ignorantibus, vel forte conniventibus."—T. Wyke. "Simone et Guidone de Monti Forte, Comite Rubeo, immo aliis nonnullis spectantibus, in crastino S. Gregorii."—Chr. Oxen.

"Onde la corte turbò forte, dando di ciò reprensione allo Re Carlo, che ciò non doveva sofferire, se l'havesse saputo, e se nol sapeva, non lo dovea lasciar passare impunito."—G. Villani.

[4] In the Pleas of 1275, Walter de Baskervill is spoken of as outlawed for the death of Henry (murdrati per Simonem de Monte Forti), and was therefore probably one of Guy's comrades at Viterbo. Baskervill pleaded in defence that he could not be tried for anything done in a foreign country, and subsequently he was allowed, 1278, to recover his lands, by the Kenilworth decree, from Roger de Clifford, the latter, however, retaining his life interest.—Placit. 3° Edw. I. pp. 195, 264.

wickedly killed—alas! what a calamity!—your and our kinsman Henry. We, firmly resolving to pursue these wretches to their ruin and extermination[1], as if the atrocity had been committed on ourselves or on our children, have ordered Henry Count Valdemonte and Agnani, our Vicar-General in Tuscany, to pursue and seize these most abominable criminals, so that it may be made manifest by deeds how deeply their guilt has touched our inmost soul. Wherefore we earnestly beseech your Greatness not to be confounded or dejected, but to persist in your accustomed constancy. Viterbo, March 13[2]."

King Philip's letter to the King of the Romans, written "not without vehement bitterness and grief of heart," described in greater detail that the two Kings were hearing the solemnities of the mass in the church of the Minor Friars, while Guy and Simon, "at the same day and hour, attacked Henry with armed hand, when he was in a certain other chapel of Viterbo, opposite his lodging, hearing mass or praying, and there at the instigation of the devil killed him."

The church at Rome, then represented by the conclave, issued its denunciation on the murderers; and Pope Gregory, six months after his election, renewed it, calling them "sons of Belial, led on by a diabolical spirit." The presence of Edward I. at the Papal Court on his return from Syria, seems, however, to have been the active cause of quickening the steps of justice, for up to that time no arrest had taken place and no judicial process begun. Gregory X., lamenting the delay, in a public and solemn notice of the crime[3] (March 1, 1273), summoned Guy de Montfort to appear within fifteen days before him to answer the charges of murder, fratricide, sacrilege, and the insult done to God, to the Church, and to the Princes, of which common report denounced him and his late brother Simon[4] to have been guilty.

[1] "In exterminium et ruinam iniquorum ipsorum."
[2] Rymer.
[3] Rymer.—Lansd. MS., 397.
[4] "Simone fatali sorte rebus humanis exempto."—Rymer.

An escort was offered him from the boundaries of the territory of his father-in-law in order to prevent any excuse of his fearing to approach Edward I., who had even offered to remove his residence if Guy would swear to come. Count Rosso soon afterwards received a similar summons[1], as he not only arrived at Viterbo at the same time with Guy, but had also accompanied him when approaching the spot where the murder was perpetrated, had been present with his suite near the place while so foul a deed was committed, and had subsequently harboured Guy.

The criminals, instead of obeying, sent Almeric de Montfort on their behalf to excuse their non-appearance, and plead for delay until Edward's departure from Italy, fearing his avowed desire of revenge; Guy even ventured to allege that he had the justest reasons at the time for the murder of Henry, and that having been stripped by Edward of all his substance he was now compelled by his destitution to league with men of violence. The Pope of course rejected all such excuses as trifling; and as to his plea of poverty, reminded him that in fact he had lost nothing, for that the property in England had never belonged to him at all, his elder brothers having had prior claims to the succession of their late parents; while as to his Sicilian lands, the King had justly recalled the grant of them on his sudden flight after the murder.

Almeric vainly tendered Guy's confession of the crime and bargained for mercy: the Pope, though Guy did not appear, deprived him of all faculty of inheritance, and doomed him to perpetual infamy, to confiscation and forfeiture of his jurisdiction in the lands of his wife, decreeing that no descendant, even to the fourth generation, should ever hold office or dignity, while every one was authorized to seize Guy and bring him to prison[2].

---

[1] In a letter to Raynerio, the supreme authority in Florence, March 6, 1273. The summons was to be delivered in or near "civitate Luan [? Sovana] consueto ejus domicilio." —Rymer.

[2] Processus, April 1, 1273. —Rymer.

THE MURDER AT VITERBO.

The zeal of the Pope, however, seemed to relax, when not excited by the presence of his powerful friend, King Edward[1]. In a few months afterwards (from Lyons, November 29) he wrote to that monarch, that "on his passage through Florence, Guy, by his wife and others, had implored compassion with every sign of a humbled and contrite heart; with his accomplices he had even prostrated himself on the road before the Pope two miles out of Florence, barefooted and with no other garments than shirt and hose, having ropes round their necks, and begging in that lowly posture with tears and prayers for any punishment, so that a door of mercy might be opened for him[2]."

Simon de Montfort had already escaped from human punishment, by his death in a castle near Sienna, in the year of the murder, "after a brief wandering on the earth with the curse of Cain upon him[3]." Guy, however, was now consigned by the relenting Pope to the penance of a cell for more than ten years, "until the apostle[4] (in the words of the chronicler) granted him favour and mercy." The motives of Martin IV. in his release, 1283, seem, however, to have been more worldly than apostolic; for the Pope needed his military services in Romagnuola against Montefeltro, and the immediate success of Guy, who recovered much territory for the Papal see, quickly repaid the obligation. His father-in-law, Count Rosso, being dead, he left the siege of Urbino by the

[1] Edward I. paid 350 marcs to William de Valence, as a debt from Henry of Almaigne, Windsor, Sept. 1274.—Rymer.
[2] Lugdun. III. Kal. Dec. Gerard de Roscillon was despatched by the Pope with this letter.—Rymer.
[3] Chr. Roff. According to Ann. Dunst. he died in France, as well as his brother Richard. "Simon passa en France et y mourut sans posterité."—Moreri, Dict. "Simon, Earl of Bigorre, was ancestor of a family of Montfort in that part of France." —Sandford's Gen. Hist. p. 87. It is probable that he was the father of Richard Signor di Gambatesa, who, by marrying Thomasa, the heiress of the Campobasso family, became the ancestor of the lords of Gambatesa and Campobasso, who continued to flourish in the kingdom of Naples till the 15th century. His death, however, before March, 1273, is certain and notorious.
[4] "Puis en souffroit Guy grant penitence, car il en fu en chartre en un fort chastel, et y demoura tant que l'apostoile li fist grace et misericorde."—Gesta Philippi III. Nangis.

Pope's sanction, in order to secure the inheritance of his wife and children from the encroachment of Count Santa Flora. A few years later, in 1288, again in the service of Charles d'Anjou, he was taken prisoner in a naval fight off Sicily, while endeavouring to relieve Catania, which had been seized by Reginald on the King's behalf. The Sicilian admiral, Roger de Laurea, sent him and his other French captives to various prisons; but though all the others were released by ransoms, Guy alone could never regain his liberty, either by entreaties or large offers of money.

At one period an agreement seems to have been come to for his release, on payment of 10,000 ounces of gold (4000 to be paid at once, and 6000 in ten months). There is extant an earnest letter from one of his friends at Naples, calling on all his relations in France to contribute towards this sum, and stating that the Guelf party in Tuscany had already promised to raise 6600 florins, besides 1000 from a vassal. As his life would be in danger in default of payment, his friends are urged to do the best they can as quickly as possible[1].

The influence of the English King is said to have occasioned[2] this severe treatment of Guy, and "the hand of God (observes the annalist) reached him in its own due time, for he finished his days miserably in a Sicilian prison[3]."

Though accident thus brought home misery to one of the murderers, yet the murder was never effectually punished by the arm of human law. The savage deed cannot be palliated

---

[1] This appeal is made to Raoul de Cleremonte, constable of France, Amalto de Montfort, and to Jehana de Montfort, Conte de Esquillache and de Moterescaiens.—Rymer. Florence had promised 1000, Sienna 2000, and Orvieto 3000 florins.

[2] Nangis, Gesta Philippi III., "Dolo tentus ut dicitur Regis Edwardi."

[3] Muratori, Ann. Guy, by his marriage with Margaret, only daughter of Count Rosso, had two daughters—Thomasa, who married Pietro di Vico, Prefect of Rome; and Anastasia, who married, 1293, Romano Orsini, Grand Justiciary of Naples, invested as Count di Nola by Charles II. Almeric de Montfort, after Guy's death, acted as guardian to his nieces, and died 1292.—See Campanile, "Dell' Armi," &c. p. 44. The Harl. MS. 6461, 19, p. 70, adds, incorrectly, to the children of Simon de Montfort, " de quibus nulla proles." Guy died 1288.—Moreri.

by any reference to the provocation so many years before, but it would appear still more strange if the unfortunate Prince, as many accounts assert[1], was in no way a party to the death of the great Simon de Montfort. There is no express proof as to his being present at Evesham or not; we have seen that he had been sent on an embassy to France, May 17, and may possibly not have returned before that battle. His cold-blooded murder seems to denote that the de Montforts at least thought his active enmity had earned their life-long vengeance. Some such strong impulse seems required to account for the crime, especially in the case of Simon, whom we have seen, in all the fresh excitement of anger and grief, shielding the father of his present victim from the fury of his soldiers at Kenilworth, and who had himself been indebted for his life to Prince Edward when a captive at Northampton.

Among some zealous Royalists there had yet lingered an apprehension that the de Montforts, if recalled from exile, might have troubled the state, and the murder at Viterbo appeared in their eyes as a providential means of rendering their pardon hopeless[2].

The retribution of this atrocity, which worldly policy delayed and mitigated, has been signally awarded by poetry. Dante has for ever fixed the shadowy image of Guy de

---

[1] According to Chr. Norm. Duchesne, Henry was not in the battle of Evesham, and had endeavoured to procure the recal of the exiles. It adds that Simon had guaranteed his safety at Viterbo in the presence of the two Kings. It is very improbable that Henry was mistaken for Prince Edward, as Chr. Lanerc. asserts.

[2] " Irruit in templum maledicti
    stirps Guenenonis,
Perfodit gladiis hunc Symonis atque
    Guidonis:
Disposuit Deus ut per eos vir tantus
    abiret,
Ne revocatis liis gens Anglica tota
    periret."

Given as an epitaph on Prince Henry in Lansd. MSS., 229, and Chr. Roff. From the allusion in it to the traitor, Gano de Pontieri (the Ganellone of Dante, Inf. 32. 122), who betrayed Charlemagne at Roncesvalles, it appears of foreign origin, and may have been inscribed at Viterbo in the church. "Gui—ayant tué dans l'église de S. Laurent de Viterbe (le Prince Henri) qu'il accusoit d'avoir fait mettre en pièces le corps du Comte de Leicester son père."—Moreri, Dict. [Perhaps Henry was specially odious as a renegade from de Montfort's party.]

Montfort, plunged up to his throat in a bubbling pool of hot blood, and shunned even by other murderers in hell :—

" Un ombra d'un canto sola,	A spirit by itself apart retired,
Colui fesse in grembo a Dio	He in God's bosom smote the
Lo cor, che'n su Tamigi ancor si	heart
cola¹.—Inf. 12. 119.	That still beside the Thames for vengeance bleeds.

The heart of the unfortunate Prince was sent to Westminster Abbey in a golden vase, and was there allowed to be enclosed in the same tomb with the body of Edward the Confessor². It is said that a gilt statue on his monument held the embalmed heart, with the label, " I bequeath to my father my heart pierced with the dagger." These may have been the last words of the dying Prince³. His bones, when brought to England, were buried honourably at Hailes in Gloucestershire, May 21⁴.

Such funeral honours, however, could not comfort the bereaved father: he who had formerly been spared by the mercy of the de Montforts, now felt their tardy and distant vengeance as a mortal blow. His only surviving son Edmund was at the time on his way to Syria, in company with his cousin of the same name, the King's son, as Crusaders⁵;

¹ The characteristic allusion of Dante (ancor si cola) to the ancient superstition of the blood trickling afresh from a murdered corpse, either to denounce the murderer, or to excite others to revenge, has not been rendered by Cary and others. A friend, the Rev. Henry Wellesley, having pointed this out, has also supplied the novel translation of the last line.
² Chr. Roff. His old shrine was translated with much ceremony to a new one adorned with gold and precious stones, being borne on the shoulders of King Henry III., Richard King of the Romans, Prince Edward, Edmund Earl of Lancaster, Earl de Warenne, Philip Basset, and as many as could touch it. The deposit of the heart is also mentioned by Dart (Hist. Westm. Abbey), and Crull (Westm. Abb., p. 175). G. Villani says the heart was placed on a column at London bridge, which is very improbable, and Landino speaks of his burial in London, "where the other Kings are buried." The mention of the Thames by Dante probably caused the confusion.
³ Landino. There is no trace or record, however, of any such monument in the Abbey.
⁴ Chr. Oxenede and Ann. Waverley speak of his burial at Hailes on May 21; a funeral mass in his honour was celebrated at Norwich, July 22. The Lansd. MS. 229, says the body was buried at Viterbo between two Popes, and all his bones carried to Hailes.
⁵ T. Wyke. MS. Lansd. 229. The seal of Edmund de Alemania, Earl

he anxiously recalled him to England on learning the fatal loss; but although gratified by his return, he soon after, April 2, 1272, went down sorrowing to the grave.

As the wealthiest man of his times, the King of the Romans[1], in pursuance of a vow made in a moment of peril at sea, had amply endowed a monastery at Hailes[2], where was also deposited what was then esteemed a possession very lucrative from its attractions, a drop of blood reputed to be that of our Saviour. The importation of this relic[3], duly

of Cornwall (at p. 95, Sandford) represents him as a knight galloping, with his arms on shield—on the reverse, the same arms on a large shield are upheld by a strap from the mouth of an eagle.

[1] Arms of K. of Romans in east window of Bedall church, and of Richmond, Yorkshire.

[2] The Franciscan Alexander Hales, a native of this place, owed his education to the King of the Romans, and was so acute a reasoner as to be called the Irrefragable Doctor; he had the distinction of being master to two eminent saints of the Romish calendar, Buonaventura and Thomas Aquinas.

[3] The Earl brought this blood to Hailes "upon Holyrode day in Herviste, where God daylie shewithe miracles throwe the virtnes of that precious blood;" and therefore Pope John XXIV. allowed the Abbot to grant absolution for all but reserved sins after two confessions, and one confession "*to asoyle them in the poynt of dethe of all synnes, noone excepted.*" Pope Eugene IV. gave absolution for four confessions at Corpus Christi, and seven years and three lents to all who give "eny thinge to the worship of God and that precious blod." Pope Callixtus III. "granted full remission at Corpus X^{ti}, and at Holyrood in May and harvest;" also xv Cardinals, each by himself, gave 100 days pardon to those who honor it, and "put to ther helpynge hondes to the wellfare of that forsayde monasterii of Hayles." Leland, Collect.

Vol. VI. p. 283. Edmund, Earl of Cornwall, obtained this blood in Germany, according to Hollinshed, "by fair entreaty and money, of a nobleman, Lord of Seyland" (Dugd.), and gave one-third of it to Hales, and two-thirds to the College of Bons Hommes which he founded at Ashridge, Herts, 1283 (Deo et beatæ Mariæ ac rectori Bonorum virorum fratrum ecclesiæ, in honore pretiosi sanguinis Jhesu Christi apud Esserugge), and where he was himself buried, together with the heart of the sainted Bishop of Hereford, Thomas de Cantilupe (v. p. 257 ante), in a tomb "miro tabulatu fabricatâ" in the north part of the choir. The saint's heart, however, was subsequently (mandatis apostolicis) removed, and with the holy blood translated, "in tabernaculo quodam deaurato sibi competenti." Dugd. Mon. 6. 514. The seal of the monastery, accidentally found in 1821, appears to represent the golden cross, which enshrined the relic, above a vase or bottle. In 1295 Edmund, Earl of Cornwall, gave "crucem auream cum pede de aumail, quæ nobilissiman portionem sanguinis preciosissimæ Crucis Christi in se insertam continuit."—Chr. Hayles; Dugd. Mon. Perhaps this relic gave rise to the proverbial saying, "As sure as God is in Gloucestershire." This is called in "Ray's Proverbs" a foolish and profane proverb, unfit to be used; and explained as having more rich abbeys, &c. than other shires; but the Hailes relic may have caused this expression of pious faith.

authenticated under the hand of Pope Urban IV., produced a great sensation at the time, 1270, and brought the monastery into high repute for many ages, until at length the rough chemistry of Henry VIII.'s commissioners detected it to be the blood of a duck[1]. In this spot his widow Beatrice[2],

---

[1] This seems to rest on the testimony of William Thomas, clerk of the Council to Edward VI., who may have been present at the examination of the relic before the King. He says (MS. Bodl. N. E. B. 2. 7), "See here the craft of thes develisse soule-quellers: it behoved eche person that cam thither to se it, first to confess hymself, and then, paying a certeyn to the comon of that Monastery, to enter into a chappell, uppon the aulter whereof this blod shuld be showed him.—(The monk confessor presented)—a pixe of cristall great and thicke as a bowle on the one side, and thyne as a glasse on the other syde—(two monks specially appointed) *every Saturday killed a duck*, and renewed therewith this consecrate blud, as they themselves confessed, not onlie in secret, but also openly before an approved audyence."—On Nov. 24, 1539, John Hilsey, Bishop of Rochester, preached at Paul's Cross, and shewed the relic to be "no blood, but *hony clarified and coloured with saffron*, as it had been evidently proved before the King and Council."—"The blood was invisible to man under mortal sin, no better than the blood of a duck renewed every week in a crystal very thick on one side but very thin and transparent on the other."—See Herbert's Henry VIII. p. 431; Fuller's Church History, 6. 333; Fox, Acts and Monum. 2. 431; Collier's Eccles. Hist. 2. 149.—The original report of the King's Commissioners, however, make no mention of duck's blood, nor of the different thickness of the sides of the glass. The certificate of *Hugh Latimer, Bishop of Worcester, of Henry Holbech, Prior of Worcester, of Stephen Whaley, Abbot of Hayles, and of Richard Tracye, Esq., High Sheriff of Gloucestershire*, dated Oct. 28, in 30th year of Henry VIII., reports that "they have viewed a certeyne supposed relycke caulyd the blod of Hailes, which was inclosed *within a rownde berall garnyshed and bownd on ev'y syde with sylv'*, which we cawsed to be openyd in the presence of a greate multytude of people—(they took it out)—being within a lytle glasse, and also tryed the same according to owr powers, wittes, and discretyons by all meanys, and by force of the view and other tryals thereof we thinke, deame, and judge the substaunce and mattier of the sayde supposyd Relycke to be an unctuowse gumme colouryd, which being in the glasse appeiryd to be a glisterynge redd resemblynge partly the color of blod—and after we did take owt part of the sayd substaunce and mattier ewt of the glasse, then it was apparunte glisterynge yeolow color lyke Ambre, or basse golde, and dothe cleve to as gumme or byrdlyme." It was enclosed within a coffre and sealed, and so delivered to Richard Tracye; and it casts suspicion on the Commissioners to find that the Manor of Hailes is now in the family of the Tracys.—End of Hearne's Benedictus Abb. Petroburg.—Oxon. 1735.

[2] Concia, his second wife, mother of Edmund, dying in 1261, when she was buried at Hayles, the Prince remarried June 16, 1269, Beatrice, daughter of a German baron, Theodoric de Falkenberg, and niece of Engelbert, Archbishop of Cologne (1262—1275), who retired to Bonn in 1268, disgusted at a rebellion of the Colognese. His tomb and effigy are in the cathedral of Bonn. "Non ambitu dotalitii, sed incomparabilis formæ ipsius captus illocebrâ."—T. Wyke. Lansd. MSS. 229.

whose personal beauty had but recently led the uxorious Prince in his old age to a third marriage, erected a sumptuous pyramid over his tomb. The relic, the monument, and the whole convent have been long swept away, and there survived to modern times only one incidental effect of the accumulation of vast property in this Prince's hands. As Earl of Cornwall[1] he had given charters to the numerous small towns[2] on his estates in that county, and this entitling them subsequently as burghs to send representatives to Parliament, long enabled them to sway the destinies of the empire by the chorus of their accordant voices, and thus during many centuries to influence the constitutional liberties of England.

[1] The grant of Cornwall to him was in 1224, and it was from this domain that he raised the army he had with him at the battle of Lewes. "Cornubia, ubi Richardus Comes excitavit exercitum, quem secum duxit ad bellum de Leaus."—Cott. MSS. Nero A. IV. The arms of the King, argent, a lion rampant gules within a bordure bezantée, were found in a Franciscan convent at Bordeaux, on its being pulled down, 1746. He had probably been a benefactor to it. For the same reason his arms also appear in the south aisle of Westminster Abbey.

[2] Launceston was made free 1231; Liskeard, 1240; Bodmin, Truro, and Helston afterwards. — See Lysons' Cornwall.

APPENDIX.

A.—Referred to at page 171, Note 3, and at page 194, Note 2. Reprinted from a letter addressed by Mr Blaauw to the *Sussex Express and County Advertiser*, 1863:

No historian has yet fixed the site of the Battle of Lewes. That of the first collision between Prince Edward and the Londoners, under the command of Lord Nicholas de Segrave, is accurately ascertained to be that portion of the Downs immediately above the Offham Chalkpits, where large quantities of skeletons have been at various periods exhumed by the men engaged in flint-digging,—the greater portion of which is to the north-east of Steere's Mill. Here the killed were evidently buried after the battle in small pits sufficient for six or nine bodies. The greatest number dug up in any one pit was nine.

Where the more extensive portion of the battle was fought between the other two divisions of Simon de Montfort's army and his reserve with the two divisions of the Royal Forces, has not as yet been fixed upon; for it is a singular fact that the traces of a battle-field have not been recognized upon any part of the Downs. The remains of no single warrior have ever been found from Plumpton Plain to Steere's Mill, or to Kenward's or Spital Mill. Nor are there any traces on the side hill from the Race Course to Houndean Bottom, so that the wide expanse of Downs from the northern boundary to Ashcombe, with the exception of the one mentioned above, the Offham Chalkpits, affords not the slightest trace of a battle; and yet it is supposed by some writers that there were nearly 100,000 men engaged in it, viz. 40,000

Baronial troops and 60,000 Royalists. Of the accuracy of this number great doubt is expressed. Half the number is more probably nearer the truth, as the estimated loss of the battle ranges between 3000 and 20,000. The Monk of Lewes sets it at 2700, which might perhaps represent those who fell in the streets of Lewes, and those who fought in the rencounter between the King and Simon de Montfort. Taking a medium calculation, and setting the number to be 5000, it is quite evident that there must be the site of the burial of not less than 3500 yet unknown and undiscovered, and were these buried on any part of the Downs traces of them would long before this have been exposed, for nearly every portion of the Downs has, within the past century, been sufficiently turned up to mark such a spot if any existed.

In 1264 the Downs extended to the very walls of Lewes, and to the gates of the Priory in Southover, and, with the exception of a very few buildings, an uninterrupted sward surrounded the western side of the town, so that any party leaving Lewes Castle would, immediately they passed the Wallands, be upon the Downs; and a similar party, leaving the walled boundary of the Priory of St Pancras, find themselves upon smooth turf open to sight on all sides; so that the troops under Prince Edward would, after leaving Lewes Castle, be upon the Downs as soon as they reached the Paddock, and hence on the Wallands to Offham Hill would have an easy and uninterrupted ride on their way to meet the Londoners. A similar open field would be presented to King Henry and his brother, the King of the Romans, with their troops when they emerged from the Priory grounds. These commanders and their troops could readily and uninterruptedly march from Southover over the Hides to the gentle slopes of the Downs at the Spital and towards Ashcombe.

From facts which have recently come to the knowledge of the writer of this article, he is confirmed in the belief that the greater portion of the Battle of Lewes was fought in the vicinity of Lewes County Gaol to the very walls of the town.

At the onset of the battle the Barons' army was drawn up in battle array, the right wing commanded by Henry, the eldest, and Guy, the third son of de Montfort, on the ground near the site of the last Sheep Fair, extending near to "Hope in the Valley," at the foot of the Haredean. The left wing of the Royal forces, under the King of the Romans, was opposed to these Confederate forces, and ultimately succumbed to them. These entered the battle-field no doubt from the top of Southover.

The centre of the Barons' army descended the hill to near the Lewes Gaol, where they encountered Henry and his centre, who had emerged from the Priory, and took his route, no doubt, up the sides of the Hides and Southover House Paddock. The reserve of the Confederate forces was held back at Kenward's Mill, where de Montfort could command, as it is stated he did, a full view of the battle-field.

It is evident that the King's forces were taken by surprise; consequently some time elapsed before they were prepared to leave their quarters, and during this time the Barons' army was descending from the heights of the race-hill towards Lewes. Prince Edward was the first in the field, and his impetuosity of attack succeeded in overcoming the Londoners, who formed the left wing of the Confederate army, and the time estimated from the first alarm that the Barons' army was ahead, would be sufficient to enable the Royal Prince to reach the ascent to the Offham Hill, about three-quarters of a mile from the Castle. His sanguinary attack occupied but little time before he drove the Londoners over the precipitous side hill of the Offham Chalkpits that formed a temporary respite in the retreat down to the brooks; but this was only temporary, for the Prince's forces could again come upon them by descending the valley opposite Offham turnpike-gate. From here the pursuit of the discomfited Londoners extended into the Weald, and a portion of them were pursued along the high ground to Hamsey Church, where they passed the swamps to Malling Mill, near which upwards of 80 were killed, and afterwards buried in a pit that was discovered at the time of lowering Malling Hill. Another party, the more numerous of the affrighted warriors, passed through the Weald on their escape to London, and were met with by some Royalist troops at Croydon, where a severe hand-to-hand fight took place, and the dead were buried in George Street of that town. These were discovered a few years since in lowering the road leading to the Brighton Railway Station.

The King and his forces, who were lying within the walls of the Priory, being taken by surprise, lost some time in getting in order; so that before Henry could possibly leave his quarters the Barons were gradually approaching Lewes, and it doubtless was only by great exertions he got from Lewes as far as the Spital Barn. He could not possibly have reached the heights of the Downs, as there was not time for such a movement after the period of the alarm being given, which did not take place till after the Barons came in sight of the Priory Church Tower, and this could not be seen until the Barons had passed the Sheep Pond, southward of the Lewes Race Course; consequently it is clear that the Barons' right wing and centre had commenced descending the Spital Hill. From these and other facts we have concluded that the battle-field on which Simon de Montfort defeated Henry and his forces was in the close vicinity of the Lewes County Gaol, and extended from thence to the walls of the town at Westgate, and to the walls of the Priory Gateway. We are further strengthened in our opinion by the fact that in 1810 Mr Barrett, the late respected road-surveyor, lowered the Brighton turnpike-road; and during his excavations near the eastern carriage entrance to the County Gaol he discovered three large pits filled with skeletons, containing by estimate quite 500 bodies in each. These he subsequently reburied in the grounds of St Ann's almshouses. His carts were engaged several days in carrying them to their present resting-place. The discovery of these pits readily proves that a battle had been fought in their vicinity; and if, as we suppose, these are the bodies of those who were engaged in the final struggle for victory, it may, without any stretch of imagination, be considered that the site selected by us was that of the battle.

Near about the time that Henry was overwhelmed by his opponents, his brother, the King of the Romans, was equally discomfited by the rapidity of the attacks of his foes on the right wing of the Barons. His defeat was so rapid that he nearly fell into the hands of the Barons, and would have done so had he not made his escape to a water-mill at hand. This water-mill was on the Winterbourne stream, the remains of which were traceable about 80 years ago.

The spot we have selected for the site of Montfort's carriage, in which were confined Augustine de Harestock [Hadestock], Richard Dycard [Pycard], and Stephen de Chelmereford, three aldermen of London, who were, by mistake, killed by Prince Edward's party on their return to the battle-field, was on the high ground near Steere's Mill—a spot eminently calculated to mislead the King's party as the head-quarters of the Barons' Commander-in-Chief, especially as he had fixed his banner on the carriage.

We believe that by taking it for granted that the battle-field was between Lewes and the Spital Mill, and becoming acquainted with the localities, the reader of the records of the battle will find no difficulty in reconciling it with all the details that have been furnished by the writers of the day when it was fought. It may be said that, in giving our views, we have dogmatically asserted as facts what are mere suppositions; but we sincerely believe in our statements, and trust they will furnish some reliable addition to the researches of the antiquary as well as be interesting to the reader.

B.—Referred to at p. 328: from Archives du Royaume, J. 630. Inventaire de Dupuy, Angleterre III.

Alienora Dei gracia regina Anglie, domina Hybernie, et ducissa Aquitanie, Petrus comes Sabaudie et Johannes Mansellus Thesaurarius Eboracensis omnibus ad quos presentes littere pervenerint salutem. Notum facimus quod cum per composicionem et pacem inter excellentissimum dominum Ludovicum illustrem regem Francie ac karissimum dominum nostrum Henricum regem Anglie illustrem initam, teneretur idem dominus rex Francie dare ipsi domino regi Anglie id quod quingenti milites constare deberent rationabiliter ad tenendum per duos annos, secundum quod in forma pacis ejusdem plenius continetur, prefato quod domino rege Anglie aliorum arbitrium non curante super hoc expectare, ad hunc amicabilem finem devenissent quod predictus dominus rex Francie pro eo quod constare deberent quingenti milites tenendi, ut predictum est, ipsi domino regi Anglie in centum triginta quatuor milibus librarum Turonensium teneretur, de qua quidem summa pecunie idem dominus rex Anglie septuaginta sex milia librarum Turonensium jam ab eodem domino rege Francie receperat in pecunia numerata, Nos, ab ipso domino rege Anglie per patentes ipsius litteras super hoc plenam potestatem habentes, totum residuum illius pecunie, videlicet quinquaginta octo milia librarum Turonensium, deductis, duobus milibus libris Turonensibus quas idem dominus rex Anglie dedit et concessit subsidio terre sancte per dilectum nostrum Johannem de Valencenis militem in hujusmodi subsidium expendendis, nomine ipsius regis Anglie ab ipso rege Francie recepimus in pecunia numerata, et ita cum satisfactum sit integre predicto domino regi Anglie de totali debito supradicto, Nos nomine procuratorio domos et res miliciæ Templi et hospitalii Ierosolimitani tam citra mare quam ultra, quas priores et magistri earumdem domorum sponte predicto domino nostro regi Anglie per suas patentes litteras super hiis, ut dicitur, obligaverant pro domino rege Francie memorato, et omnes obligaciones alias, si que super hiis alie facte fuerint, quitamus ex nunc et remittimus penitus et expresse, volentes quod si littere predictorum priorum et magistrorum ipsarum domorum Templi et Hospitalii, vel alie super predictis obligacionibus facte, forte invenirentur ab aliquo, nullius essent valoris a modo nec obtinerent alicujus roboris firmitatem, Promittentes etiam bona fide quod, quam citius commode poterimus, litteras patentes ejusdem domini regis Anglie super hujusmodi obligacionum remissione et quitacione expressa eidem regi Francie faciemus haberi. In cujus rei testimonium presentes litteras sigillis nostris fecimus sigillari. Datum Parisiis die Dominica post ascensionem Domini M°.CC°.lx°. quarto, mense Junio.

    Three seals appended. 1. Queen Eleanor's, without inscription, the lower half of her figure remaining, the rest broken. 2. Peter de Savoy's perfect, with his arms, inscribed S. Petri de Sabaudia. 3. John Mansel's broken, the middle part of an old Roman Imperial coin.

C.—Referred to at p. 330: from Arch : du roy : J. 1034. Suppl : au Trésor des Chartes.

Conseiles donnés au Roi d'Angleterre pour l'administration de son Royaume.

A nostre Seigneur le Roy monstre chil ki a grant volenté de

li servir toute se vie, si comme il a montré et dit a plusieurs du consel ki li deussent monstrer et dire le pourfit et l'onneur et le bien de vous et de votre roiaume, encores le vous mechion en escrit, si ke vous en puissies mix user pour deffrende et recouvrer votre roiaume et votre terre, et dont vous porres avoir plus grand defaute, chést à savoir, d'or et d'argent. Dieu et droiture est avoekes vous et li plaist ke vous le vollies siever, car tout le plus de la boene gent de crestienté vous voelent sievir a che faire, mais ke vous aiiez poir d'aus aidier d'argent. Argent ares vous asés, mais ke vous voeillez ordener levie de le bone gent de vostre roiaume d'Engleterre, lequelle cose il font volentiers mais ke vous chele vie voellies ordener et monstrer avoeques, si comme autre roy ont fait en tans de guerre.

Au coumenchement cascuns Archeveskes et eveskes aient XII chevaus, IIII clers et IIII escuiers, desquel cascuns ara de sen Seigneur une reube par an, et leur seigneur III, et nient plus. Li dras ke li eveske usera soit de le valeur de IIIs l'aune, des clers IIs et VId l'aune, et des escuiers IIs l'aune et nient plus.

Item, ke toutes les dames du roiaume d'Engleterre se tiegnent a leur reubes ke eles ont, et ke cascun an eles aient une reube de IIIs l'aune ausi comme li eveske et li chevalier ont, et nient plus.

Item, tant comme an mengier des archeveskes et eveskes il aient II mes de char an diner, l'un quit en yaue et l'autre en rost. Au souper 1 mes de char rostie et nient plus, et au premier mes, il aient chervoise à boire, et au second vin, au souper cherevoise sans vin.

Item, ke nus archeveskes, eveskes, contes, barons ne riches hom ne faichent nul genuer aus feste ni doignent a mengier à nului, si ne soit a gent ki soient leur ostes ke il herberguent avoec aus, et soient pris en le maniere devant dite.

Item, ke notres sires li rois, contes, barons et toute maniere de gent tienent et tenir fachent de mengier et de boire et de restaure tant comme le were dure.

Item, ke chascuns escuiers et chevaliers ki aient XXX livres de rente aient cheval et soient varni d'armes.

Item, ke chascuns bourgois et franc hom ki ait de biens à le valeur de Vc marcs d'estellins aient kevel et soient varni d'armes.

Item, cascun markeant Lombart et li autre estraine paieront volontiers pour cascun sac à laine de l'euvre et pour cascun lest de quir, V marcs.

Item, de toutes markeandises entrans en le tere ou isans hors de le tere d'Engleterre, ke on pait de cascun XXs, XIId du vendour a maintenir le were.

Item, de toutes markeandises vendues dedens le roiaume soit paiè pour cascuns XXs du vendeur, IId a maintenir le were.

Item, pour cascun quartier de fourment vendu soit paié du vendeur IIId, de l'orge IId, du soille IId, de l'avaine Id, des fêves Id, des pois Id, du mestellou Id, a maintenir le were.

Item, de cascun buef et de cascune vake paie du vendeur IIIId, pour porc IId, pour mouton IId, pour veel IId.

Item, ke tout markeant estraine puisent venir et markeander sain et sauf par tout le roiaume d'Engleterre, paiant leur droiture devant dit hormis chiaux du roiaume de Franche ou ke il soient en were contre le roiaume d'Englletterre ou en tains de were contre nostre sener le roi.

Et puis ke li estraine marcheant voelent aide à le were maintenir, bien le doivent voloir et soutenir les gens du roiaume d'Engleterre, et ke nostres sires li rois voelle aidier et grase faire à tous ses chevaliers et esquiers, ki serout en sen serviche en le were du roiaume, soient respitië de leuer detes, tante comme il seront en le were hor du roiaaume, et sachies, Sire se vous voles hastierment faire l'ordounanche de le laine, pourche ke li tans aproche, ke l'ordonnanche plaira bien as markeans estraines de paier V. marcs pour le sac : vous en vares avantage dedens VI. mois CX. mille marcs, mais ke vos gent de levier vous voellent aidier passer à tous de markeans.

D.—Referred to at p. 331; from Arch : du roy : J. 1024 Suppl : au Trés : des Chartes.

A tot ceus qi cest escrit vrunt u arunt Richard par la grace de Deu Roy des Romeins tot jors cressaunt salut en Deu. Sache vostre universites nos estre tenut à Madame Aleanor nostre soer contesse de Leycestre, à tot ses enfaunt et a tote lor gent à estre lor leal ami et enterin et lor serom eydannt e conseylant à tot nostre poer à lor dreyture porchacer en Engleterre et à totes lor besoynes fere envers totes gent sauve la foy nostre Seyneur le rey de Engleterre e la mon seur Edward soen fiul, et de ce volons à nostre Senor e leaument promectons a fere luy nostre lectre overte dedent les octaves de la Seint Michel prechein suannt, e de ce fere luy baylom en pleage not honorables peres en Deu Walter par la grace de Deu evesque de Wirecestre e Roger evesque de Cester, e mon seur Warin de Bassingeburne, qi par not prieres en cest escrit unt mis lor seaus. Donné en la priore de Kenilwerthe le Dimeinche prechein avant la feste de la Nativité Nostre dame en l'an du rengne le Rey quarante nevime.

Traces of three seals appended.

E.—Referred to at p. 334. From the Registres de Champagne, Vols. IV. and V. p. 474, Art. 8.

Eschivardus de Chabenes, Comes de Bigorre et Icedanus frater ejus Simoni de Monteforti comiti Leycestriæ—quod dominus Gaston Bearnensis devastavit nobis totam terram, et nos non possumus defendere—damus totum Comitatum Bigorre cum pertinenciis suis bono animo et spontanea voluntate quia magis volumus quod vos habeatis et vestri quam extranei—Datum Tarbe in Transfiguratione Domini in camera episcopi, anno domini Millo. CCo. LVIo.

Esquinardus de Chabanes, Comes Bigorre dedimus et concessimus et hac presenti carta confirmamus bono animo et nostra spontanea voluntate domino Simoni de Monte Forti Comiti Leycestriæ karissimo avunculo nostro et hæredibus suis et assignatis totum Comitatum nostrum Bigorre et S. Chanzon et Montem de Marchan et Vicecomitatum de Marchan cum omnibus pertinenciis suis, quia magis volumus quod dominus Simon et hæredes et assignati sui habeant et teneant prædictum Comitatum una cum terris prædictis et omnibus suis pertinenciis quam inimici nostri a quibus expediri comitatum nostrum et terras prænominatas defendere non possumus, promittens pro nobis et hæredibus nostris præfato Simoni et hæredibus et assignatis hanc donationem et concessionem ac præsentis cartæ confirmationem juramento corporaliter præstito nullis temporibus nec ullo modo vanire presumamus, et ad majorem securitatem sigillo venerabilis patris domini Episcopi Lincolniensis una cum sigillo nostro præsentem cartam procuravimus calceari. Datum in Parisiis in festo beatæ Ceciliæ Virginis, 1258.

A tous ceux qui cet ecrit verront et arront, Symons de Montfort, fils et heritier monseigneur Simon de Montfort Comte de Leycestre salut. Sachiez que je donne et ottroie pour moi et mes heritiers à noble et cher Seigneur Thiebault par la grace de Dieu Roy de Navarré et Comte de Champagne et à ses heritiers le chastle de Lourde et ses appartenances et tout le droit que nous avons ou avoir pouvons en le Comté de Bigorre, le quel Conté' le devant dit Comte mon pere dou don et dou grant mon Seigneur Eschivat de Chabannes, avant le comte de Bigorre, et pour ce que je veuil que cest mon don et grant soit ferme et establie en tous jours, en temoins de ce je ai mis mon scel à cet escrit qui fut fest au mois d'Ottobre, l'an Notre Seigneur mil deux cenz sexante et cinc.

There is a similar deed sealed by Eleanor Countess of Leycester, of the same date. William, Bishop of Le Puy, claimed Bigorre as held of his see, and took it into custody on behalf of Thiebault in 1267, in order to protect it from the suits of the King of England, and of Esquivat de Chabannes.

F. p. 220, Note 4.—It has occurred to me that the siege of Tonbridge, to which the passage cited from the Hundred Rolls refers, might be considered the early one of May 1 (see p. 209). I therefore quote the following additional entry : " Et quod dominus Gilbertus comes de Clare cepit de hundredo de Faversham XV. libras pro insultatione castri de Tunnee'gge (sic) quam fecerunt per districtionem domini Johannis de la Hay et dum comes fuit cum domino Rege." John de la Hay was an eminent baronial partisan ; and the only time which unites the two conditions of his holding a command in Kent, and the Earl of Hertford being in the King's company with the view to reduce Tonbridge, is the occasion of the return from Lewes to London. The fines which the Earl's bailiffs levied seem to have been for insufficient musters or late appearance in the field, and are repeatedly complained of.—Rotuli Hundredorum, I. pp. 206, 208, 209, 210, 211. P.

G.—Mr Blaauw had begun collecting materials for a catalogue of the partisans of the Barons. He had transcribed from the Inquisitiones de Rebellibus, preserved in the Records of the Tower, all that relate to Sussex. But he ended by striking them out; feeling, I have no doubt, that the evidence they give is insufficient, as they only show that certain lands were occupied upon different persons, who are not, however, described as "rebelles" or "inimici regis," and may have suffered for a lord's fault or by an act of usurpation. He, however, left uncancelled letters 84, 398, 399, and 406, from the Tower records; and these, which contain from 50 to 100 names of Royalists or rebels, I have used with advantage in the subjoined lists, though I have not always been able to identify the persons alluded to.

Our chief sources for the personal history of the war, are the Chronicles, such as Rishanger and Wykes, supplemented by lists of names like those printed in the Appendix to Rishanger; certain lists of "Rebelles" in the Calendarium Genealogicum, e. g. pp. 175, 246; lawsuits for the restitution of property in the Abbreviatio Placitorum, and the facts of all kinds collected by Dugdale in the Baronage. All this evidence is more or less doubtful and difficult. Our chroniclers and clerks were not very studious of orthography. The two Royalists of note who fell at Evesham are called in a MS. copied by Stow (Harl. 542), Hugo Stragmiles and Adam de Ridmallis, and in the Miracula Simonis de Montfort, appear as Hugo de Troiâ and Adam de Ridmark. I cannot doubt that the same names are intended, but cannot identify either person, unless the first be a Hugo le Strang or L'Estrange, miles, and the second an Adam de Ridware who held part of two fees on William de Percy's property. The rebels in the Calendar were men of landed property which the Crown had declared forfeit: but even with this assistance I cannot recover several of their names. In the Abbreviatio Placitorum cases of forcible entry, robbery, and usurpation of lands during the civil war are very numerous; but except where we get clear evidence that the aggressor was in arms against the King, or the sufferer a Royalist, I have not inserted their names. There can be little doubt that every county had men like the Earl of Derby, who saw nothing in the great conflict of King and people but an opportunity for private plunder and revenge.

Nevertheless, for the great nobility of the kingdom, the Earls and Barons, the evidence is on the whole sufficient, and an analysis of it will, I think, throw some light on the war. In the year 1264 there were twelve great English Earls. Deducting, however, from these the King's brother, half-brother and son, there were only nine who could be said to represent the independent baronage: and even of these the Royalist de Warenne was the King's second cousin, and the Royalist Earl of Hereford descended through his grandmother from a bastard of Henry I. The Royalist Earl of Warwick had been bought over by his earldom in 1263. The six Earls who espoused the popular side might, therefore, fairly claim to speak for the whole English nobility.

The English barons had by this time dwindled down from 206, their number altogether in John's reign, to 161. Of these we can identify 50 as certainly, and nine as probably, Royalist: 59 as certainly, and five as probably, insurgent: and eight as precluded by age or infirmity from taking part. Of 30 we know little or nothing. At first sight these numbers appear to show that the kingdom was pretty evenly divided, but that the barons had a slight majority. As, however, every insurgent had to compound after Evesham for his estates, the chances are that few, if any, have escaped notice; and I suspect accordingly that the King had in fact a small majority. There are considerations, however, more important than the mere adding up of names. Nothing will serve better as a rough test of the military and political strength of either side than the number of castles its partisans owned. Now the Royalist Earls had 30, the insurgent Earls only 19; the Royalist barons 38, and the insurgents only 22 or 24. It must be remembered that the King still had many castles in his own hands; Rochester and Dover, for instance, though given up to parliamentary seneschals in 1258, were held for him in 1264. Others, like Windsor and Bristol, had never been parted with; and *some, like those attached to the earldoms of Devon and Albemarle, were in his care during a minority. The result was that he could choose counties like Kent and Sussex—where almost every man was against him, but where he held almost every strong place—for the base of his operations.

The local distribution of the two causes is, on the whole, very clearly marked. If we take a line skirting the western boundaries of Hampshire, Berkshire, Oxfordshire, Warwickshire and Derbyshire, the country to the east is baronial, to the west and north Royalist. I believe the main reason of this to have been that the eastern portion includes London and the chief commercial parts of the kingdom, which suffered more from Henry's misrule, and Oxford, where the scholars were almost unanimous against him; whilst the west and north were inhabited by a martial nobility who were too distant and too formidable to be oppressed, and to whom a war on the commercial districts was eminently acceptable. But there is no doubt the personal influence of the great nobles had something to do with the difference. The Earls of Leicester, Norfolk, Hertford, Lincoln, Oxford and Derby carried with them the minor nobility and gentry of the counties in which their castles and estates were, and the sprinkling of west country names on the Barons' side is, I suspect, chiefly attributable to the fact that the Earl of Hertford was also Earl of Gloucester, and that young Humphry de Bohun and John FitzJohn took part heartily for De Montfort. Altogether, however, the district I have indicated contributed 41 out of 59 barons to the constitutional cause, and only 18 out of 50 to the Royalist. Even of these 18 two were notoriously bought over by the King.

ROYALIST EARLS.

Edward, Earl of Chester[1], having the castles of Chester, Lancaster, Diganwy, Caer Vaelan, Rhuddlan, Beeston, Newcastle-under-Line, Shrewsbury, Bridgenorth, Richmond, and Tickhill.

Richard, Earl of Cornwall, having the castles of Restormel, Tintagol, Mere (in Wilts), Okehampton, Berkhampstead, Wallingford and Knaresborough.

William de Valence, Earl of Pembroke, having the castles of Goodrich, Kilgaran and Hertford.

John de Warenne, Earl of Surrey, having the castles of Lewes, Reigate, Conisborough, Sandal, Stamford, Dinas Bran, and Leones. From a case recorded in the Abbrev. Placit. p. 168, this Earl

---

[1] For proof of Edward's Earldom see Ormerod's Cheshire, I. p. 423. New Rymer, I. p. 423. Dugdale's Baronage, I. p. 46. Rishanger Chron. p. 20. Brut y Tywysogion, A. 1263.

APPENDIX. 367

seems at one time to have been Baronial, and procured a pardon accordingly.

Humphrey de Bohun, Earl of Hereford and Essex, having Caldecot castle. He was Royalist at Lewes, but in the Barons' army at Evesham.

William Mauduit, Earl of Warwick, of Warwick castle.

The families of Redvers of Devon and Fortibus of Albemarle were represented at this time by a minor, Aveline. The Dowager Countesses made a little private war on one another during the troubles, and Isabella de Fortibus seems to have leaned to the Baronial side. Abbrev. Placit. pp. 160, 173. But the castles of the two families were probably in the King's hands. They were, for Devon, Plympton and Carisbrook; for Albemarle, Cockermouth, Skipton, and Skipsea.

INSURGENT EARLS.

Simon de Montfort, Earl of Leicester, having the castles of Kenilworth and Odiham.

Gilbert de Clare, Earl of Gloucester and Hertford, having the castles of Tonbridge, Hanley, Monmouth, Usk, Caerleon and Trogy.

Roger Bigod, Earl of Norfolk, having the castles of Framlingham and Strigul.

Henry de Lacy, Earl of Lincoln, having the castles of Pontefract, Clithero, Halton and Denbigh.

Robert de Vere, Earl of Oxford, having the castles of Castle Camps and Hedingham.

Robert de Ferrars, Earl of Derby, having the castles of Peak, Tutbury and Chartley.

NEUTRAL.

Peter de Dreux, Earl of Richmond, being also Duke of Brittany, took no part in English politics.

ROYALIST BARONS.

William Aguillon of Portingeres castle, *Suss.* and *Surr.*
James Alditheley or Audley of Audley castle, *Staff.*
Eustace de Balliol of *Durham, Cumb.* and *West.*
John de Balliol of Barnard and Fotheringay castles.
William Bardolf of *Linc., Norf.* and *Suss.*
Philip Basset of Wycombe, *Bucks.*

Warine de Bassingbourne of Benefeld castle in *Northants*.
John Beauchamp of Hacche in *Somerset*.
William Beauchamp of Elmley castle.
Nicholas de Bolteby of *Northumb*.
Ralf de Boteler of Oversley castle, *Warw*.
William de Braose (called of Gower), of Bramber and Knapp castles.
Peter Brus of Skelton and Kendall castles.
Robert Brus of Lochmaban castle in Scotland.
John de Burg[1], senior, of *Norfolk*, of Asshe in *Hants*, and of *Som.*, *Northants*, *Ess.* and *Herts*.
Pain Chaworth of *Glouc*.
Roger de Clifford of Clifford and Corfham castles.
John Comyn of Badenoch, of Crigelton and Galloway castles in Scotland.
Thomas Corbet of *Salop*.
William le Deneys of *Somers*.
Oliver de Dynan of *Dev*.
John FitzAlan of Arundel, Whitchurch, Clun and Shrawarden castles.
Reginald FitzHerbert or FitzPeter of *Glouc.*, *Salop*, *Here.*, *Wales*, &c.
Fulk FitzWarren of Whittington castle.
Peter de Genevil of Ludlow castle.
John de Grey of *Der.* and *Notts*.
Walter de Grey of Rotherfield, *York* and *Linc*.
William de Greystoke of *Cumb*.
Hamo L'Estrange of *Salop*.
Roger Leybourn of Leybourn castle, *Kent*.
Philip Marmion of *Leic.* and *Warw*.
Roger de Merley of Morpeth castle.
Hugh de Mortimer of Ricard's castle.
Roger de Mortimer of Wigmore and Radnor castles.
Geoffrey de Neville of Hornby castle and of *York.*, *Lanc.*, *Linc*.

[1] John de Burg, senior, was made Sheriff of Norfolk by the Barons after the battle of Lewes. As, however, he obtained redress after Evesham for injuries sustained during the war, I think he must have been ostensibly Royalist. New Rymer, I. p. 442. A. P. p. 157.

APPENDIX. 369

Robert de Neville[1] of Brancepeth and Raby castles.
Henry de Percy of *Northants, Sur.* and *Suss.*
Ralph de Ribald[1] of Middleham.
Robert de St. John[2] of Basing.
Peter de Savoy of Pevensey castle.
William de Say of *Kent* and *Norf.*
Roger de Someri of Dudley and Welagh (*Worces.*) castles.
Robert de Stuteville of *Warw.*
Robert de Tattershall[3] of Tattershall castle (*Linc.*), and Buckenham castle, *Norf.*
Roger de Tony of Kirtling castle (*Camb.*), and Castle Maud in the Welsh Marches.
Gilbert de Umfraville[4] of Prudhoe and Harbottle castles.
John of Vaux, or de Vallibus, of *Norf., Northants* and *Suff.*
John de Verdon[4] of Brandon castle, *Warw.*
Robert Waleran of Kilpec castle.
Alan de la Zouch of *Leicest.*

To this list we may probably add, Robert Bertram of Bothale (*Northumb.*), who got seisin of his lands soon after Evesham: Roger de Chandos of Snodhill castle, *Here.*, whose son had livery in 1265-6: John de Courtenay of *Devon, Dorset,* &c., who was made governor of Totness in 1261-2: Robert FitzJohn or Clavering of *Northumb.*, son of a Balliol and ward of Will. de Valence: John FitzHerbert of *Sussex*, a royal surety: William Paganel of Carlton, *York*, whose lands were restored him in 1260: Geoffrey de Scales of *Essex*, whose younger son Thomas was Royalist, Abbrev. Plac. 177: Ralph de Sudley of *Herefordshire;* a royal governor in 1269, and connected with the Beauchamps of *Elmley:* Gilbert Talbot of *Glouc.* and *Here.*, a Royalist governor in 1269, and grandson of Basset of Wycombe.

---

[1] Ralf de Ribald, with his two sons-in-law Robert de Neville and Robert de Tattershall, was Royalist at first, but made his peace with the barons after Lewes.
[2] I insert Robert de St John as Royalist because he was allowed to fortify in 1260, and was made governor of Porchester in 1266.
[3] See note 1, preceding page.
[4] Gilbert de Umfraville and John de Verdon seem to have been for a time on the Barons' side. Dugdale's Baronage, I. p. 505. Abbrev. Plac. p. 167.

INSURGENT BARONS.

Giles of Argentine of *Camb., Ess., Herts* and *Hunts.*
Thomas de Astley of *Warw., Leic.* and *Northants.*
John de Balun of *Here.* and *Glouc.*
William Bardolf of *Linc., Norf.* and *Northants.*
Ralph Basset of Drayton.
Ralph Basset of Sapercote.
John Beauchamp of Bedford.
Maurice Berkeley of Berkeley castle.
Roger Bertram of Mitford castle, *Northumb.*
William de Blund of *Norf., Suff., Ess.* and *Beds.*
Humphrey de Bohun of Hay, Huntington, Brecknock and (?) Hereford castles.
Ralph de Camoys of *Camb., Hunts, Northants,* &c.
Walter de Colevil of *York, Leicest., Rut.,* &c.
Robert de Crevequer of *Kent.*
William de Criketot of *Suffolk.*
Nicholas de Cryoll of *Kent.*
Norman D'Arcy of *Linc.*
Hugh le Despenser of *Rut., Ess., Northants., Beds,* &c.
William Devereux or De Ebroicis (?) of Lenhall castle, *Here.*
Walter de Dunstanvill of Salop and Wilts.
Henry Engaine of *Hunts.* and *Northants.*
John de Eyvill of Hod castle, *York.*
John FitzJohn or FitzGeoffrey of Evyas Lacy castle, and of *Bucks.*
Robert FitzPayne of *Somer., Dors., Wilts,* &c.
Robert FitzWalter of Baynard's castle.
Gerard de Furnivall of Wardon, *Northants.*
Gilbert de Gaunt of *Linc.,* &c.
John Giffard of Brinsfield and St Briavel's? castles.
Richard de Grey of *Leices.*
Henry de Hastings of Bolsover castle.
Henry Hoese or Hussey of *Suss.*
Roger de Huntingfield of *Suf.*
John L'Estrange of Ruton castle.
Robert L'Isle of Rougemont, *Beds.*

Geoffrey de Lucy of *Hants, Kent, Sur.* and *Suss.*
Roger Luvetot of Derby and Notts.
Robert Marmion, *Linc.*
Geoffrey de Mandevill of Mershwood, *Wilts.*
Robert de Mandevill of Mershwood, *Wilts.*
William W. Marescal of *Norf., Linc.* and *Somer.*
William Marmion of *Suff.*
William de Monchensy of *Norf., Northants.,* and *Ess.*
Roger de Montalt of Rising and Mold castles.
Peter de Montfort of Beaudesert and Henley-in-Arden castles.
Thomas de Multon of Egremont and *Linc.*
Hugh de Nevill of Stoke Courcy castle.
John de Nevill of Notts.
Adam de Newmarch, *Linc.* and *York.*
Henry de Pomeroy of Devon.
Robert de Ros of Belvoir castle.
Roger de St John of Oxon.
Nicholas de Segrave of Warw. and Leices.
John de Stutevill of Derby.
Richard de Tany of *Ess.* and *Herts.*
Robert de Tregoz of Evyas Harold castle.
John de Vesci of Alnwick castle.
Robert de Vipont of Appleby and Burgh castles.
Baldwin Wake of *York* and *Cumb.*
Walter de Wayvill or Wahull, *Beds.*

In conjunction with this list we may perhaps notice, William de Beauchamp of Chalveston or Eton in *Beds*, who was made sheriff after Lewes (see however, p. 379); Thomas de Clinton of Warwickshire, whose second son, John, was an insurgent; Gilbert Peche of Brunne, two of whose brothers were on the Barons' side, and Robert Valoins of Suffolk, whose uncle, William le Blund, fell fighting against the King at Lewes. Dugdale thinks that Henry Lovel of Castle Cary was connected with the eminent rebel, John Lovel; and two other Lovels, Robert and Thomas, were among the garrison of Kenilworth.

MINORS, AGED, INFIRM, OR OUT OF ENGLAND.

Stephen de Bayeux of *Linc.*, *Somers.* and *Dors.* If alive, seventy-five years of age.

George Cantilupe of Abergavenny and Kilgaran castles. Only thirteen years old in 1265. (Compare Annals of Dunstaple, p. 257, and Calend. Geneal. p. 197.)

Henry Delaval of Seaton in Northumb. was over 60 in 1258.

Hugh FitzRalph of Notts and Derby was probably an old man, as he had been a governor of royal castles in 1235.

Thomas de Furnivall of Derby and Notts. Probably on pilgrimage or dead.

Robert de Ghisnes had sold his lands in Northants, and probably was no longer counted in the English baronage.

Robert de Gresley of Manchester was a minor.

Geoffrey de Luterell was mad.

UNACCOUNTED FOR.

Richard Basset of Weldon in *Northants.*

Walter Bek of Eresby.

Philip de Columbers of Staway in *Somerset.*

Hugh and Stephen de Cressie of *Norf.* and *Suff.*

Maurice de Croune of Surrey.

Philip D'Albini of Berks.

Edmund D'Eyncourt of *Notts.*

Richard de Dover of Chilham castle in *Kent.* (This pedigree is in hopeless confusion. The family descended from a bastard of King John, but John de Chilham was on the Barons' side.)

Henry FitzRandolf of *Northumb.*

Ralph de Gaugi of *Northumb.*

Robert de Gurney of *Gloucest.*, &c.

Henry or John de Heriz of *Notts.*

William Heron of *Northumb.*

William de Keynes of *Dorset.*

Philip de Kyme of *Kesteven.*

Henry de Longchamp of *Hants.* (He had married a Heringod, and two of that name were in the rebellion.)

Henry de L'Orti of *Devon* and *Cornwall.*

Matthew de Lerainc.

APPENDIX. 373

Nicholas Martin of *Devon* and *Som.*
William or Simon de Montacute.
Peter de Mauley of *Yorkshire.* His father had been godfather to Prince Edward.
Nicholas Moels of Cadbury.
John de Mohun of *Somerset* and *Devon.*
Roger de Mowbray[1] of Bedford castle and *York.*
Ralph Musard of Musardere castle, *Derb.* and *Gloucest.*
Peter de Scoteni of *Linc.*
William le Scrope of Bolton.
Robert de Stafford of *Staff.* married a daughter of the Royalist, Thomas Corbet.
Reginald de Valletort of Trematon castle.
John de Wolverton of Bucks.

A list of the gentry who fought on either side must obviously be very imperfect. Only a few were important enough to be named by the chroniclers, and the remainder are chiefly known to us by the list of confiscations. England probably contained at this time some twelve thousand men who had taken out their knighthood, or might be compelled to do so; and it is reasonable to assume that half of these took part in the war. Nevertheless I cannot account for more than from 390 to 400 names, and out of these less than 100 are of royalists. Still I think we may assume that these names fairly represent the distribution of the different sides, and their evidence is unmistakeable. On the king's side more than half (about 50 out of about 100) come from the North, West, or South-West, though no names from the Counties Palatine of Cheshire and Cornwall are included; and though the other half of England must have contained two-thirds of the population. On the Baronial side (omitting more than 30 names which I cannot identify) more than 220 belong to the Eastern, South-Eastern, or Midland Counties; less than 40 to the Northern, Western, or South-Western. Northamptonshire, Kent, and Sussex contribute in more than their due proportion to the constitutional cause; no doubt because those counties were especially the theatre of war.

[1] As Roger de Mowbray died in 1266, in the Isle of Axholme, it may be that he was killed in a skirmish of the times when the barons fortified it. In this case he was probably Royalist, as his widow and heirs were not impaired in estate. But his father William had died there.

London was dealt with separately, and only supplies one or two names, as of Stephen Bukerel, to my list.

ROYALIST GENTRY.

* A little uncertain. † Professedly royalist but of doubtful fidelity. County not quite certain. A.P. Abbreviatio Placitorum.

Robert de Amundeville*. *Dur.* Ralf de Ardern and his father. *War.* Walter de Audrey*. *Dur.* Hugh of Balliol. *Dur.* William Bagot. *Staff.* and *Sal.* Anselm de Basset†. *Som.* Thomas Berkeley. *Glou.* Hugh le Bigot. *Yor.* Three or four sons of William Beauchamp. *Wor.* John Bechhampton. *Wil.* William de Berwick†. *Som.* William de Borham. *Ess.* John de Bolemer. *Norf.* Henry de Bracton. *Dev.* Richard de Braham. *Bed.* Robert de Briwes. *Norf.* and *Lin.* Walter Bryndebere? *Bed.* Henry de Burewhull. *Norf.* and *Welsh Marches.* Robert le Bygod. *Sus.* William de Chaeny. *Camb.* or *Welsh Marches.* Robert le Chamberlain. *Hants.* Walter de Caple. *Glouc.* and *Wor.* Patric Chaworth. *Glou.* Robert de Cheny. *Welsh Marches?* Geoffrey de Chesewyk. *Kent.* Roger de Clifford, Junior. *Her.* William la Cousche. *Camb.*

William de Ecchynge*. A. P. 177. ? same as William de Etling. New Rymer, I. p. 455. *Welsh Marches.* Hugh of Elencourt. *Glou.* and *Wor.*

Charles Fitz-Charles? *Sus.* Marmaduke Fitz-Geoffrey*. *Dur.* Robert Fitz-Pain. *Dev. Dor. Wil.* &c. Ralf Fitz-Ralf. *Northern.* Ralf Fitz-Ranulf. *Norf.* and *Northern.*

Adam de Gesemue. *Northern.* William de Gouiz. *Dor.* Matthew de Gamages. *Welsh Marches.* Osbert Gifford, *Oxon.* Gilbert Hansard. *Dur.* Simon de Halle. *Norf.* and *Welsh Marches.* Henry de Henfeld. *Leic.* Robert de Hilton*. *Dur. Yor.* John of Hirlawe. *Nthumb.* Robert de Hovel. *Suf.* William de Hugeford. *Sal.*

Adam de Kidmallis, or Ridmark. ? de Ridware. *York.* William de Lafford, senior. *Bed.* Geoffrey de Langley. *War.* Nicholas de Leukenor. *Mid.* and *Ess.* Robert and Roger Le Strange. *Sal.* Hugo Le Strange?, or Hugo de Trojâ, of a London family of that name.

APPENDIX. 375

John de Mautravers. *Dor.* William de Mautravers. *Dor.* and *Berks.* Stephen de Meinill. *Northern.* Robert de Mere.* *Som.* A. P. p. 173. Walter de Merton. *Sur.* and *Norf.* Roger de Mules. *Dev.* John Mussegros. *Glou.* and *Som.* William de Napford, or Nafford. *War.* Peter de Neville. *Nthants.* and *Leic.* John Norman. *Ess.*

John Paynel. *Berks.* Robert Pierpoint. *Linc.* and *Notts.* ? Alan Plukenet. *Here.* Hugh de Percy. *Sur.* and *Sus.* Geoffrey le Salar. *Suss.* ? Ralf le Sauser. *Mid.* John le Sauvage. *Sus.* Thomas de Scalars. *Herts.* Alice de Scales. *Camb.* William de St Omer. *Her.* and *Wor.* A. P. 160. William de Stenesby. *Sus.* ? William de Suwell. *Sus.* ? A. P. 177.

Roger de Torny. *Yor.* John, Hugh and Robert de Turberville. *Welsh Marches.* Marmaduke and Richard de Tweng. *Yor.* Robert Tybetot. *Yor.* and *Dev.*

Roger and William de Whelton. *Beds.* A. P. 169. William de Wilton. *Kent.*

Henry la Zouche. *Herts.* and *Bed.* William and Yvo la Zouche. *Eastern* or *Midland* ?

BARONIAL GENTRY.

William de Albaniaco. *Glou.* Henry de Albemare. Richard de Amundevill. *Salop. Sus. Wilts.* William Angevin. James de Appelby*. *Linc.* ? *Dev.* Edmund of Ardern. *War.* ? Thomas de Ardern. *War.* Nicholas le Archer. *Nthants.* Ralf, Roger, and Thomas de Arcy. *Linc.* Reginald de Argentein. *Ess. Camb.* &c. William de Arundel. Ralf de Arundel ? *Cornwall.* Guncelin de Badlesmere. *Kent.* Ingelram de Baillol. *Leic.* Roger de Balun. *Nthants.* Walter de Barkeswille, prob. same as Walter de Baskerville. *Her.* and *Sal.* John of Bath. *Berks. Herts. Oxon.* &c. Guy Baysselle ? same as Guydo Brussell. John de Becclesangar. *Kent.* John de Belham : Monachus. Henry and Richard de Berham. *Ess.* ? John de Beufo. *Linc.* or *Norf.* ? Henry de Beyville. *Dor.* Roger le Bigot. *Yor.* or *Linc.* ? Philip de Blakemore. *Dev.* Andrew le Blund. *Ess.* ? Simon de Bodiham. *Here.* John of Bodiham. *Linc.* John de Bohun. *Glou.* John, brother of Francy de Bohun. *Sus.* Richard de Borard. *Linc.?* Harvey de Boreham. *Ess.* Nicholas de Bosco. John de Boseville. *Suff.* Reginald de Bottreaux. *War.* Peter de Bourton. J. Boxcrisse. William de Boytune. *Suff.* John de Bracebridge. *War.?* Thomas de Bray. *Bucks.* R. de Brocton. *Sal.* Bernard de Brus. *Hunts.* or *Rut.* Guydo Brussell. *Norf.* Stephen Bukerel. *Mid.* Robert Burdet. *Leic.* John de Burgh, junior. *Nthants,* &c. W. de Burmugham. *Bucks.* Robert Butevilayn. *Notts. Bed.* and *Linc.?*

William Camerarius (prob. Chamberlain of Hants. ?). Nicholas de Cantilupe. *Nthants.* Nicholas Carrok. *Kent.* Richard de Casterton. *Rut.?* John of Caston. *Camb.* Gregory and Hugh de Caudewelle. *? Here.* William de la Cene. *?* de Chen. *Linc.* Robert Chadde. John de Chilham. *Kent.* John de Chokesfeld or Clakesfeld. *Kent.* Thomas de Clare, *Glou.,* latterly royalist. Walter le Clerk. *Nthants.* John de Clinton. *War.* Richard de Cnolle. Galfridus Cocus. *Wilts.* Philip de Colevile. *Camb.* or *Nthants.* Hugo de Coleworth. *Nthants.* Fulk Constable. *York.?* Richard Corbet. *Hunts.* and *Nthants.* Robert Corbet. *Sal.* Richard de Corpestey. *Sus.* Philip de Covel. *Linc.?* Henry de Cramanvile. *Kent. Ess.* and *Suff.* John and Walter de Cranford. *Nthants.* Walter de Crepping. *Ess.* Richard de Crevequer. *Kent.* Robert de Crevequer. *Kent.* Bertram del Criel. *Kent.* Laurence del Crok. Thomas de Cronesley. *Leic.* Alan de Crowethorne. Geoffrey de Crulefeld. *Hants.* Richard de Culworth. *Ess.* John de Cumbe, of John de la Haye's household. Robert de Cumden.

Philip de Daventre. *Hunt.* and *Beds.?* Philip de Dayvill or Sayvill. *Yor.* See *Eyvill.* John le Despenser. *Leic.* and *Linc.* Geoffrey de Donham. *Linc.* John de Dovor. *Hunt.* and *Ess.* Philip de Doyly. *Linc.* Hugh de Dunster. *Suff.* John de Dykelinge. *Ess.* John de Dyne. *Oxon.* Ralf de Dyvâ. *Oxon.*

Gilbert Einefeld. *Mid.?* Gilbert de Ellesfeld. *Oxon* and *Berks.* John of Estregate. *Mid.* John Esturmy. *Suf.* Richard Everard. *Suf.* Henry and William de Eyvill. *Yor.*

W. de Ferrariis. *Rut.* Henry Fitz-Aucher. *Wilts.* Robert Fitz-Nicholas. *Sus.* Robert Fitz-Nigel[1]. *Berks* and *Bucks.*

---

[1] Robert Fitz-Nigel (killed at Evesham) was heir of Agnes Basset, and perhaps therefore connected with Basset of Wycombe. *Calend. Geneal.* I. p. 43. See p. 153, note 1.

APPENDIX. 377

Simon Fitz-Simon[1]. *Bed.* Eustace de Foleville. *Leic.* and *Linc.* Henry le Fonun, Constable of Odiham. A. P. 175. William de Furnivall. *Nthants.* and *Notts.* John Genevile. *Here.* William de Cterstone. *Kent.* Osbert Giffard. *Som. Dev.* and *Oxon.*; changed sides. Hugo Gobyun. *Leic.* and *Bed.* Turgis de Godwineston. *Kent.* ? Walter de Gloves. *Bed.* or *Leic.* ? W. de Goldington. *Norf.* Brian de Gorvâ. *Leic.* Robert de Gotely. *Sus.* Hugo de Graham. John de Grey. *Leic.* Richard de Grey. *Kent.* Adam Gurdon. *Hants.* John de Gurney. *Nthants.* Brian de Guwiz. *Dor. Som.* W. de Gyleford. *Sur.* ?
John de Habñ. Ralf Haquet. *Bucks.* and *Worc.* William de Harecurte. *Oxon.* Saer de Harcourt. *Leic.* Robert de Hardres. *Kent.* Wil. de Hardreshill. *Lin.* and *Nthants.* Henry de Hastings. *Leic.* Matthew de Hesting or Hasting. *Kent. Sus.* Nicholas de Hautlo. *Camb.*? Richard and John de Havering. *Hants.* Richard de Havering. *Dor.* John de la Haye. *Lin. Nthants. Kent. Sus.* and *Glou.* Thomas de Heyham. *Kent.* Richard de Hemyngton. *Norf.* Simon Herin. *Norf.*? Ralf de Heryngot. *Sur.* William Heringod. *Kent.* Thomas de Hestelee. ? Astley: see p. 369. Philip de Heymile. ? Hay, miles. Hugh de Hopville. Roger de la Hyde. *Nthants.*
Robert de Irland. *Sus.*
Andrew de Jarpenvill. *Bucks.*
Ralf Kaket: see Haket. William de Kekewell. *Sus.* Richard de Kemsing. *Kent* ? the same as Richard, Rector of Kemsing. *Kent.* John Kyriel. *Kent.*
William de Lacu. *Staf.* William de Lafford, junior. *Bed. Leic.* and *War.* Walter de Lecton. *Camb.* William of Leicester: Clericus. Michael of Lenham. *Kent* ? *Sus.*? John de la Lind. *Linc. Sus.* Robert de L'Isle. *Lin. Norf.* and *Suf.* Walter de London: Clericus. Henry de Longchamp. *Hants.* Robert Lovel. *Dur.* John Lovel. *Nthants. Camb. Hunts.* and *Wilts.* See Luvel. Robert de Lusches. *Oxon.* John Luvel. *Oxon.* Robert Luvel. J. Luvel. *Norf.* William de Lymar. *Leic.* John de Lymonges. *Kent* or *Nthants.*

---

[1] "Qui primo vexillum erexit contra regem Henricum." MS. quoted in Rishanger, p. 125.

Robert Maloree. *Linc.* or *Yor.*? Henry de Manneston. H. de la Mare. *Oxon.* William Martell. *Leic.* John and William de Maundeville. *Som. Dur.* and *Wilts.* Thomas Maunsel. *Bucks.* or *Kent*? William Melker de Stoke. Thomas de Moland (Molendinis). *Mid.*? Sampson de Moles. ? de Mule : see. *Surr.* Roger de Monteny. *Camb. Norf.* and *Suf.* Simon, Henry, Guy, Amalric and Richard de Montfort. *Leic.* Robert de Montfort. *War.* William de Montefort. Jordan de Moulton. *Linc.* John de Mucegros, Constable of Salisbury. *Glouc. Som. Nthants.*? Waleran Munceaux. *Suf. Ess.* and *Oxon.* H. Murdak. *Oxon.* Robert Mutun or Motun. *Leic.*

Hugh and John Neville. *Ess.* Peter de Neville. *Leic. Rut.* Stephen de Neville, *Leic.* Robert de Newyngton. *Glou.*? Matthew Noel and his brother. *Herts.* and *Bed.* Roger de Noers. *Bed.*

Richard de Offenthone. *Linc.* David de Offyntone. Ralf de Oteringdene. *Kent.*

John Page. *Norf.* or *Kent*? Robert Paignell. *Oxon.* Grimbald Pancefot. *Her.* and *Wor.*: see p. 266. note 1. Walter de Panes. *Glou.*? Symon de Pateshyll. *Bed. Hunt. Linc.* Hugh Peche. *Camb.* Robert Peche. *Suf.* John of Peckham. *Kent.* Henry de Pembrigge. *Leic.* Walter Pentheceustre. *Sur.* Ralf Perot. *Bed.* Henry Perot. *Bed.*? Henry de Pevenesse. *Kent.* or *Sus.*? Hugo Peverel. *Devon.* Stephen de Pirie. *Kent.* Ralf de Pomeroy. *Dev.* and *Som.* William de la Poyle or Puxle. *Mid.* Hugo Poynz. *Som.* William de Preston. *Leic.* Simon le Prude. *Norf.*

Felicia de Queye. *Bed.* Roger Quintin. *Norf.*?

John de Reygate. *Leic.* Adam de Riddenn. Anselm and William de Ripple. Roger Roulee. *Hunt.*? Amaric de Ruscelles. *Norf.* Geoffrey Russell. *Sus.* John de Rye. *Leic.*

Jordan de Sackville. *Suf.* Thomas de Sandwich : Clericus. *Kent.* Richard St John. *Oxon.*? Roger de St Philibert. *Oxon. Berks.* or *Suf.*? W. de St Philibert. *Nthants.* Henry de Schorn. John of Scordebec. Peter de Segrave. *War.* and *Leic.* R. de Sepinges. Philip le Serjeant. *Nthants.*? A. P. 159. Laurence de Shauekuntewelle. Geoffrey de Skeffington. *Leic.* J. de Snaves (see Suanes). John Fitz-Adam de Someri.

Herts. Sampson de Soles. *Kent.* Eustace de Solevill. Stephen Soudan. ? Sodanke. *Kent.* John Spinard. *Kent.* John de Stotevill. *Northumb.* Semann de Stoke. *Notts.* John de Suanes. *Kent.* Thomas de Suthesse. *Kent.* John de Suthun: Clericus. R. and Reginald de Sutton. *Nthants. Notts.* The first is probably the same as Robert le Sutton. *Nthants.* A. P. 159. Walter and Henry de Swynesford. *Norf.* and *Suf.*? John Talebot. *Sus.* Lucas de Tanny. *Ess.* and *Herts.* Roger de Tilmanneston. *Kent.* William de Tracy. *Glou.* and *Wilt.* Alan Travers. *Norf.*? Robert de Trek. *Sus.* Roger de Trihampton. *Kent*? Edmund Trumbert. *Yor.* Richard and William Trussell. *War.* Martin de Tunstall. *Kent.* William de Turwill. *Hants.*? or *Wilts.*? Hugo de Tywe. *Som.* and Ireland. Richard de Vernon. *Leic.* William de Vesci. *Northumb.* Reginaldus Vicecomes (? of the Viscount family or a Sheriff). Robert de Vipont. *West.* John Vissy. *Glou.*?

Hugo Wake. *Bucks.* and *Nthants.*? Nicholas Wake. *Yor.* John la Warre. *Glou.*? William de la Warre. *Her.*? or same as Wil. de Ware. *Norf.* Bartholomew de Wateringbury. *Kent.* Reginald and Simon de Waterville. *Nthants.* A. P. 166. Berenger de Watevile. *Hunt.* Eustace de Watteford. *Nthants.* Robert de Weresle. ? *Wor.* Osbert de Werford. *Leic.* Nigel de Weston. *Linc.* A. P. p. 164. William de Whelton. *Nthants.* Thomas de Winton: Clericus. Ralf de Wodekyme. W. de Wortham. *Suf.* Geoffrey de Wrokeshall. *Glou.*? John de Wyaxvill. *Nthants.*? Geoffrey de Wycheling: Clericus. *Kent.* Hamo de Wycleston. Robert de Wyleby. *Leic.* and *Cumb.* Isaac de Wylmington. *Kent.* Simon Wyolf. *Suf.*?

In connection with this list we may consider the names of John de Aur'. *Dorset.* William de Bovill. *Suffolk.* Geoffrey de Escudemor. *Wilts.* John de Mareville. *West.* John de Plessets. *Northumb.* John de St Walery. *Hants.* and Robert de Stradley. *Notts.* These were appointed "Custodes Pacis" in their respective counties after the battle of Lewes. As however the Royalists, John de Burg. Senior, *Norfolk,* and Oliver de Dynant, *Devon.* (see p. 368), figure on the same list, we must assume that in some cases the Barons were compelled to take officials from the opposite ranks. Indeed John de Aur' was superseded before the battle of Evesham by Brian de Gowiz and Oliver de Dynant by Hugo Peverel. New Rymer, Vol. I. pp. 442, 457.

These names in some cases have been identified from lists of forfeitures in a particular county, like that at p. 298, note 5, or from lists indicating the various counties to which the persons named belonged. Where this guidance was wanting I have used the Calendarium Genealogicum, the Rotuli Hundredorum, the Testa de Nevill, the Excerpta e Rotulis Finium, the Abbreviatio Placitorum, and Dugdale's Baronage. If a name appears always in connection with the same county I think we may assume the owner's identity. Often where there is only one mention of a name it would be unreasonable to doubt. Thomas de Suthesse appears only in the Testa de Nevill (p. 215), but holds part of a fee under Simon de Montfort. I have marked Stephen Soudan or Sodan as possibly of Kent, because his name occurs in a list made up largely of Kentish names, and a Hugh Sodanke had land in that county under John, while Stephen was succeeded by a son Hugh. But in several cases persons bearing the same surname were so numerous and so scattered that I have offered no conjecture. Lastly, it must be borne in mind that a man of property in the 13th century often owned patches of land in several different counties. My list does not profess to be exhaustive for these: and it may happen that a knight's name has come down to us in legal record associated with his least important holding. Still this cannot often have been the case: and as the inferences, I have tried to draw, rest on the great division of S. E. and N. W. they will not, I hope, be much affected by any corrections that local antiquarians might make.—P.

NOTE.—I am indebted to the historian of the Weald of Kent, Mr R. Furley, for pointing out to me that Simon de Montfort held the manor of Sutton Valence in Kent in right of his wife. (*Rot. Hund.* p. 323.) If Sutton castle was then built, as Mr Furley thinks, it was an important position; and must be added to the list of baronial fortresses.

INDEX.

A

Absolution, translation of, 91; read at St Paul's cross, 92; by Pope Urban IV., 96, n. 3
Addington given by King William I., to Tezelin his cook, 27, n. 3
Adrian V., Pope, 106, n. 1
Albemarle, Earl of, 85
Albemarle, Isabella Countess of, 231, 326
Alditheley, James de, 227, n. 5
Aldithel, James of, 76
Aliens exiled under pain of death, 70; persecution of, 102, n. 1; at battle of Lewes, 210, 233.
Amesbury, Queen Eleanor retires to convent of, 111, n. 1
Amiens, the award of, 112; annulled by King Louis, 114; results to King's side, 117; King at, 113
Anecdotes of alleged miracles performed by de Montfort's corpse, 289
Anglia Sacra, quoted, 18, n. 1
Angoulême, Count of, 23, n. 1, 25
Anguillara, Count, 343, 346; castle of, 343, n. 5
Anjou, Count d', 216; Charles d', 236; accepts Sicilian crown, 339; Beatrice wife of Charles, 339, n. 1
Aquabella, 16, n. 3
Aquablanca, Peter de, 20, 36
Aquinas, Thomas, quoted, 5, n. 1
Ardern, Ralph de, betrays de Montfort's movements to P. Edward, 271, n. 1
Argentein, Giles de, 301
Arms used in battle, 192, n. 2, 3; bearing of, without licence, forbidden, 230
Armour, 193, n. 1

Arundel, Isabella de Warrenne, Countess of, reproves the King, 58
Astley, Thomas de, slain, 278

B

Bacon, Roger, 79, n. 2; 120, 192, n. 5; 315, n. 1
Bacon, Lord, quoted, 80
Baliol, Guy de, 278, 300
Baliol, Eustache de, 248, n. 4
Baliol, John, Lord of Galloway, 157, 248, 308, n. 1
Barantin, Drago de, Governor of Windsor castle, 222
Bardolf, William, Councillor at Oxford, 151, 112, n. 1, 153, 179; prisoner, 198
Barons, letter to King Henry from, 142; threatens King, 119
Baskerville, concerned in the death of Prince Henry, 344, n. 4
Basset, Fulk de, Bishop of London, 21
Basset, Philip de, 97, n. 1; 107, 113, n. 1; 127, 153, 177, 184, 199, 308, n. 1
Basset, Ralph, 184; warden of Leicester, 230; refuses to survive de Montfort, 274: slain, 276, 298, n. 5.
Bassingburne, Warren de, 242, n. 1; 265, 275, 279, n. 1; 300, 331
Battle, 199; King at, 133, n. 6, 222, 324
Battle, preparations for, 164, 165
Bearn, Gaston Count de, 55, 884, n. 1
Beatrice, Countess of Provence, 19
Beatrice, widow of King of the Romans, 352, n. 2
Beauchamp, John de, 279, n. 8

INDEX.

Beaumont, Louis de, Bishop of Durham, 26, *n.* 1
Bec, Abbot of, 236
Befs, John, 203, *n.* 6; 204, *n.* 1
Berkhampstead, 241
Berkstead, Stephen de, Bishop of Chichester, 233, *n.* 2
Bertha, song of Master, 337
Besil, Mathew de, taken prisoner by barons at Gloucester, 103
Bigod, Roger, Earl of Norfolk and Marshal of England, 79; at Amiens, 113, *n.* 1; sides with barons, 179
Bigorre, Escivat Count de, 333, *n.* 5; de Montfort surrenders land to, 334
Bigot, Hugh le, 85; Justiciary of England, 70; displaced as Governor of Dover, 42, *n.* 3; 113, *n.* 1; flight, 206, 134–292
Blonde of Oxford, quoted, 19, *n.* 4
Blund, William de, 44 *n.* 1, 174; slain, 196, 210
Bohun, Humphrey de, attacked by P. Edward, 101; loses castles of Hay and Huntingdon, 101, *n.* 2; prisoner, 198
Bohun, Humphrey de, Jun., 112, 114, 178, 233, 280, *n.* 1.
Bolimar, John de, 310, *n.* 1
Boniface VIII., protest of barons, 29
Boniface, Archbishop, at Amiens, 113; opinion of Oxford, 120; conditions of return, 123, 233
Boreham, Harvey de, 176, *n.* 2
Boseham, summons proclaimed at, 259
Boteville, Roger, prisoner, 128
Botiller, Ralph de, 30
Boulogne, P. Henry attacked at, 236; bishops summoned to, 238
Bracton, Judge, quoted, 80, *n.* 1
Brackley, conference at, 122
Braose, Eleanor de, wife of de Bohun, 101
Braose, William de, claims Sedgewick castle, 113, *n.* 4; 132 *n.* 2; pedigree, 286, *n.* 1
Braunceston, Henry de, at Amiens, 114, *n.* 1
Breamore, Prior of, 231, *n.* 3
Breaus, William de, 113
Bredenstone Tower, 29, *n.* 1
Bristol, 220, 265, *n.* 4
Brom castle, Simon de Montfort at, 44
Bruce, Robert, 158

Brune, Robert, 219
Brus, Robert, 113, 248, *n.* 4, 327
Buckerel, Stephen, 124, 311
Bulla Aurea, Hungarian charter, 246
Burdett, Robert, 298, *n.* 5
Burgh, Hubert de, 13
Burgundy, Duke of, 216
Bury, Rich. de, Bishop of Durham, quoted, 78, *n.* 2
Burgh, John de, 169, 178, *n.* 3; warden of Norfolk, 230
Bury, Abbot of, 83
Bussy, William de, 72

C

Campbell, Lord, quoted, 31, *n.* 3
Canterbury, Boniface, Archbishop of, 76; massacre of Jews at, 131; proclamation at, 236; dissension between Barons at, 256
Cantelupe, Walter de, Bishop of Worcester, 68, 76, 140, 164
Cantelupe, Thomas, at Amiens, 114, *n.* 1; Lord Chancellor, 257, *n.* 1, 2; 258, *n.* 2, 3; 260, *n.* 5
Cantelupe, Joan de, 176, *n.* 4
Car of Simon de Montfort attacked, 196
Carlaverock, 148
Caston, John de, 185
Cathedrals in progress of building, 226, *n.* 1
Census, 134, *n.* 5
Chacepore, Peter, 27
Champagne, William, Count of, 15
Chartres, King Henry met by Louis IX. at, 62
Chaucer quoted, 246, 303
Chaworth, Patrick and Pain, 265
Chelmareford, Stephen de, 174, *n.* 2
Chester given to Simon de Montfort, 249, 252
Chester, Ranulf, Earl of, 46
Chichester, Bishop of, 122, 233, 238, *n.* 5; excommunicated, 302, 323
Cinque Ports, excommunicated, 239
Cistern, first leaden, 226, *n.* 4
Clare, Richard de, Earl of Gloucester, opposed to the Court, 41; bought over by the King, 42, 76; dissension with de Montfort, 87; death, 98
Clare, Gilbert de, with de Montfort, 99, 139, 177, 203; excommunicated, 239; jealous of de Montfort, 253, 254; tries to entrap de Montfort, 256, 258; at Gloucester,

259; at Forest of Dean, 262; with Prince Edward at Ludlow, 266; receives estates, 300; retires from Court, 308, n. 1
Clare, Thomas de, 259, 262, 300
Clarendon, Lord, quoted, 117
Clement IV., Pope, 238, n. 2; 301, n. 3; 303; death, 340
Clement V., Letter from, 258
Clifford, Roger de, sides with the Barons, 103, 104; deserts the Barons, 117, n. 4; his wife a captive, 125, n. 2, 126, 177, 227; meets the King, 243; safe conduct, 262; urges P. Edward forward, 269, n. 3, 300
Clive, town of, 271, n. 4
Cloth, early manufacture of, 240, n. 1
Cluniac Monastery, grievances of, 145, 146, n. 1
Cnol, Edward de la, Dean of Wells, 241
Cosham, John, 187
Combe, Barons ascend the Downs at, 170
Comet, 281
Compromise at Coventry, 307
Comyn, John, 157
Confiscation of property, 298
Convention signed, 138
Corbet, Richard, 325
Cortes, Aragon and Castile supplied deputies to, 246
Council of London, 232, n. 3
Creppinge, Walter de, 279, n. 5
Crokesley, Richard de, Abbot of Westminster, 71
Cronesley, Thomas de, 298, n. 5
Crown jewels pledged, 93
Croydon, 220, n. 5
Crusades, 3, 306, 336
Cuberle, Geoffry, at Amiens, 114, n. 1

D

Dammé, village of, 234, n. 2
Dante, his opinion of Henry III., 19, 4, n. 1, 35, 37, n. 4, 303, 350
Dean, forest of, 255, 262
Deception of Prince Edward, displays Barons' banners, 272, n. 4
Deed of surrender to Count de Bigorre, 362, App. E
Derby, Earl of, signs convention, 138
Despenser, Hugh le, 112; signs convention, 138, 179, n. 2; 236, 261, 274; death, 276, 298; widow of releases Royalists, 304, n. 5
Devereux, William, slain, 279, n. 5
Discontent, causes of, 66, 136, 137
Disinherited Barons, 298, n. 3; compound for lost estates, 208, n. 3
Domesday Book, disposition of property in, 6; Brady's introduction quoted, 7, n. 1
Dover Castle surrendered, 105; attacked by King, 107; surrendered to, 117; Simon de Montfort at, 222, 241, 325
Dragon as Royal Banner, 190; displayed by de Montfort, 191
Drayton quoted, 2, 266
Drieby, Philip de, prisoner, 128
Dunstable, tournament to be held at, 256

E

Edmund, Prince, surrenders Dover Castle, 105; with Queen, 120, 234; receives Simon de Montfort's estates, 209, n. 2, 3, 4; crusader, 336, 350
Edmund, Prince, second son of King of the Romans, 84, 146, 203; crusader, 350
Edward, King, 111, 345
Edward, Prince, 38, 40, n. 1, 94, 100, 107, 138, 146, n. 1, 243, n. 2, 266, 302, n. 1, 319; Northampton, 126; successes of, 132; at Lewes, 143, 189, 191, 194, n. 3, 196, 204, 205, n. 1, 2, 208; flies to the Franciscans, 214; surrenders, 217; sent to Dover, 218; liberated on parole, 249, 262; escapes, 263; excommunicated, 265; takes Kenilworth, 268; charged with cowardice, 269, n. 3; misleads spies, 271, n. 3; surprises the Barons at Evesham, 272, 273; overpowers the Barons, 306; retakes Dover, 331, n. 3; crusader, 336
Eleanor, Queen, 22, 34, n. 3, 136, n. 1, 254, 328; keeper of great seal, 109, n. 4; attacked by Londoners, 110, n. 3; as widow retires to convent, 111, n. 1, 3
Eleanor, Princess, Countess of Leicester, 87, 243, 300; banished, 313; household expenses of, 314 to 319; retires to France, 331, 332; surrenders rights to Bigorre, 334

384 INDEX.

Eleanor of Castile, 228, *n.* 3, 229, *n.* 1, 2, 3
Eleanor, daughter of Simon de Montfort, 332, 333, *n.* 1, 2
Ely, Hugh Northwold, Bishop of, 55, 233
Engagement of King of the Romans to befriend the Countess of Montfort, 361, App. D
English troops wish to leave Wales, 265, *n.* 7
Estrange, Hamo l', 241, 300, *n.* 5
Evesham, battle of, 242, 275; de Montfort marches to, 271; baronial troops seen leaving, 272; list of slain, 279, *n.* 5: Simon de Montfort buried at, 286, *n.* 5

F

Fairs prohibited by the King, 265
Ferrers, Robert de, Earl of Derby, 180, 308
Ferrers, William de, 128
FitzAllan, John, 131, 149, 260; prisoner, 198; death, 149, *n.* 1
FitzAucher, Henry, 300
FitzJohn, John, 130, 177, 178, 262, 280
FitzNigel, Robert, 301
FitzPiers, Reginald, 201
FitzRalph, Ralph, 248, *n.* 4
FitzRichard, 311, *n.* 1
FitzSimon, Simon, 128
FitzThomas, Mayor of London, 138, 310
FitzWarren, Fulk de, 154, 155; drowned at Lewes, 210, *n.* 2
Flanders, Joan, Countess of, 47, *n.* 4
Fletching, village of, Barons at, 139, *n.* 3; prelates at, 163, 170
Flete, John de la, 311
Foliot, Reginald, 317, *n.* 3
Food, scarcity of, 134
Fortibus, William of, Earl of Albemarle, 76
France, Barons' treaty with, 84
Franciscans, Order of, 214
Frederick, Emperor, excommunicated, 243
Frideswide, Saint, 121
Fulcodio, Cardinal Guido di, 238

G

Gaunt, Gilbert de, 184, 326
Gebyon, Hugh, 128
Geoffreyson, John, 76
Gesem, Adam de, 248, *n.* 4

Gibbon thinks of writing about the Barons' War, 3, *n.* 1
Gifford, John, 101, 102, 103, 183, *n.* 2, 200; claims the ransom of de la Zouch, 255; at Forest of Dean, 261
Gloucester, Prince Edward besieged in, 108; de Clare at, 259; de Montfort at, 265; Prince Edward at, 266, *n.* 1; prisoners sent to, 269
Gloucester, Gilbert, Earl of, 71, 138, 169, 233, 256, 257; separates from barons, 261, 264; takes London, 338, *n.* 1
Gloucester, Isabella, Countess of, 41, *n.* 2, 48
Gorva, Brian de, 298, *n.* 5
Gravelines, 329
Gravesend, Richard de, 298, *n.* 5, 300
Great comet, 281, 282
Greek fire, composition of, 208, *n.* 2, 3
Gregory IX. denounced by the Emperor Frederick, 4
Gregory X., Pope, election of, 340, *n.* 4
Grethead, Bishop, 78, 120, 290, 291
Grey, Richard, 76, 107, 112, *n.* 1, 181, *n.* 1, 298, *n.* 5, 300; prisoner, 269
Grose, quoted, 14, *n.* 1
Guizot, quoted, 8, *n.* 1, 79
Gundred, Princess, 147
Gurney, John de, 310
Gynville, John, 185, *n.* 5

H

Hadstock, Augustine de, 174
Hailes, P. Henry's bones buried at, 350, *n.* 4, 351, *n.* 2, 353
Hallam, compares Simon de Montfort to Cromwell, 44, *n.* 3; quoted 245, *n.* 3
Hamsard, Gilbert, 248, *n.* 4.
Hamsey, 170
Harcourt, Saer de, 298, n. 5
Hastings, Henry de, 112, *n.* 1, 176; death, 177, *n.* 1, 194, 280, *n.* 5, 308
Hastings, Matthew de, 326, *n.* 3
Hatfield, William de Valence at Bishop of Ely's Park at, 25
Hawarden Castle, Conferences between P. of Wales and de Montfort, 270
Hay, Royalists driven from, 260
Haye, John de la, 325

INDEX. 385

Hemington, Richard de, justice at Lincoln, 104, *n.* 5
Henry II., death, 7
Henry III., 5, 82, 92, 94, 95, 97, 106, 121, 302, *n.* 2; claim to the crown, 9; betrothal to Joanna; marriage, 14; war with France, 23; at Paris, 61—88, *n.* 2, 97; bequeaths his heart, 62; does homage for Aquitaine, 89, *n.* 1; absolution granted, 90; annuls the laws made at Oxford, 92; delays at Rheims, 98; prohibits Prince Edw. from continuing hostilities, 105; meets the French king at Boulogne, 107; at Amiens, 113, *n.* 2; summons council at Oxford, 120; at Lewes, 124, 143; preparations for battle, 198—220; in London, 223, *n.* 2, 3, 4; love of the arts, 223, 226; letter to the Queen, 240; to Louis IX., 241; at Pershore, 248; London, 250; Northampton, 260; at Gloucester, 262; at Evesham, 280
Henry IV., 299, *n.* 5.
Henry, Prince, 105; taken prisoner, and liberated, 106; joins the Royalists, 117, *n.* 2, 146; sent to King of France, 236, 261; receives de Furnival's estates, 299; overcomes Earl of Derby, 307, 308, *n.* 1; at Viterbo, 338; marriage, 341; murdered, 343, *n.* 3; insulted, 343, 349, *n.* 1, 2; buried, 350
Hereford, de Montfort leaves, 270; Royalists driven from, 260
Hereford, Earl of, 85, 101, 308, *n.* 1
Hereford, Peter de Aigue Blanche, Bishop of, at Amiens, 102, 113, 234
Herietesham, Geoffry de, 309
Heringot, Ralph, slain, 210, *n.* 1
Hermite, William de St., 27
Horace, quoted, 37, *n.* 6.
Hostilities commenced, 100; stopped by K. Henry, 105
Hoveden, John de, poem by, 226, *n.* 3.
Hoveden, Roger de, quoted, 337, *n.* 1
Hubert de Burgh, 13
Hugh le Bigot, 151; made Justiciary Commander of Dover, 151
Humphrey de Bohun, Earl of Hereford, marriage, 150
Hurtald, Poictevin, 27
Hussey, Henry, 185, *n.* 2

I

Innocent IV., Pope, allows monks to perform service hooded, 27, *n.* 2, 35
Invasion, preparations to meet, 234, 235
Isabella, queen of King John, 22; death, 23
Itinerary of Prince Edward, 271, *n.* 4

J

Jews, massacre of, 130, 131; commended to the care of Mayor of London, 227, *n.* 2, 3; benefits withdrawn from, 298
Joan, Princess, 338, *n.* 2
John, King, made prisoner by Fitz-Warren, 156
Joinville, 63

K

Kaleto, John de, Abbot of Peterborough, 27, *n.* 2
Kempsey, de Montfort at, 270
Kenilworth, 181, 183; P. Edward removed to, 243; Simon de Montfort, jun., marches to, 267 *n.* 2; decree of, 308, *n.* 1; surrender of, 310, 325
Kilwarby, Archbishop, 121, *n.* 1.
King Harry's mill, 202, *n.* 1, 2, 3, 203, *n.* 5
Kingston, conference at, 93

L

Lancaster, Blanche of, 299, *n.* 5
Langton, Archbishop, 78
Leicester, taken by P. Edward, 132
Leicester, Earl of, 112, 164
Leicester, Countess of, 319
Leopardi, 27
L'Estrange, Hamo, deserts the Barons' cause, 117, *n.* 4
Letters to Queen Eleanor, 240; of advice to King, 330, 359, App. C.; from barons to Louis IX., 261, *n.* 1
Lewes, 16, 108 133, *n.* 7, 173, 187; King at, 143, 169, *n.* 5; battle of, 191; earliest murage grant, 200; resistance at, 208; treaty of, 215; Prior of, 244, *n.* 3; summons proclaimed at, 259; site of battles considered, 354
Lewisham, Prior Philip de, 72
Lewknor, Nicholas de, 300
Leybourne, Roger de, 300; sides with barons, 101, 118, *n.* 3; against 117,

C C

n. 4, 131, 177; meets the King, 243; safe conduct to meet P. Edw., 262
Lichfield, Roger de, Bishop of. 123, n. 2
Lincoln, Greathead, Bishop of, 59, 61, n. 2
List of contending earls, 364, App. G.
Llewellyn, Prince, attacks Roger de Mortimer, 100
London, fortified, 108; citizens rise against King, 124; council at, 232; citizens put to the rout at Lewes, 194; fined, 311; excommunicated, 239
London, Bishop of, 122, 236, 237, n. 3, 238, 302
Losell, Gregory de, 292
Louis IX., 5, 63; arbitrates between King and Barons, 93, 96, 109, 116; interview with the King, 107; delivers judgment at Amiens, 114
Lucy, Geoffry de, 112, n, 1
Ludlow, Royalists driven from, 260; P. Edw. at, 266
Lusignan, Geoffry de, 205, n. 6
Lusignan, Guy de, 176, 205
Lusignan, Hugh, 205, n. 6
Lymington, 231
Lynde, John de la, 114, n. 2

M

Machiavelli, quoted, 90, n. 2, 135, n. 3
Mackintosh, Sir J., quoted 295
Madox, History of the Exchequer, quoted, 37, n. 1
Mad Parliament, the name given to the council of Oxford, 65
Magna Charta, renewal in 9th year Henry III., 9, 32, 36, 64; confirmed, 67; proclaimed, 74—135.
Maltravers, William de, prisoner at Lewes, 201, n. 2, 285, n. 3
Mandeville, William and John, slain, 279, n. 2
Manfredi, King, 303
Mansel, John, 31, 83, surrenders Scarborough, 92; flies to Boulogne, 105; escapes from the Tower, 110 —112; dies abroad, 113—234
March of P. Edward from Worcester to Shrewsbury, difficulties in understanding, 271, n. 4
Marche, Count de la, 23
Mare, Henry de la, 301, n. 2
Mareschal, William, 114, n. 1, 300
Margoth, female spy disguised as a man thwarts de Montfort, 268; n. 3

Marie, authoress, 78, n. 3
Marisco, Adam de, 56, n. 2, 57, n. 3, 120, 214, n. 2; pedigree, 291, n. 5; letters of, 292—294
Marisco, Everard de, 317, n. 3
Marlborough, statute of, 244, n. 2, 245, n. 3
Marmion, Philip de, 152, n. 1
Marmyon, Robert and William, 183, n. 5
Martel, William, 298, n. 5
Maudvit, William, 183, n. 4
Maurienne, Thos., Count of, 20
Maunsel, Thos., prisoner, 128, n. 4
Meinill, Stephen de, 248, n. 4
Memorial to Pope, answer, 76, 77
Mepham, Richard de, Archdeacon of Oxford, 237, n. 3
Merton, Walter de, chancellor, 97, n. 1, 301
Meyland, Roger de, Bishop of Lichfield, 122, n. 2 ; of Chester, 331
Mise of Lewes, 215—218, 284, 297
Mitford, Roger Bertram de, prisoner, 128, n. 3
Monceaux, Waleran de, 326
Monchensi, Joan de, wife of William de Valence, 146
Monchensi, Warin de, 24, 262
Monchensi, William de, 177, 178, 233, prisoner, 269
Monks, luxurious living of, 144, 145
Monmouth, Prior of, 262 ; de Montfort at, 265, n. 5
Montalembert, Count de, quoted, 43, n. 3
Monte, Pessulano, King's butler, 27
Montfort, Count de, Simon the Bald, estates forfeited, 48 ; pedigree, 45, n. 1
Montfort, Almeric de, 46 ; prisoner, 53, n. 1 ; dies at Otranto, 54
Montfort, Simon de, 35; opposed to court, 41 ; acknowledged leader of the Barons, 42 ; acknowledged by King, 46, n. 6; married, 49; pleads his cause with the Pope, 49 ; invested as Earl Leicester, 52; crusader, 52 ; in Gascony, 55, 59, 61; scene with King, 56 ; stripped of his command, 60 ; declines regency of France, 60 ; King agrees to pay compensation, 61; surrenders Kenilworth and Odiham, 69 ; councillor, 76; witness to King Henry's ratification of act of renunciation, 85, n. 4 ; dissension with de Clare, 87;

INDEX.

gifts to shrine of St Alban's, 90, n.1; precedes the King to England, 98; accepts leadership of Barons, 98; attacked by King at London, 108; at St Alban's, 110; accident at Catesby and return home, 113, n. 5, 6; in arms again, 116; gives Prince Henry leave to bear arms against him, 117; still upholds the cause, 119; summons barons to Northampton, 125; signs convention, 138; leaves London, 139; preparations for battle, 164—168, 171, 179; attacks the King, 197; suggests truce, 208; majority of the nation on his side, 209, 210; strengthens the blockade of the priory, 214; leaves Lewes with King, 220; at Dover, 222; authorized by King to select councillors, 233; at Boulogne, 237: excommunicated, 239; spends Christmas at Kenilworth, 248, n. 3: appropriates eighteen baronies, 251, n. 3; pride of, discussed, 250—254; opposes Tournament, 256, n. 1, 258; moves north, 259; at Northampton, 260; at Gloucester with King, 262; in Wales, 265; recalled from his enterprise, 266; plans marred by his son's carelessness, 268—270; marches towards Evesham, 271; seeing the dangers. at Evesham urges the Barons to fly, but declines himself, 274; slain, 277, n. 1; treatment of corpse, 284, n. 3, 4, 286, n. 3, 4; removal of corpse, 287, n. 3; alleged miracles, 288; account of, 290; negociates with France, 292; value of estates, 299, n. 1; all followers of excommunicated, 303, n. 2; his family excluded from any benefit from Kenilworth decree, 308
Montfort, Henry de, eldest son of Simon de Montfort, embarks for Gascony, 59; at Boulogne, 73; at Paris, 94; a chief of the baronial party, 112; at Amiens, 114; at Lewes, 178; Prince Edw. at Dover under care of, 218; warden of Kent, 230; released, 249, n. 1; pride of, 253; with Prince Edward, 263; offers to bear the battle alone, 274; slain, 277, n. 4; miracles attributed to, 289, n. 4; Prince Edward and Henry under care of, at Odi-

ham, 319: joins his father, 325; surrenders rights to Count Bigorre, 334
Montfort, Simon de, second son of Simon de Montfort, at Paris, 94; prisoner, 126; released 222; warden of Surrey and Sussex, 230; summoned from Pevensey, 267, n. 1; escapes from Kenilworth, 268, n. 6; releases the Princes, 364; threatens invasions, 305; at Wilmington, 324, 325; wounded, 331; at Viterbo, 338, 340; murders Prince Henry, 342; excommunicated, 345; death, 347
Montfort, Almeric de, third son of Simon de Montfort, at Gravelines, 329; prisoner, 333, 334; released, and death at Rome, 335; sent to the Pope, 346
Montfort, Guy de, fourth son, at Lewes, 178; wounded, 278, n. 2; at Viterbo, 338, 340; murders Prince Henry, 342; excommunicated, 345, 347, n. 4; dies, 348
Montfort, Richard, fifth son, at Gravelines, 329; dies, 335
Montfort, Eleanor, daughter, prisoner, 333, n. 2
Montfort, Laura, daughter of Almeric de, 333, n. 5
Montfort, Peter de, 76, 112; at Amiens, 114; prisoner, 127, n. 2; released, 222; sent to the French King, 237, 238; slain, 278
Montfort, Peter, son of Peter, 127
Montfort, Countess of, at Vaux, 44, n. 5
Montfort, Philip, 339, n. 4
Montpelier, Henry of, 27
Mortimer, Matilda de, de Montfort's head sent to, 285, n. 4, 286, n. 1
Mortimer, Roger de, 76; attacked by Prince Llewellyn, 100; marriage, 153; favours P. Edward's escape, 263; retires from court, 307; meets the King, 243
Mount, Harry, 211, n. 3
Muccgas, John de, 326
Murage grant, 200
Musgrave John, 265

N

Navarre, Theobald, King of, treaty with King Henry, 55
Neumarket, Adam de, 127; Warden of Lincoln, 230; prisoner, 269

388 INDEX.

Neville, Hugh, 184, n. 1; prisoner, 269, n. 2
Neville, John, 184, n. 1
Neville, Robert de, Warden of the King's forces in the North, 104, n. 4, 248, n. 4
Neville, William de, Prior of Cluniac monks at Lewes, 143, n. 2
Newcastle-on-Line given in exchange to Simon de Montfort, 249
Newick, 170
Newington, Robert de, 128
Newport, de Montfort at, 265
Nicholas, de Montfort's barber, recognises the banners, 273, n. 1, 2
Norfolk, Roger, Earl of, 233, 239, n. 2
Norman, Simon, 20
Normandy formally resigned by Barons, 85
Norreys, Richard de, given Ocholt Manor, 28, n. 2
Northampton, meeting of Barons at, 125; Prince Edward attacks, 126; prisoners at, 128, n. 6; sacked, 129; legate at, 302, n. 3
Norwich, Nicholas de Plumpton, Archdeacon of, 122
Nottingham betrayed to Prince Edward, 132

O

Odiham, 322
Osney Abbey, 28
Ottoboni, Cardinal, afterwards Pope Adrian V., 106, n. 1, 302, n. 3, 308, n. 1
Oxford, great council summoned at, 36, 64; King's Proclamation to Sheriff of, 108, n. 5; students turned out of, 120; ordered to return to, 129, n. 3
Oxford, Earl of, 269
Oxford, Alice, Countess of, 326

P

Palgrave, Sir F., quoted, 65, 224, n. 1
Pandulf, raised to the bishopric of Norwich, 12, n. 1; death of, 12
Park, Geoffrey de, 187, n. 7
Parliament to meet in London, 244, n. 2; 248, n. 5; act of confirming the peace, 249, n. 2
Pasilure, Robert de, 12, 13
Pauncefot, prisoner, 128, n. 5; 266, n. 2

Peace, proposals of, at Lewes, 141; proffers of, declined, 159
Pec, fortress of given to Simon de Montfort, 249
Peckham, Archbishop, 121, n. 1
Pembroke, William, second Earl of, 48
Percy, Hugh de, 113, n. 1, 131
Percy, Lord, 148, n. 2; prisoner, 198
Persecution of all not speaking English, 102, n. 1
Pershore, meeting of King and Royalist prisoners, 243, 260
Peter's pence, 29, n. ,
Peter de Rivaulx, 12
Peter de Roche succeeded Pembroke as Regent, 10, n. 3
Peter of Savoy received the domain of Richmond, 15, 16; crusader, 16; Bishop of Hereford seized by the Barons, 102; death, 103
Peterborough abbey plundered, 230, n. 4
Pevensey, in custody of William de Valence, 146; Royalists fly to, 207; summons proclaimed at, 259, 327
Peyclinton, Robert de, 298, n. 5
Plesseiz, John of, Earl of Warwick, 76
Plugneth, Alan, 300, n. 6
Plumpton, Nicholas de, Archdeacon of Norwich, 122
Poem after Barons' victory, 209
Pointz, Hugh, 185
Police established, 230
Pope, remonstrance to by Barons, 54; unwilling to abandon the King, 237
Preston, Gilbert de, Justice at Lincoln, 104, n. 5
Preston, William de, 298, n. 5
Priory at Lewes, Barons in sight of, 171; Royalists retreat to, 199; and resist at, 208
Prisoners, exchange of, 227, n. 4
Proclamation of Henry, 75, 108, n. 3, 188, 236, 264
Provisions, prices of, 40, 60, 239, 314—329
Puvilesdon, Thomas de, 124, n. 2, 179, 311, n. 3
Pycard, Richard, 174
Pyramus, Denis, 79

Q

Quittance, deed of, 358, App. B

INDEX. 389

R

Raban, Elias de, 27
Reasons in behalf of Barons, 61
Relic at Hailes, 351, *n*. 3, 352, *n*. 1, 353
Reygate, John de, 298, *n*. 5
Richard I., absence abroad, 7
Richard II. deposed, 299
Richard Prince, 18, 20, 36, 37, *n*. 3, 195, 198, 203, 218, 252, *n*. 1, 331, 353, *n*. 1; redeems captive crusaders, 53; deprived of the government of Gascony, 57; arbitrates, 97, 105, *n*. 1; at Northampton, 126; letter, 161; at Lewes, 189, 202, prisoner, 304; dies, 351, App. B
Rivallis, Peter de, 27
Rivaulx, Peter de, 12; death, 13, *n*. 2
Rival, Roger de, 278
Robertsbridge, abbey of, 223
Roches, Peter de la, 12
Rochester, defended by Earl de Warenne, 122; siege of, 131; well at, 132, *n*. 1
Rochefort, Guy de, 72
Rodes, Gerard de, 106, 107
Ros, Robert de, 112, *n*. 1, 263, 266
Rouen, Archbishop of, 237
Rout of Londoners, 194, 195
Royalists retreat to Priory, 199; to France, 207; summoned, 259, *n*. 4
Royal menagerie, gifts to, 226
Ryegate defended by Earl de Warenne, 122

S

Sackville, Jordan de, 185
Sainte Chapelle, 63, *n*. 4
St Edmund, 78
St Hermite, William de, 72
St John, Roger de, 261, 265, *n*. 1
St Pol, Count, 78
Salisbury, constableship of, 326, *n*. 2
Sandwich, Ralph de, 265, *n*. 5
Sandwich, Richard de, Bishop of London, 112, 140
Savoy, Boniface, Archbishop of Canterbury, 17; death, 18, *n*. 2, 76, 292
Savoy, Philip, 17, 254
Say, William, 187, *n*. 2, 220, *n*. 3
Scotney, Walter de, 72
Sedgewick, castle of, 113, *n*. 4
Segrave, Gilbert de, 175, 194
Segrave, Nicholas, 112, *n*. 1, 175, 280, 298, 301

Segrave, Steven de, 14
Shakespeare, quoted, 13
Shrewsbury, Prince Edward marches towards, 271
Sicily, crown of, accepted by Prince Edward, 35; renounced by Barons, 77, 238, 239
Skeffington, Geoffrey de, 298, *n*. 5
Somery, 198, 308, *n*. 1
Stamford, Henry de, Bishop of Durham, 26, *n*. 1
Statutes sworn at Oxford, 67; proclaimed, 74; revoked, 115; annulled, 297
Stokes, Seman de, 326
Stoteville, Robert de, 248, *n*. 4, 301
Suffield, Walter de, 144
Summons for the Parliament, 244; from Woodstock, 245
Surrey, population of, 135
Sussex, population of, 135
Sutton, Robert de, 301

T

Talisman against fire, 81, *n*. 1
Tallages, 247, 283
Tancred, quoted, 247
Tany, Richard de, 301
Tarento, William de, 22
Tattishall, 198
Tickhill, lordship of, 117; castle of 307
Tipetot, Robert, 265, *n*. 3
Tony, Michael, 311
Tony, Robert de, 185, *n*. 6
Tothill Fields, 137, *n*. 2
Tournaments forbidden, 256, *n*. 1, 258
Treaty with France (5th Article) quoted, 85, *n*. 1, at Lewes (Mise), 215, *n*. 2
Tregoz, Robert, Baron de, 185, *n*. 1; slain, 279, *n*. 5
Tuberville, Hugh, 241, *n*. 3
Tunbridge, 133, *n*. 2, 220, 363

U

Urban IV., Pope, 96, 352

V

Valence, Aymer de, 25, 77; bishop, 55; goes into exile, 71
Valence, Guy de, 146
Valence, Joan de, 73, 230
Valence, William de, 23, 24; death, 25: rupture with de Clare, 64, 126, 254, 130, 146; escapes, 206;

lands at Pembroke, 260; summoned, 262
Valentia, John de, mediates at Brackley, 122
Vaux, John de, deserts Barons' cause, 117, n. 4
Vere, Robert de, Earl of Oxford, 169, 233, 269
Vernon, Richard de, 298, n. 5; at Kenilworth, 268; grant, 300
Vesey, John, 112, n. 1, 182, 183, n. 1, 280
Vipont, Robert, 112, n. 1, 181

W

Wace, Robert, 79, n. 1
Waddington, William of, translator of "Manuel," 79
Wake, Baldwin, 112, 127; death, 129, n. 2; prisoner, 269, 280
Wake, Nicholas, 127
Walascho, Pope's envoy, 181, n. 3
Wales, Llewellyn, Prince of, 270
Waleran, Robert, 97, n. 1, 241, 242, n. 2
Wallingford, 241, 242, 260
Waltone, Simon de, 103
War, fresh outbreak of, 116, 125
Wardens of the counties summoned to attack the Rebels, 267
Warenne, Earl de, 148, 234; agrees to the Oxford statutes, 70; defends the King at Ryegate and Rochester, 122, 131, 132, n. 2; at Lewes, 134; marriage, 146; flight, 205; at Kenilworth, 268; estates seized by de Clare, 254; summoned, 259, 262; lands at Pembroke, 260, n. 5
Warre, John de la, 325, n. 5
Washington, 166, n. 2

Waterville, Reginald, 128
Waverley, Ralph, Abbot of, 317, n. 8
Welsh auxiliaries, desert de Montfort, 275, n. 2
Wengham, Henry de, 68, n. 3
Westminster Abbey, 136, n. 5, 350, n. 2, 3
Westminster, Edward of, 253, n. 3
Westminster Hall, 33, 64
Westminster Palace burnt, 223, n. 3, 4
Whitsand, King embarks at, 116
Wicliffe, sent to Rome, 76, n. 5
Widmarsh, Prince Edward at, 263
Wigmore, 264, 284, 287, n. 4
Wilmington, 324, n. 1
Wilton, William de, 210
Wimbledon, Peter, rector of, 27
Winchelsea, 133, 324
Winchester, Earl of 43, n. 1
Winchester, Bishop of, 122, 237, 238
Winchester, great council at, 245, n. 3; young Simon de Montfort plunders, 267; Parliament at, 298
Windsor fortified, 108
Wolvesham, recusants from "Mad Parliament" escape to, 69
Woodstock, 248
Worcester, Bishop of, 122, 164, 237, 238, 261, 331; absolves baronial troops, 272, n. 2; death, 303, n. 1
Worcester, Nicholas de Ely, Bishop of, 308, n. 1
Worcester, troops summoned to meet at, 264, bridges destroyed at, 265; Prince Edward at, 266
Wyke, quoted, 240
Wyvile, Robert de, 298, n. 5

Z

Zouch, Alan de la, 201, n. 3, 4

HISTORICAL WORKS.

MODERN EUROPE. From the Fall of Constantinople to the Establishment of the German Empire, A.D. 1453-1870. By THOMAS HENRY DYER, M.A. Second Edition, revised and continued. In 5 vols. demy 8vo. 2*l*. 12*s*. 6*d*.

HISTORY OF ENGLAND, during the Early and Middle Ages. By C. H. PEARSON, M.A., Fellow of Oriel College, Oxford. Second Edition, much enlarged. Vol. I. 8vo. 16*s*. Vol. II. 8vo. 14*s*.

HISTORICAL MAPS of ENGLAND during the first Thirteen Centuries. With Explanatory Essays and Indices. By C. H. PEARSON, M.A. Imp. folio. Second Edition. 31*s*. 6*d*.

THE BARONS' WAR. Including the Battles of Lewes and Evesham. By W. H. BLAAUW, M.A. Second Edition, with Additions and Corrections by C. H. PEARSON, M.A. Demy 8vo. 10*s*. 6*d*.

MARTINEAU'S (HARRIET) HISTORY OF ENGLAND FROM 1800-15. Being a Reprint of 'The Introduction to the History of the Peace.' With new and full Index. 1 vol. 3*s*. 6*d*.

MARTINEAU'S (HARRIET) HISTORY OF THE THIRTY YEARS' PEACE, 1815-46. With new and copious Index. 4 vols. 3*s*. 6*d*. each.
These histories contain a vast store of information, only with much labour attainable elsewhere, on all the great social and political questions of the important and interesting period of which they treat—a period separated by so short an interval from our own time that to every educated person who takes an intelligent interest in the questions of the present day a thorough knowledge of its history is indispensable.

LIVES OF THE QUEENS OF ENGLAND, from the Norman Conquest to the Reign of Queen Anne. By AGNES STRICKLAND. Library Edition. With Portraits, Autographs, and Vignettes. 8 vols. post 8vo. 7*s*. 6*d*. each. Also a Cheaper Edition in 6 vols. 5*s*. each.

LIVES OF THE LAST FOUR PRINCESSES OF THE ROYAL HOUSE OF STUART. Forming an appropriate Sequel to the 'Lives of the Queens of England.' With a Photograph of the Princess Mary, after a picture by Honthorst. Crown 8vo. 12*s*.

THE LIFE OF MARY, QUEEN OF SCOTS. By AGNES STRICKLAND. 2 vols. post 8vo. 5*s*. each.

HUME, SMOLLETT, & HUGHES' HISTORY OF ENGLAND. 18 vols. [sold separately] post 8vo. 4*s*. each.

THE STORY OF THE IRISH BEFORE THE CONQUEST. From the Mythical Period to the Invasion under Strongbow. By LADY FERGUSON. Fcap. 8vo. 5*s*.

HISTORY OF THE IRISH REBELLION IN 1798. By W. H. MAXWELL. With Portraits and Etchings on Steel by George Cruikshank. Tenth Edition. 7*s*. 6*d*.

THIERRY'S HISTORY OF THE CONQUEST OF ENGLAND BY THE NORMANS; its Causes, and its Consequences in England, Scotland, Ireland, and the Continent. Translated from the 7th Paris edition by WILLIAM HAZLITT. With short Memoir of Thierry, Index, and Portraits of Thierry and William the Conqueror. 2 vols. 3*s*. 6*d*. each.

JESSE'S MEMOIRS OF THE PRETENDERS AND THEIR ADHERENTS. With Index and Portraits. Post 8vo. 5*s*.

JESSE'S MEMOIRS OF THE COURT OF ENGLAND DURING THE REIGN OF THE STUARTS, including the Protectorate. 3 vols. With Index and 42 Portraits. 5*s*. each.

NUGENT'S (LORD) MEMORIALS OF HAMPDEN, HIS PARTY AND TIMES. With a Memoir of the Author, copious Index, an Autograph Letter, and Portraits. Post 8vo. 5*s*.

CARREL'S HISTORY OF THE COUNTER-REVOLUTION IN ENGLAND for the Re-establishment of Popery under Charles II. and James II. By ARMAND CARREL. Together with Fox's (Right Hon. C. J.) History of the Reign of James II., and Lord Lonsdale's Memoir of the Reign of James II. With Portrait of Carrel after Viardot. 3*s*. 6*d*.

JAMES'S (G. P. R.) HISTORY OF THE LIFE OF RICHARD CŒUR DE LION, King of England. With Index and Portraits of Richard and Philip Augustus. 2 vols. 3*s*. 6*d*. each.

HISTORICAL WORKS.

COXE'S MEMOIRS OF THE DUKE OF MARLBOROUGH. With his original Correspondence, collected from the family records at Blenheim. Edited by Archdeacon W. COXE, M.A., F.R.S. Revised Edition by JOHN WADE. With Portraits and Index. 3 vols. post 8vo. 3s. 6d. each.

*** An Atlas of the plans of Marlborough's campaigns, 4to. 10s. 6d.

COXE'S HISTORY of the HOUSE OF AUSTRIA. From the Foundation of the Monarchy by Rhodolph of Hapsburgh to the Death of Leopold II., 1218-1792. By Archdeacon COXE. Together with a Continuation from the Accession of Francis I. to the Revolution of 1848. To which is added Genesis, or Details of the late Austrian Revolution (translated from the German). With Portraits of Maximilian, Rhodolph, Maria Theresa, and Francis Joseph. 4 vols. with Indexes, 3s. 6d. each.

LIFE OF THE EMPEROR KARL THE GREAT [Charlemagne]. Translated from the Contemporary History of Eginhard, with Notes and Chapters on Eginhard, the Franks, Karl, and the Breaking-up of the Empire. With a Map. By WILLIAM GLAISTER, M.A., B.C.L., University College, Oxford. Crown 8vo. 4s. 6d.

GERMANY, MENZEL'S HISTORY OF, from the Earliest Period to a recent date. With Index and Portraits of Charlemagne, Charles V., and Metternich. 3 vols. 3s. 6d. each.

RUSSIA, HISTORY OF, from the Earliest Period. Compiled from the most authentic sources, including Karamsin, Tooke, and Ségur. By WALTER K. KELLY. With Index and Portraits of Catherine, Nicholas, and Menschikoff. 2 vols. 3s. 6d. each.

OCKLEY'S HISTORY OF THE SARACENS and THEIR CONQUESTS IN SYRIA, PERSIA, AND EGYPT. Comprising the Lives of Mohammed and his Successors to the Death of Abdalmelik, the Eleventh Caliph. By SIMON OCKLEY, B.D., Professor of Arabic in the University of Cambridge. Sixth Edition. With Portrait of Mohammed. 3s. 6d.

CONDE'S HISTORY OF THE DOMINION of THE ARABS IN SPAIN. Translated from the Spanish by Mrs. FOSTER. With Engraving of Abderahmen Ben Moavia, and Index. 3 vols. 3s. 6d. each.

MACHIAVELLI'S HISTORY OF FLORENCE and of the Affairs of Italy, from the Earliest Times to the Death of Lorenzo the Magnificent; together with the Prince, Savonarola, various Historical Tracts, and a Memoir of Machiavelli. With Index and Portrait. 3s. 6d.

HUNGARY, its History and Relution: together with a copious Memoi Kossuth from authentic sources. W Index and Portrait of Kossuth. 3s. 6d.

ROSCOE'S (W.) LIFE of LOREN: DE MEDICI, called 'the Magnificent,' cluding the Copyright Notes and Illus tions, and Index. With his Poems, Lett &c. Tenth Edition revised, with Men of Roscoe by his Son, and Portrait Lorenzo (after Vasari). 3s. 6d.

ROSCOE'S (W.) LIFE and PON' FICATE OF LEO X., with the Copyri Notes, Appendices of Historical Dc ments, the Dissertation on Lucretia Bor Final Edition, revised by THOMAS ROSC with Index, and two Portraits of Rose and one of Leo X. 2 vols. 3s. 6d. each

RANKE'S HISTORY OF Tl POPES, their Church and State, especially of their Conflicts with Prot antism in the 16th and 17th Centuries. Tr: lated by E. FOSTER. With Portrait: Julius II., Innocent X., and Clement 3 vols. 3s. 6d. each.

RANKE'S HISTORY OF SERV AND THE SERVIAN REVOLUTIC With an Account of the Insurrection Bosnia. Translated by Mrs. KERR. which is added, The Slave Provinces Turkey, from the French of Cyp Robert and other sources. 1 vol. 3s. 6

KINGS OF ROME, History of By T. H. DYER, LL.D. With a Prefa Dissertation on the Sources and Evide of Early Roman History. Demy 8vo.

DECLINE OF THE ROMAN I PUBLIC. From the Destruction of thage to the Consulship of Julius Ca By GEORGE LONG, M.A. 5 vols. 8vo. per vol.

'If any one can guide us through the al inextricable mazes of this labyrinth, it is Long.'—*Saturday Review*.

MASON (A. J.). THE PERSE(TION OF DIOCLETIAN; an Histo Essay. By ARTHUR JAMES MASON, M Fellow of Trinity College, Cambri Demy 8vo. 10s. 6d.

'This is one of the most striking and ori contributions to ecclesiastical history whicl come under our notice for some time.'—*Spect*
'Mr. Mason has worked vigorously and pendently, and in a right direction. We d pretend to be convinced by him on all points he has given us, at least, a good deal of m for thought.'—*Saturday Review*.

GIBBON'S ROMAN EMPII Complete and Unabridged, with Varie Notes, including, in addition to the Autl own, those of Guizot, Wenck, Nieb Hugo, Neander, and other Scho Edited by an English Churchman. 7 With copious Index, and two Maps a Portrait of Gibbon. 3s. 6d. each.

HISTORICAL WORKS. 3

GUIZOT'S HISTORY OF THE ORIGIN OF REPRESENTATIVE GOVERNMENT IN EUROPE. Translated by A. R. SCOBLE. With Index. 3s. 6d.

GUIZOT'S HISTORY OF THE ENGLISH REVOLUTION OF 1640. From the Accession of Charles I. to his Death. With a Preliminary Essay on its Causes and Success. Translated by WILLIAM HAZLITT. With Portrait of Charles, after Vandyke. With Index. 3s. 6d.

GUIZOT'S HISTORY OF CIVILISATION, from the Fall of the Roman Empire to the French Revolution. Translated by WILLIAM HAZLITT. With Portraits of Guizot, Charlemagne, and Louis IX. 3 vols. with Index, 3s. 6d. each.

JAMES (G. P. R.), THE LIFE and TIME OF LOUIS XIV. With Index, and Portraits of Louis XIV. and Mazarin. 2 vols. 3s. 6d. each.

DE LOLME ON THE CONSTITUTION OF ENGLAND; or an Account of the English Government, in which it is compared both with the Republican form of Government and the other Monarchies of Europe. Edited, with Life of the Author and Notes, by JOHN MACGREGOR, M.P. 3s. 6d.

LAMARTINE'S HISTORY of THE GIRONDISTS; or, Personal Memoirs of the Patriots of the French Revolution, from unpublished sources. Translated by H. T. RYDE. With Index, and Portraits of Robespierre, Madame Roland, and Charlotte Corday. 3 vols. 3s. 6d. each.

LAMARTINE'S HISTORY of THE RESTORATION of MONARCHY in FRANCE (a Sequel to his History of the Girondists). With Index, and Portraits of Lamartine, Talleyrand, Lafayette, Ney, and Louis XVII. 4 vols. 3s. 6d. each.

LAMARTINE'S HISTORY of THE FRENCH REVOLUTION OF 1848. With Index and Frontispiece. 3s. 6d.

MICHELET'S HISTORY of THE ROMAN REPUBLIC. Translated by W. HAZLITT. With Appendix, Index, and a Portrait of Michelet. 3s. 6d.

MICHELET'S HISTORY of THE FRENCH REVOLUTION, from its earliest indications to the flight of the King in 1791. With Index and Frontispiece. 3s. 6d.

MIGNET'S HISTORY OF THE FRENCH REVOLUTION, from 1789-1814. With Index and Portrait of Napoleon. 3s. 6d.

PHILIP DE COMMINES, MEMOIRS OF. Containing the Histories of Louis XI. and Charles VIII., Kings of France, and Charles the Bold, Duke of Burgundy. Together with the Scandalous Chronicle, or Secret History of Louis XI., by JEAN DE TROYES. Edited, with a Life of De Commines and Notes, by Andrew R. SCOBLE. With Index, and Portraits of Charles the Bold and Louis XI. 2 vols. 3s. 6d. each.

SULLY, MEMOIRS OF THE DUKE OF, Prime Minister to Henry the Great. Translated from the French, with Notes, an Historical Introduction, Index, and Portraits of Sully, Henry IV., Coligny, and Marie de Medicis. 4 vols. 3s. 6d. each.

SCHLEGEL'S (F.) LECTURES ON THE PHILOSOPHY OF LIFE and THE PHILOSOPHY OF LANGUAGE. Translated by A. J. W. MORRISON. With Index. 3s. 6d.

SCHLEGEL'S (F.) LECTURES ON THE PHILOSOPHY OF HISTORY. Translated from the German, with a Memoir of the Author, by J. B. ROBERTSON. With Index and Portrait. 3s. 6d.

SCHLEGEL'S (F.) LECTURES ON MODERN HISTORY, together with the Lectures entitled Cæsar and Alexander, and The Beginning of Our History. Translated by L. PURCELL and R. H. WHITELOCK. With Index. 3s. 6d.

TYTLER'S (PROF.) THE ELEMENTS OF GENERAL HISTORY. New Edition. Revised and brought down to Christmas, 1874. Small post 8vo. 3s. 6d.

THE STUDENT'S TEXT-BOOK OF ENGLISH AND GENERAL HISTORY, from B.C. 100 to the Present Time, with Genealogical and Literary Tables, and Sketch of the English Constitution. By D. BEALE. Crown 8vo. 2s. 6d.

THE STUDENT'S CHRONOLOGICAL MAPS OF ANCIENT AND MODERN HISTORY. By D. BEALE. Medium 8vo. 3s. 6d.

A PRACTICAL SYNOPSIS OF ENGLISH HISTORY; or, A General Summary of Dates and Events for the use of Schools, Families, and Candidates for Public Examinations. By Arthur Bowes. 5th edition. Revised to date. Demy 8vo. 2s.

[TURN OVER.

ENGLISH CHRONICLES.
Post 8vo. 5s. per Volume.

BEDE'S ECCLESIASTICAL HISTORY, and the Anglo-Saxon Chronicle. With Notes, Analysis, Index, and Map. By Dr. GILES.

CHRONICLES OF THE CRUSADERS. Richard of Devizes, Geoffrey de Vinsauf, Lord de Joinville.

FLORENCE OF WORCESTER'S CHRONICLE, with the Two Continuations: comprising Annals of English History to the Reign of Edward I.

GIRALDUS CAMBRENSIS' HISTORICAL WORKS: Topography of Ireland; History of the Conquest of Ireland; Itinerary through Wales; and Description of Wales. With Index. Edited by THOMAS WRIGHT.

HENRY OF HUNTINGDON'S HISTORY OF THE ENGLISH, from the Roman Invasion to Henry II.; with the Acts of King Stephen, &c.

INGULPH'S CHRONICLE of the ABBEY OF CROYLAND, with the Continuations by Peter of Blois and other Writers. By H. T. RILEY.

MATTHEW PARIS'S CHRONICLE. In 5 vols. FIRST SECTION: Roger of Wendover's Flowers of English History, from the Descent of the Saxons to A.D. 1235. Translated by Dr. GILES. 2 vols. SECOND SECTION: From 1235-1273. With Index to the entire Work. 3 vols.

MATTHEW of WESTMINSTE FLOWERS OF HISTORY, espe such as relate to the affairs of Britai A.D. 1307. Translated by C. D. Yo In 2 vols.

ORDERICUS VITALIS' ECC SIASTICAL HISTORY OF ENGL AND NORMANDY. With Chroni St. Evroult. Translated, with Note T. FORESTER, M.A. In 4 vols.

ROGER DE HOVEDEN'S NALS OF ENGLISH HISTORY; A.D. 732 to A.D. 1201. Edited by RILEY. In 2 vols.

ROGER OF WENDOVER. *Matthew Paris.*

SIX OLD ENGLISH CHR(CLES, viz.:—Asser's Life of Alfred the Chronicles of Ethelwerd, Gildas, nius, Geoffrey of Monmouth, and R of Cirencester.

WILLIAM OF MALMESBU CHRONICLE OF THE KING ENGLAND. Translated by SHARP

PAULI'S (Dr. R.) LIFE of ALF THE GREAT. Translated from th man. To which is appended A Anglo-Saxon Version of Crosius, literal Translation, and an Anglo-Grammar and Glossary.

COOPER'S BIOGRAPHICAL DICTIONARY. Conta concise Notices (upwards of 15,000) of Eminent Persons of all Ages and Countries, an particularly of distinguished Natives of Great Britain and Ireland. By THOMPSON Co F.R.S., Editor of 'Men of the Time,' and Joint Editor of 'Athenæ Cantabrigi 1 vol. 8vo. 12s.

'It is an important original contribution to the literature of its class by a painstaking scholar It seems in every way admirable, and fully to justify the claims on its behalf put forth by its ec *British Quarterly Review.*

'The mass of information which it contains, especially as regards a number of authors, more obscure, is simply astonishing.'—*Spectator.*

'Comprises in 1210 pages, printed very closely in double columns, an enormous amount of ation.'—*Examiner.*

THE ONLY AUTHORIZED AND UNABRIDGED EDITION.

WEBSTER'S DICTIONARY OF THE ENGLISH L GUAGE. Including Scientific, Technical, and Biblical Words and Terms, with thei fications, Pronunciations, Alternative Spellings, Derivations, Synonyms, and nu Illustrative Quotations. With a Supplement containing over 4600 new Word Meanings. In 1 volume of 1628 pages, with 3000 Illustrations. 4to. cloth, 21s.

THE COMPLETE DICTIONARY contains, in addition to the matter, several valuable Literary Appendices, and 70 extra pages of Illustrations, g and classified, and a New Biographical Dictionary of upwards of 9700 names. 1919 In cloth, 31s. 6d.

'Certainly the best practical English Dictionary extant.'—*Quarterly Review*, Oct. 1873.

Prospectuses, with Specimen Pages, sent post free on application.

LONDON: GEORGE BELL & SONS, YORK STREET, COVENT GAR

www.ingramcontent.com/pod-product-compliance
Lightning Source LLC
Chambersburg PA
CBHW050846300426
44111CB00010B/1150